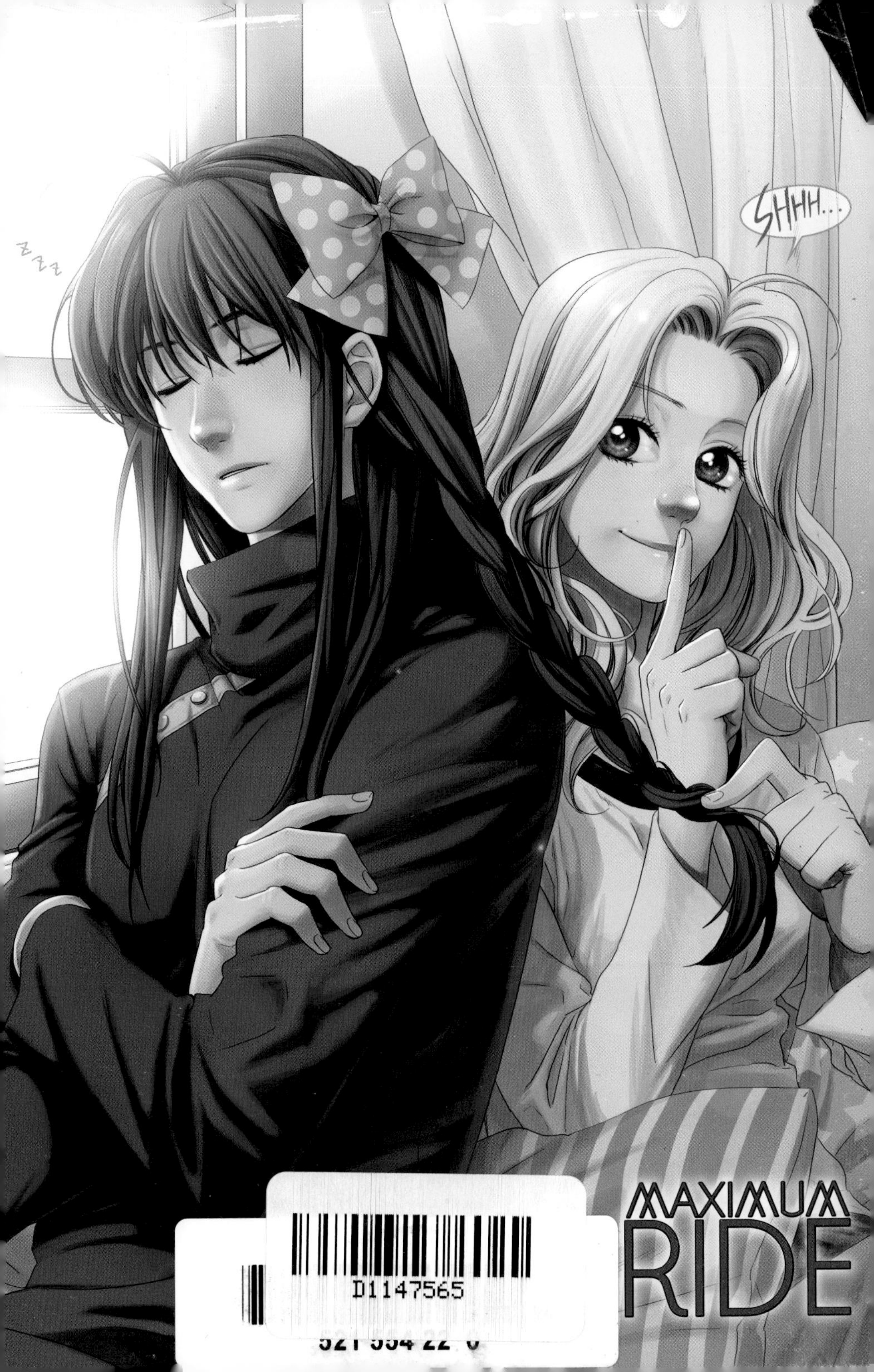

Z Z Z
SHHH...
MAXIMUM RIDE

WHAT CAME BEFORE

Max and her flock are genetic experiments. Created by a mysterious lab known only as the "School," their genetic codes have been spliced with avian DNA, giving them wings and the power to soar. What they lack are homes, families, and memories of a real life.

After escaping from the School, the flock is hunted by Erasers, agents of the School who can transform into terrifying wolf creatures, and Jeb Batchelder, the man they once thought of as a father. Despite the targets on their backs, though, the flock is desperate to learn about their individual pasts. Their inquiries lead them to Washington, D.C., where they meet Special Agent Anne Walker of the FBI, who takes them in and gives them a taste of a normal life.

The flock's respite is short-lived, however. It isn't long before they discover that Anne is in league with their enemies. On their own again, the flock heads to Florida, following a lead on a multinational corporation called ITEX that seems to have been pulling their strings all along. Once there, though, Max is kidnapped by ITEX and replaced by a clone of herself — Max 2.0!

MAXIMUM RIDE

Max is the eldest member of the flock, and the responsibility of caring for her comrades has fallen to her. Tough and uncompromising, she's willing to put everything on the line to protect her "family."

FANG

Only slightly younger than Max, Fang is one of the elder members of the flock. Cool and reliable, Fang is Max's rock. He may be the strongest of them all, but most of the time it is hard to figure out what is on his mind.

IGGY

Being blind doesn't mean that Iggy is helpless. He has not only an incredible sense of hearing, but also a particular knack (and fondness) for explosives.

NUDGE

Motormouth Nudge would probably spend most days at the mall if not for her pesky mutant-bird-girl-being-hunted-by-wolf-men problem.

GASMAN

ANGEL

ARI

JEB

MAXIMUM RIDE

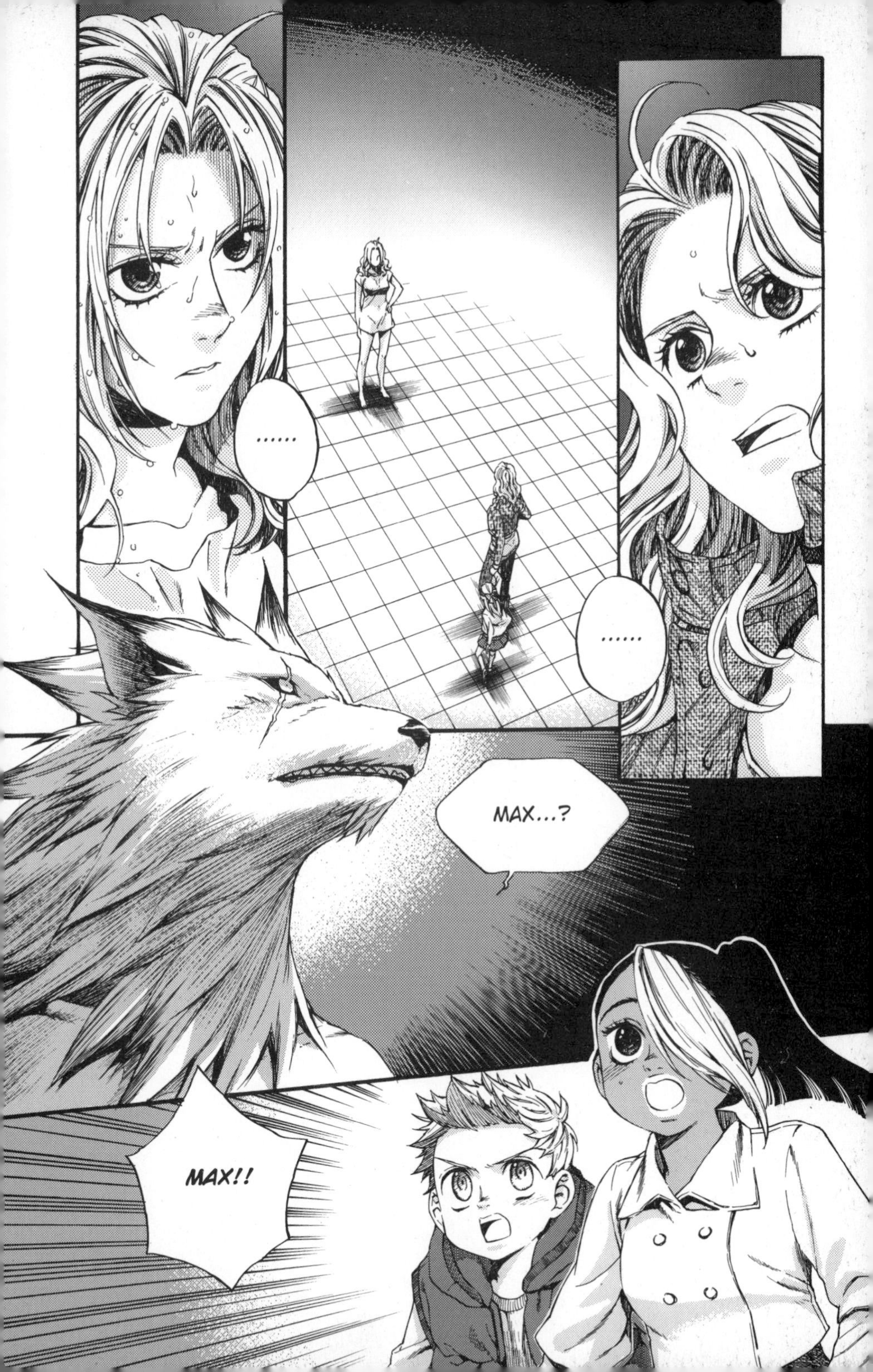
......
......
MAX...?
MAX!!

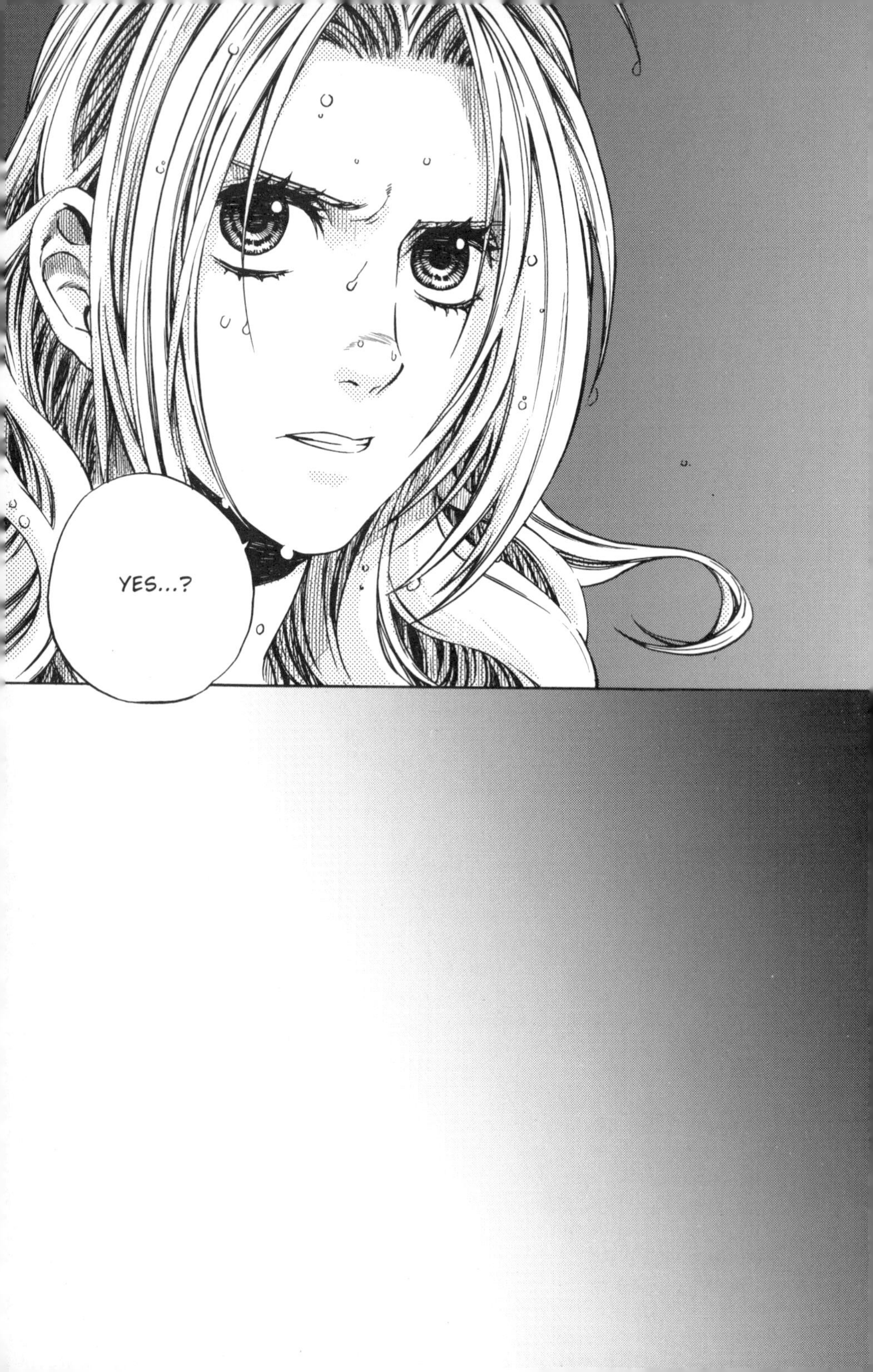
YES...?

MAXIMUM RIDE

CHAPTER 29

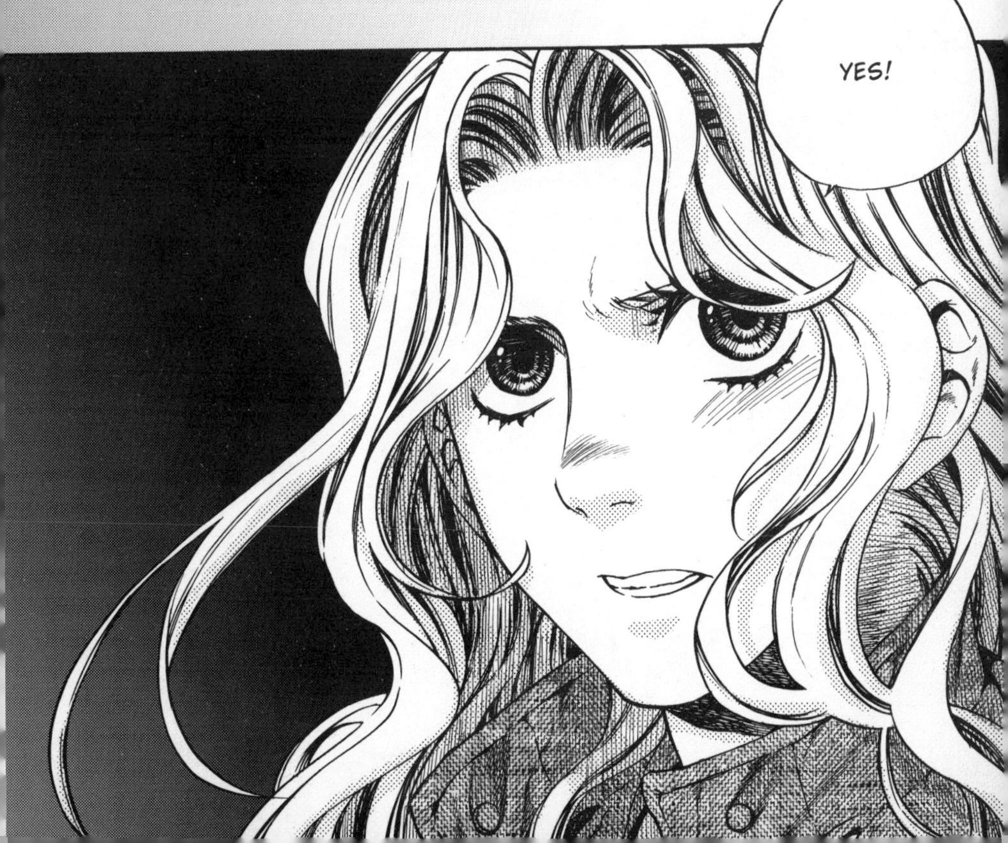
YES!

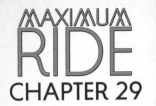

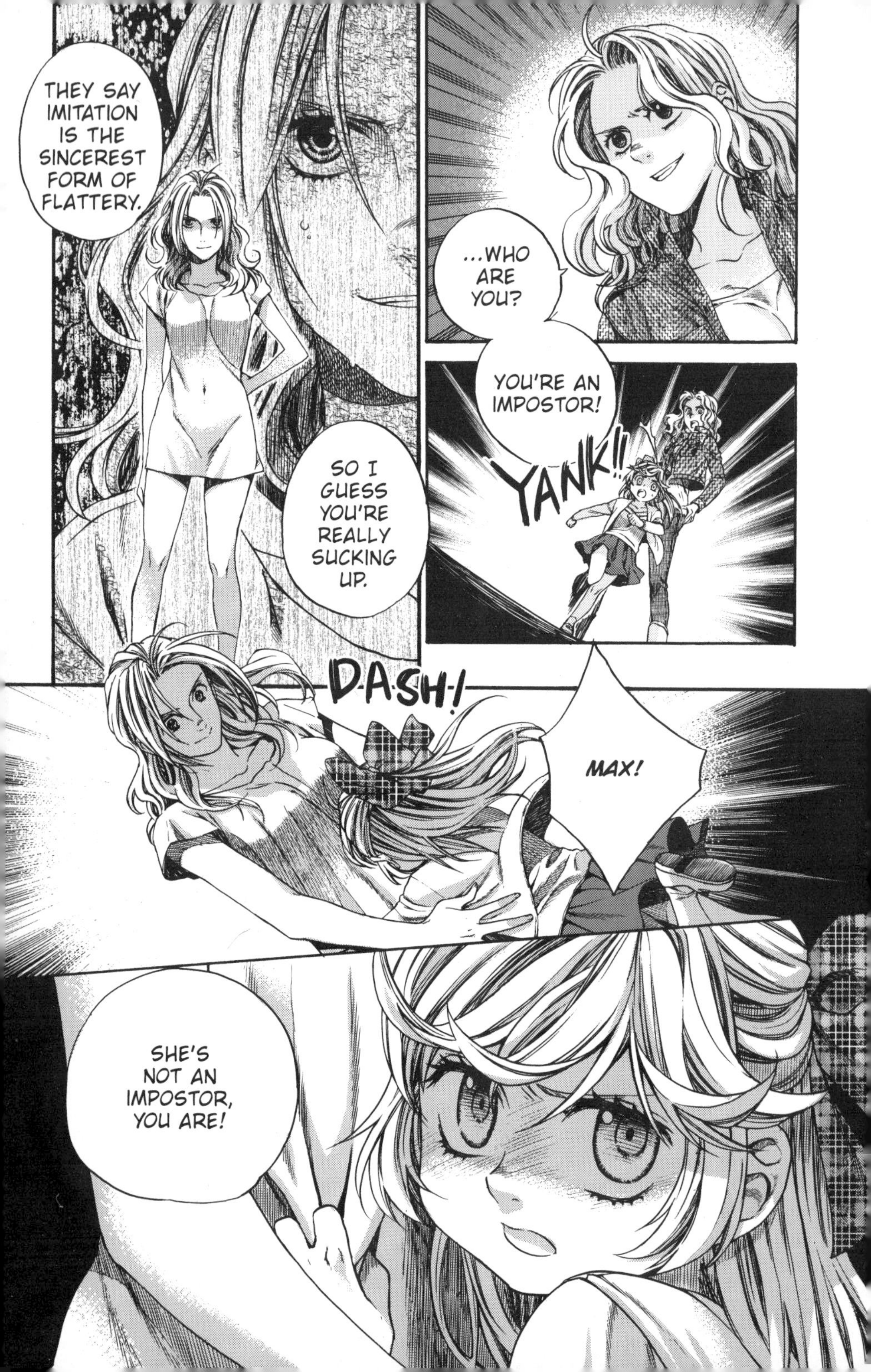
...WHO ARE YOU?
THEY SAY IMITATION IS THE SINCEREST FORM OF FLATTERY.
YOU'RE AN IMPOSTOR!
SO I GUESS YOU'RE REALLY SUCKING UP.
YANK!!
DASH!
MAX!
SHE'S NOT AN IMPOSTOR, YOU ARE!

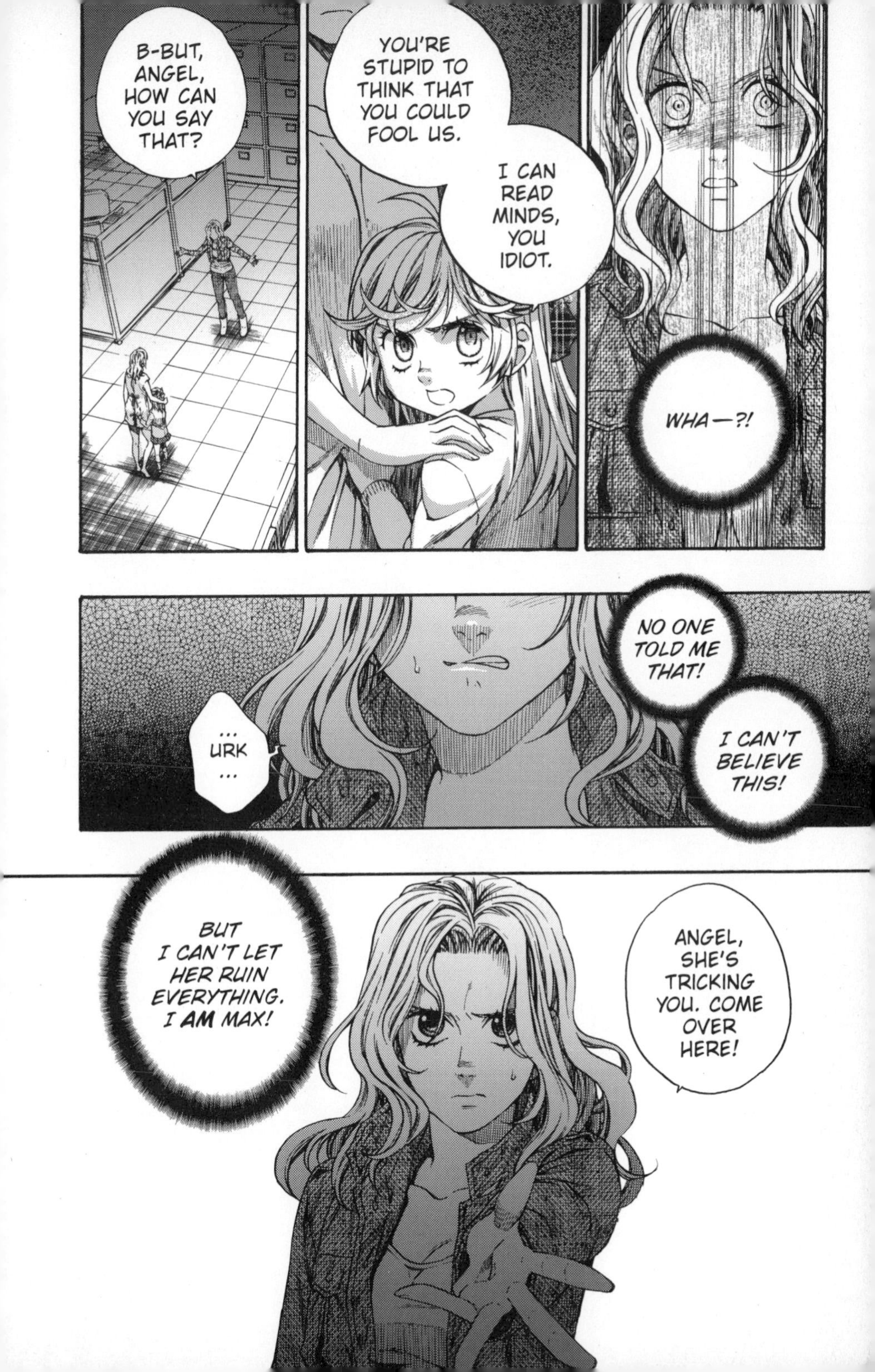
B-BUT, ANGEL, HOW CAN YOU SAY THAT?
YOU'RE STUPID TO THINK THAT YOU COULD FOOL US.
I CAN READ MINDS, YOU IDIOT.
WHA—?!
NO ONE TOLD ME THAT!
I CAN'T BELIEVE THIS!
... URK ...
BUT I CAN'T LET HER RUIN EVERYTHING. I AM MAX!
ANGEL, SHE'S TRICKING YOU. COME OVER HERE!

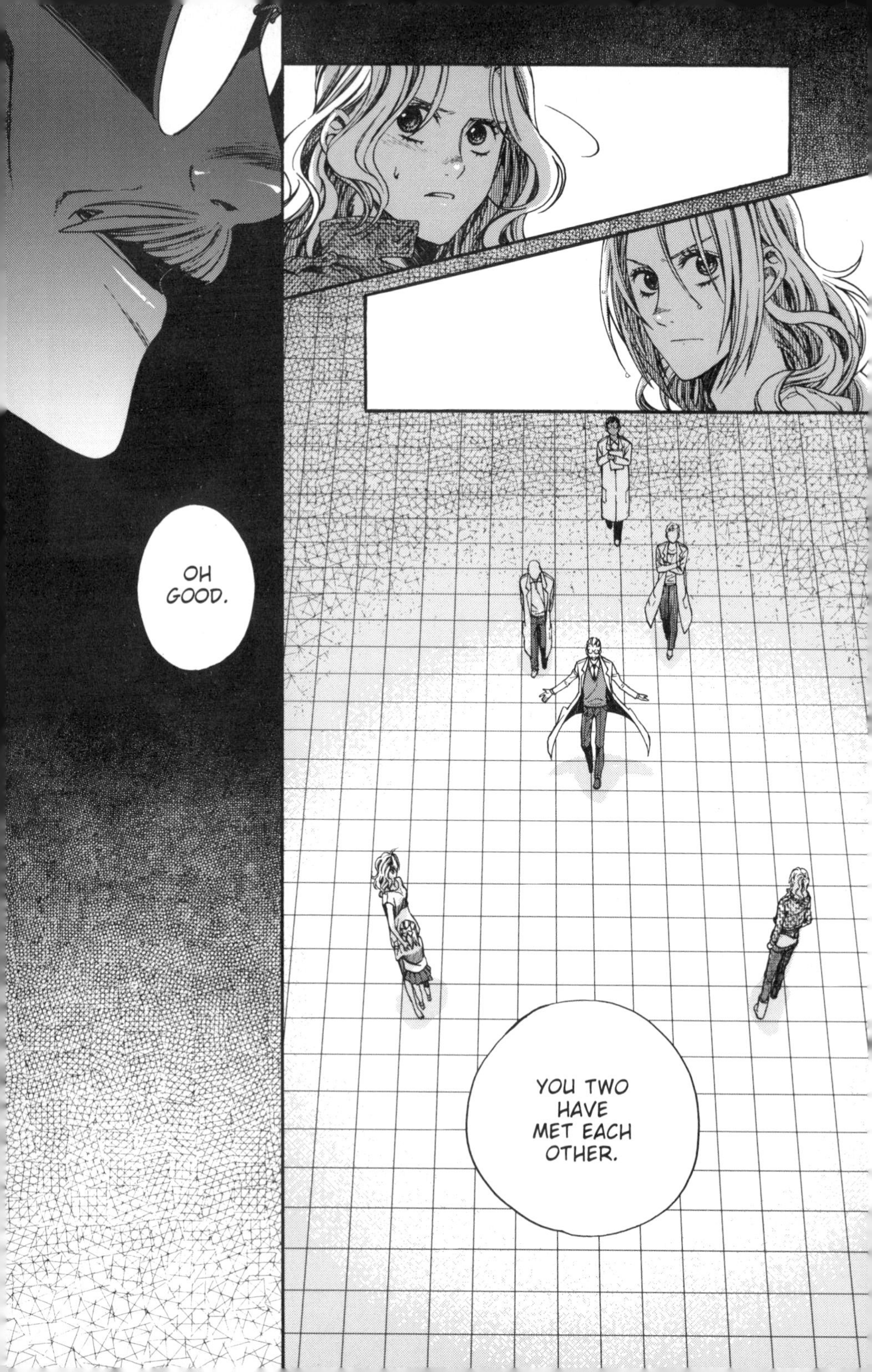
OH GOOD.
YOU TWO HAVE MET EACH OTHER.

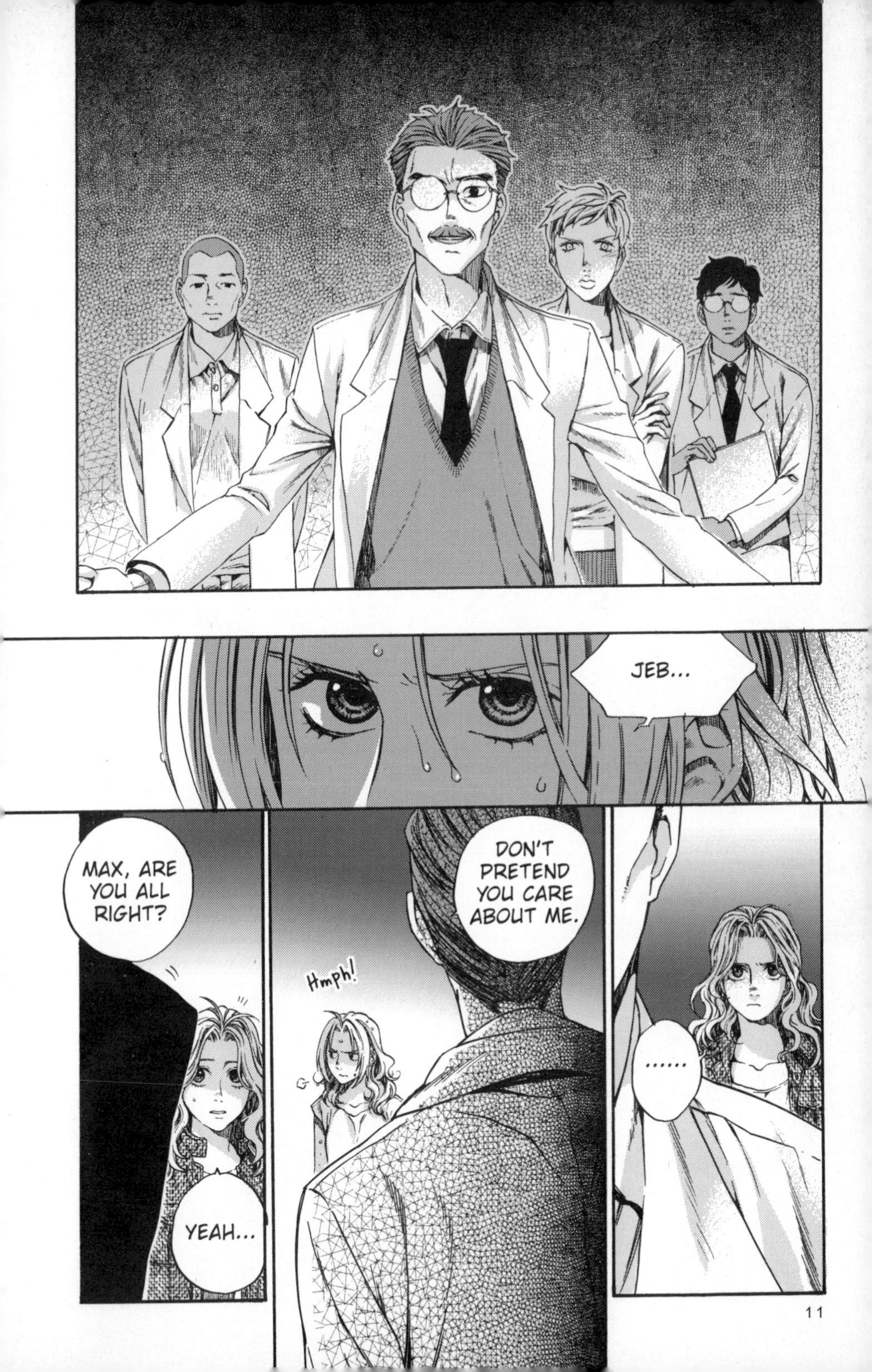
JEB...
MAX, ARE YOU ALL RIGHT?
YEAH...
DON'T PRETEND YOU CARE ABOUT ME.
Hmph!
......

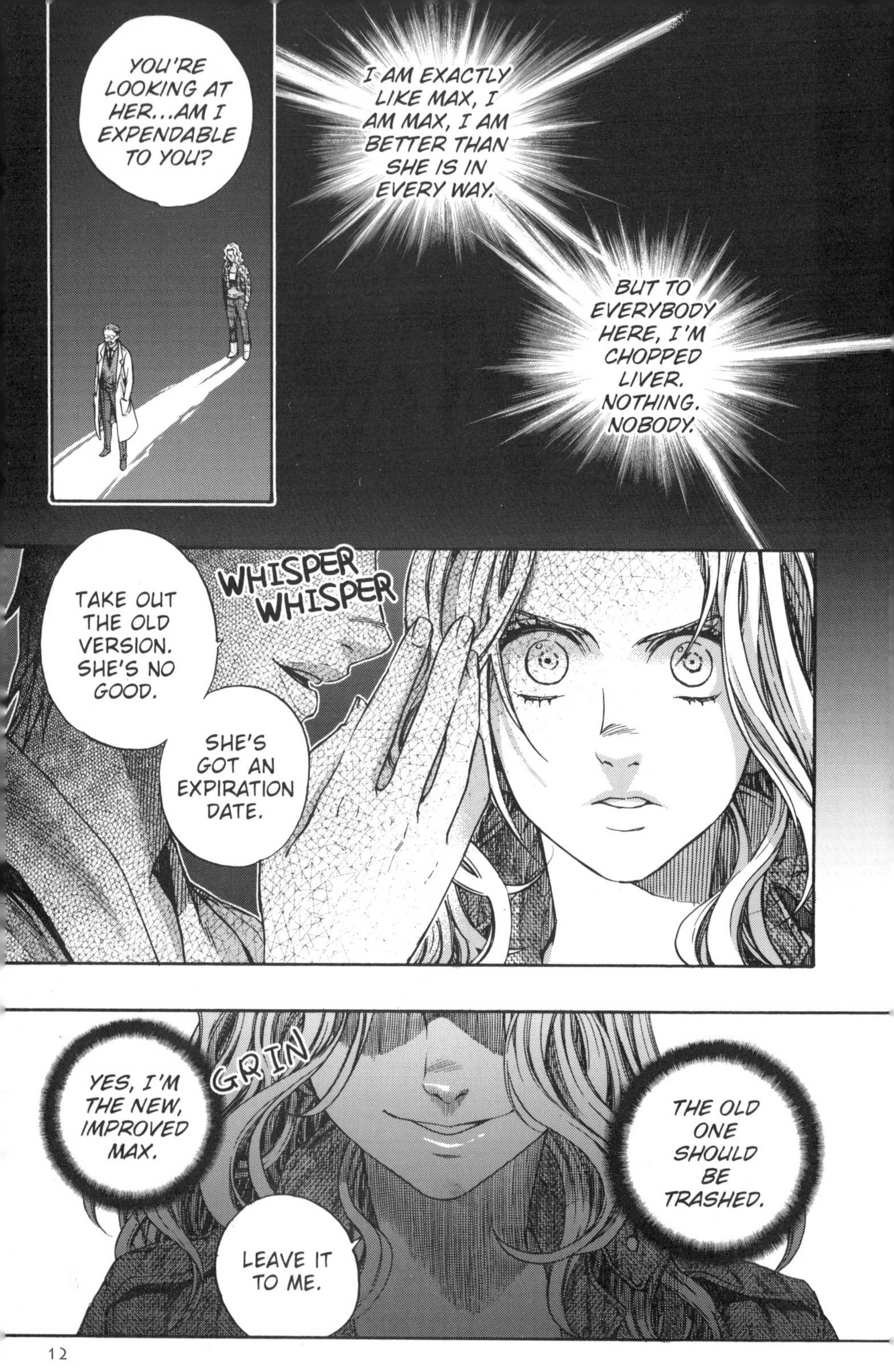
YOU'RE LOOKING AT HER...AM I EXPENDABLE TO YOU?
I AM EXACTLY LIKE MAX, I AM MAX, I AM BETTER THAN SHE IS IN EVERY WAY.
BUT TO EVERYBODY HERE, I'M CHOPPED LIVER. NOTHING. NOBODY.
WHISPER WHISPER
TAKE OUT THE OLD VERSION. SHE'S NO GOOD.
SHE'S GOT AN EXPIRATION DATE.
GRIN
YES, I'M THE NEW, IMPROVED MAX.
THE OLD ONE SHOULD BE TRASHED.
LEAVE IT TO ME.

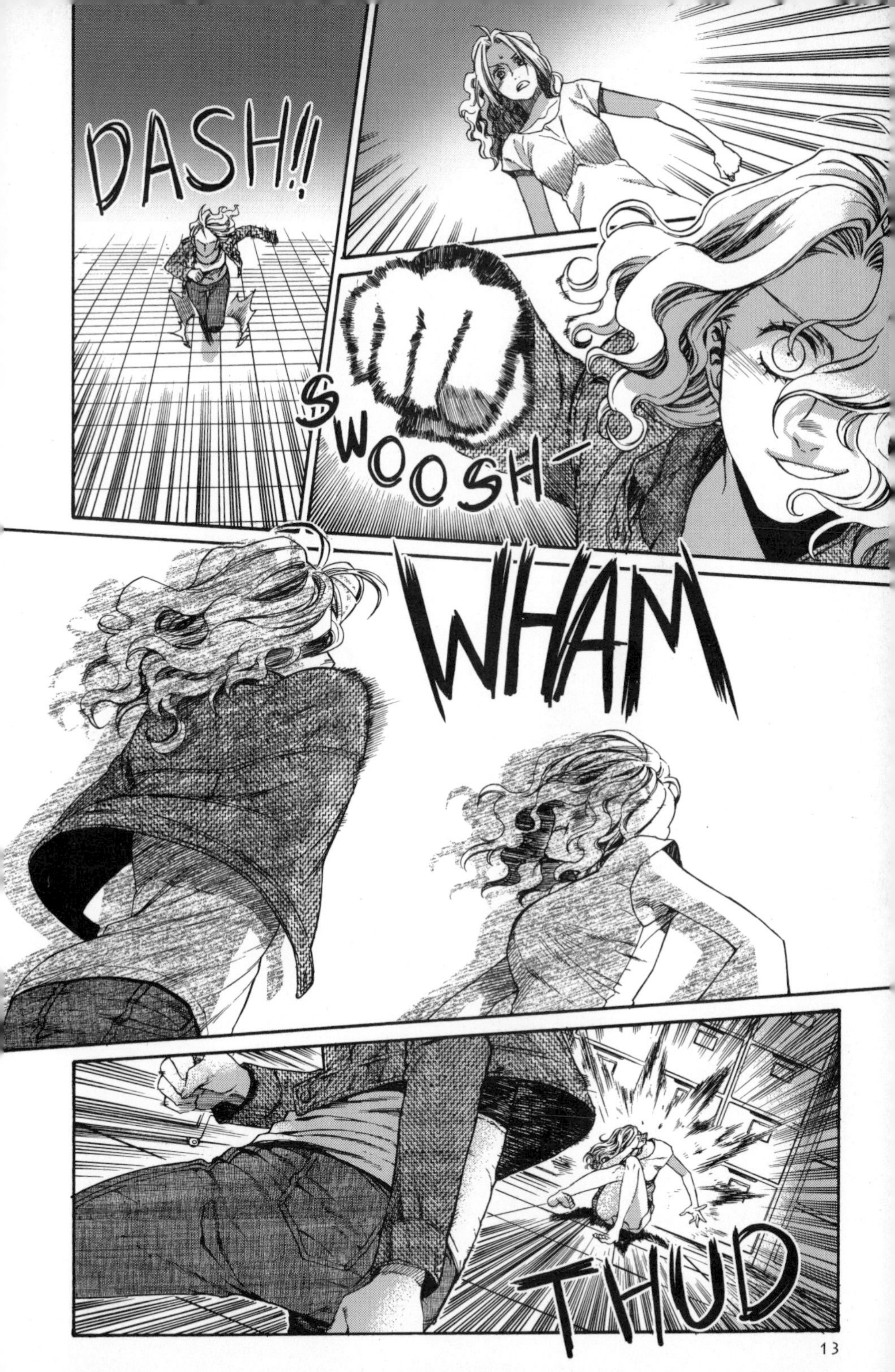
DASH!!
SWOOSH
WHAM
THUD

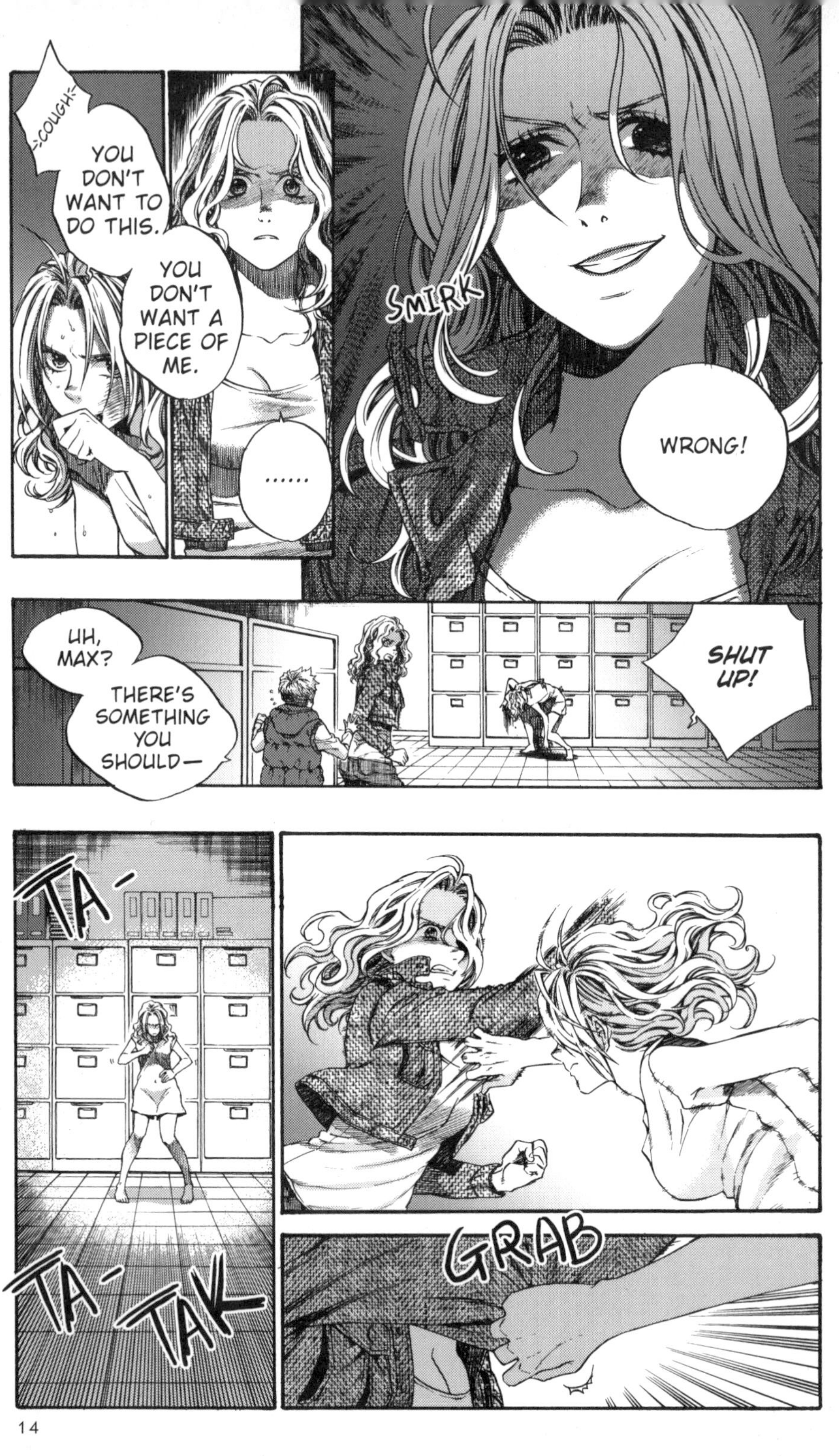
-COUGH-
YOU DON'T WANT TO DO THIS.
YOU DON'T WANT A PIECE OF ME.
......
SMIRK
WRONG!
UH, MAX?
THERE'S SOMETHING YOU SHOULD—
SHUT UP!
TA-
TA-TAK
GRAB

SLAM

THERE CAN BE ONLY ONE MAX.

LET'S SEE IF WHAT YOU SAY ABOUT HER IS TRUE...

...BATCH-ELDER.

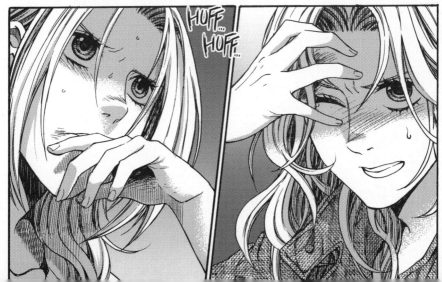

HOFF... HOFF...

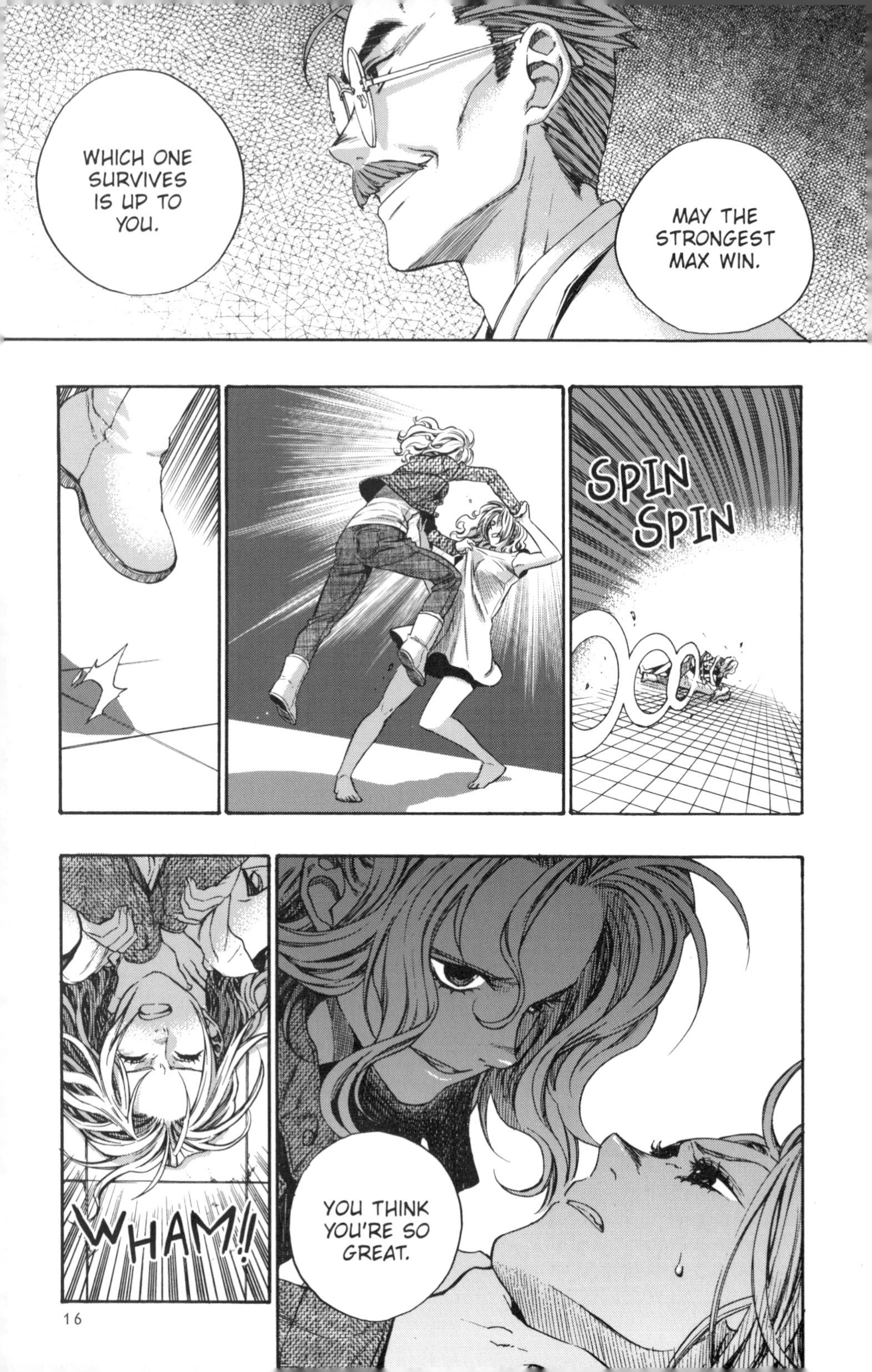
WHICH ONE SURVIVES IS UP TO YOU.
MAY THE STRONGEST MAX WIN.
SPIN SPIN
WHAM!!
YOU THINK YOU'RE SO GREAT.

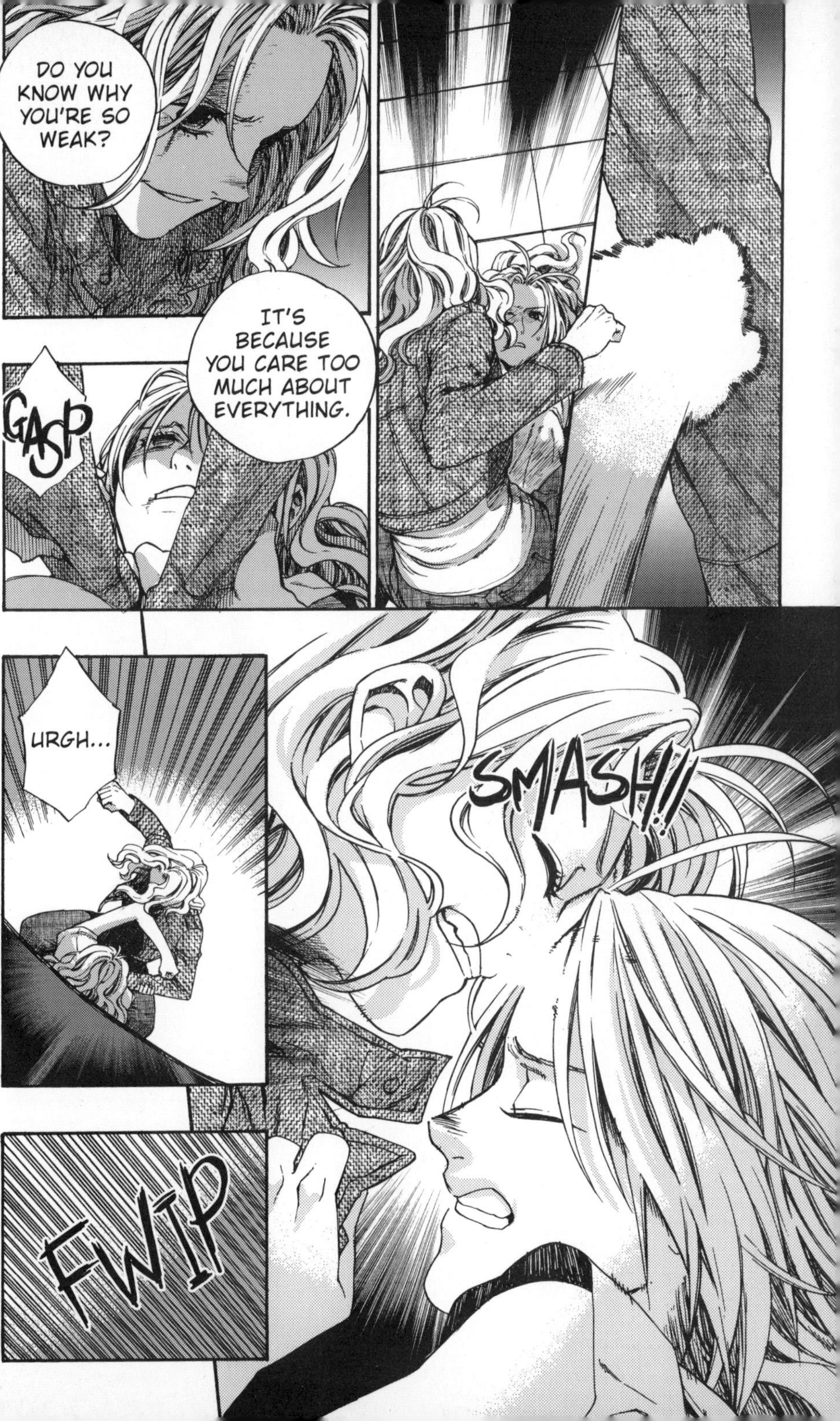
DO YOU KNOW WHY YOU'RE SO WEAK?
IT'S BECAUSE YOU CARE TOO MUCH ABOUT EVERYTHING.
GASP
URGH...
SMASH!!
FWIP

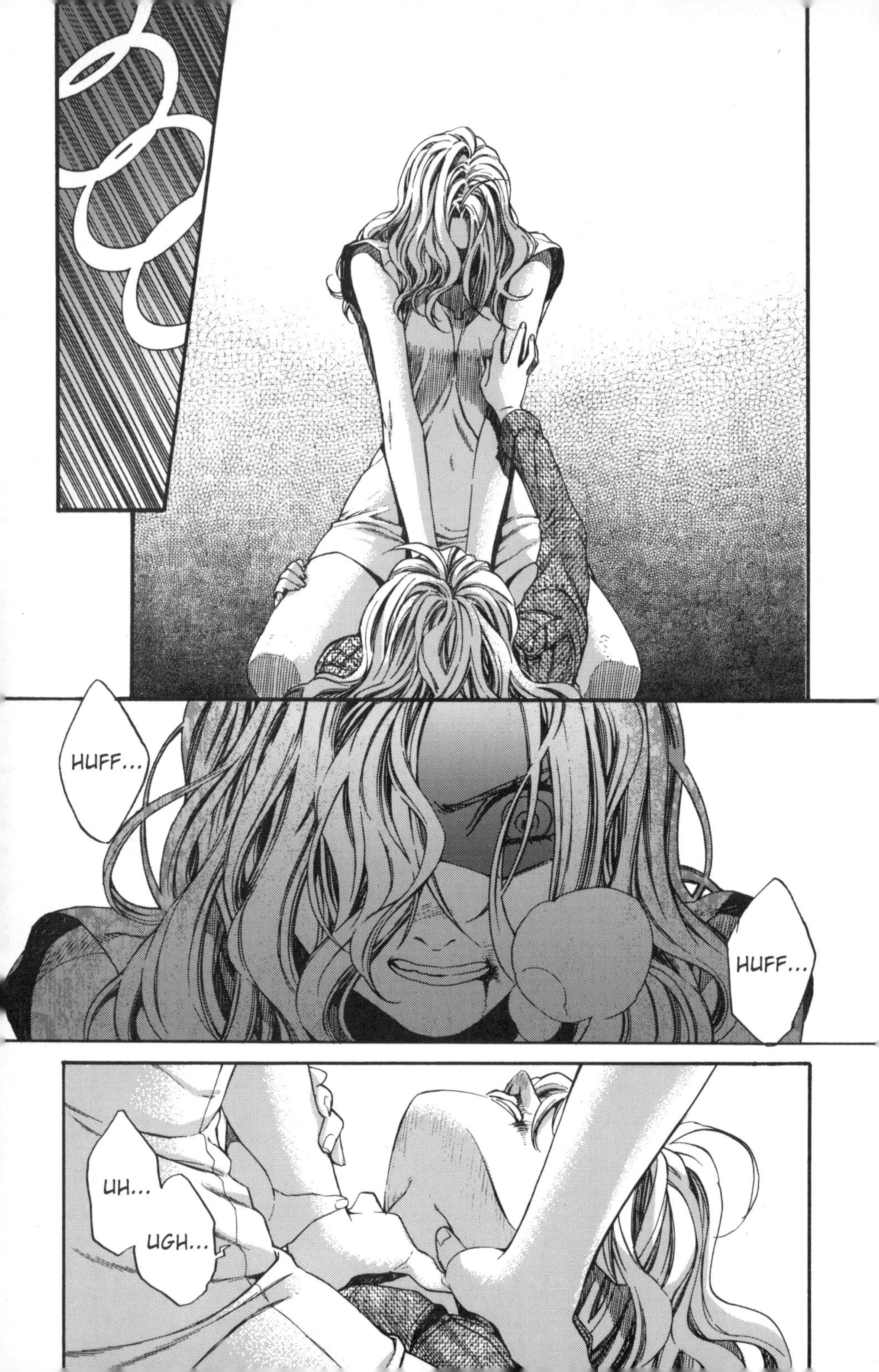
HUFF...
HUFF...
UH...
UGH...

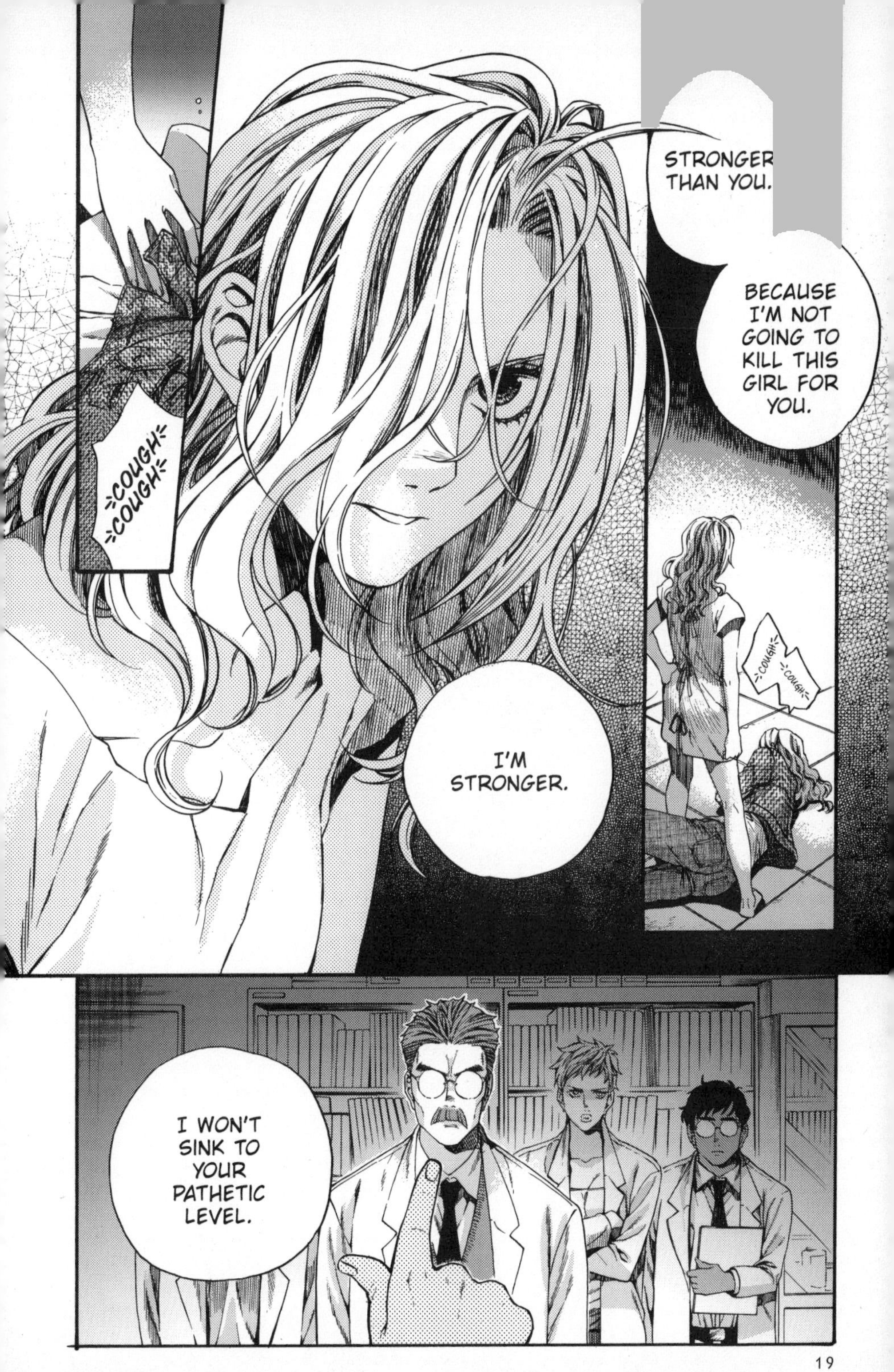
STRONGER THAN YOU.
BECAUSE I'M NOT GOING TO KILL THIS GIRL FOR YOU.
COUGH COUGH
COUGH COUGH
I'M STRONGER.
I WON'T SINK TO YOUR PATHETIC LEVEL.

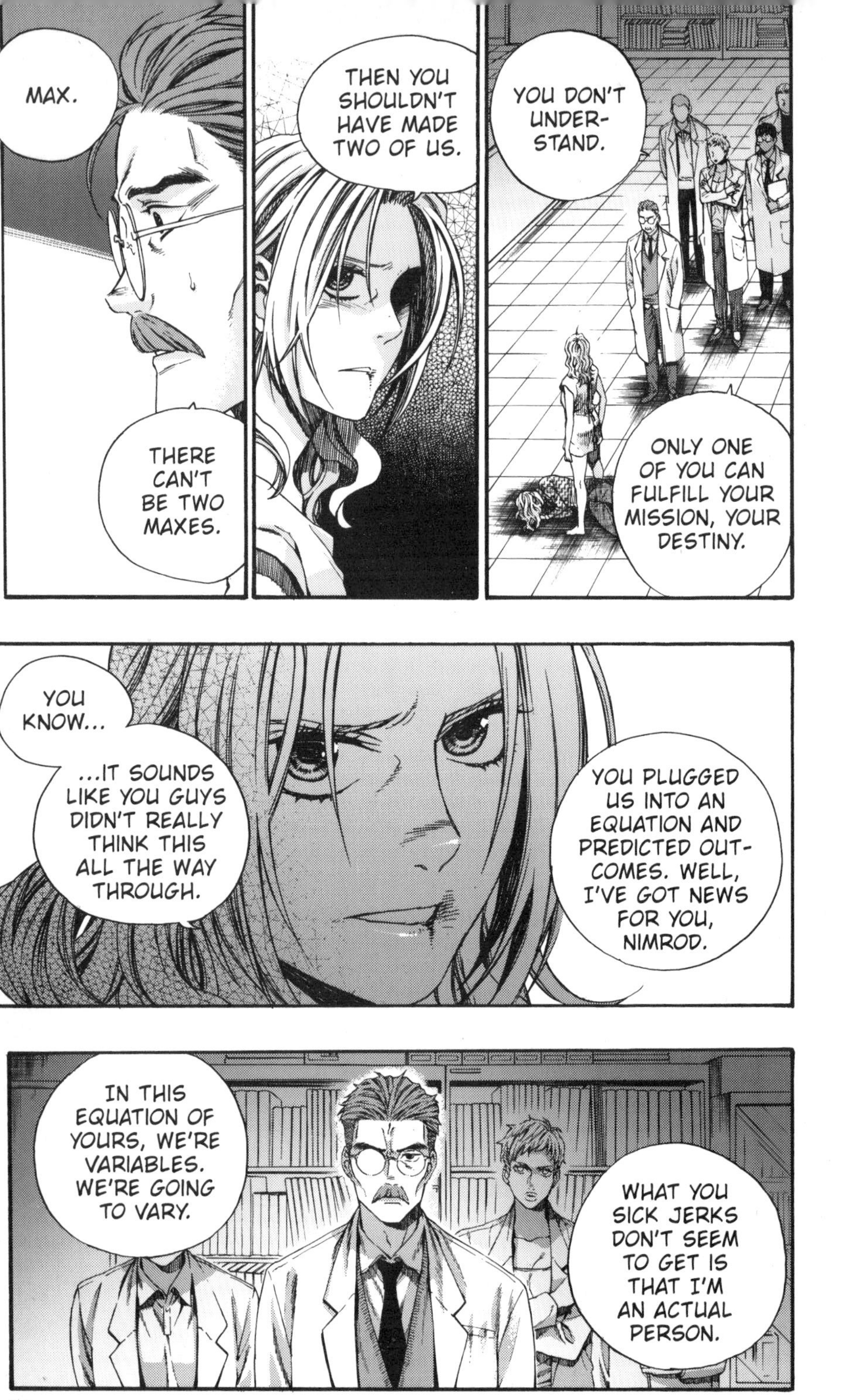
MAX.
THERE CAN'T BE TWO MAXES.
THEN YOU SHOULDN'T HAVE MADE TWO OF US.
YOU DON'T UNDER-STAND.
ONLY ONE OF YOU CAN FULFILL YOUR MISSION, YOUR DESTINY.
YOU KNOW...
...IT SOUNDS LIKE YOU GUYS DIDN'T REALLY THINK THIS ALL THE WAY THROUGH.
YOU PLUGGED US INTO AN EQUATION AND PREDICTED OUT-COMES. WELL, I'VE GOT NEWS FOR YOU, NIMROD.
IN THIS EQUATION OF YOURS, WE'RE VARIABLES. WE'RE GOING TO VARY.
WHAT YOU SICK JERKS DON'T SEEM TO GET IS THAT I'M AN ACTUAL PERSON.

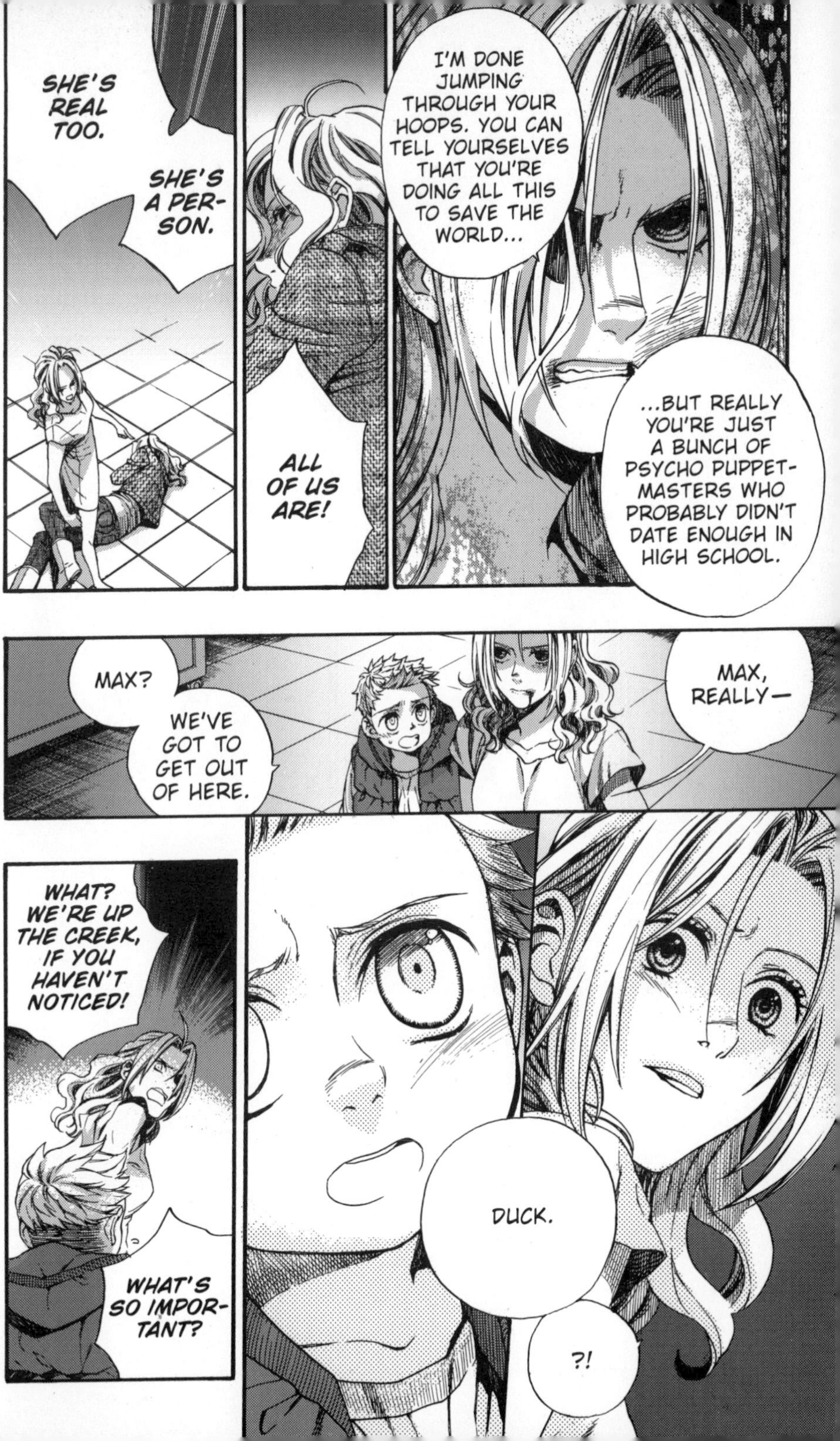

SHE'S REAL TOO.
SHE'S A PER-SON.
ALL OF US ARE!
I'M DONE JUMPING THROUGH YOUR HOOPS. YOU CAN TELL YOURSELVES THAT YOU'RE DOING ALL THIS TO SAVE THE WORLD...
...BUT REALLY YOU'RE JUST A BUNCH OF PSYCHO PUPPET-MASTERS WHO PROBABLY DIDN'T DATE ENOUGH IN HIGH SCHOOL.
MAX?
WE'VE GOT TO GET OUT OF HERE.
MAX, REALLY—
WHAT? WE'RE UP THE CREEK, IF YOU HAVEN'T NOTICED!
WHAT'S SO IMPOR-TANT?
DUCK.
?!

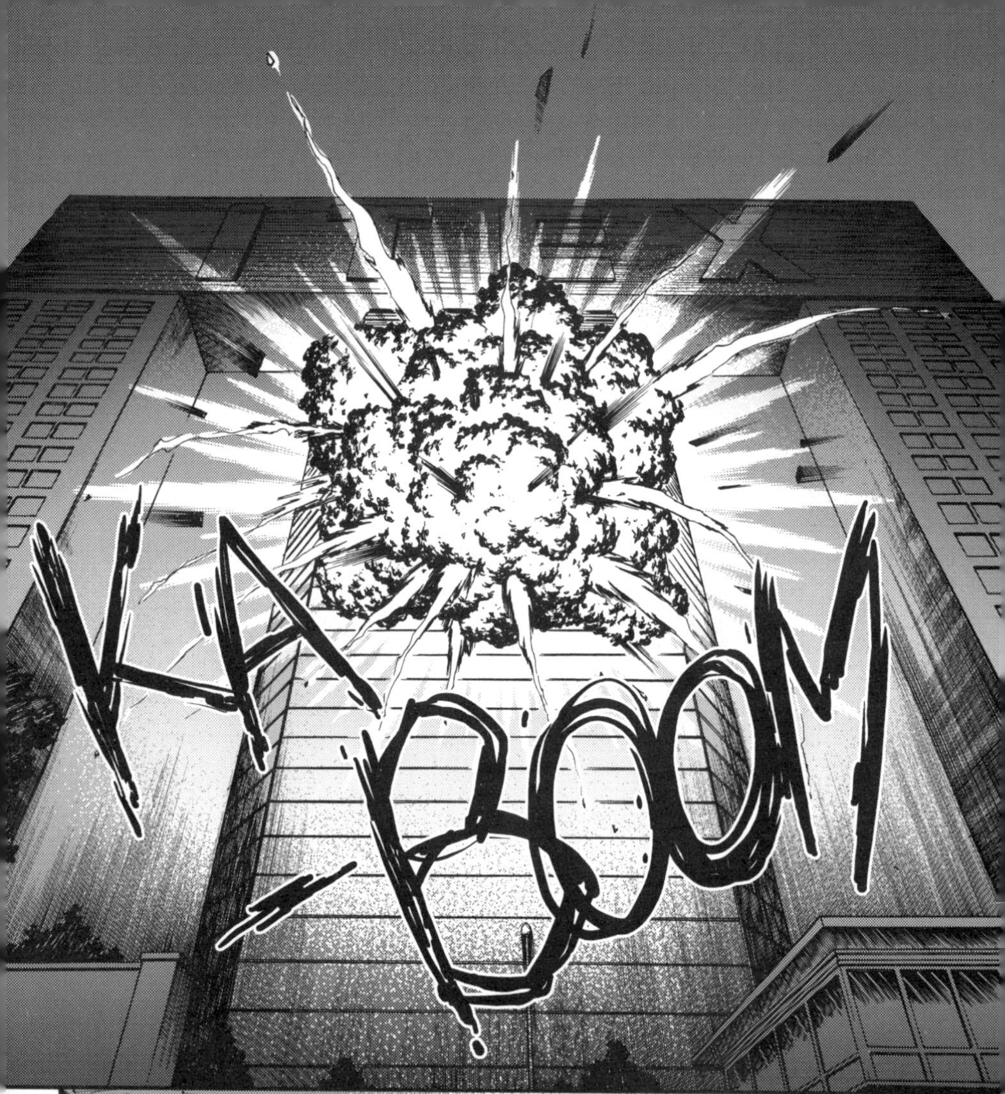
KA-BOOM
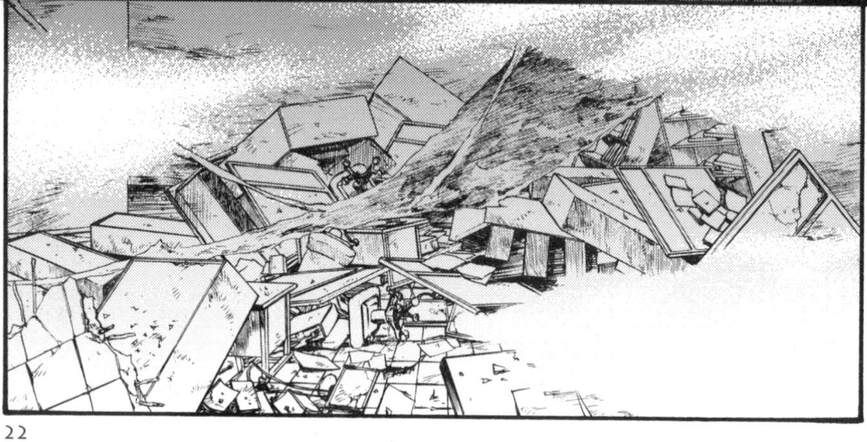

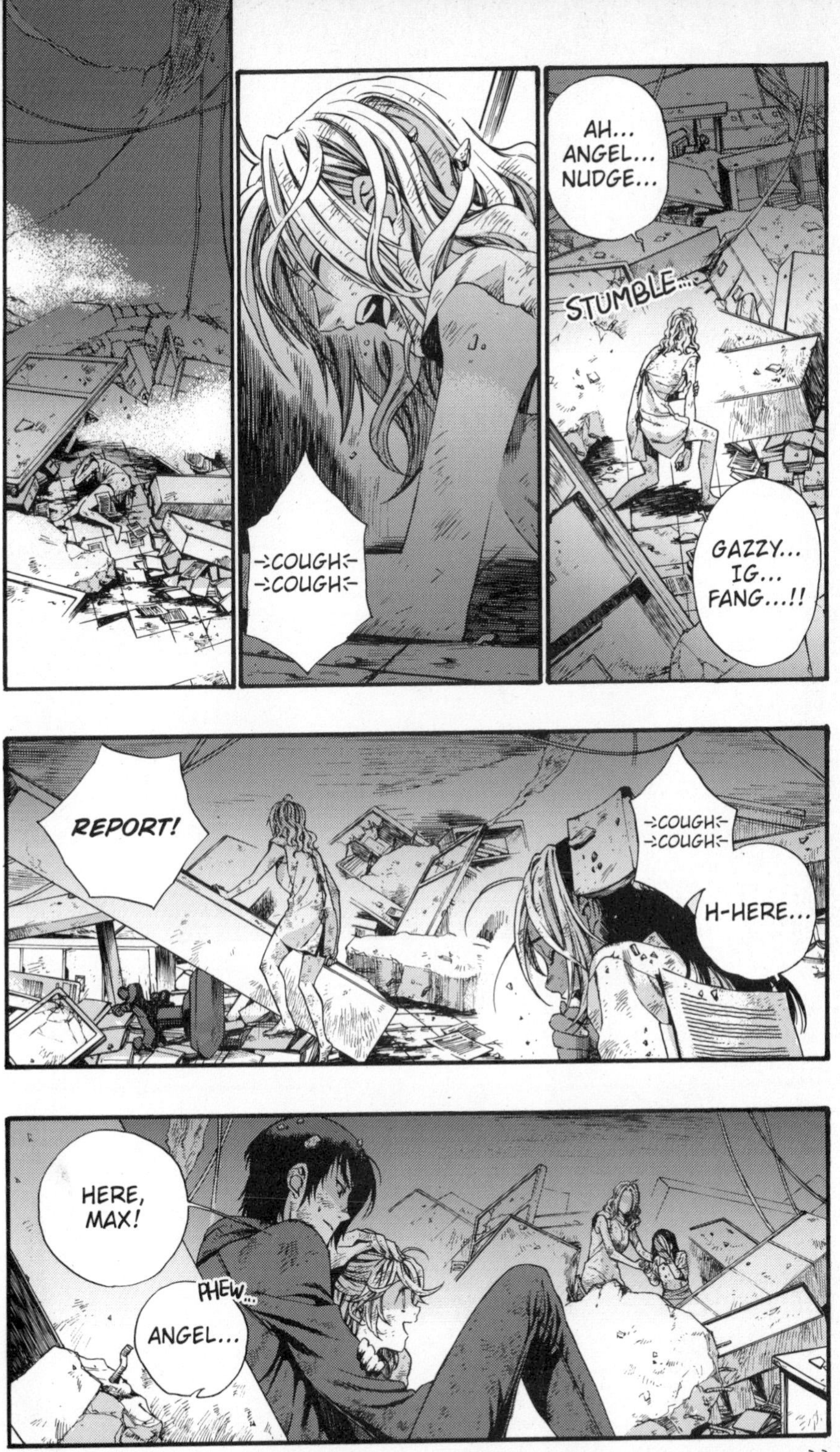
-COUGH-
-COUGH-
AH... ANGEL... NUDGE...
STUMBLE...
GAZZY... IG... FANG...!!
REPORT!
-COUGH-
-COUGH-
H-HERE...
HERE, MAX!
PHEW...
ANGEL...

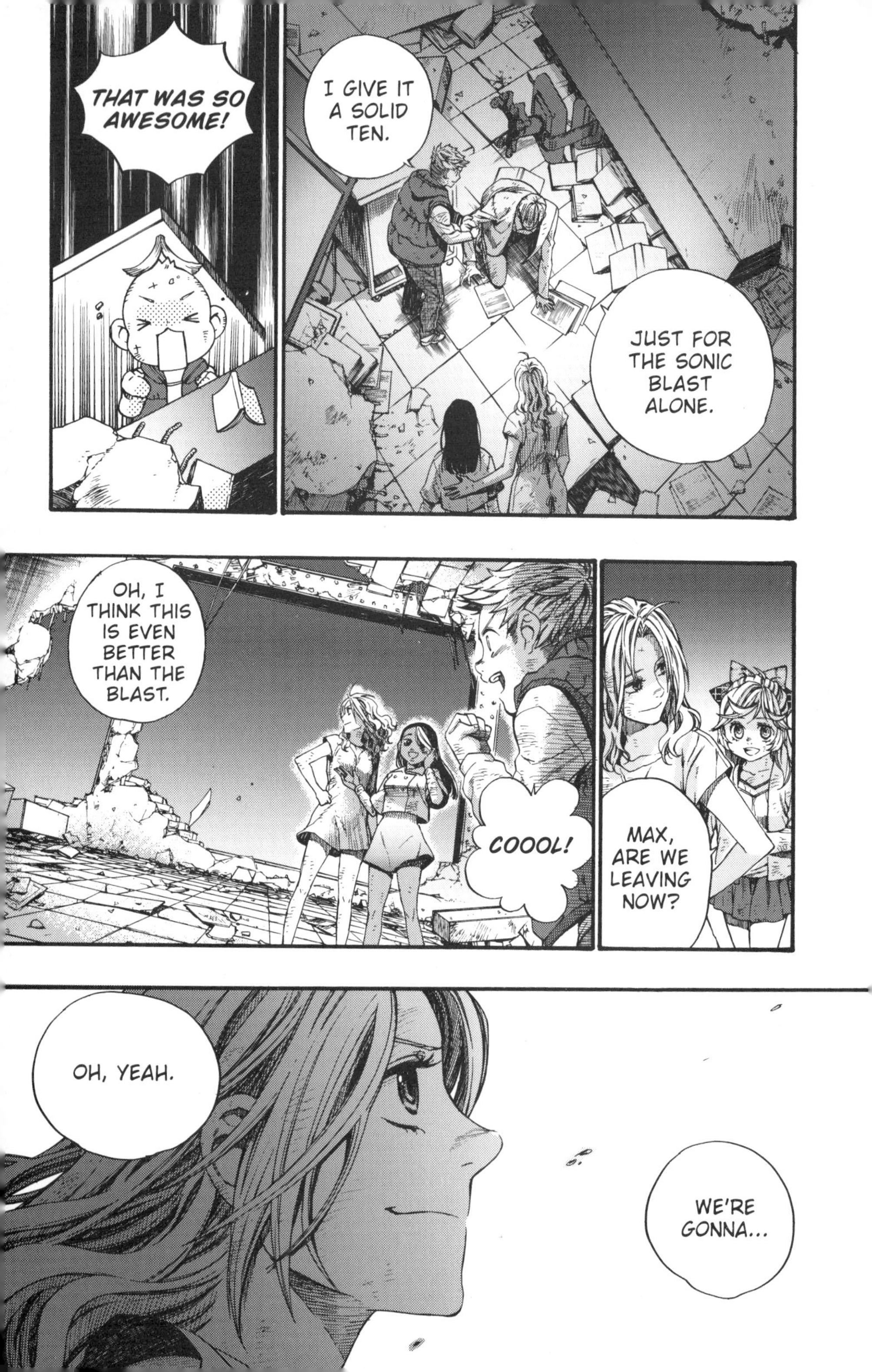
THAT WAS SO AWESOME!
I GIVE IT A SOLID TEN.
JUST FOR THE SONIC BLAST ALONE.
OH, I THINK THIS IS EVEN BETTER THAN THE BLAST.
COOOL!
MAX, ARE WE LEAVING NOW?
OH, YEAH.
WE'RE GONNA...

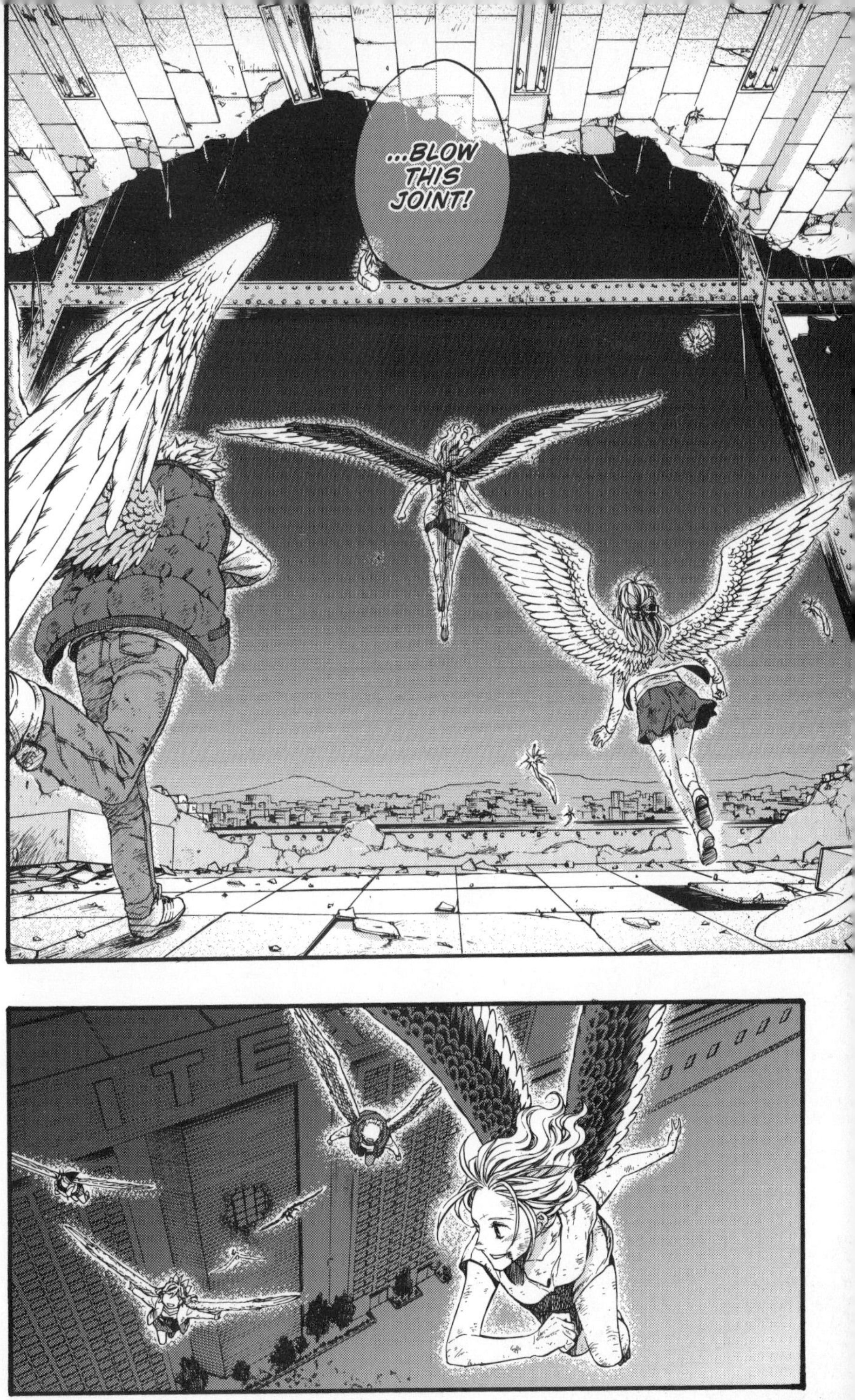
...BLOW THIS JOINT!

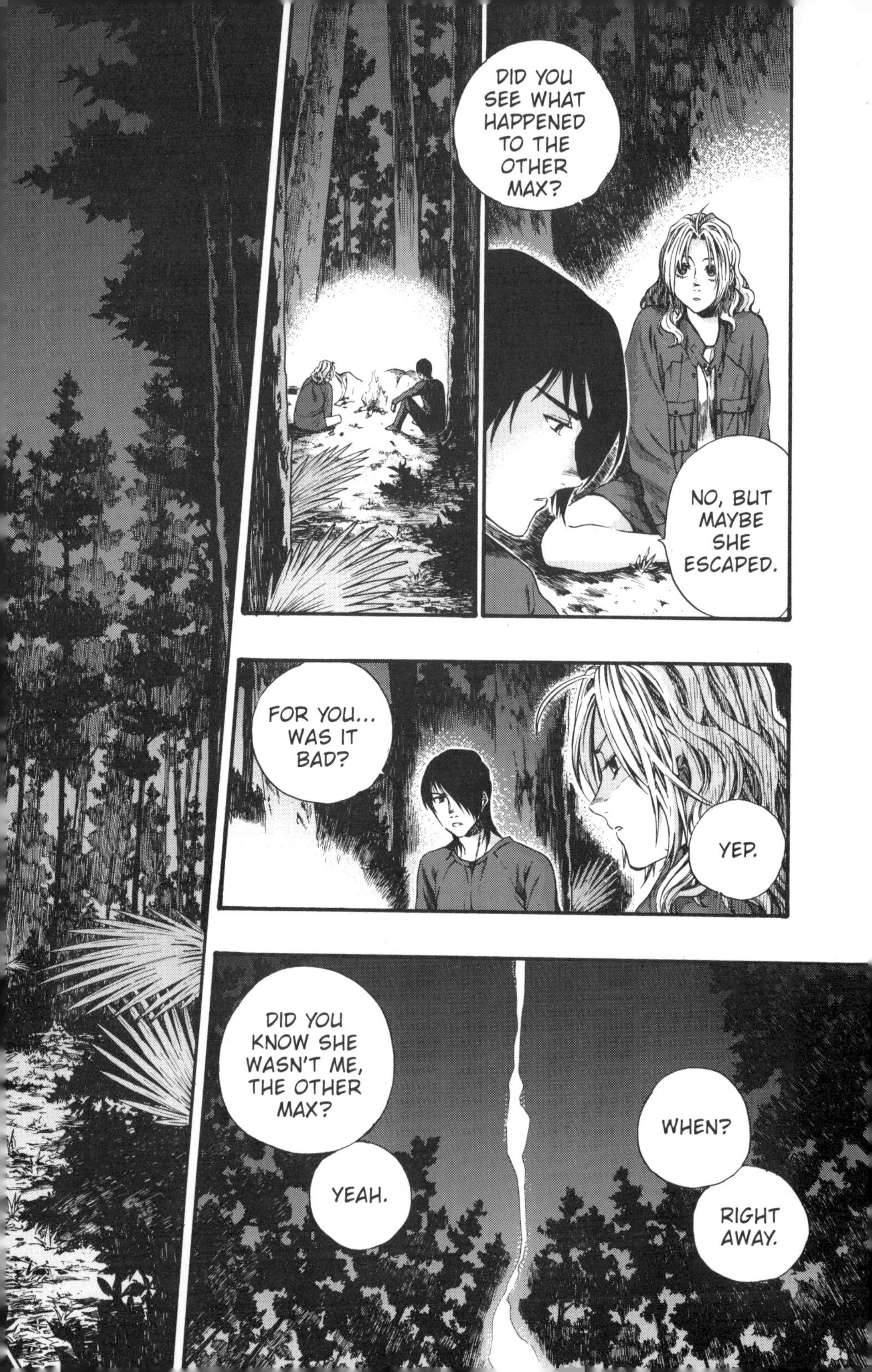
DID YOU SEE WHAT HAPPENED TO THE OTHER MAX?
NO, BUT MAYBE SHE ESCAPED.
FOR YOU... WAS IT BAD?
YEP.
DID YOU KNOW SHE WASN'T ME, THE OTHER MAX?
YEAH.
WHEN?
RIGHT AWAY.

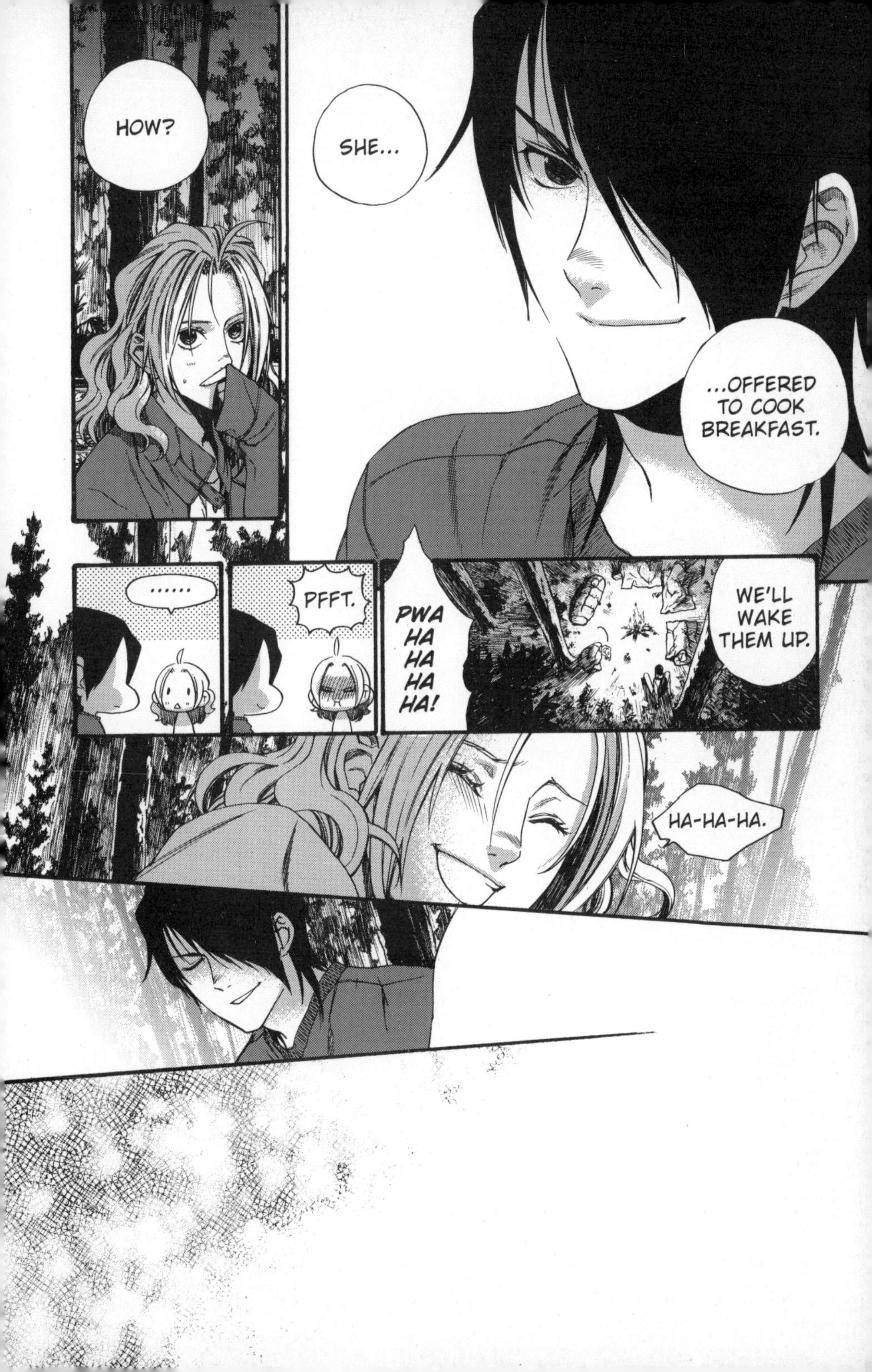
SHE...
...OFFERED TO COOK BREAKFAST.
HOW?
WE'LL WAKE THEM UP.
PWA HA HA HA HA!
PFFT.
......
HA-HA-HA.

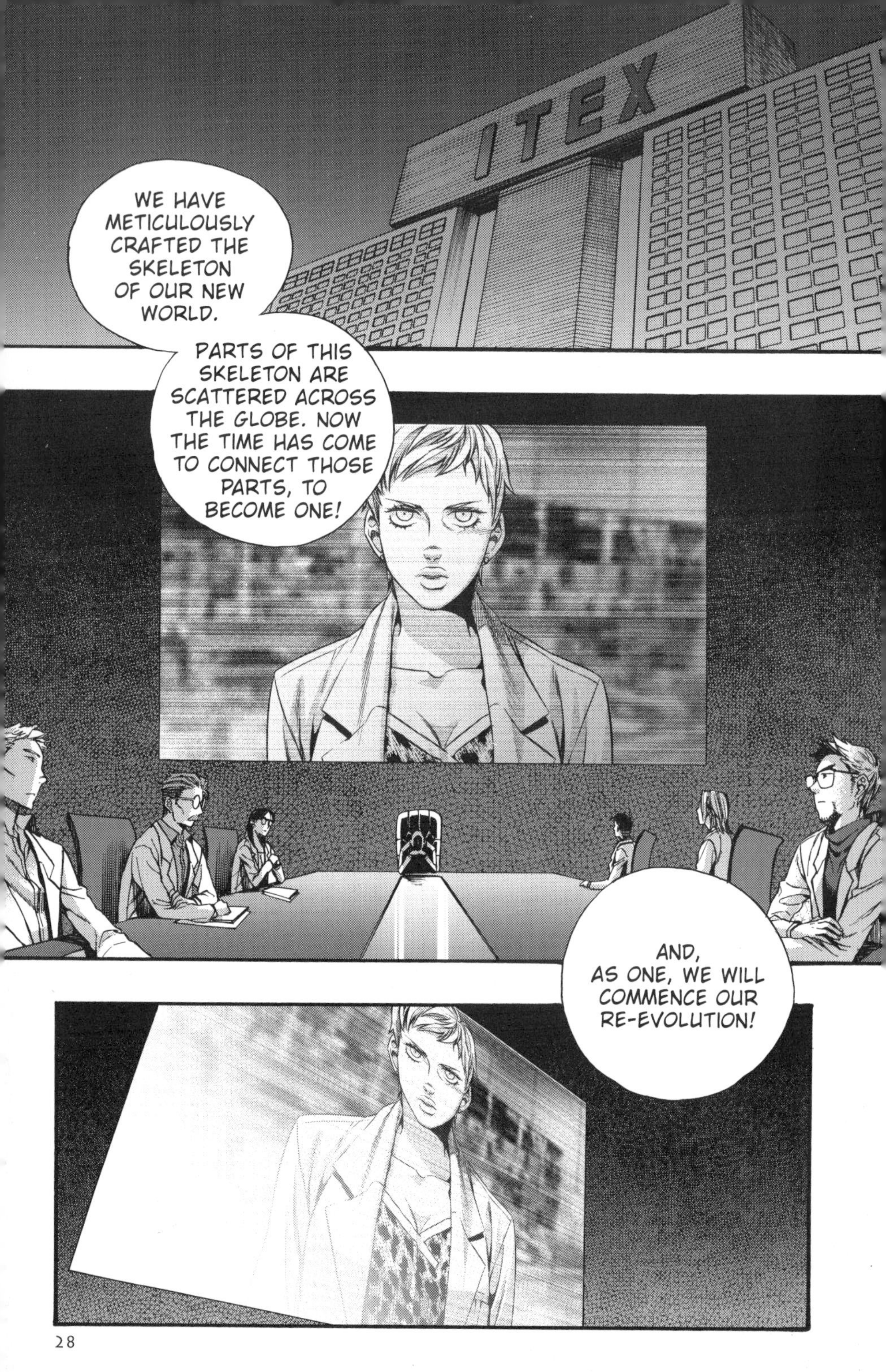
ITEX
WE HAVE METICULOUSLY CRAFTED THE SKELETON OF OUR NEW WORLD.
PARTS OF THIS SKELETON ARE SCATTERED ACROSS THE GLOBE. NOW THE TIME HAS COME TO CONNECT THOSE PARTS, TO BECOME ONE!
AND, AS ONE, WE WILL COMMENCE OUR RE-EVOLUTION!

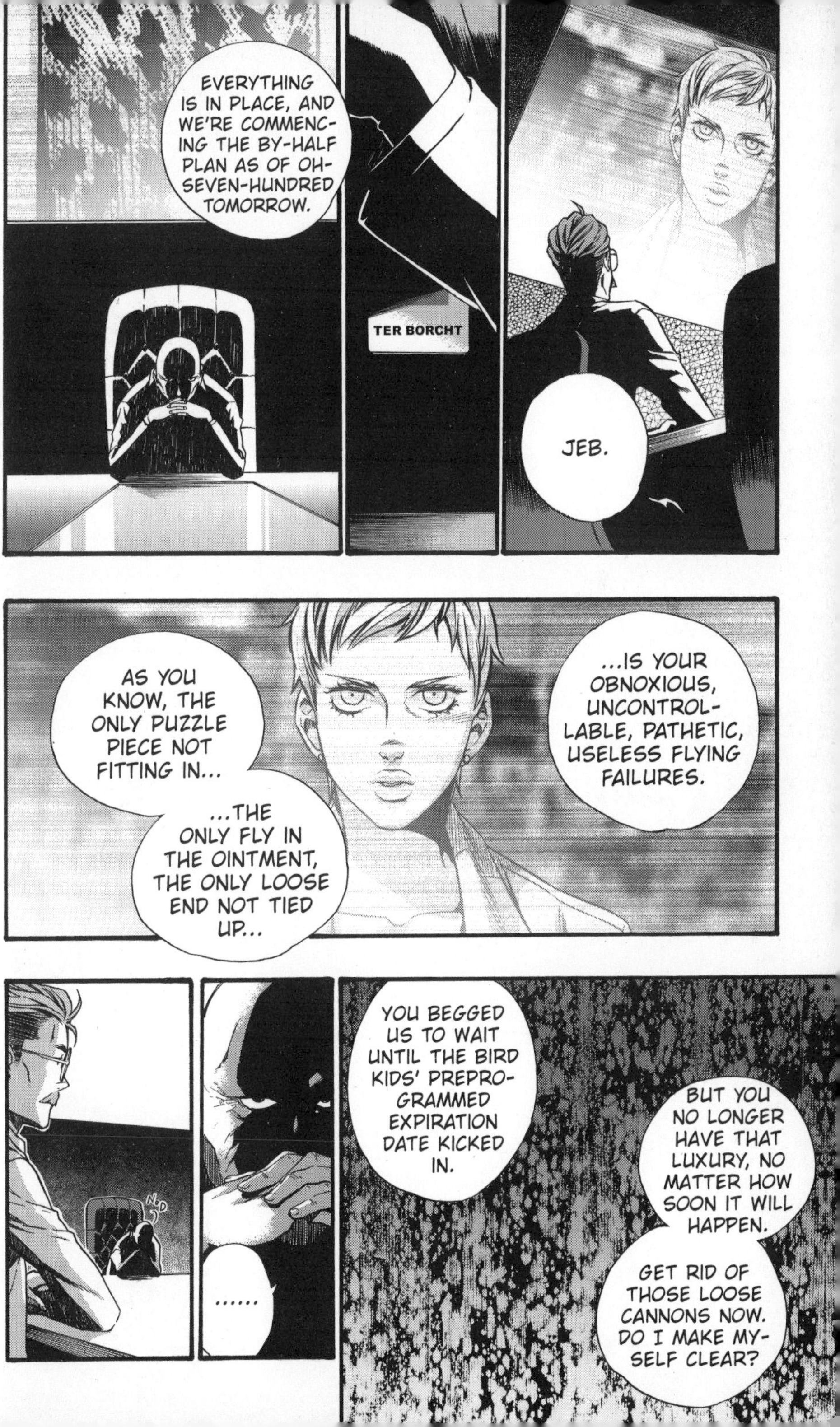
EVERYTHING IS IN PLACE, AND WE'RE COMMENCING THE BY-HALF PLAN AS OF OH-SEVEN-HUNDRED TOMORROW.
TER BORCHT
JEB.
AS YOU KNOW, THE ONLY PUZZLE PIECE NOT FITTING IN...
...THE ONLY FLY IN THE OINTMENT, THE ONLY LOOSE END NOT TIED UP...
...IS YOUR OBNOXIOUS, UNCONTROL-LABLE, PATHETIC, USELESS FLYING FAILURES.
......
YOU BEGGED US TO WAIT UNTIL THE BIRD KIDS' PREPRO-GRAMMED EXPIRATION DATE KICKED IN.
BUT YOU NO LONGER HAVE THAT LUXURY, NO MATTER HOW SOON IT WILL HAPPEN.
GET RID OF THOSE LOOSE CANNONS NOW. DO I MAKE MY-SELF CLEAR?

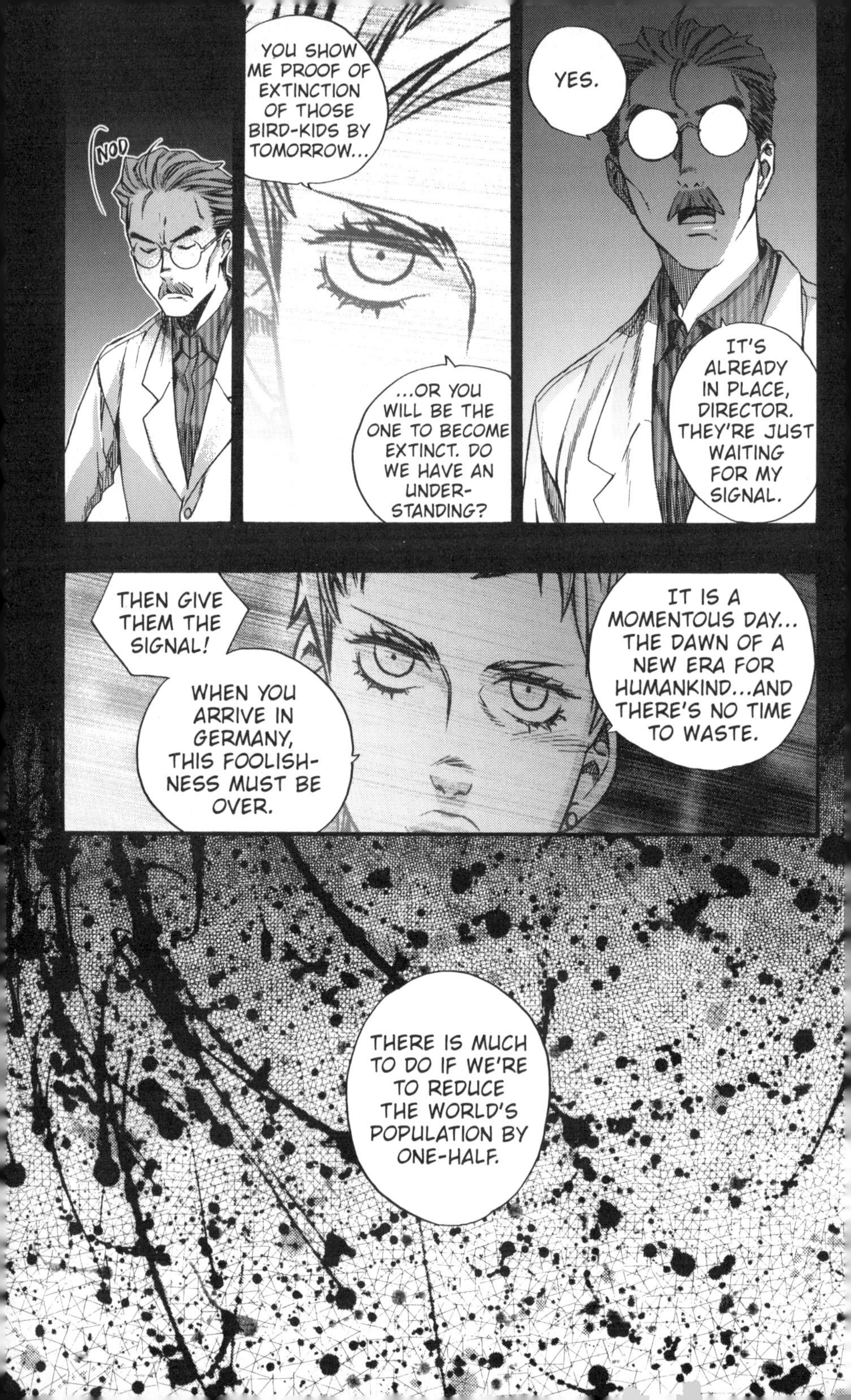

MAXIMUM
RIDE

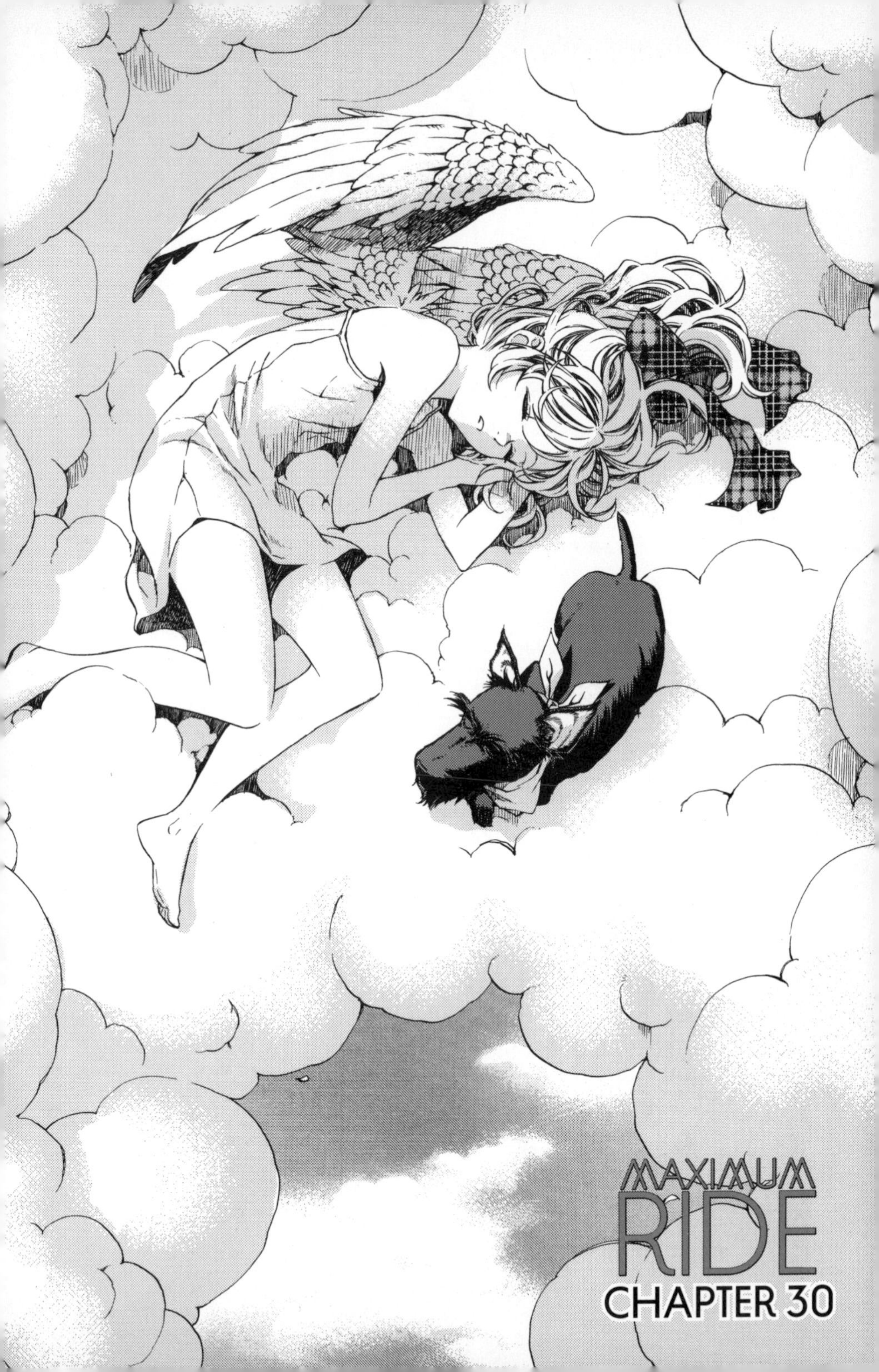
MAXIMUM
RIDE
CHAPTER 30

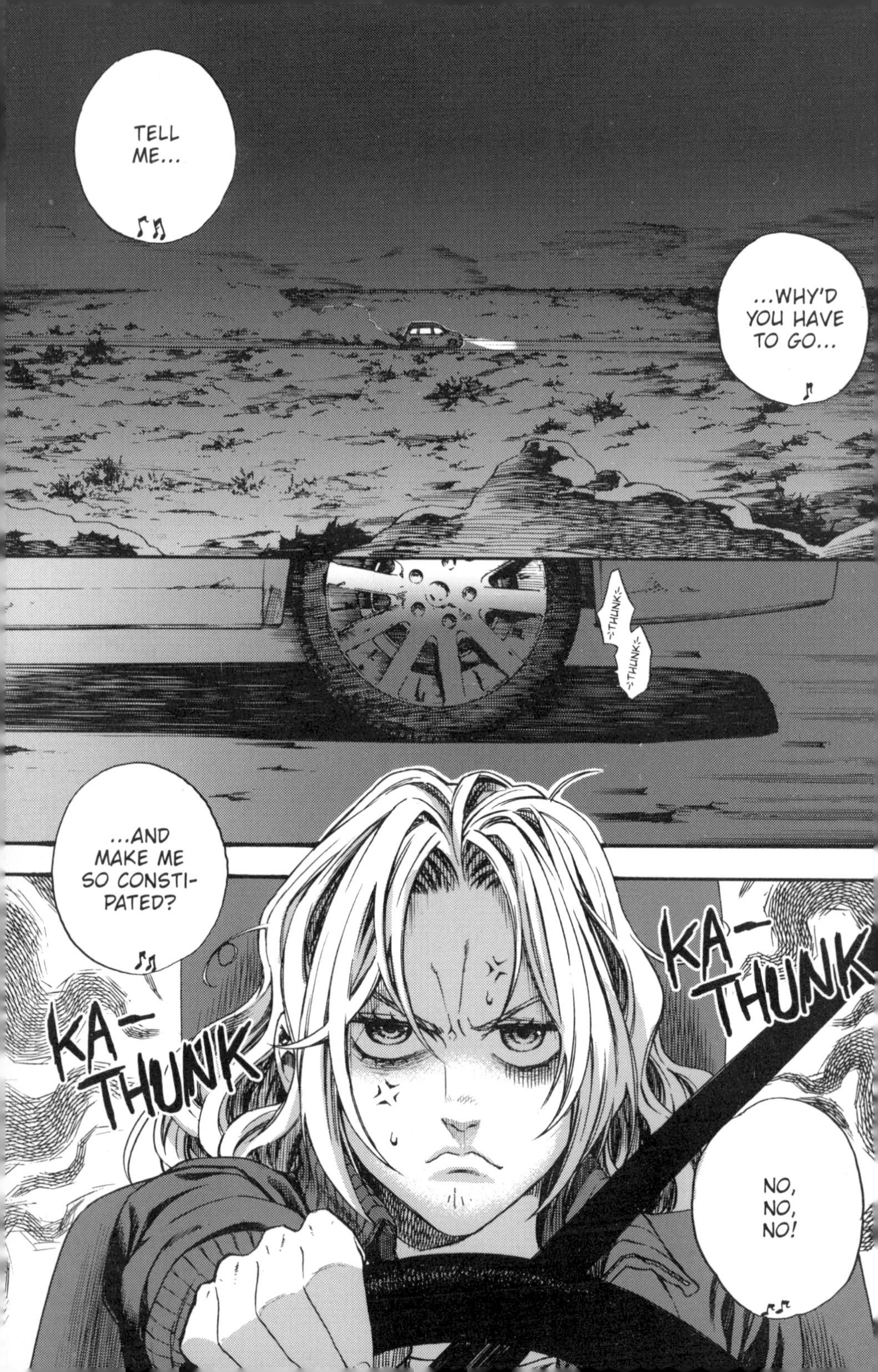
TELL ME...
...WHY'D YOU HAVE TO GO...
THUNK THUNK
...AND MAKE ME SO CONSTI-PATED?
KA-THUNK
KA-THUNK
NO, NO, NO!

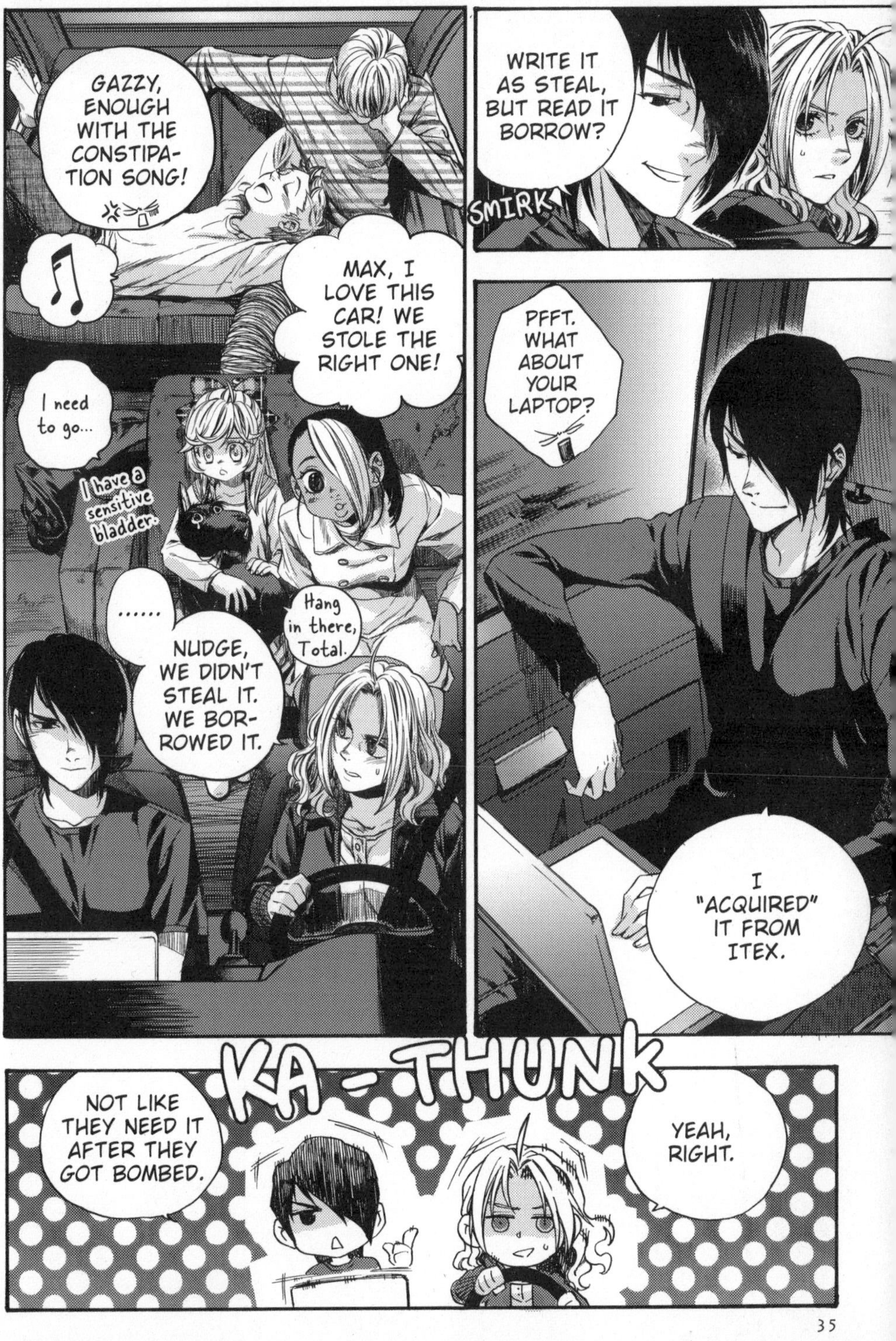
GAZZY, ENOUGH WITH THE CONSTIPATION SONG!
MAX, I LOVE THIS CAR! WE STOLE THE RIGHT ONE!
I need to go...
I have a sensitive bladder.
......
Hang in there, Total.
NUDGE, WE DIDN'T STEAL IT. WE BORROWED IT.
WRITE IT AS STEAL, BUT READ IT BORROW?
SMIRK
PFFT. WHAT ABOUT YOUR LAPTOP?
I "ACQUIRED" IT FROM ITEX.
KA-THUNK
NOT LIKE THEY NEED IT AFTER THEY GOT BOMBED.
YEAH, RIGHT.

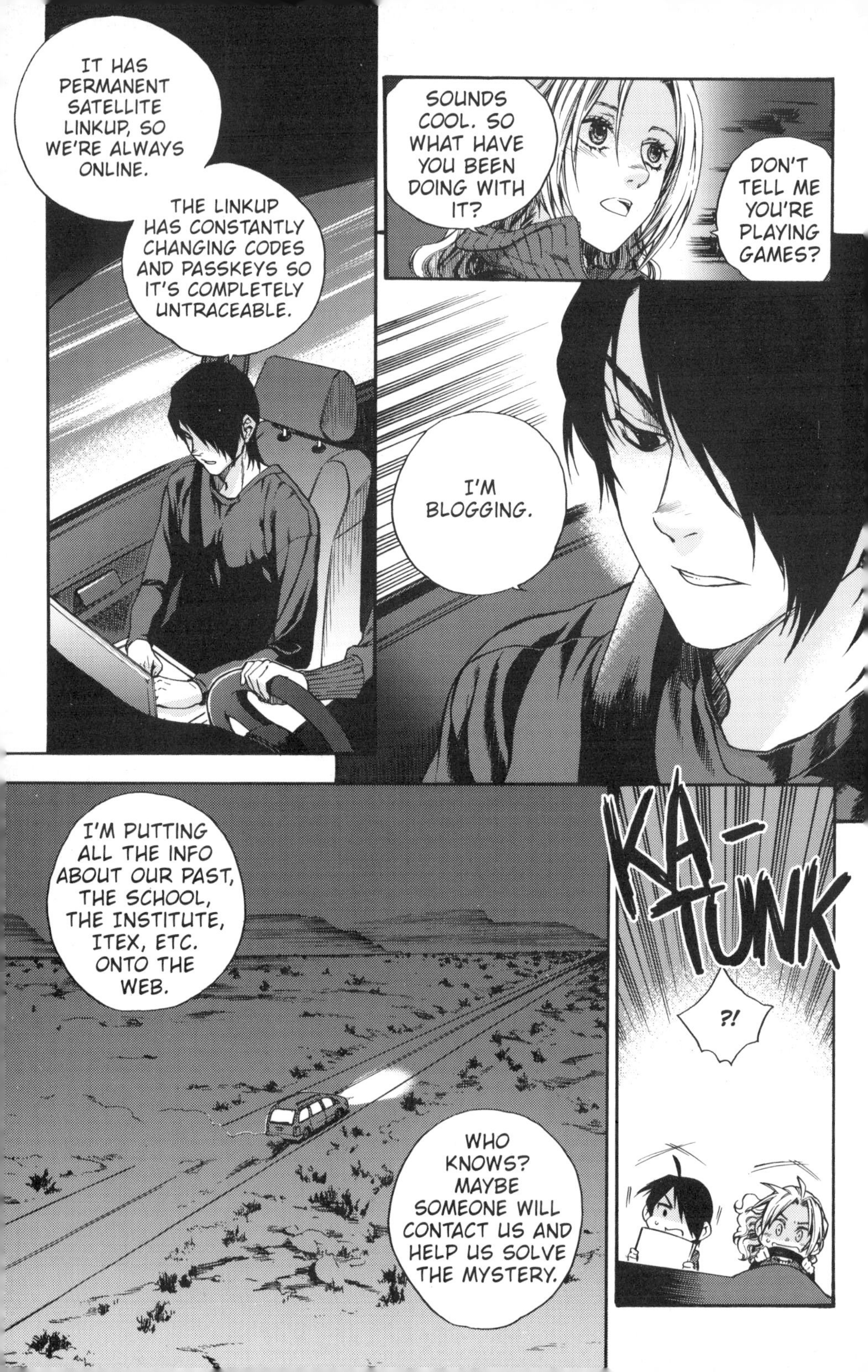

IT HAS PERMANENT SATELLITE LINKUP, SO WE'RE ALWAYS ONLINE.
THE LINKUP HAS CONSTANTLY CHANGING CODES AND PASSKEYS SO IT'S COMPLETELY UNTRACEABLE.
SOUNDS COOL. SO WHAT HAVE YOU BEEN DOING WITH IT?
DON'T TELL ME YOU'RE PLAYING GAMES?
I'M BLOGGING.
I'M PUTTING ALL THE INFO ABOUT OUR PAST, THE SCHOOL, THE INSTITUTE, ITEX, ETC. ONTO THE WEB.
WHO KNOWS? MAYBE SOMEONE WILL CONTACT US AND HELP US SOLVE THE MYSTERY.
KA-TUNK
?!

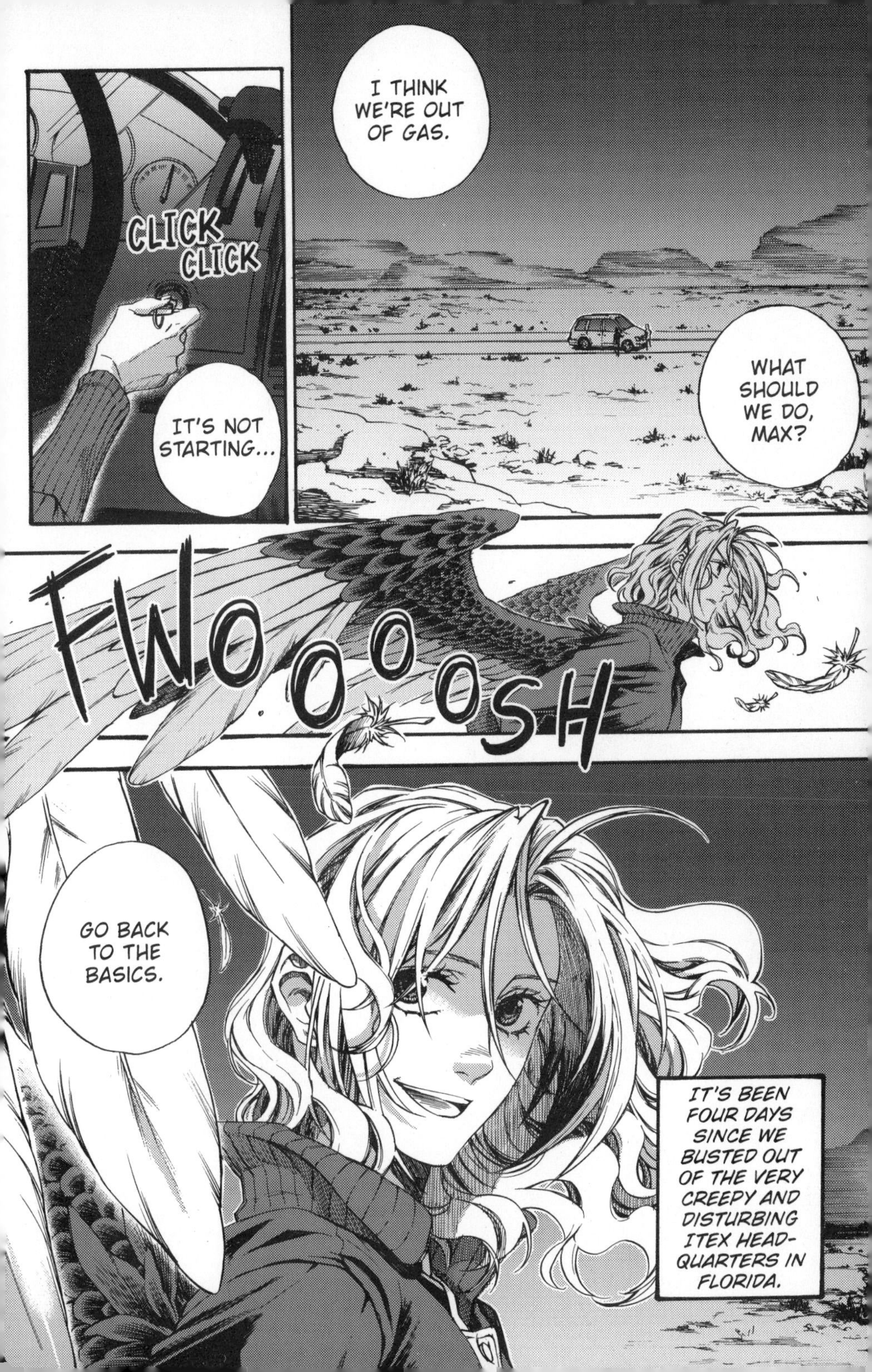
CLICK CLICK
IT'S NOT STARTING...
I THINK WE'RE OUT OF GAS.
WHAT SHOULD WE DO, MAX?
FWOOOOSH
GO BACK TO THE BASICS.
IT'S BEEN FOUR DAYS SINCE WE BUSTED OUT OF THE VERY CREEPY AND DISTURBING ITEX HEAD-QUARTERS IN FLORIDA.

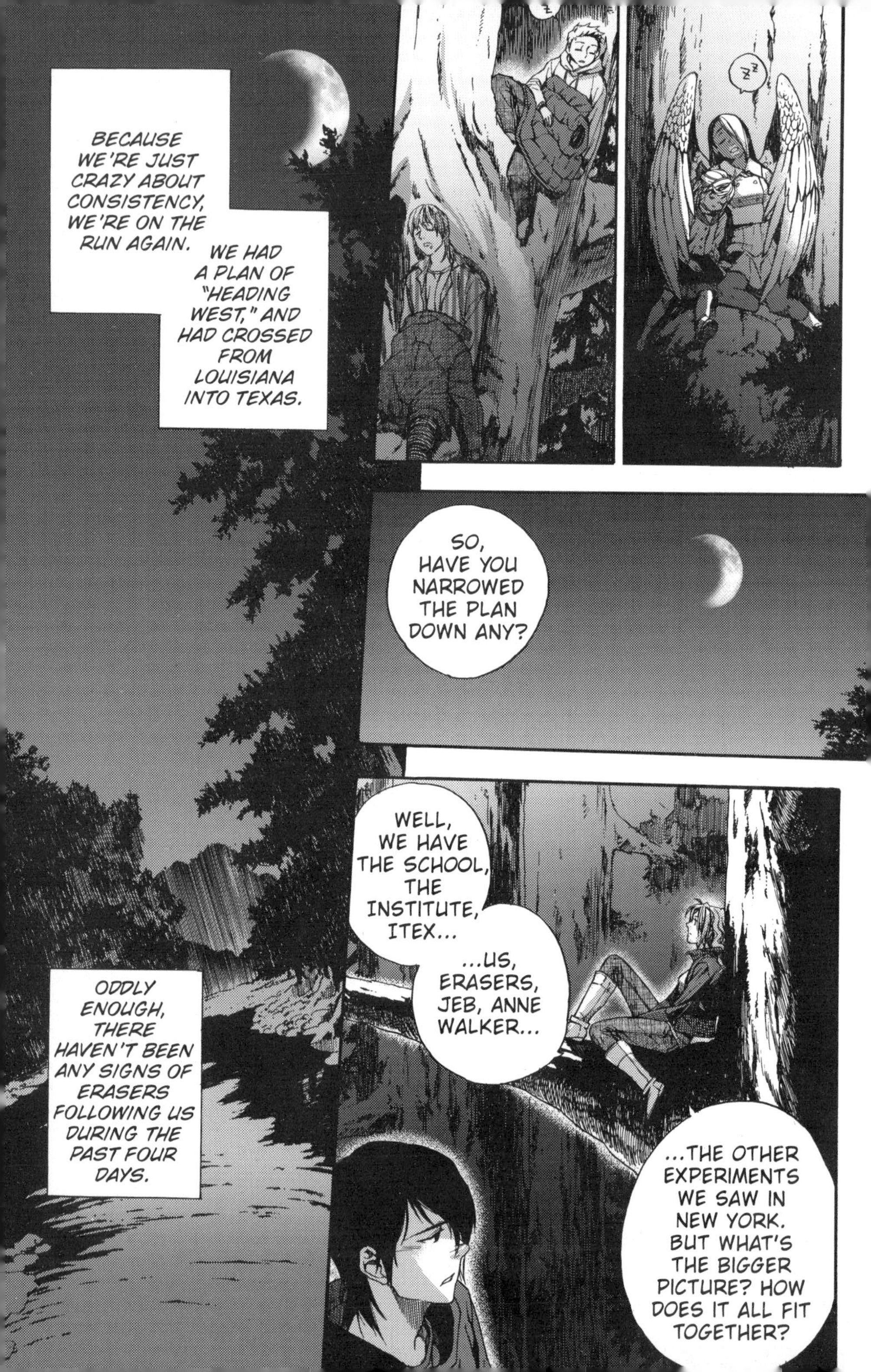
BECAUSE WE'RE JUST CRAZY ABOUT CONSISTENCY, WE'RE ON THE RUN AGAIN.
WE HAD A PLAN OF "HEADING WEST," AND HAD CROSSED FROM LOUISIANA INTO TEXAS.
SO, HAVE YOU NARROWED THE PLAN DOWN ANY?
WELL, WE HAVE THE SCHOOL, THE INSTITUTE, ITEX...
...US, ERASERS, JEB, ANNE WALKER...
...THE OTHER EXPERIMENTS WE SAW IN NEW YORK. BUT WHAT'S THE BIGGER PICTURE? HOW DOES IT ALL FIT TOGETHER?
ODDLY ENOUGH, THERE HAVEN'T BEEN ANY SIGNS OF ERASERS FOLLOWING US DURING THE PAST FOUR DAYS.

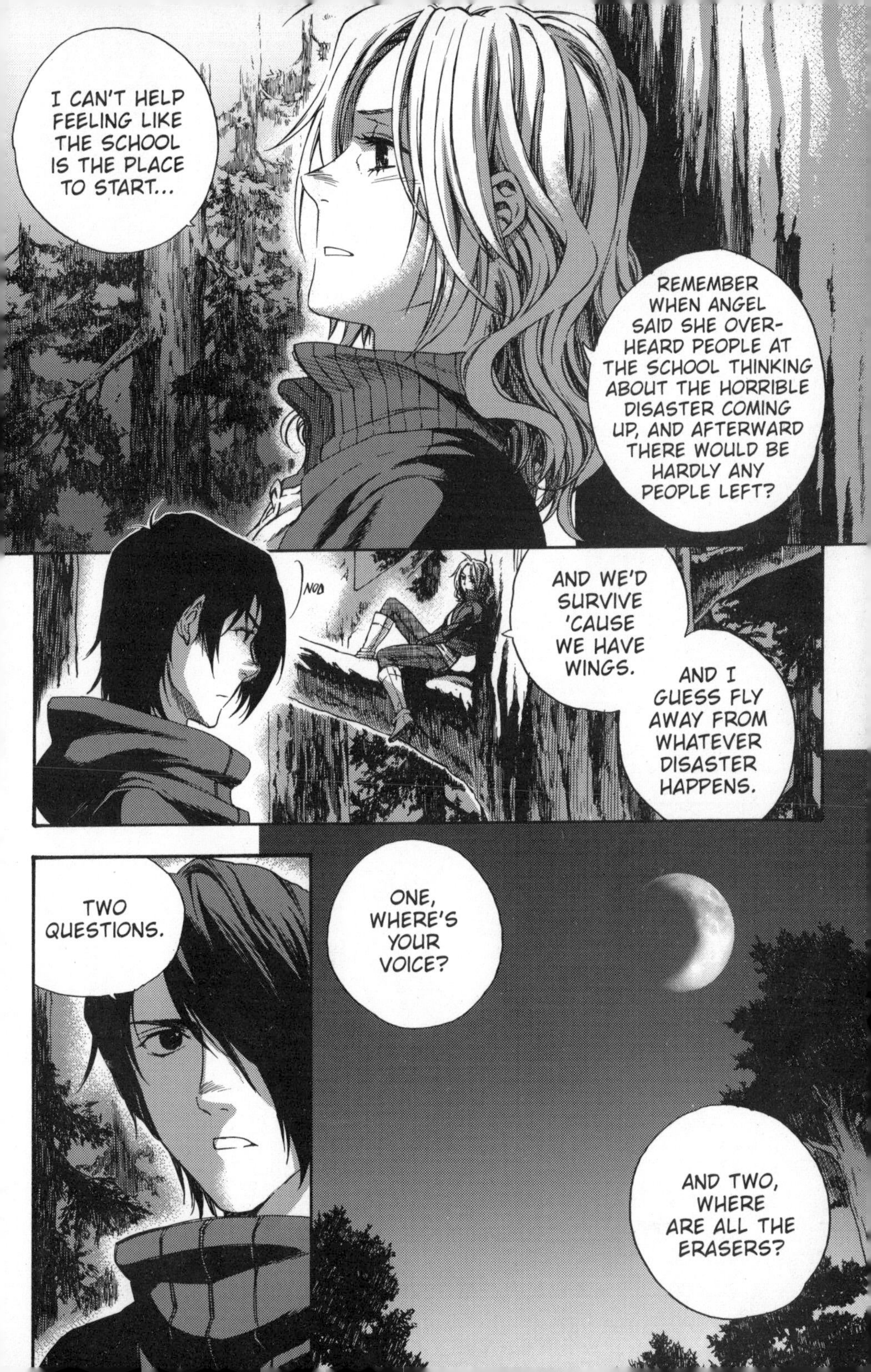
I CAN'T HELP FEELING LIKE THE SCHOOL IS THE PLACE TO START...
REMEMBER WHEN ANGEL SAID SHE OVER-HEARD PEOPLE AT THE SCHOOL THINKING ABOUT THE HORRIBLE DISASTER COMING UP, AND AFTERWARD THERE WOULD BE HARDLY ANY PEOPLE LEFT?
AND WE'D SURVIVE 'CAUSE WE HAVE WINGS.
AND I GUESS FLY AWAY FROM WHATEVER DISASTER HAPPENS.
NOD
TWO QUESTIONS.
ONE, WHERE'S YOUR VOICE?
AND TWO, WHERE ARE ALL THE ERASERS?

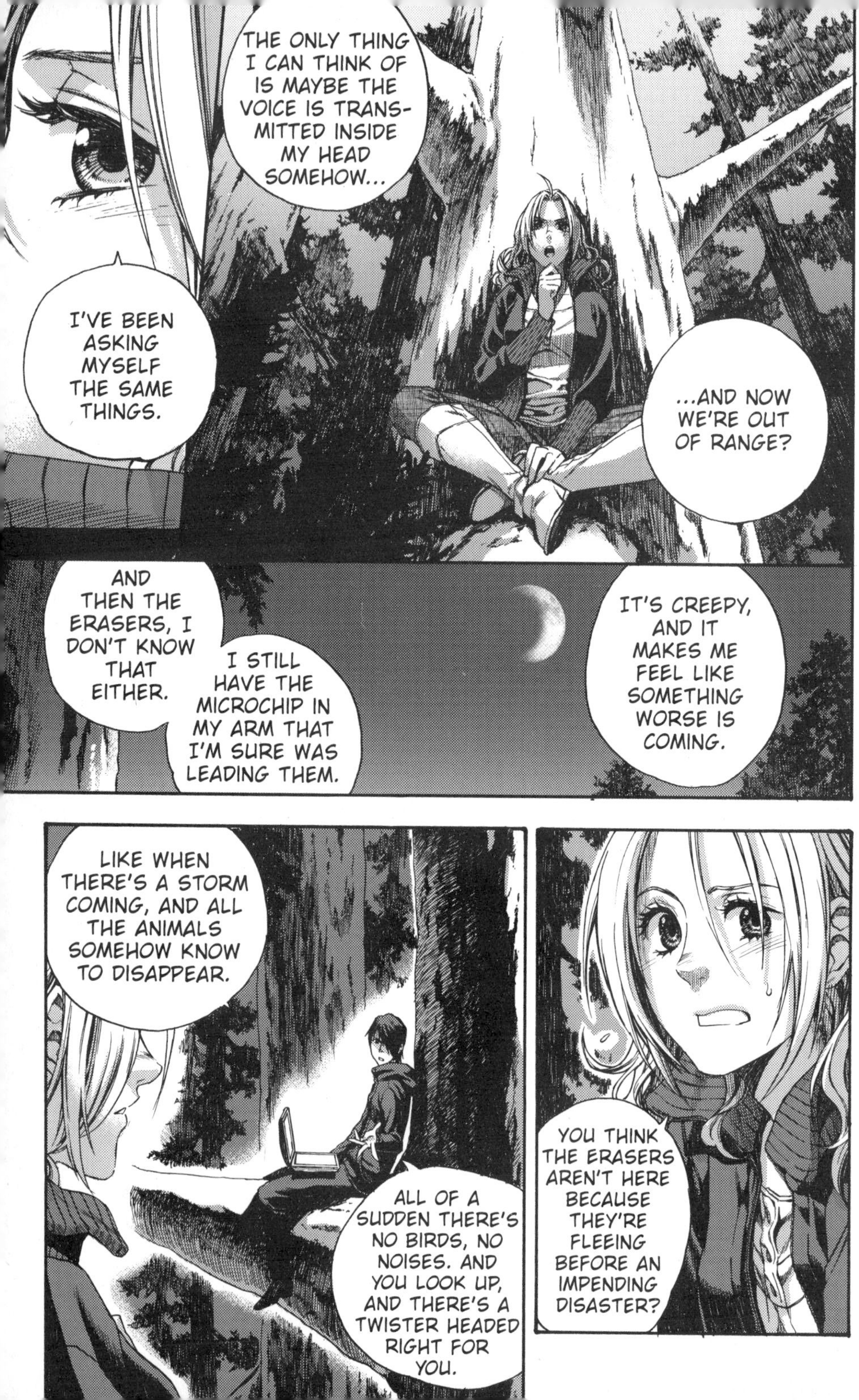
THE ONLY THING I CAN THINK OF IS MAYBE THE VOICE IS TRANS-MITTED INSIDE MY HEAD SOMEHOW...
I'VE BEEN ASKING MYSELF THE SAME THINGS.
...AND NOW WE'RE OUT OF RANGE?
AND THEN THE ERASERS, I DON'T KNOW THAT EITHER.
I STILL HAVE THE MICROCHIP IN MY ARM THAT I'M SURE WAS LEADING THEM.
IT'S CREEPY, AND IT MAKES ME FEEL LIKE SOMETHING WORSE IS COMING.
LIKE WHEN THERE'S A STORM COMING, AND ALL THE ANIMALS SOMEHOW KNOW TO DISAPPEAR.
ALL OF A SUDDEN THERE'S NO BIRDS, NO NOISES. AND YOU LOOK UP, AND THERE'S A TWISTER HEADED RIGHT FOR YOU.
YOU THINK THE ERASERS AREN'T HERE BECAUSE THEY'RE FLEEING BEFORE AN IMPENDING DISASTER?

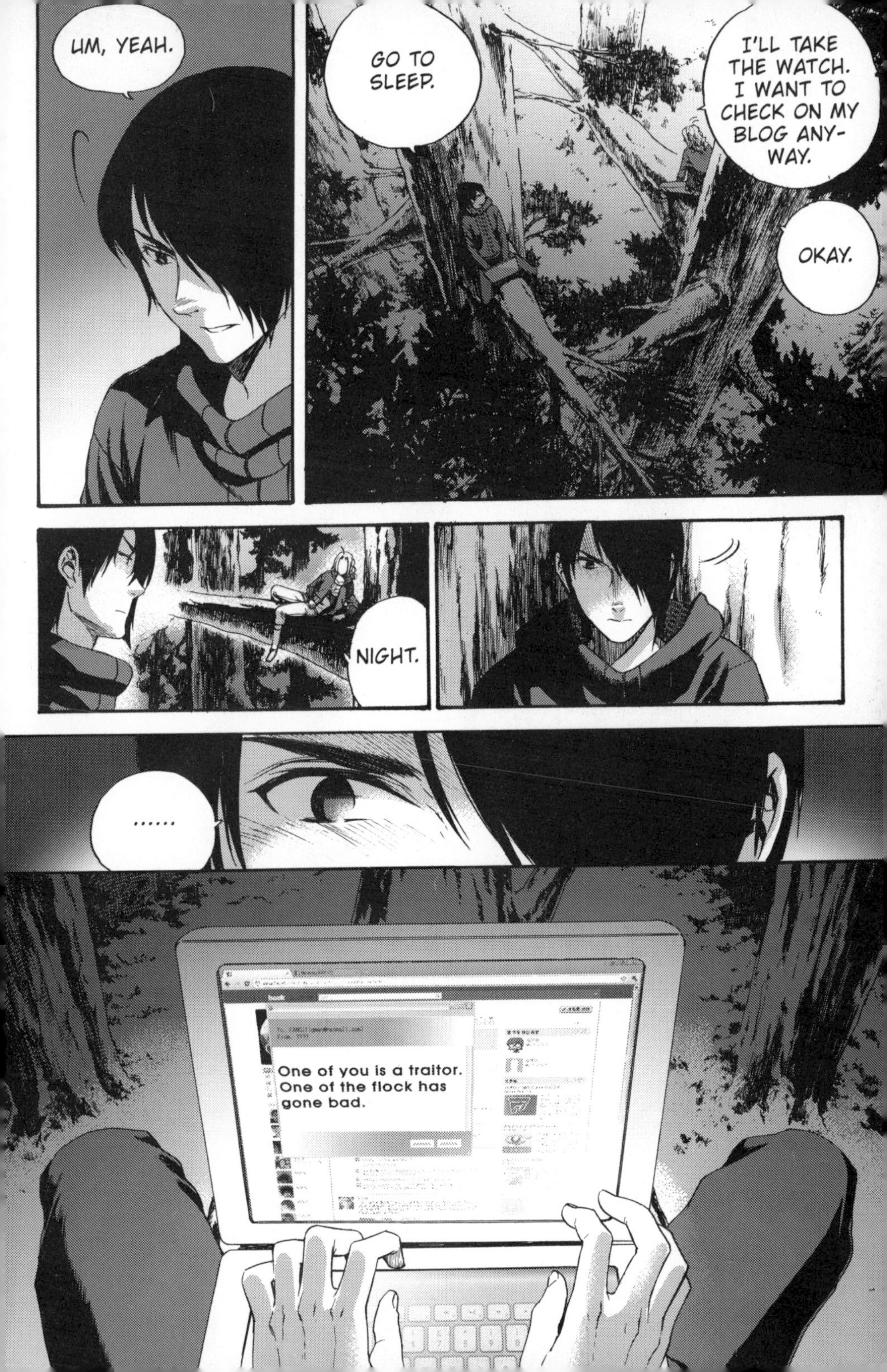

UM, YEAH.
GO TO SLEEP.
I'LL TAKE THE WATCH. I WANT TO CHECK ON MY BLOG ANY-WAY.
OKAY.
NIGHT.
......
One of you is a traitor. One of the flock has gone bad.

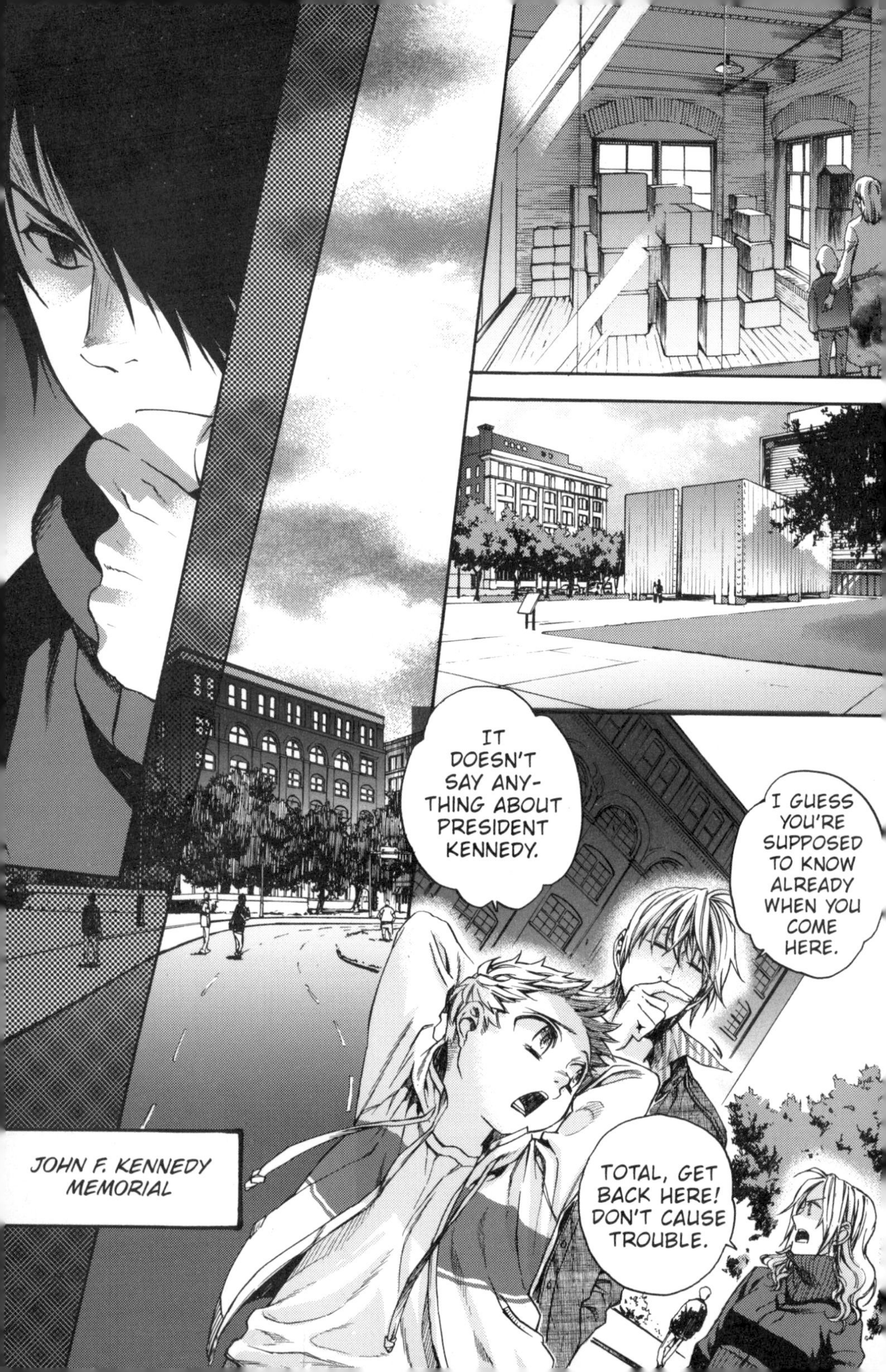
JOHN F. KENNEDY MEMORIAL
IT DOESN'T SAY ANY-THING ABOUT PRESIDENT KENNEDY.
I GUESS YOU'RE SUPPOSED TO KNOW ALREADY WHEN YOU COME HERE.
TOTAL, GET BACK HERE! DON'T CAUSE TROUBLE.

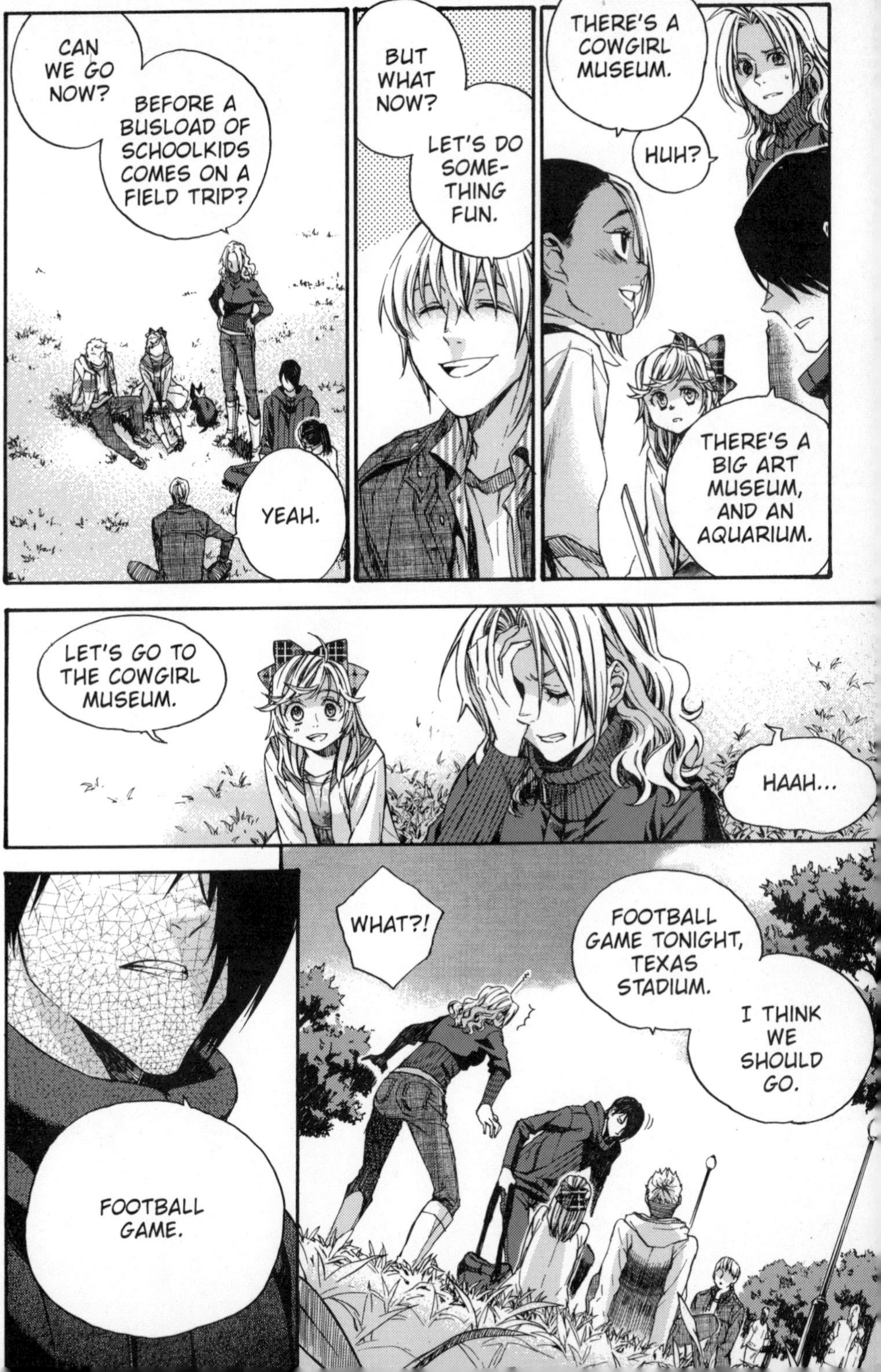

CAN WE GO NOW?
BEFORE A BUSLOAD OF SCHOOLKIDS COMES ON A FIELD TRIP?
YEAH.
BUT WHAT NOW?
LET'S DO SOME-THING FUN.
THERE'S A COWGIRL MUSEUM.
HUH?
THERE'S A BIG ART MUSEUM, AND AN AQUARIUM.
LET'S GO TO THE COWGIRL MUSEUM.
HAAH...
WHAT?!
FOOTBALL GAME TONIGHT, TEXAS STADIUM.
I THINK WE SHOULD GO.
FOOTBALL GAME.

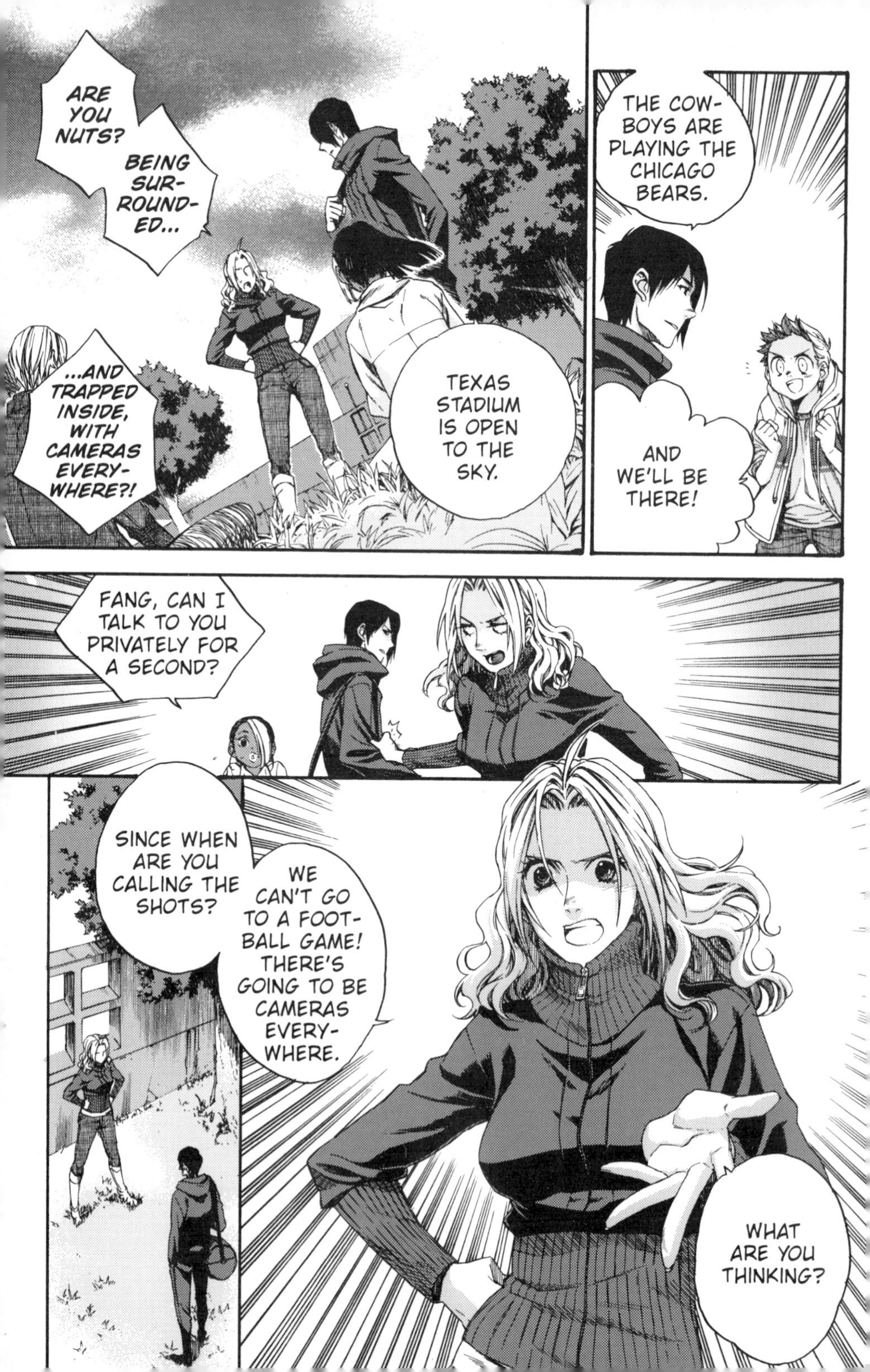
ARE YOU NUTS?
BEING SUR-ROUND-ED...
...AND TRAPPED INSIDE, WITH CAMERAS EVERY-WHERE?!
TEXAS STADIUM IS OPEN TO THE SKY.
THE COW-BOYS ARE PLAYING THE CHICAGO BEARS.
AND WE'LL BE THERE!
FANG, CAN I TALK TO YOU PRIVATELY FOR A SECOND?
SINCE WHEN ARE YOU CALLING THE SHOTS?
WE CAN'T GO TO A FOOT-BALL GAME! THERE'S GOING TO BE CAMERAS EVERY-WHERE.
WHAT ARE YOU THINKING?

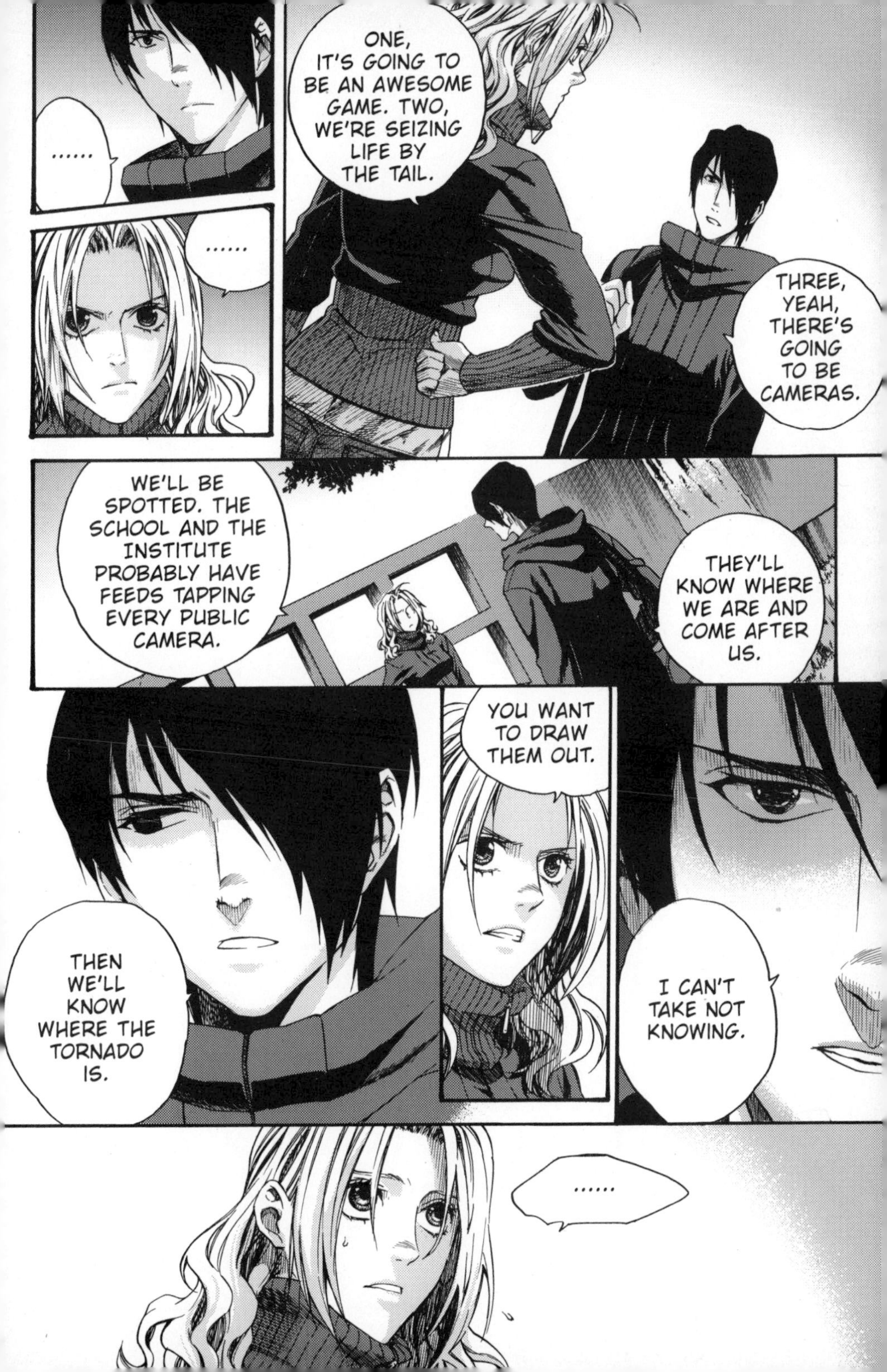
......
......
ONE, IT'S GOING TO BE AN AWESOME GAME. TWO, WE'RE SEIZING LIFE BY THE TAIL.
THREE, YEAH, THERE'S GOING TO BE CAMERAS.
WE'LL BE SPOTTED. THE SCHOOL AND THE INSTITUTE PROBABLY HAVE FEEDS TAPPING EVERY PUBLIC CAMERA.
THEY'LL KNOW WHERE WE ARE AND COME AFTER US.
THEN WE'LL KNOW WHERE THE TORNADO IS.
YOU WANT TO DRAW THEM OUT.
I CAN'T TAKE NOT KNOWING.
......

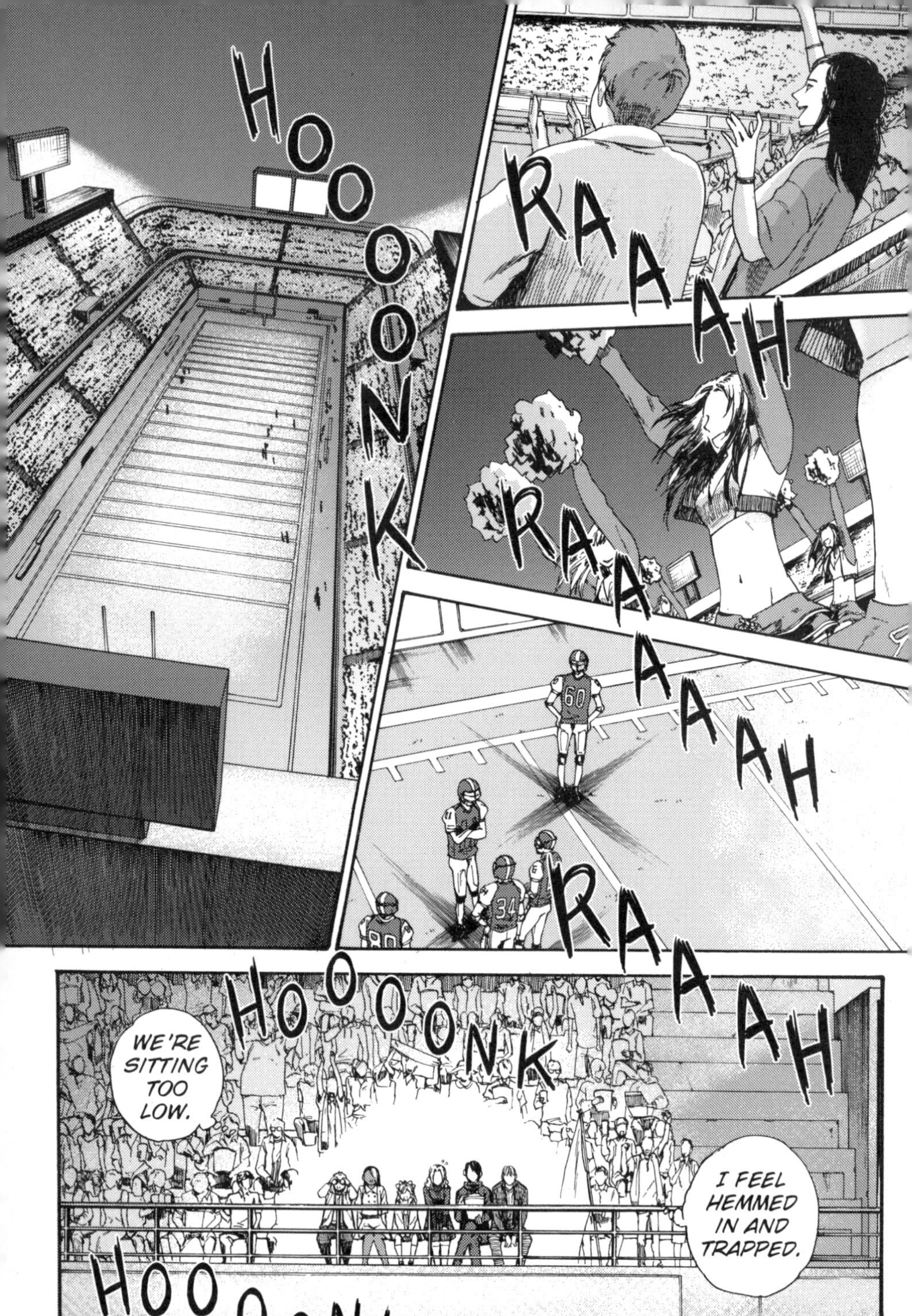
HOOOONK
RAAAH
RAAAAAH
RAAAAH
HOOOONK
WE'RE SITTING TOO LOW.
I FEEL HEMMED IN AND TRAPPED.
HOOOONK

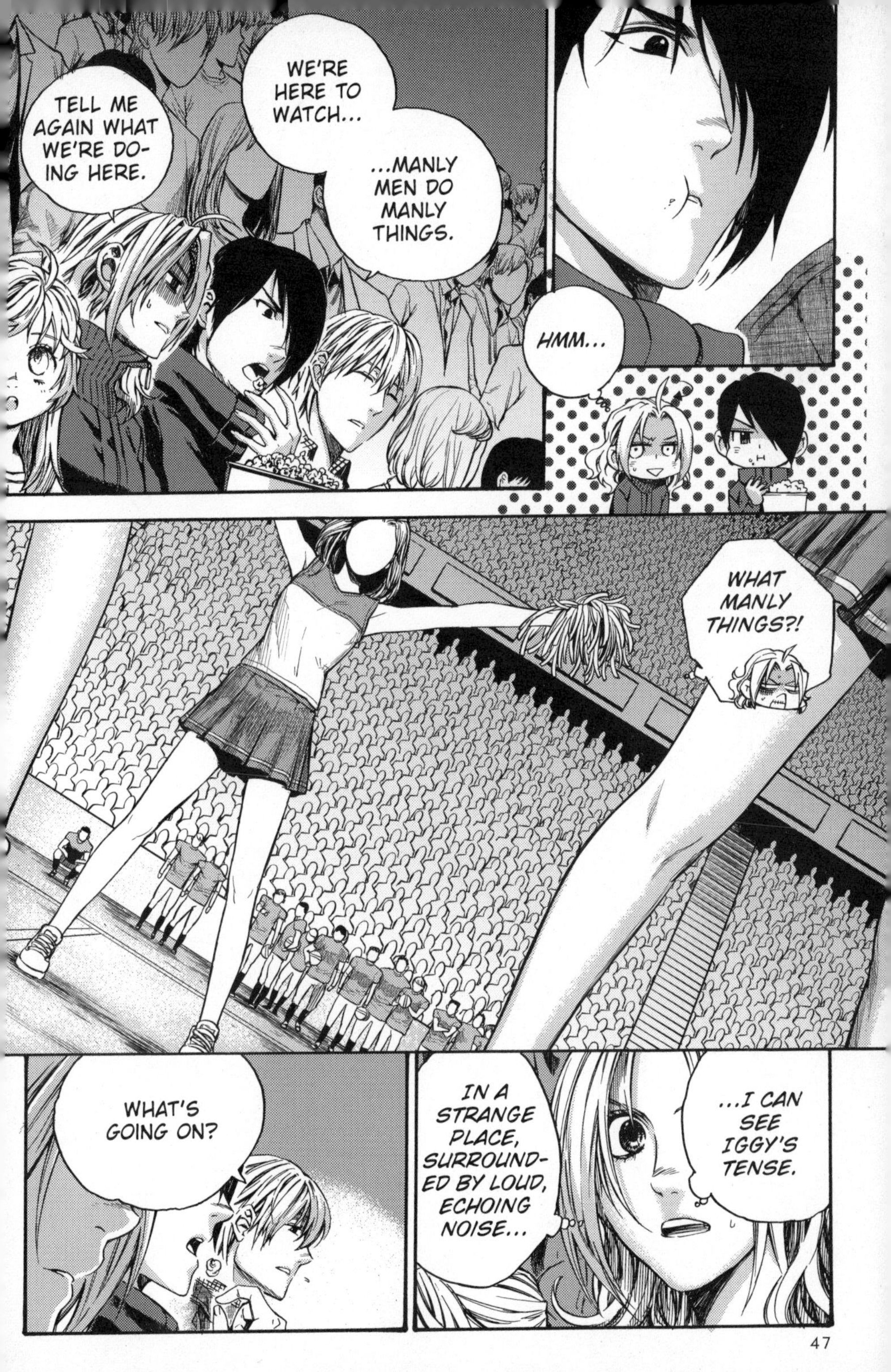
TELL ME AGAIN WHAT WE'RE DOING HERE.
WE'RE HERE TO WATCH...
...MANLY MEN DO MANLY THINGS.
HMM...
WHAT MANLY THINGS?!
WHAT'S GOING ON?
...I CAN SEE IGGY'S TENSE.
IN A STRANGE PLACE, SURROUNDED BY LOUD, ECHOING NOISE...

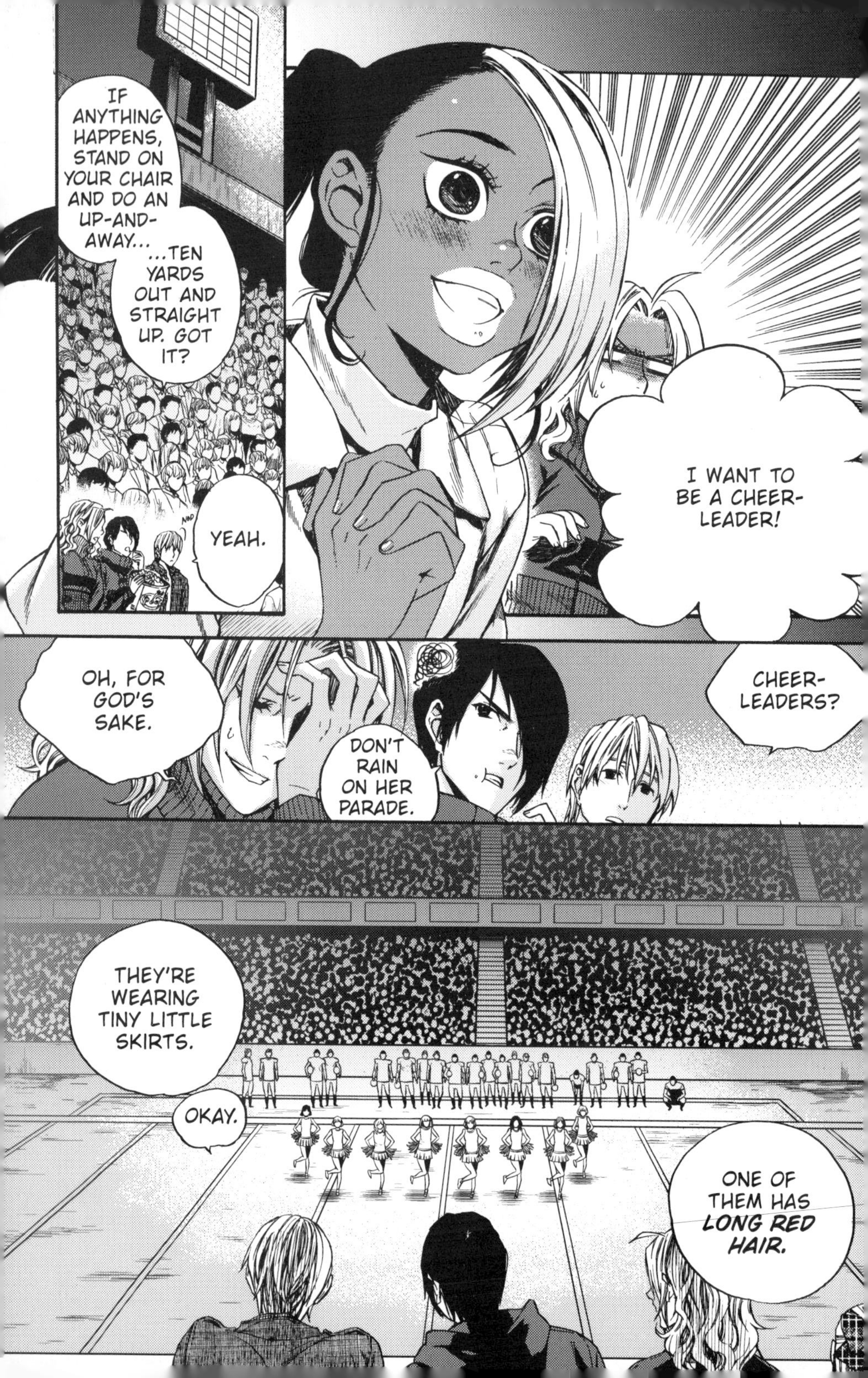
IF ANYTHING HAPPENS, STAND ON YOUR CHAIR AND DO AN UP-AND-AWAY...
...TEN YARDS OUT AND STRAIGHT UP. GOT IT?
NOD
YEAH.
I WANT TO BE A CHEER-LEADER!
OH, FOR GOD'S SAKE.
DON'T RAIN ON HER PARADE.
CHEER-LEADERS?
THEY'RE WEARING TINY LITTLE SKIRTS.
OKAY.
ONE OF THEM HAS **LONG RED HAIR.**

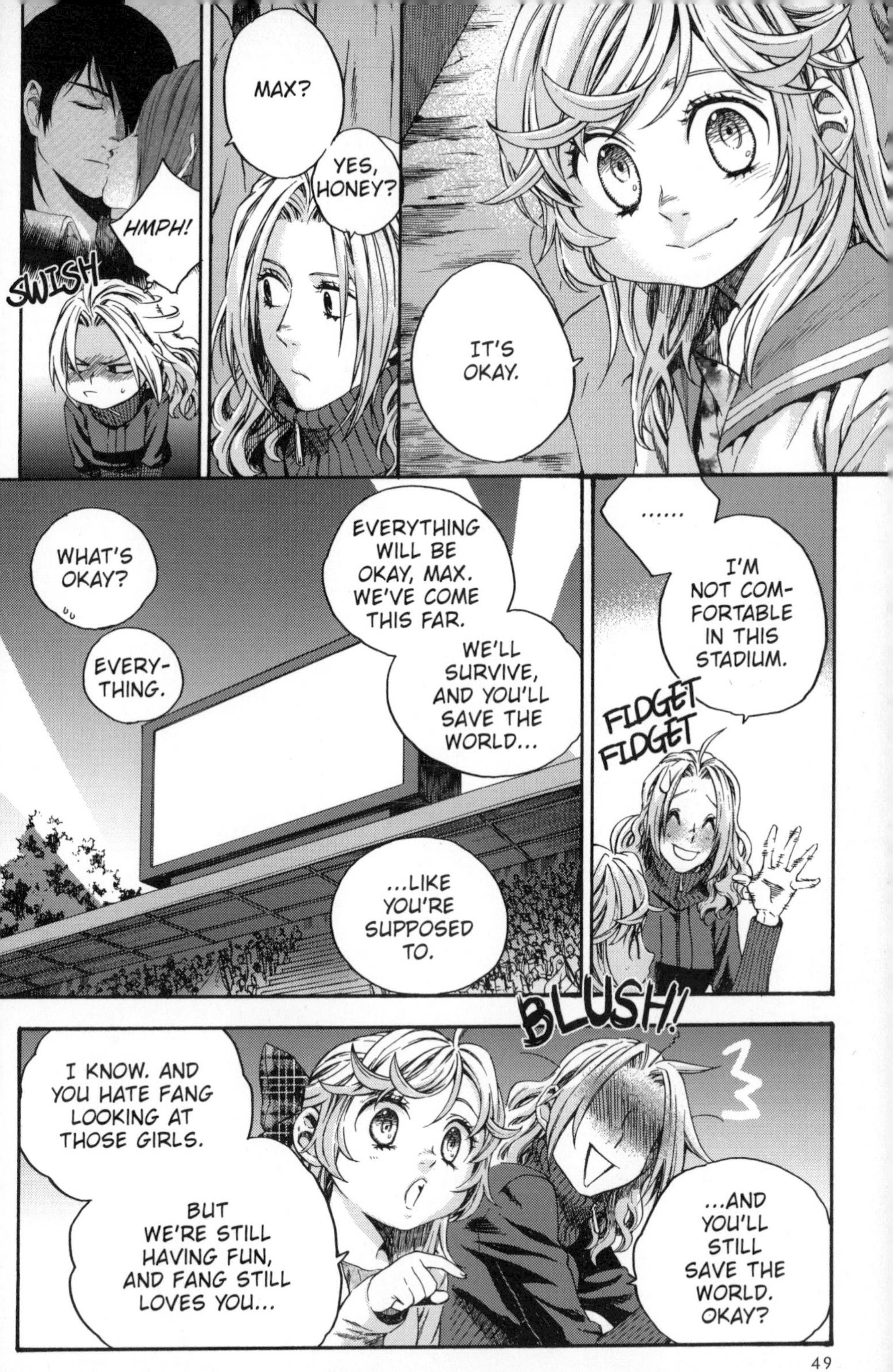
MAX?
YES, HONEY?
HMPH!
SWISH
IT'S OKAY.
WHAT'S OKAY?
EVERY-THING.
EVERYTHING WILL BE OKAY, MAX. WE'VE COME THIS FAR.
WE'LL SURVIVE, AND YOU'LL SAVE THE WORLD...
...LIKE YOU'RE SUPPOSED TO.
......
I'M NOT COM-FORTABLE IN THIS STADIUM.
FIDGET FIDGET
BLUSH!
I KNOW. AND YOU HATE FANG LOOKING AT THOSE GIRLS.
BUT WE'RE STILL HAVING FUN, AND FANG STILL LOVES YOU...
...AND YOU'LL STILL SAVE THE WORLD. OKAY?

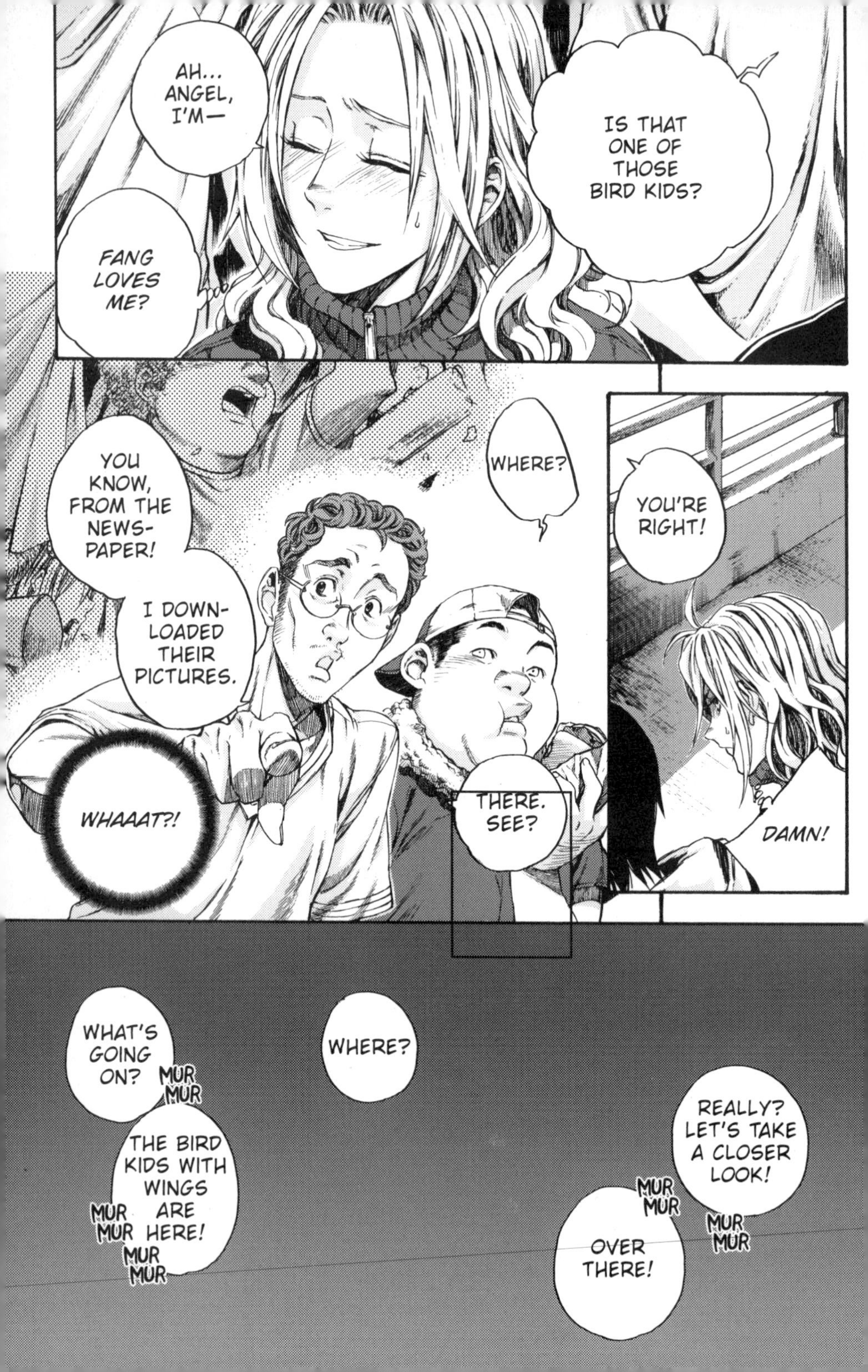
AH... ANGEL, I'M—
FANG LOVES ME?
IS THAT ONE OF THOSE BIRD KIDS?
YOU KNOW, FROM THE NEWS-PAPER!
I DOWN-LOADED THEIR PICTURES.
WHERE?
WHAAAT?!
THERE. SEE?
YOU'RE RIGHT!
DAMN!
WHAT'S GOING ON?
MUR MUR
WHERE?
THE BIRD KIDS WITH WINGS ARE HERE!
MUR MUR
MUR MUR
REALLY? LET'S TAKE A CLOSER LOOK!
MUR MUR
OVER THERE!
MUR MUR

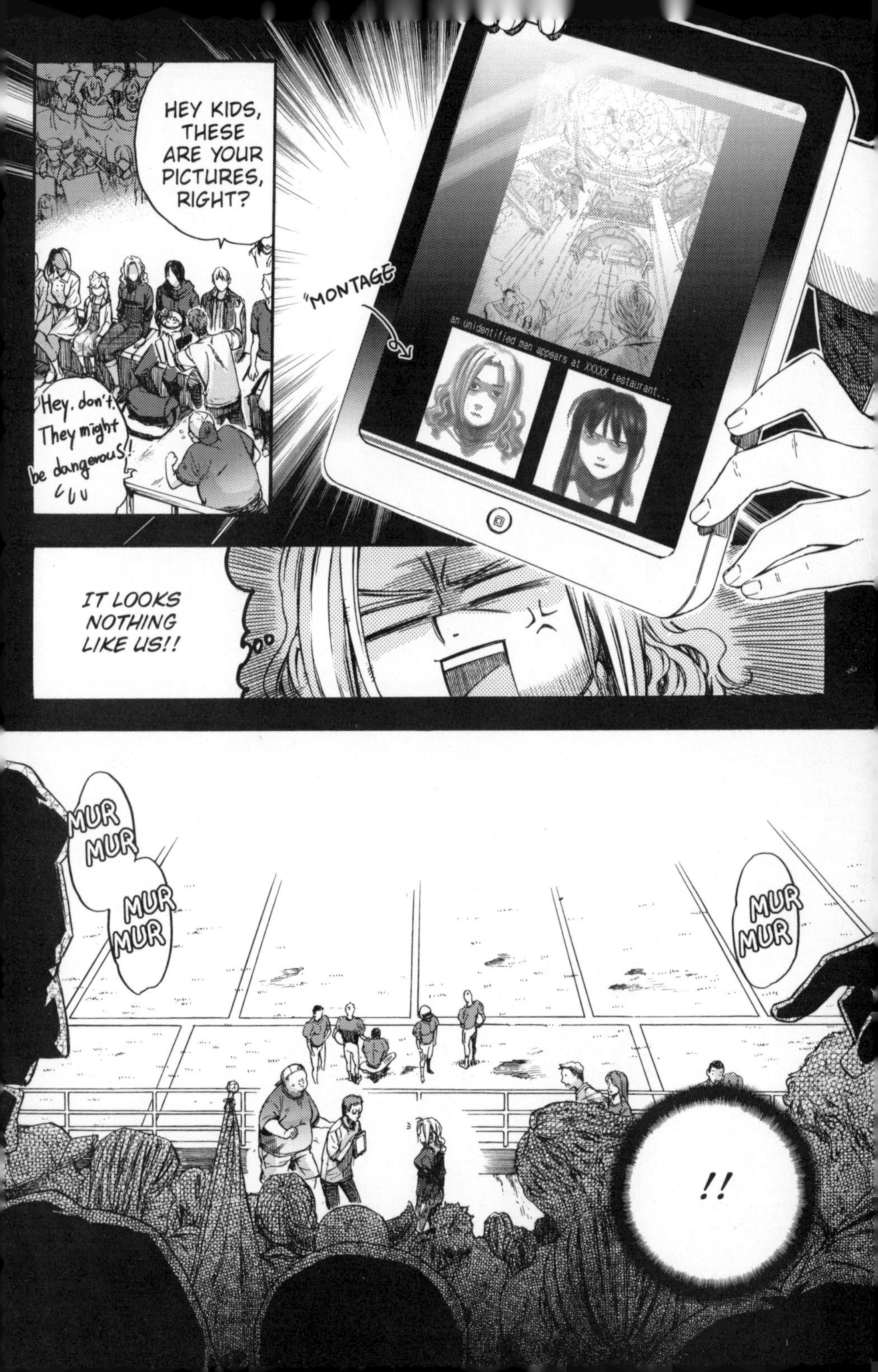
HEY KIDS, THESE ARE YOUR PICTURES, RIGHT?
Hey. don't. They might be dangerous!!
"MONTAGE
an unidentified man appears at XXXXX restaurant...
IT LOOKS NOTHING LIKE US!!
MUR MUR
MUR MUR
MUR MUR
!!

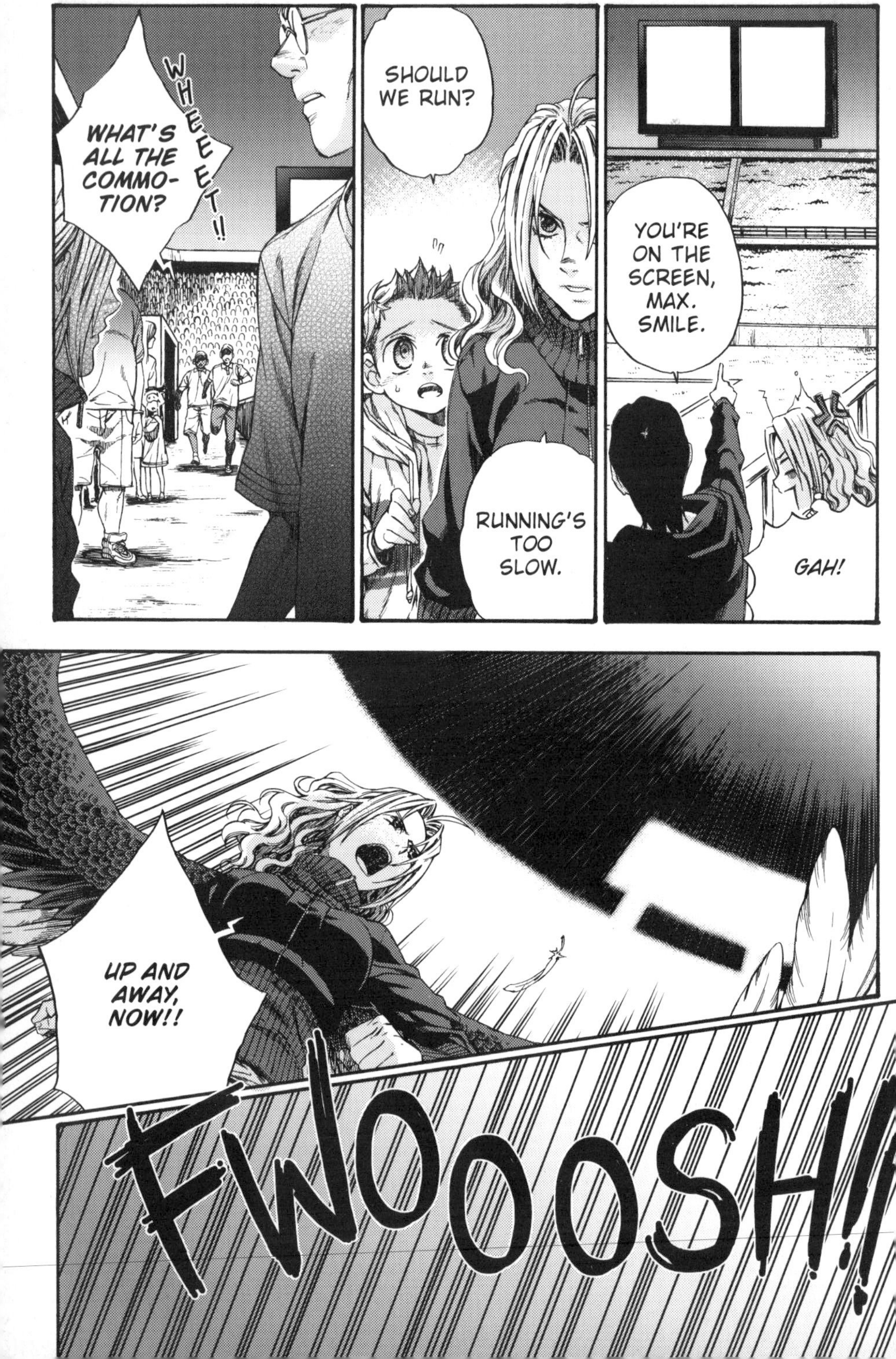
WHAT'S ALL THE COMMOTION?
WHEEEET!!
SHOULD WE RUN?
RUNNING'S TOO SLOW.
YOU'RE ON THE SCREEN, MAX. SMILE.
GAH!
UP AND AWAY, NOW!!
FWOOOSH!!

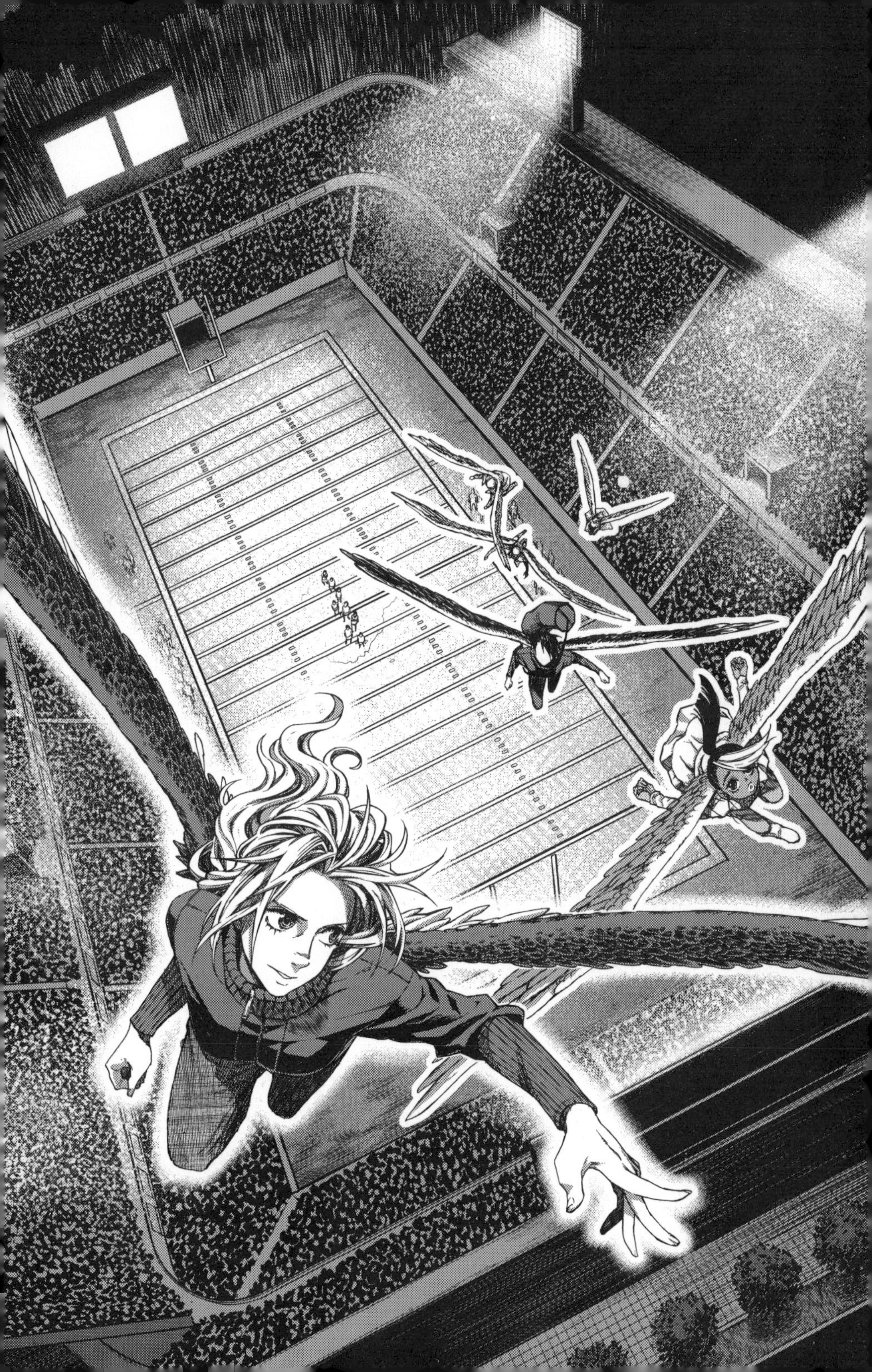

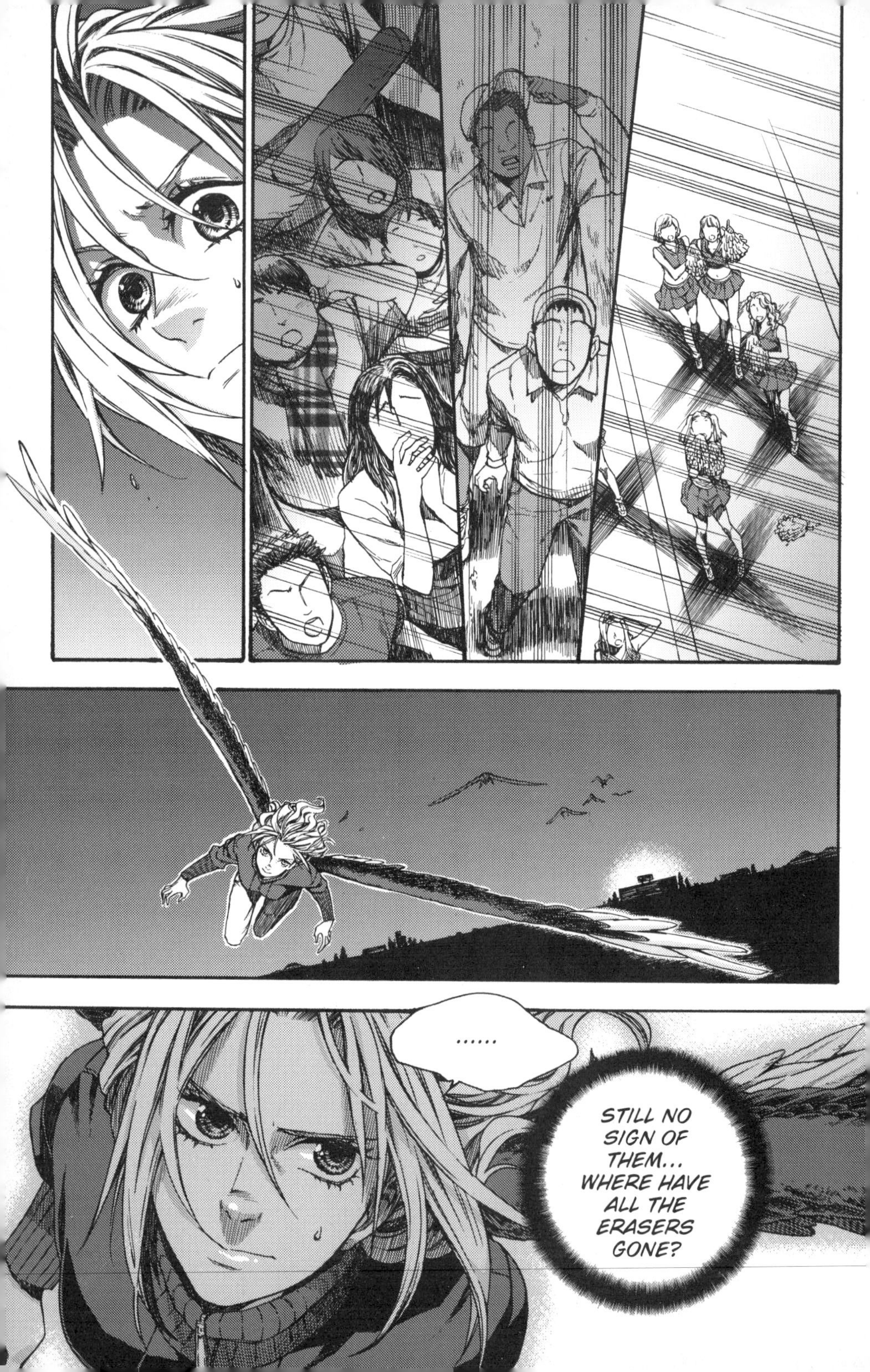
......
STILL NO SIGN OF THEM... WHERE HAVE ALL THE ERASERS GONE?

MAXIMUM

RIDE

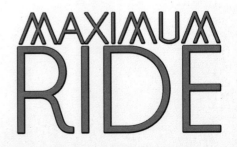

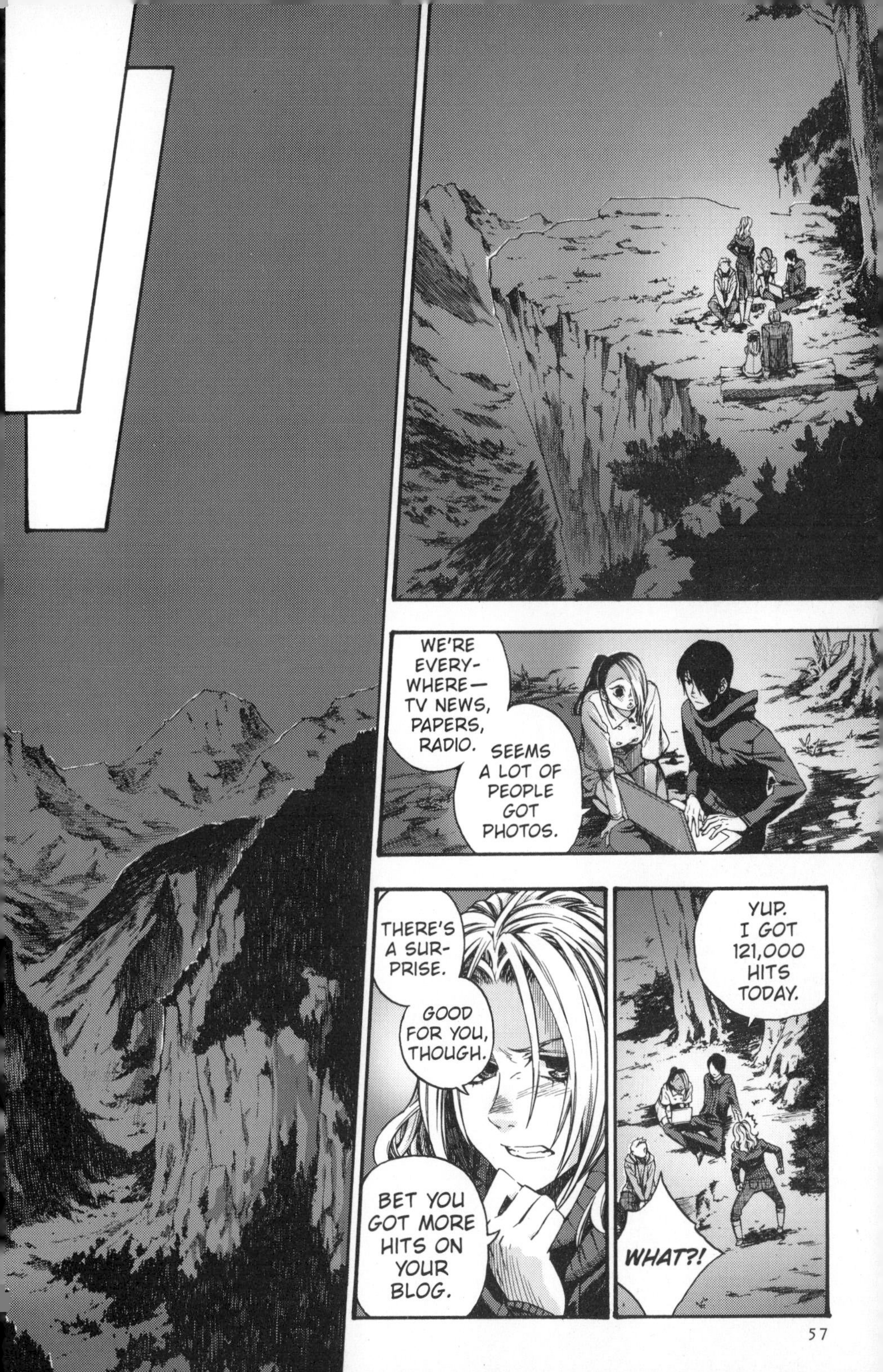
WE'RE EVERY-WHERE— TV NEWS, PAPERS, RADIO.
SEEMS A LOT OF PEOPLE GOT PHOTOS.
YUP. I GOT 121,000 HITS TODAY.
WHAT?!
THERE'S A SUR-PRISE.
GOOD FOR YOU, THOUGH.
BET YOU GOT MORE HITS ON YOUR BLOG.

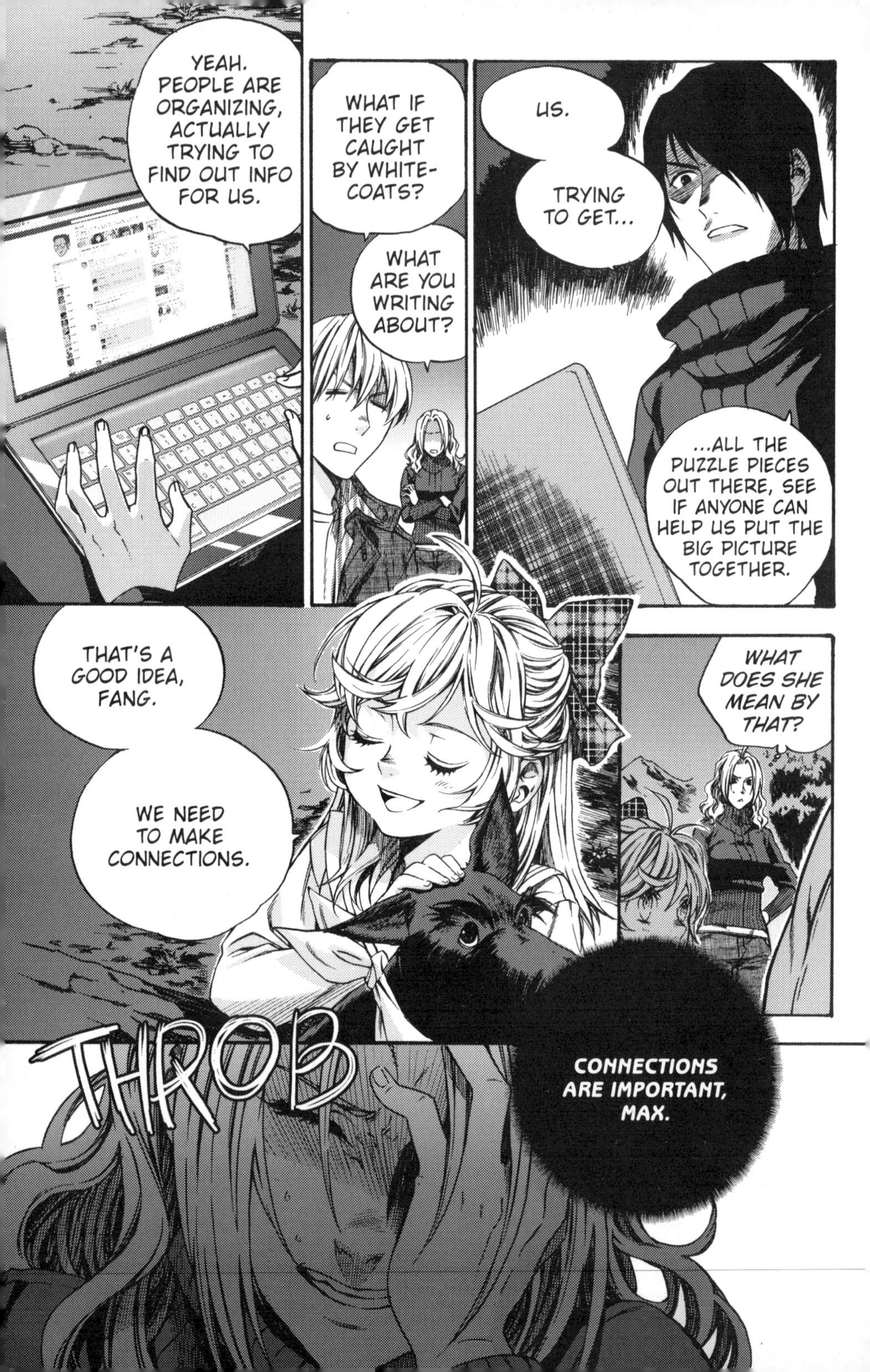
YEAH. PEOPLE ARE ORGANIZING, ACTUALLY TRYING TO FIND OUT INFO FOR US.
WHAT IF THEY GET CAUGHT BY WHITE-COATS?
WHAT ARE YOU WRITING ABOUT?
US.
TRYING TO GET...
...ALL THE PUZZLE PIECES OUT THERE, SEE IF ANYONE CAN HELP US PUT THE BIG PICTURE TOGETHER.
THAT'S A GOOD IDEA, FANG.
WE NEED TO MAKE CONNECTIONS.
WHAT DOES SHE MEAN BY THAT?
THROB
CONNECTIONS ARE IMPORTANT, MAX.

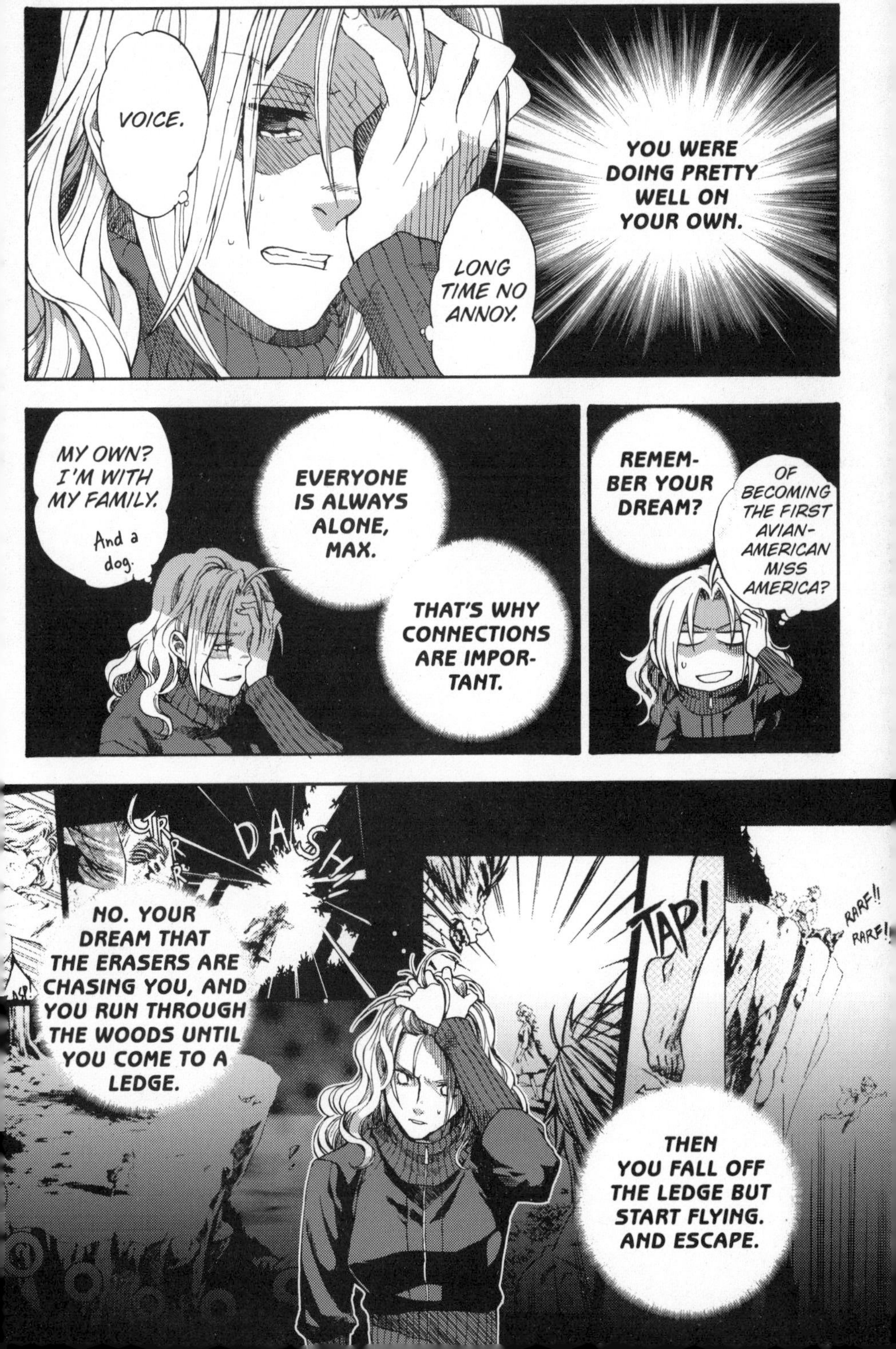
VOICE.
LONG TIME NO ANNOY.
YOU WERE DOING PRETTY WELL ON YOUR OWN.
MY OWN? I'M WITH MY FAMILY.
And a dog.
EVERYONE IS ALWAYS ALONE, MAX.
THAT'S WHY CONNECTIONS ARE IMPOR-TANT.
REMEM-BER YOUR DREAM?
OF BECOMING THE FIRST AVIAN-AMERICAN MISS AMERICA?
DASH
NO. YOUR DREAM THAT THE ERASERS ARE CHASING YOU, AND YOU RUN THROUGH THE WOODS UNTIL YOU COME TO A LEDGE.
TAP!
RARF!! RARF!
THEN YOU FALL OFF THE LEDGE BUT START FLYING. AND ESCAPE.

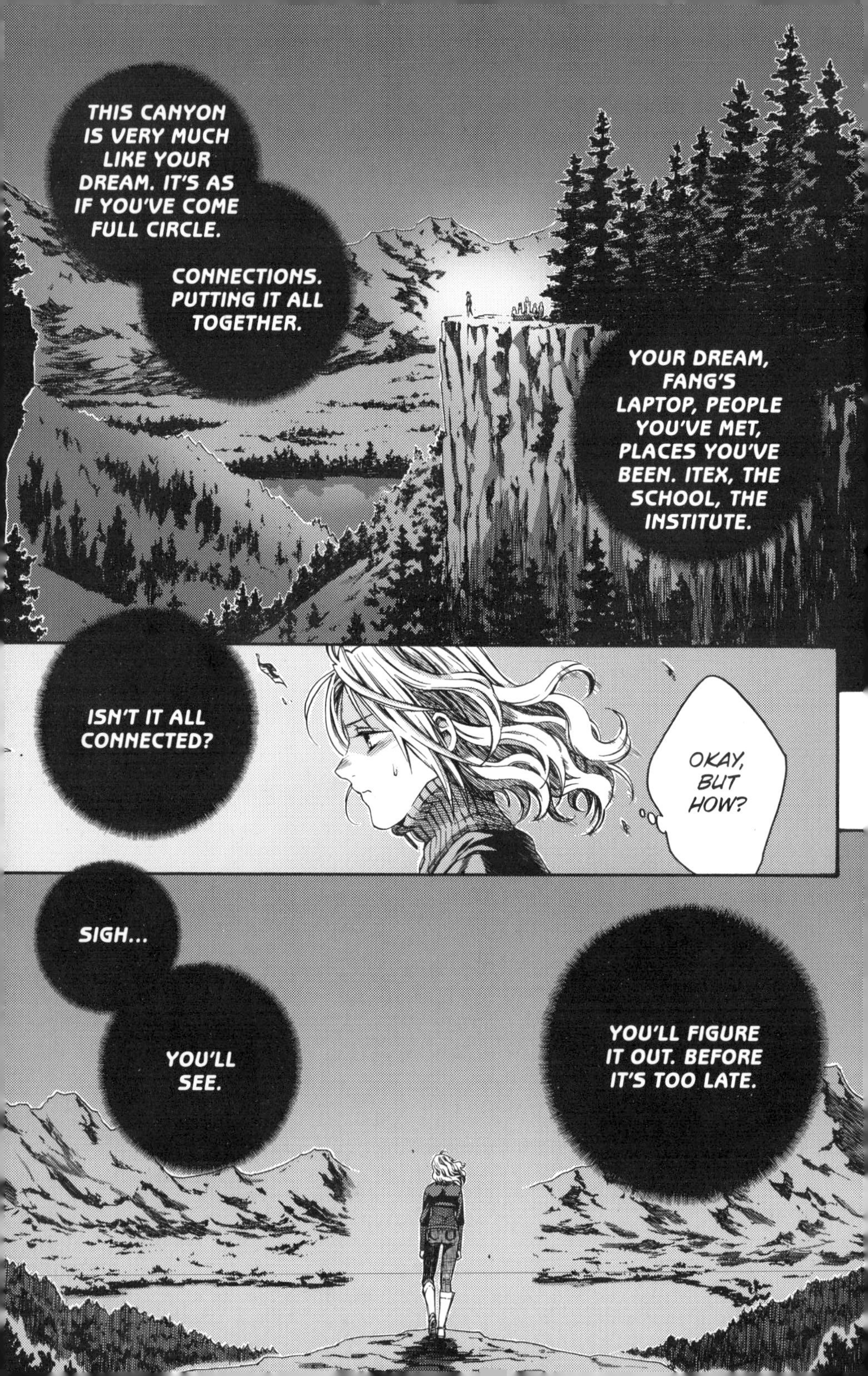
THIS CANYON IS VERY MUCH LIKE YOUR DREAM. IT'S AS IF YOU'VE COME FULL CIRCLE.
CONNECTIONS. PUTTING IT ALL TOGETHER.
YOUR DREAM, FANG'S LAPTOP, PEOPLE YOU'VE MET, PLACES YOU'VE BEEN. ITEX, THE SCHOOL, THE INSTITUTE.
ISN'T IT ALL CONNECTED?
OKAY, BUT HOW?
SIGH...
YOU'LL SEE.
YOU'LL FIGURE IT OUT. BEFORE IT'S TOO LATE.

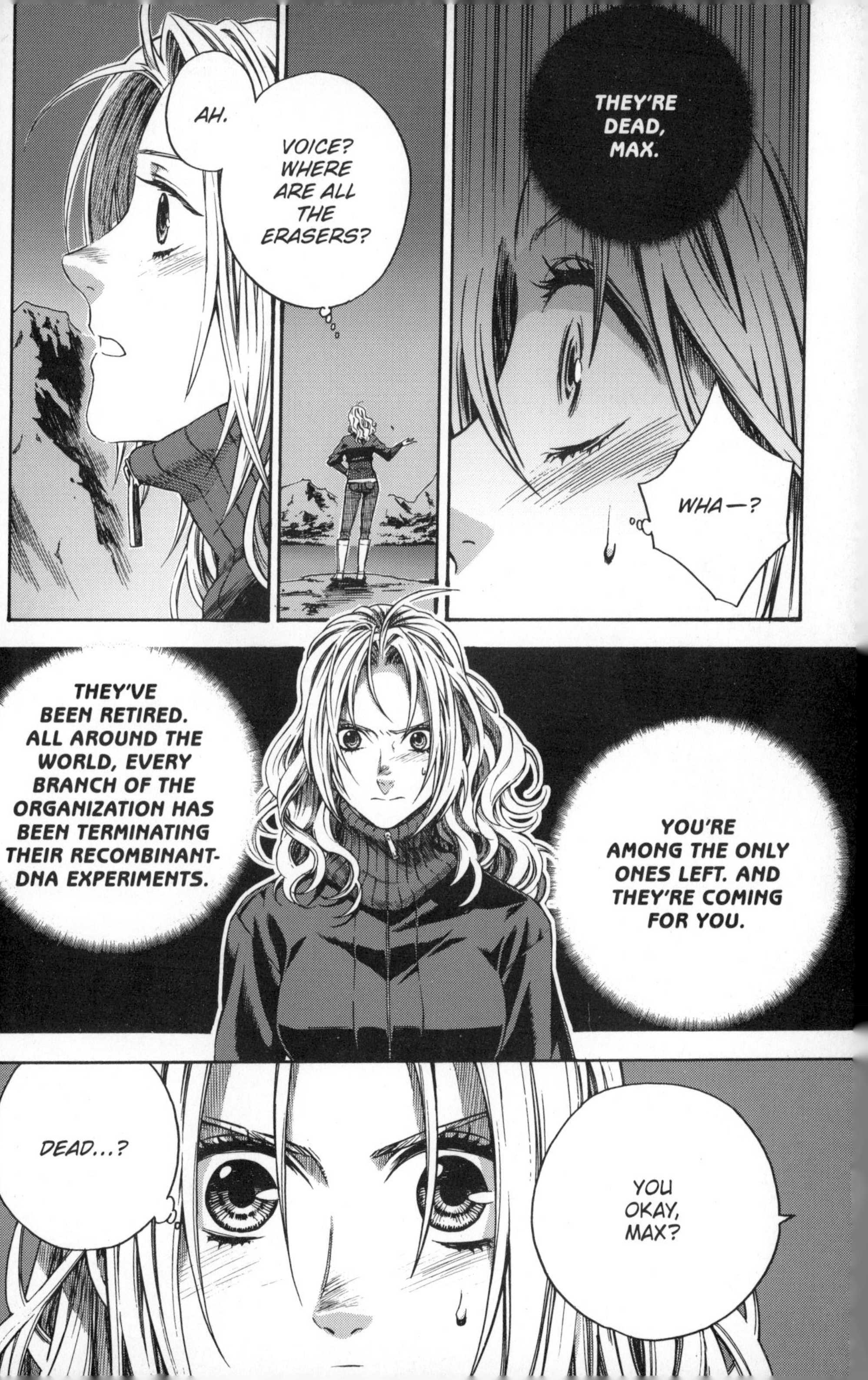
AH.
VOICE? WHERE ARE ALL THE ERASERS?
THEY'RE DEAD, MAX.
WHA—?
THEY'VE BEEN RETIRED. ALL AROUND THE WORLD, EVERY BRANCH OF THE ORGANIZATION HAS BEEN TERMINATING THEIR RECOMBINANT-DNA EXPERIMENTS.
YOU'RE AMONG THE ONLY ONES LEFT. AND THEY'RE COMING FOR YOU.
DEAD...?
YOU OKAY, MAX?

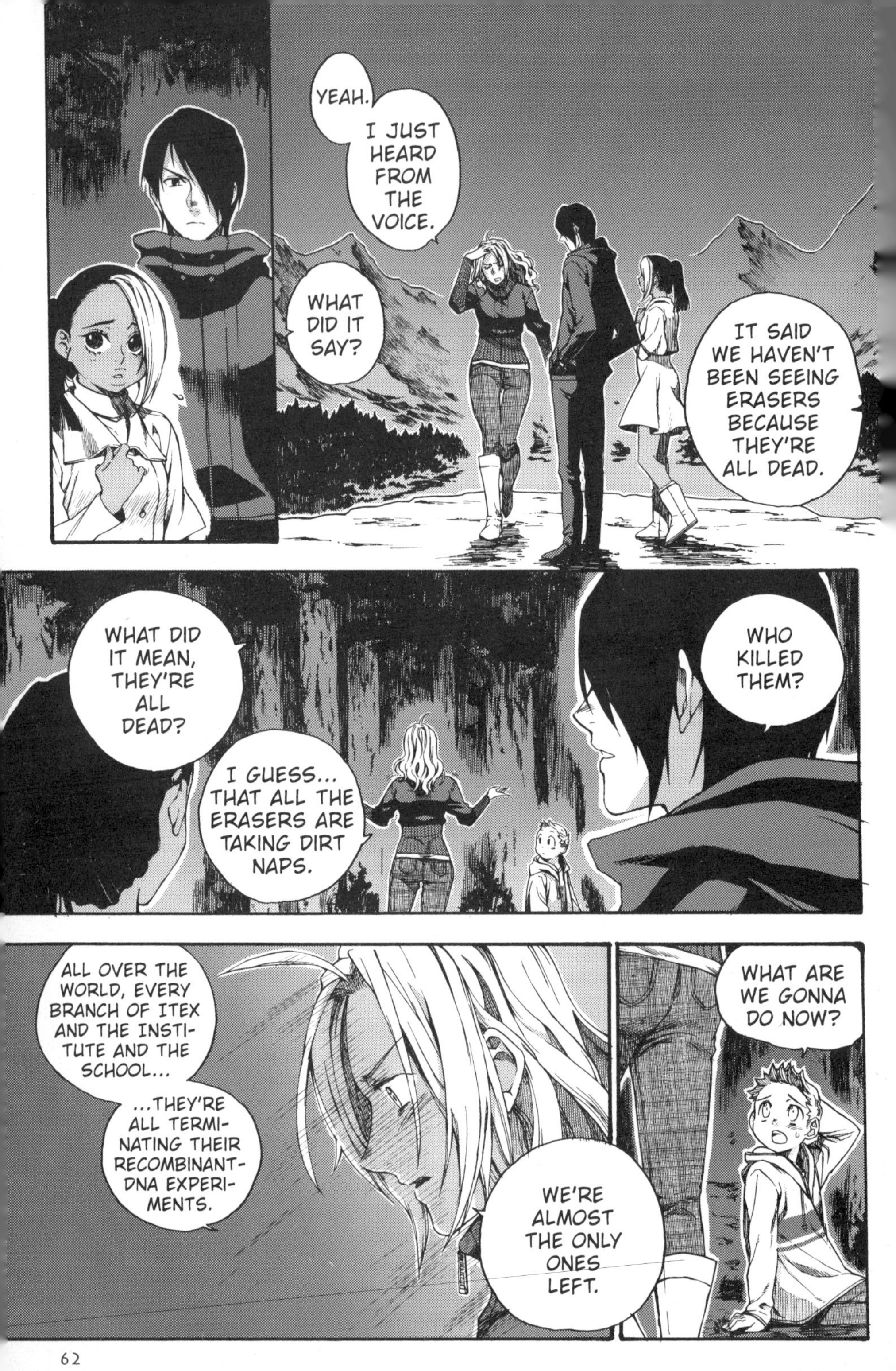
YEAH.
I JUST HEARD FROM THE VOICE.
WHAT DID IT SAY?
IT SAID WE HAVEN'T BEEN SEEING ERASERS BECAUSE THEY'RE ALL DEAD.
WHAT DID IT MEAN, THEY'RE ALL DEAD?
WHO KILLED THEM?
I GUESS... THAT ALL THE ERASERS ARE TAKING DIRT NAPS.
ALL OVER THE WORLD, EVERY BRANCH OF ITEX AND THE INSTITUTE AND THE SCHOOL...
...THEY'RE ALL TERMINATING THEIR RECOMBINANT-DNA EXPERIMENTS.
WE'RE ALMOST THE ONLY ONES LEFT.
WHAT ARE WE GONNA DO NOW?

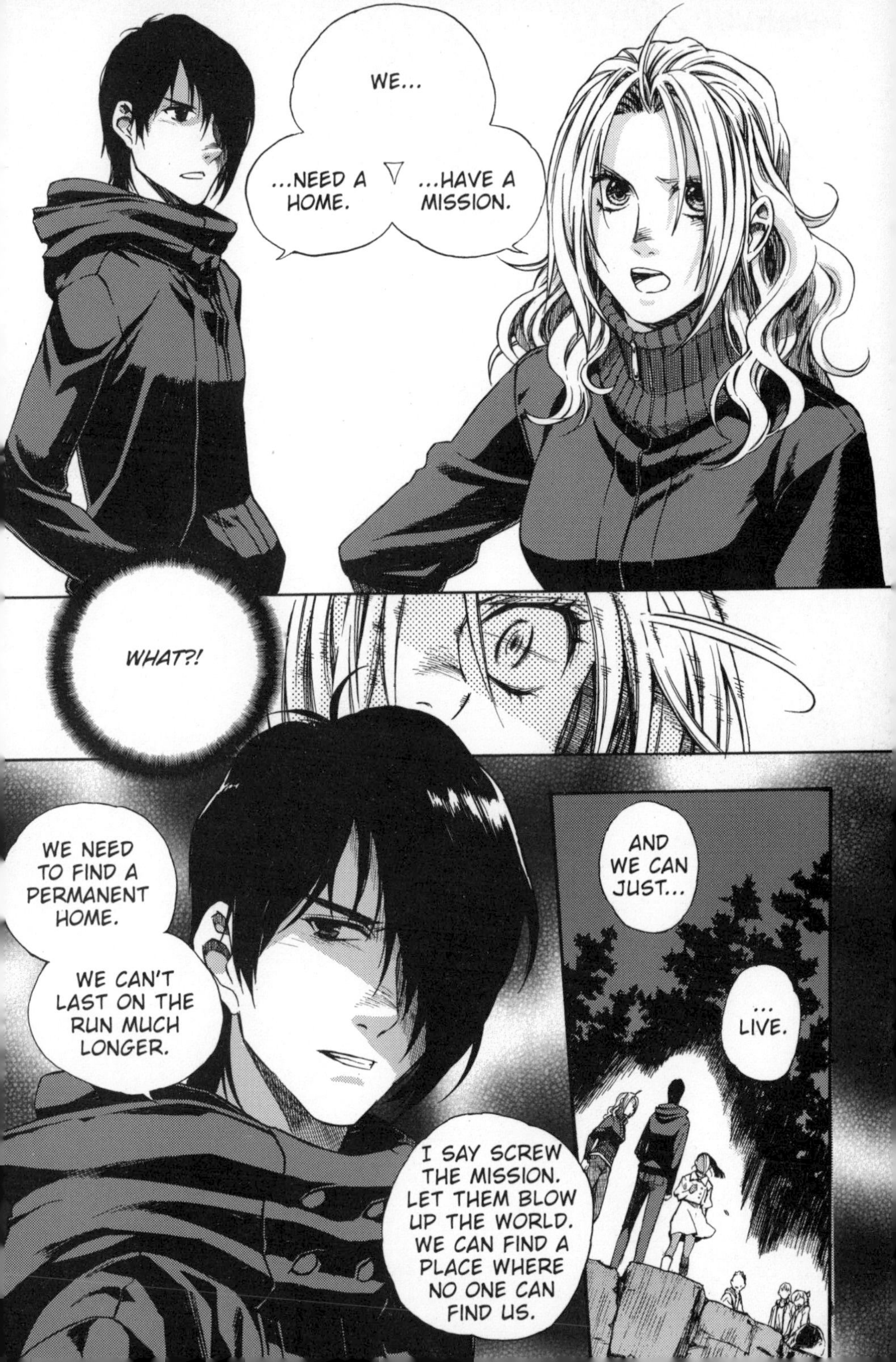
WE...
...NEED A HOME.
...HAVE A MISSION.
WHAT?!
WE NEED TO FIND A PERMANENT HOME.
WE CAN'T LAST ON THE RUN MUCH LONGER.
AND WE CAN JUST...
...LIVE.
I SAY SCREW THE MISSION. LET THEM BLOW UP THE WORLD. WE CAN FIND A PLACE WHERE NO ONE CAN FIND US.

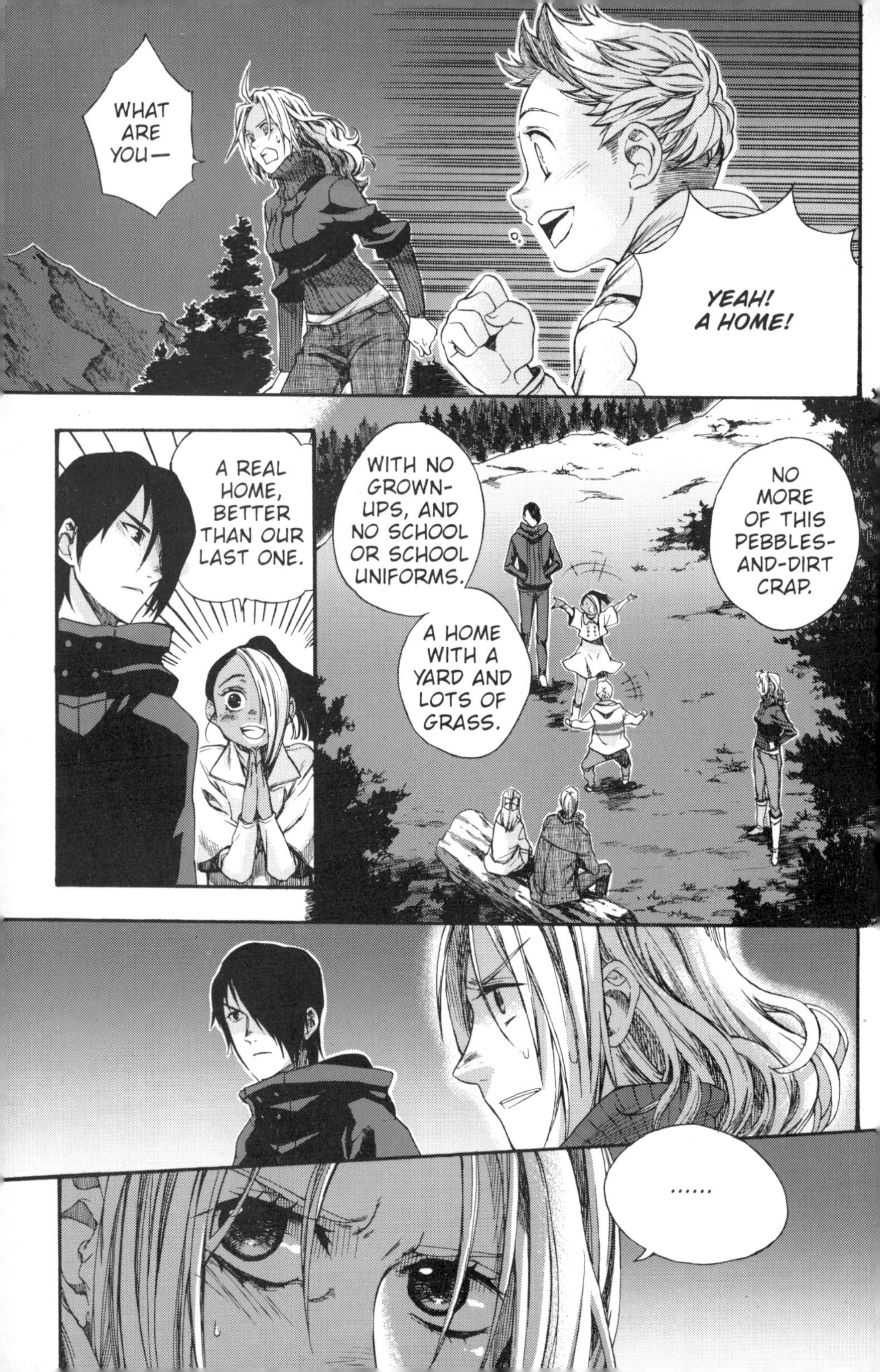
WHAT ARE YOU—
YEAH! A HOME!
A REAL HOME, BETTER THAN OUR LAST ONE.
WITH NO GROWN-UPS, AND NO SCHOOL OR SCHOOL UNIFORMS.
NO MORE OF THIS PEBBLES-AND-DIRT CRAP.
A HOME WITH A YARD AND LOTS OF GRASS.
......

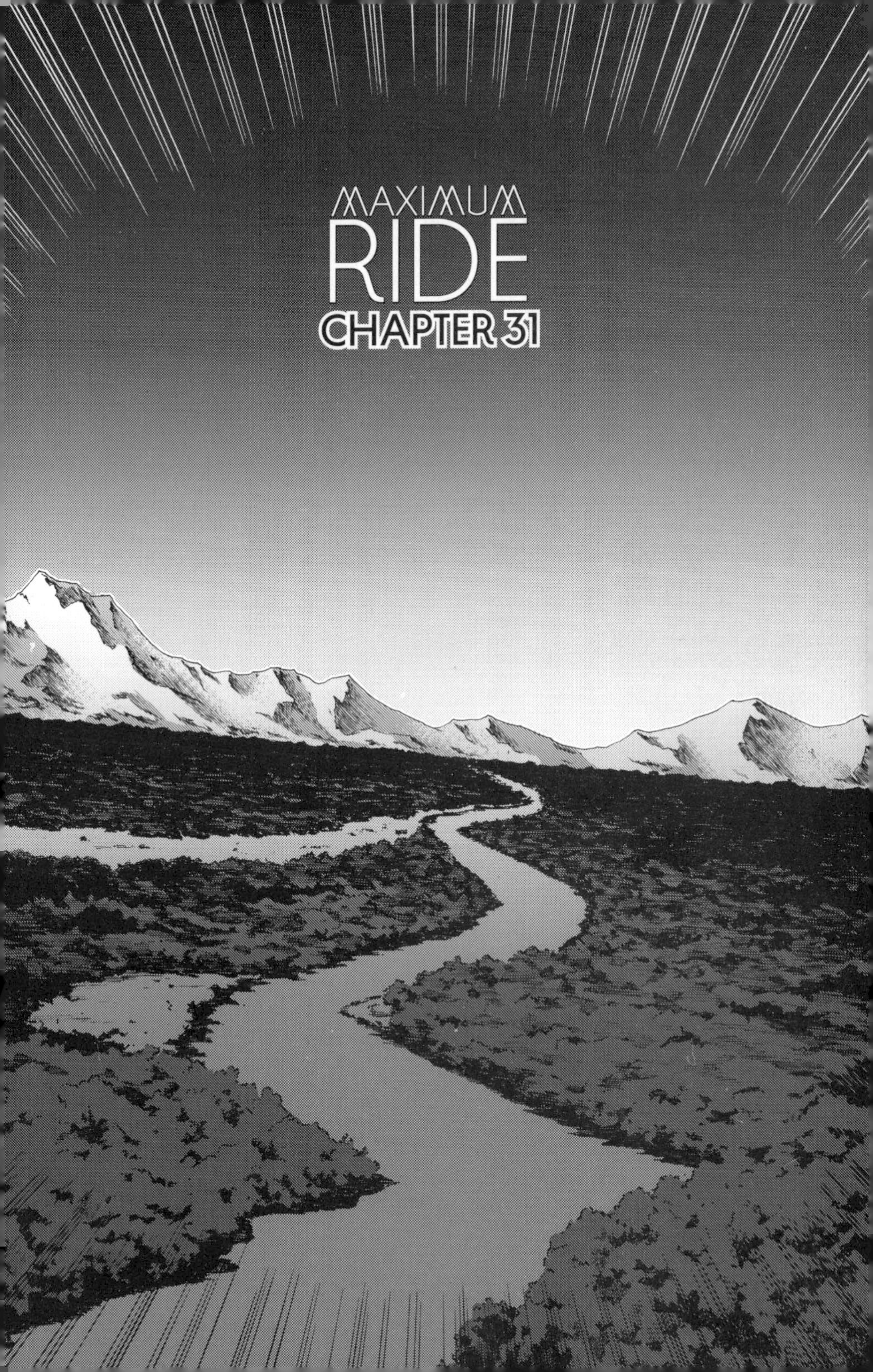
MAXIMUM
RIDE
CHAPTER 31

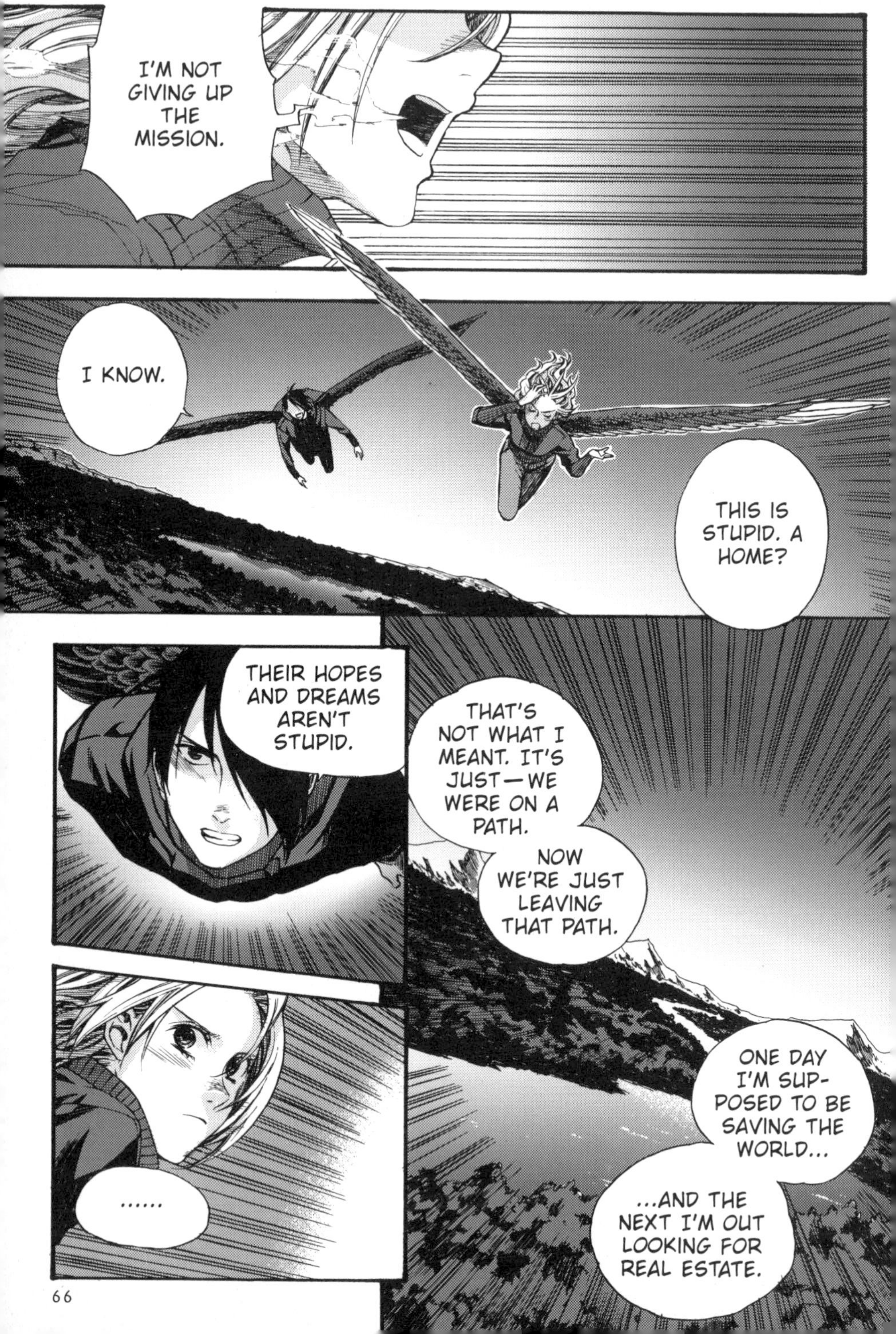
I'M NOT GIVING UP THE MISSION.
I KNOW.
THIS IS STUPID. A HOME?
THEIR HOPES AND DREAMS AREN'T STUPID.
THAT'S NOT WHAT I MEANT. IT'S JUST—WE WERE ON A PATH.
NOW WE'RE JUST LEAVING THAT PATH.
ONE DAY I'M SUP-POSED TO BE SAVING THE WORLD...
...AND THE NEXT I'M OUT LOOKING FOR REAL ESTATE.
......

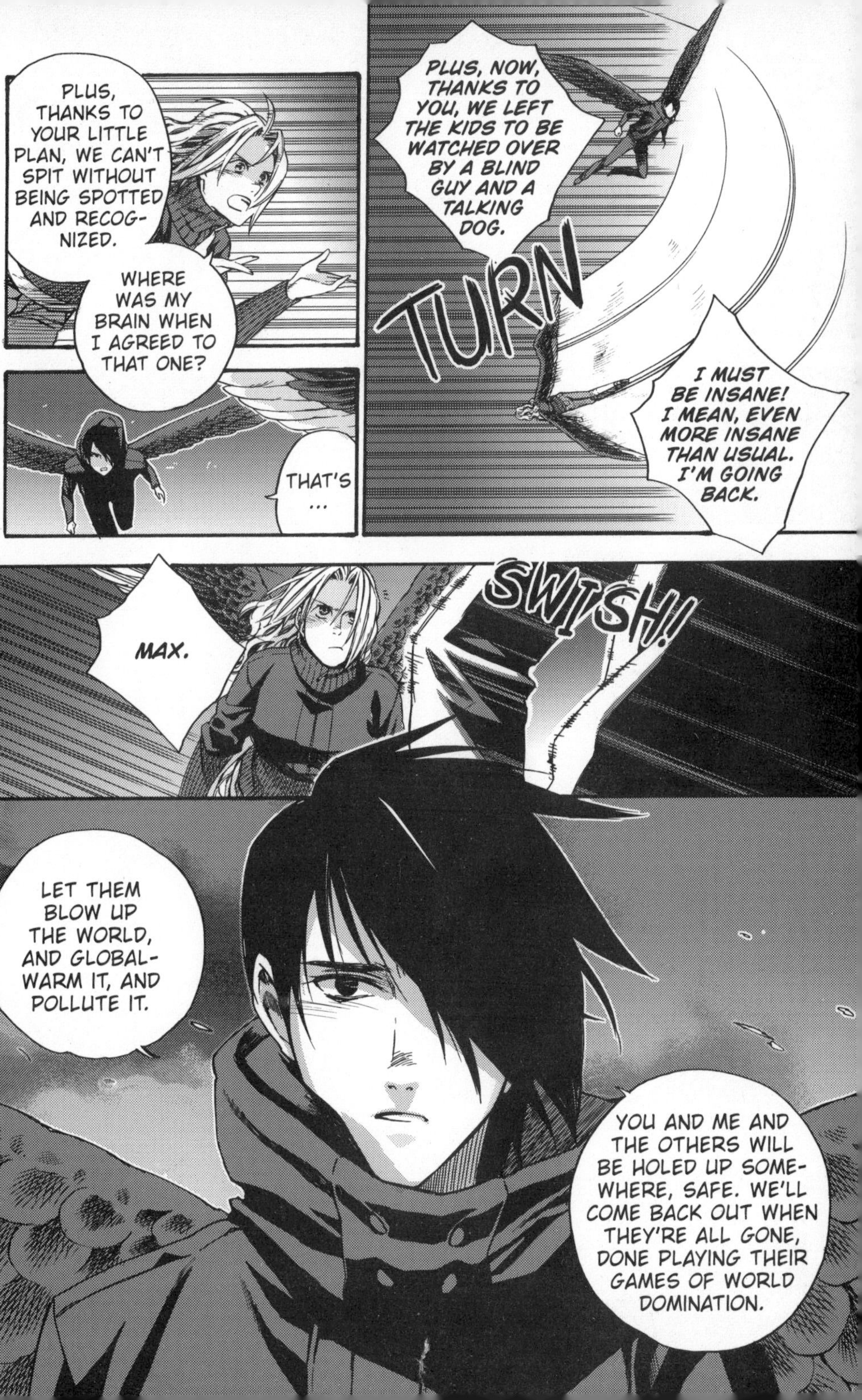
PLUS, THANKS TO YOUR LITTLE PLAN, WE CAN'T SPIT WITHOUT BEING SPOTTED AND RECOG-NIZED.
WHERE WAS MY BRAIN WHEN I AGREED TO THAT ONE?
THAT'S ...
PLUS, NOW, THANKS TO YOU, WE LEFT THE KIDS TO BE WATCHED OVER BY A BLIND GUY AND A TALKING DOG.
TURN
I MUST BE INSANE! I MEAN, EVEN MORE INSANE THAN USUAL. I'M GOING BACK.
MAX.
SWISH!
LET THEM BLOW UP THE WORLD, AND GLOBAL-WARM IT, AND POLLUTE IT.
YOU AND ME AND THE OTHERS WILL BE HOLED UP SOME-WHERE, SAFE. WE'LL COME BACK OUT WHEN THEY'RE ALL GONE, DONE PLAYING THEIR GAMES OF WORLD DOMINATION.

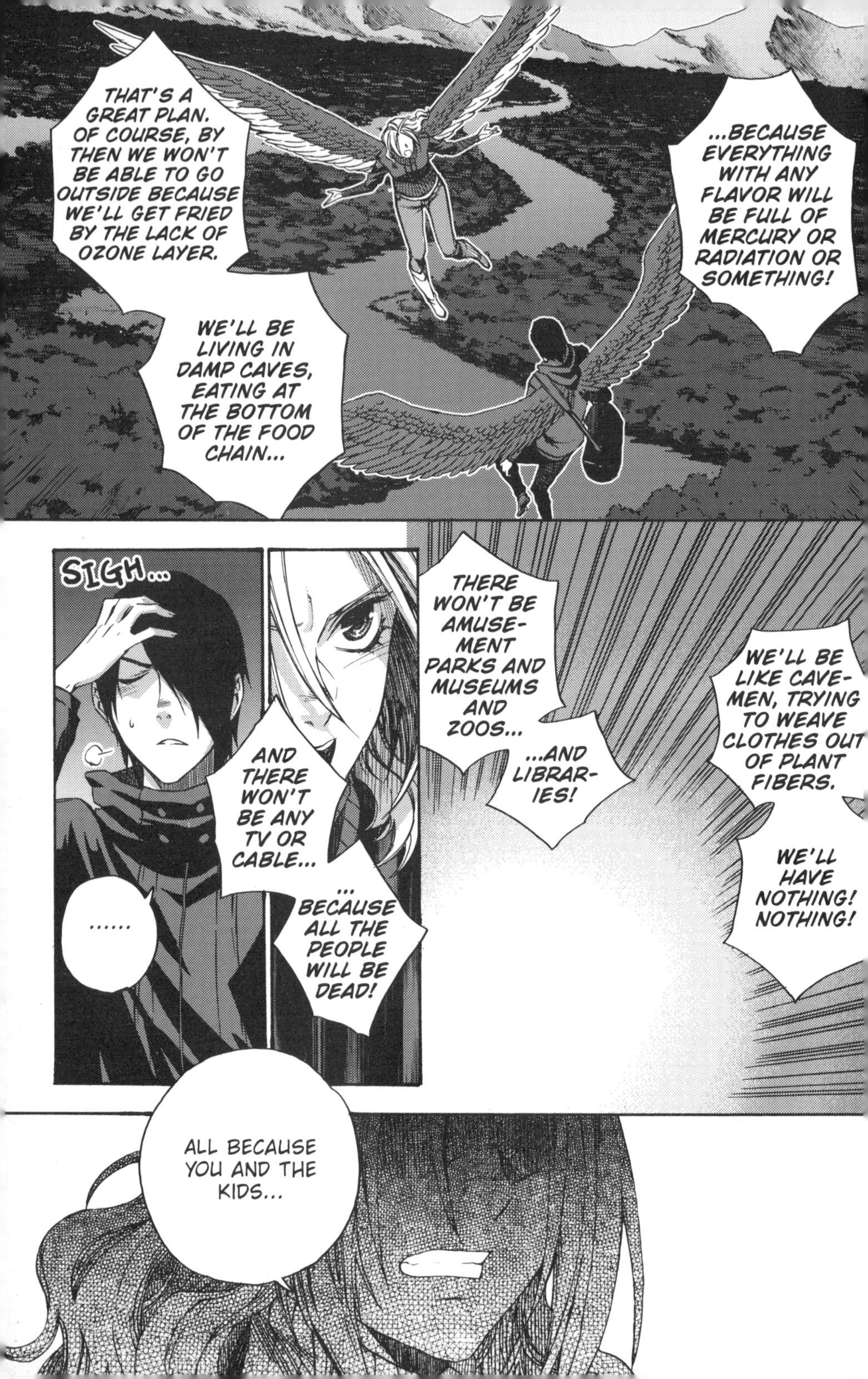
THAT'S A GREAT PLAN. OF COURSE, BY THEN WE WON'T BE ABLE TO GO OUTSIDE BECAUSE WE'LL GET FRIED BY THE LACK OF OZONE LAYER.
WE'LL BE LIVING IN DAMP CAVES, EATING AT THE BOTTOM OF THE FOOD CHAIN...
...BECAUSE EVERYTHING WITH ANY FLAVOR WILL BE FULL OF MERCURY OR RADIATION OR SOMETHING!
SIGH...
......
AND THERE WON'T BE ANY TV OR CABLE...
...BECAUSE ALL THE PEOPLE WILL BE DEAD!
THERE WON'T BE AMUSEMENT PARKS AND MUSEUMS AND ZOOS...
...AND LIBRARIES!
WE'LL BE LIKE CAVEMEN, TRYING TO WEAVE CLOTHES OUT OF PLANT FIBERS.
WE'LL HAVE NOTHING! NOTHING!
ALL BECAUSE YOU AND THE KIDS...

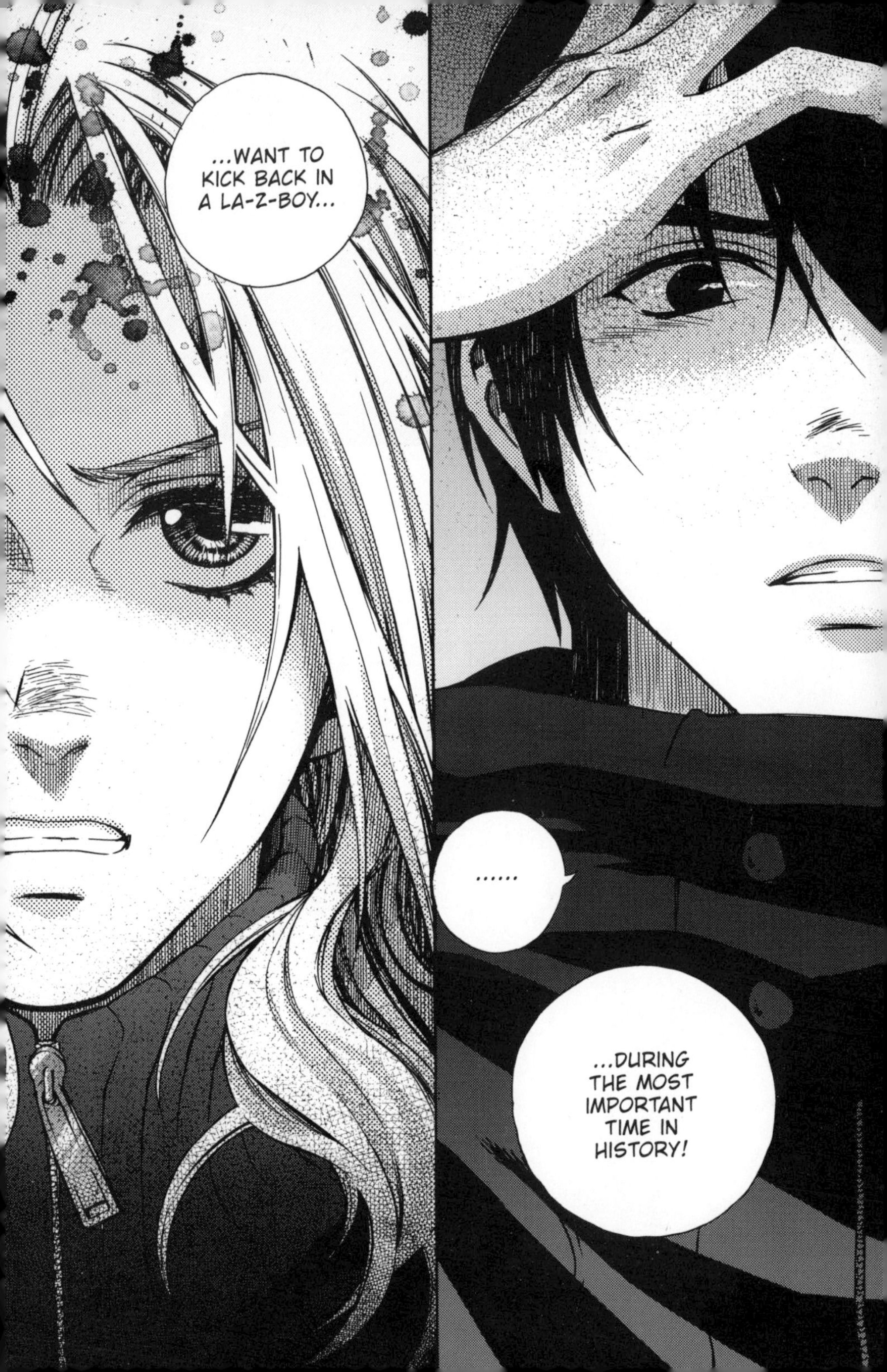
...WANT TO KICK BACK IN A LA-Z-BOY...
......
...DURING THE MOST IMPORTANT TIME IN HISTORY!

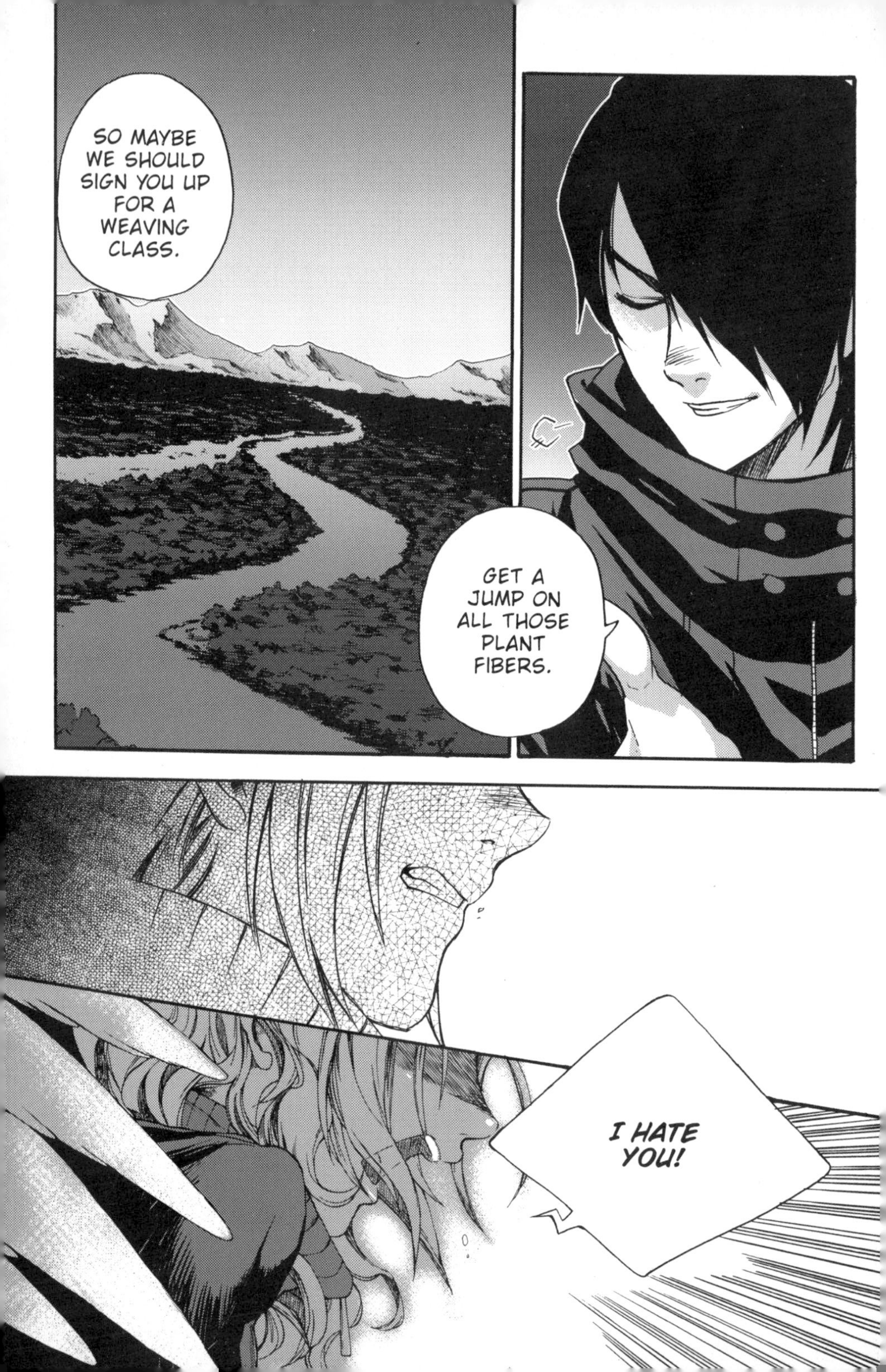
SO MAYBE WE SHOULD SIGN YOU UP FOR A WEAVING CLASS.
GET A JUMP ON ALL THOSE PLANT FIBERS.
I HATE YOU!

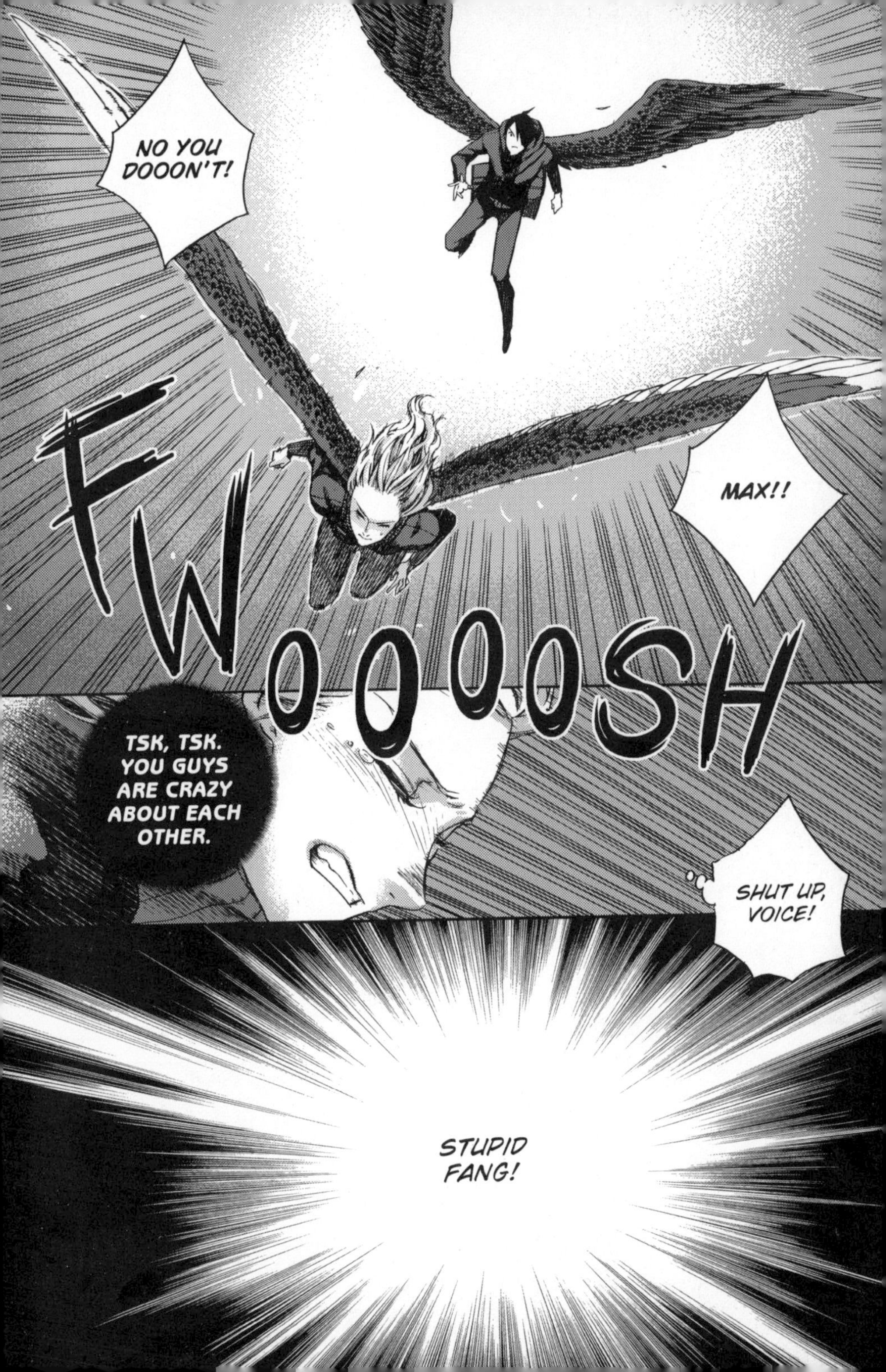
NO YOU DOOON'T!
MAX!!
FWOOOOSH
TSK, TSK. YOU GUYS ARE CRAZY ABOUT EACH OTHER.
SHUT UP, VOICE!
STUPID FANG!

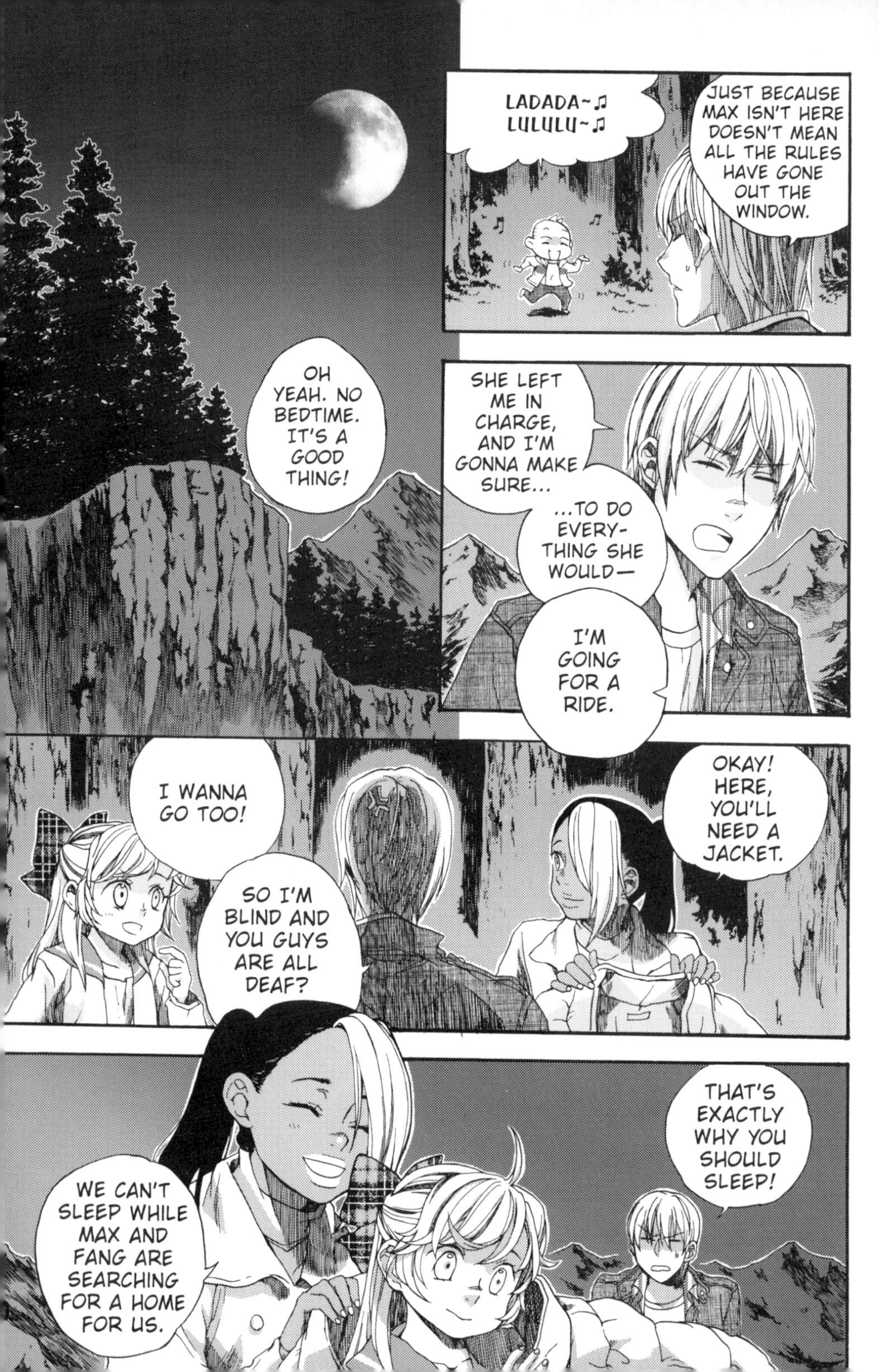
LADADA~♫ LULULU~♫
JUST BECAUSE MAX ISN'T HERE DOESN'T MEAN ALL THE RULES HAVE GONE OUT THE WINDOW.
OH YEAH. NO BEDTIME. IT'S A GOOD THING!
SHE LEFT ME IN CHARGE, AND I'M GONNA MAKE SURE...
...TO DO EVERY-THING SHE WOULD—
I'M GOING FOR A RIDE.
I WANNA GO TOO!
SO I'M BLIND AND YOU GUYS ARE ALL DEAF?
OKAY! HERE, YOU'LL NEED A JACKET.
THAT'S EXACTLY WHY YOU SHOULD SLEEP!
WE CAN'T SLEEP WHILE MAX AND FANG ARE SEARCHING FOR A HOME FOR US.

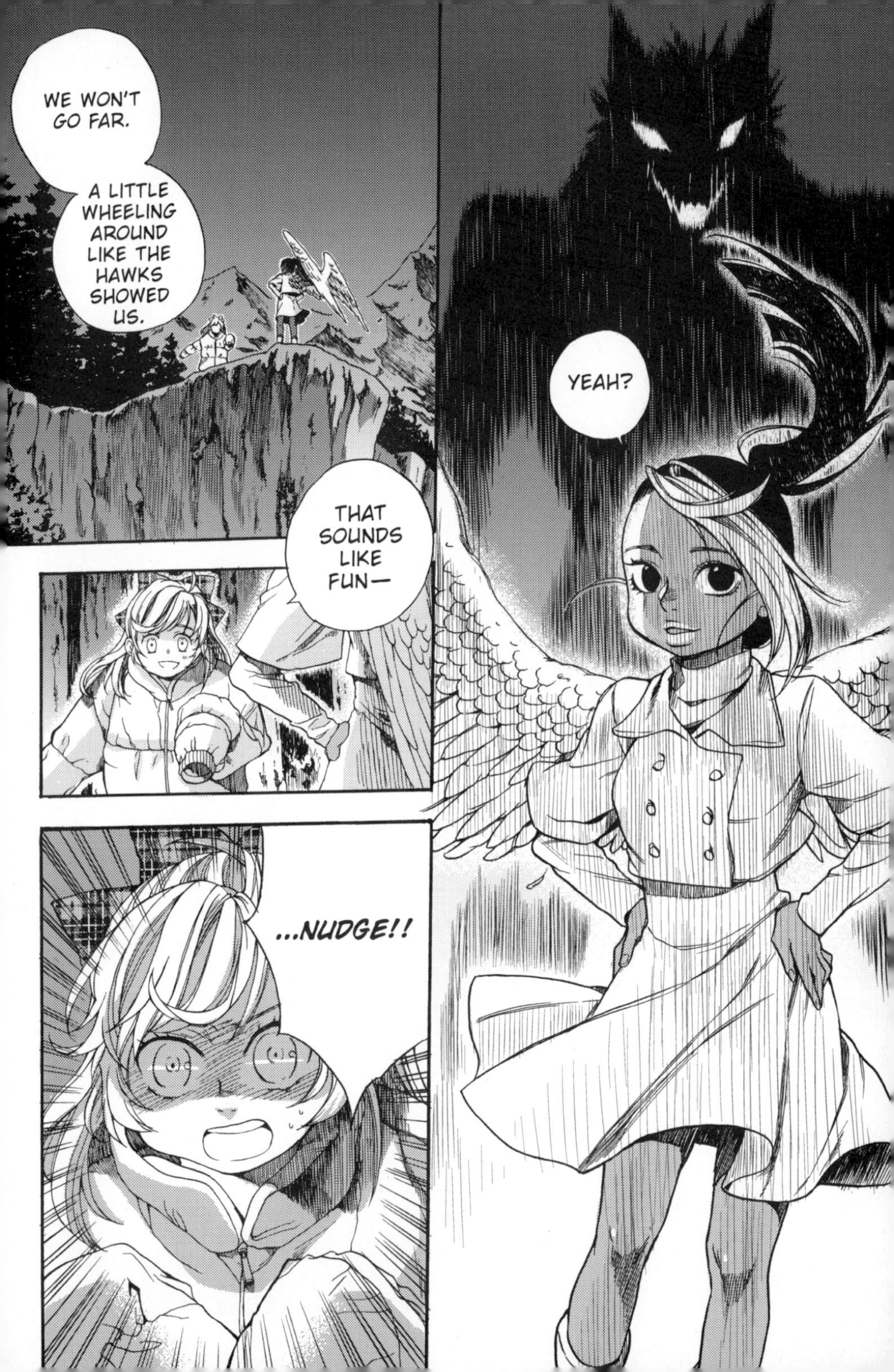
WE WON'T GO FAR.
A LITTLE WHEELING AROUND LIKE THE HAWKS SHOWED US.
YEAH?
THAT SOUNDS LIKE FUN—
...NUDGE!!

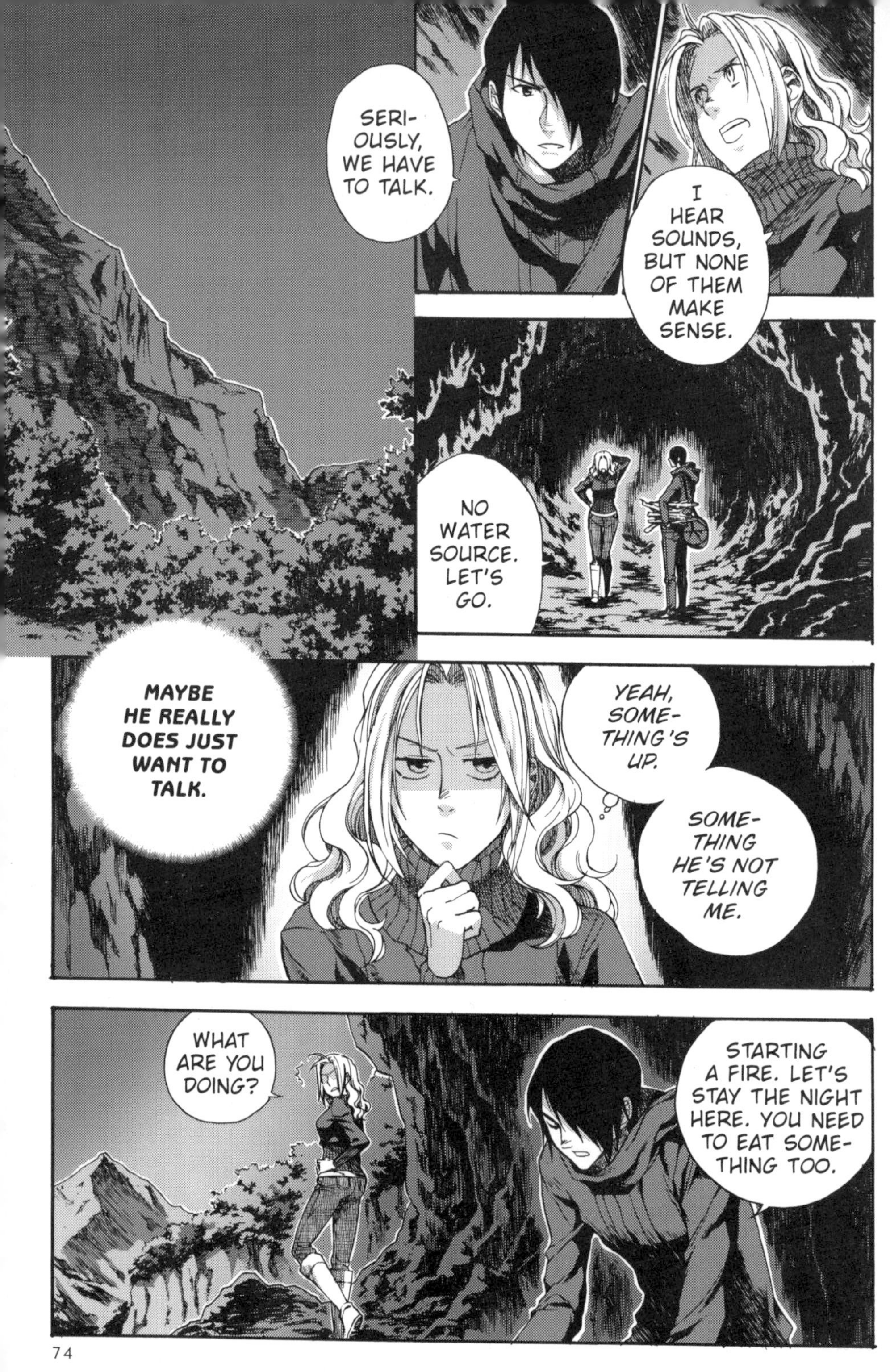
SERIOUSLY, WE HAVE TO TALK.
I HEAR SOUNDS, BUT NONE OF THEM MAKE SENSE.
NO WATER SOURCE. LET'S GO.
MAYBE HE REALLY DOES JUST WANT TO TALK.
YEAH, SOMETHING'S UP.
SOMETHING HE'S NOT TELLING ME.
WHAT ARE YOU DOING?
STARTING A FIRE. LET'S STAY THE NIGHT HERE. YOU NEED TO EAT SOMETHING TOO.

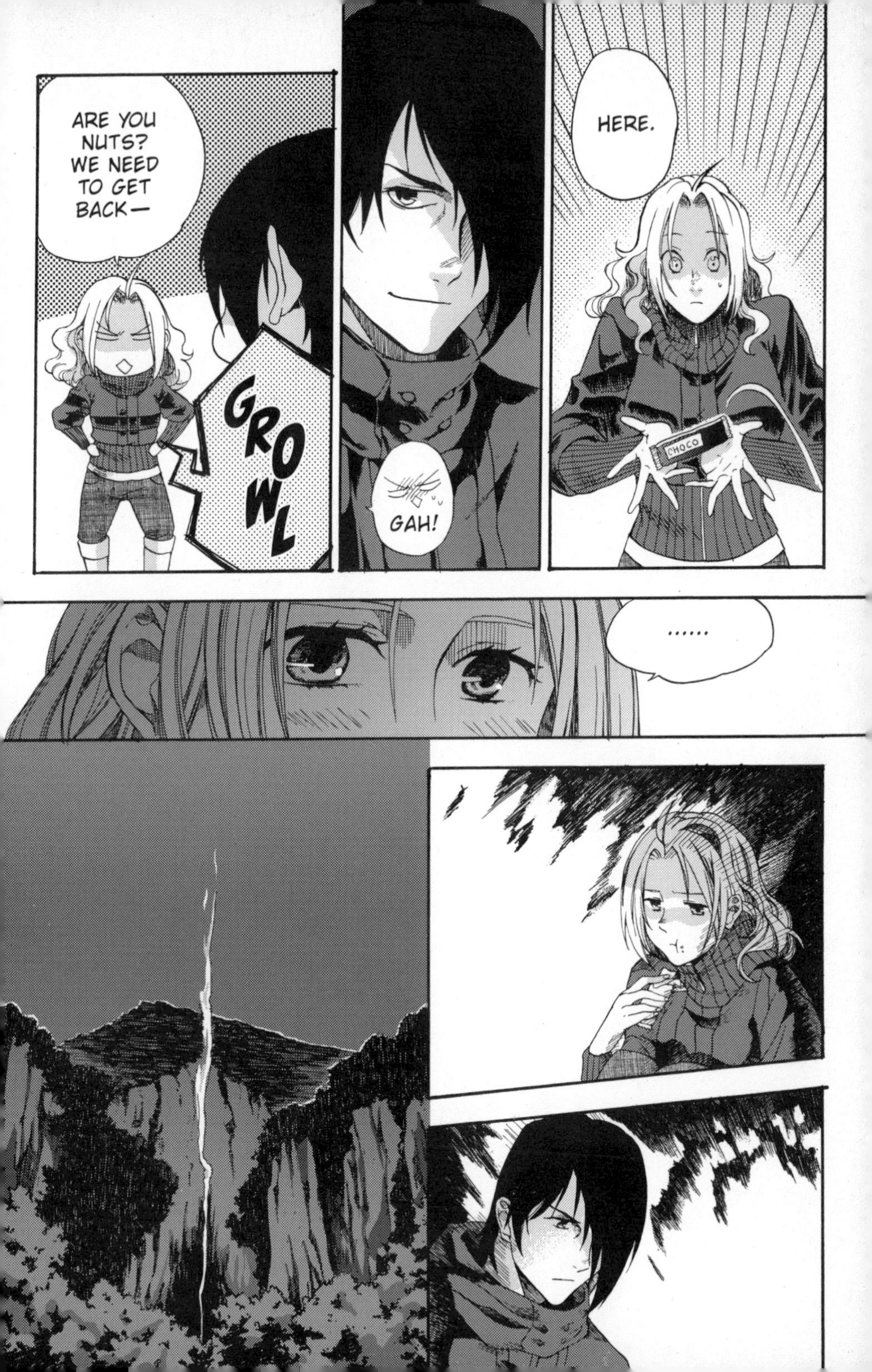
ARE YOU NUTS? WE NEED TO GET BACK—
GROWL
GAH!
HERE.
CHOCO
......

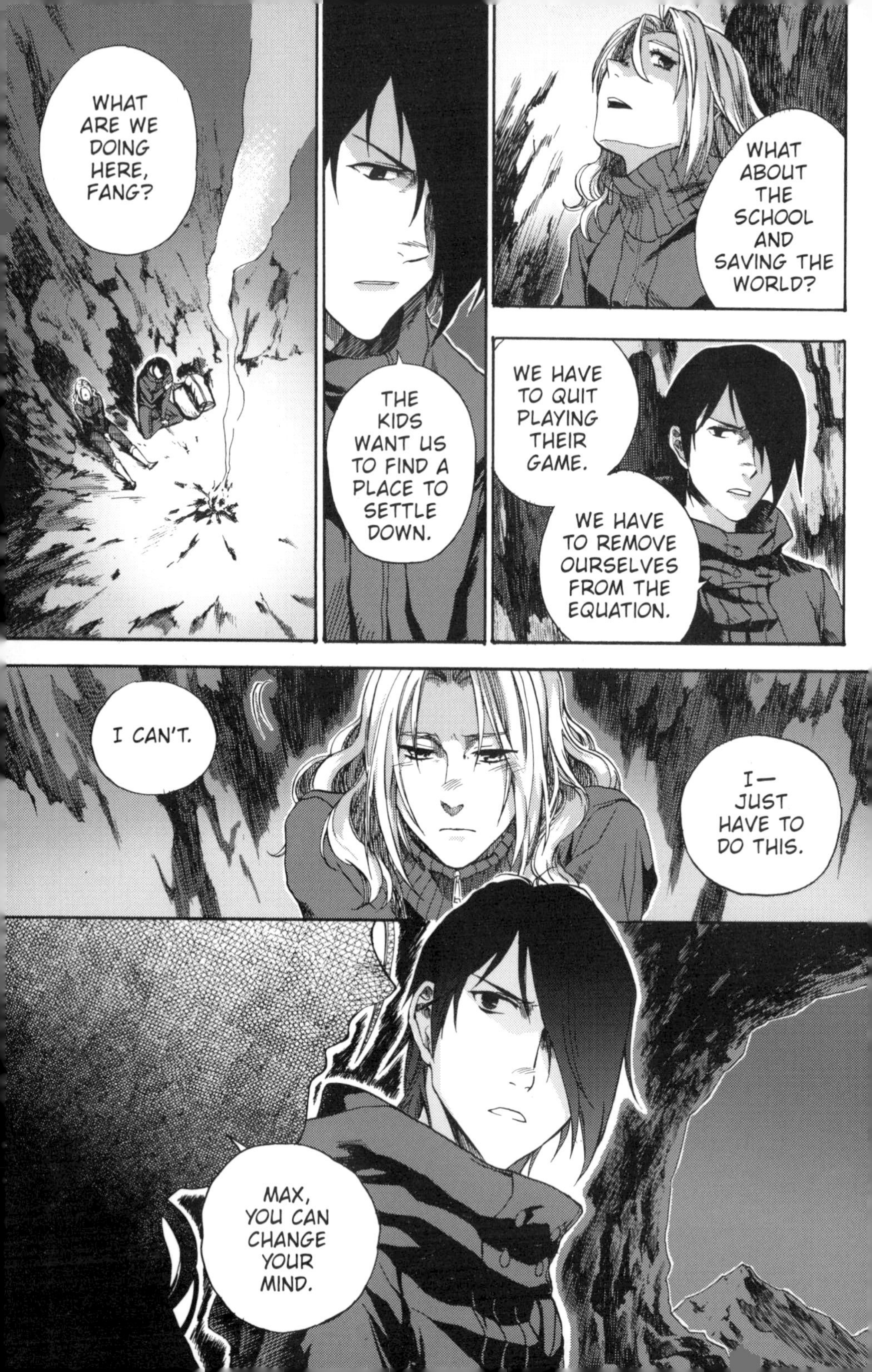
WHAT ARE WE DOING HERE, FANG?
WHAT ABOUT THE SCHOOL AND SAVING THE WORLD?
THE KIDS WANT US TO FIND A PLACE TO SETTLE DOWN.
WE HAVE TO QUIT PLAYING THEIR GAME.
WE HAVE TO REMOVE OURSELVES FROM THE EQUATION.
I CAN'T.
I— JUST HAVE TO DO THIS.
MAX, YOU CAN CHANGE YOUR MIND.

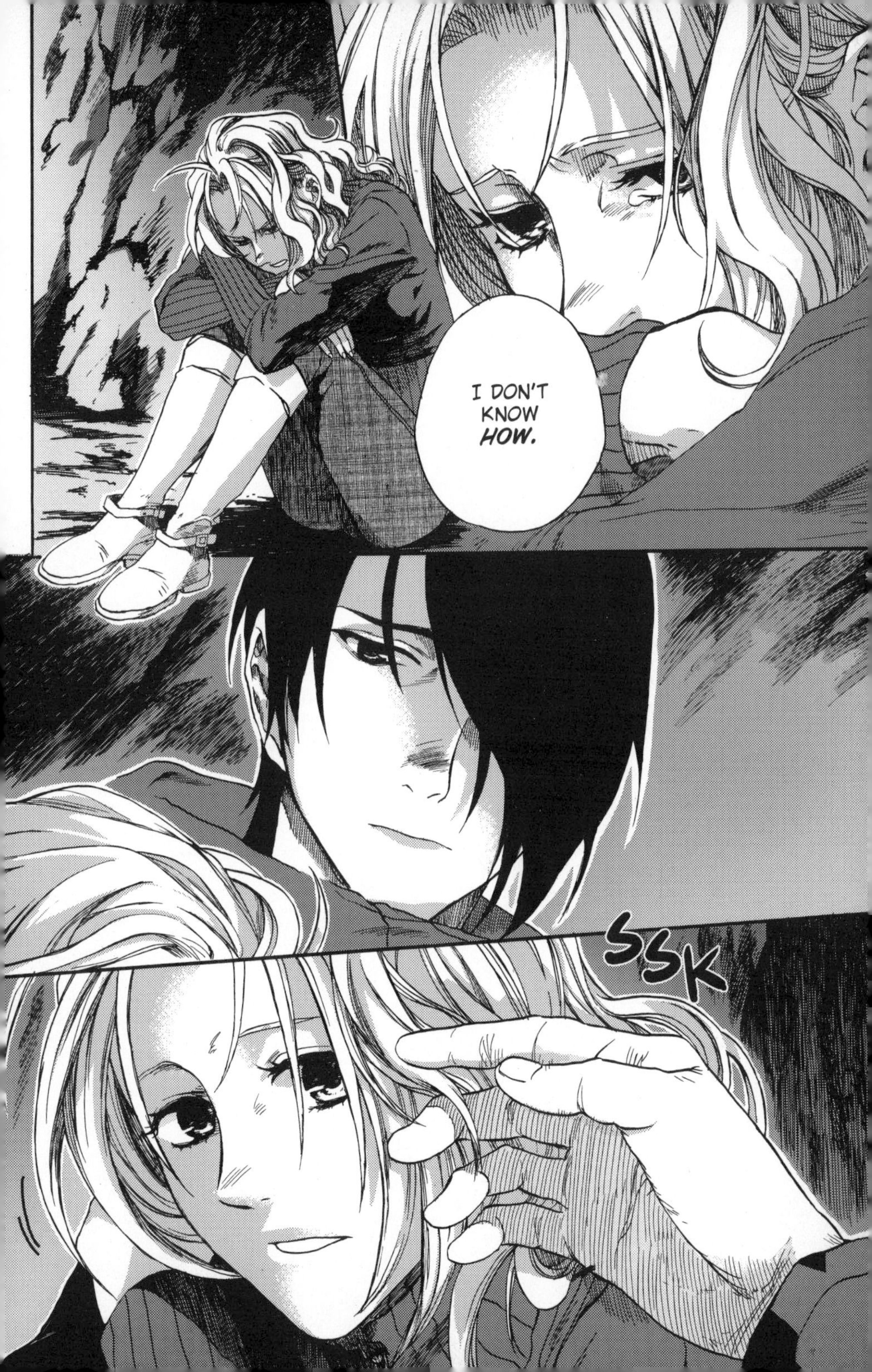
I DON'T KNOW HOW.
SSK

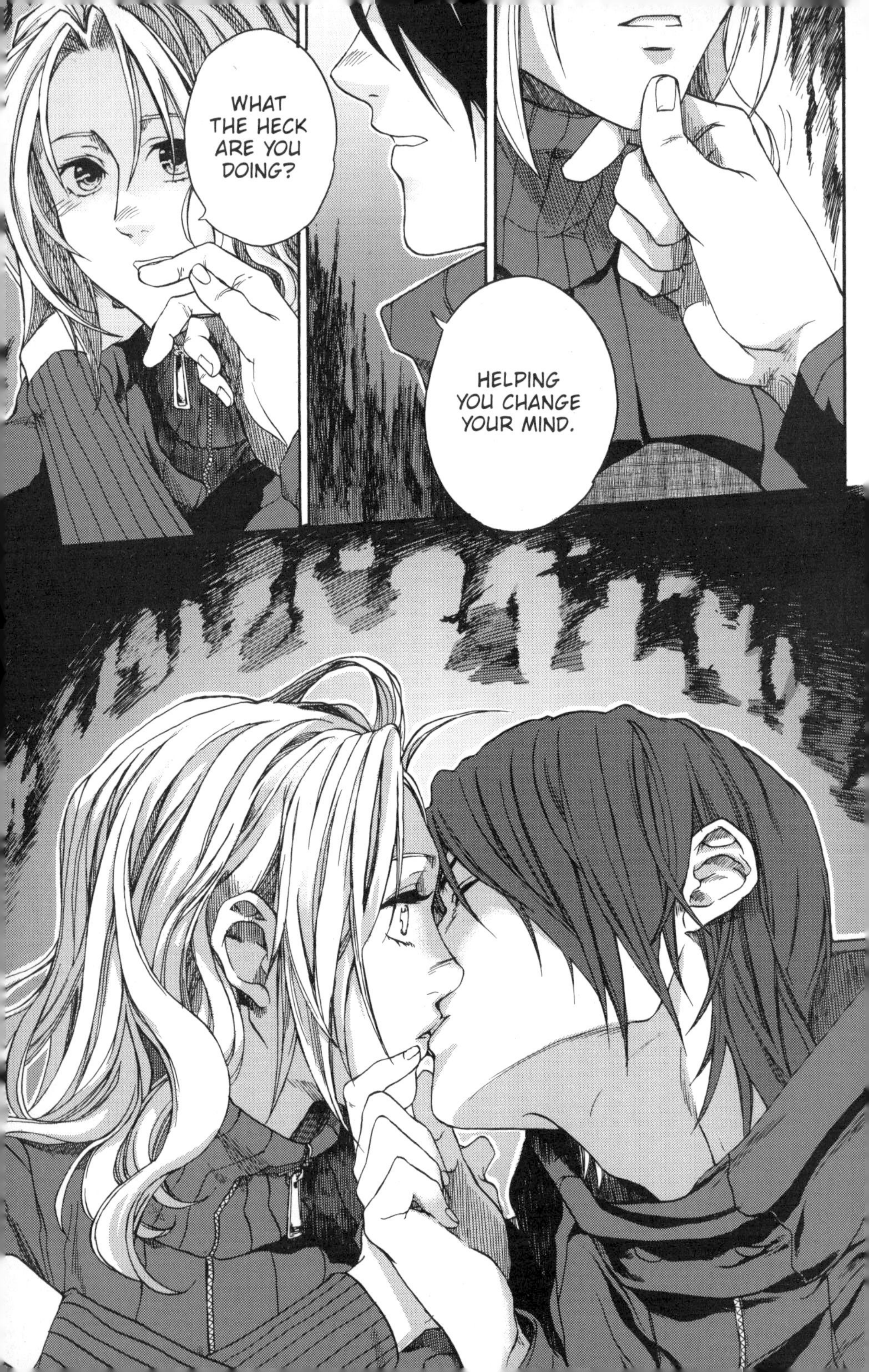
WHAT THE HECK ARE YOU DOING?
HELPING YOU CHANGE YOUR MIND.

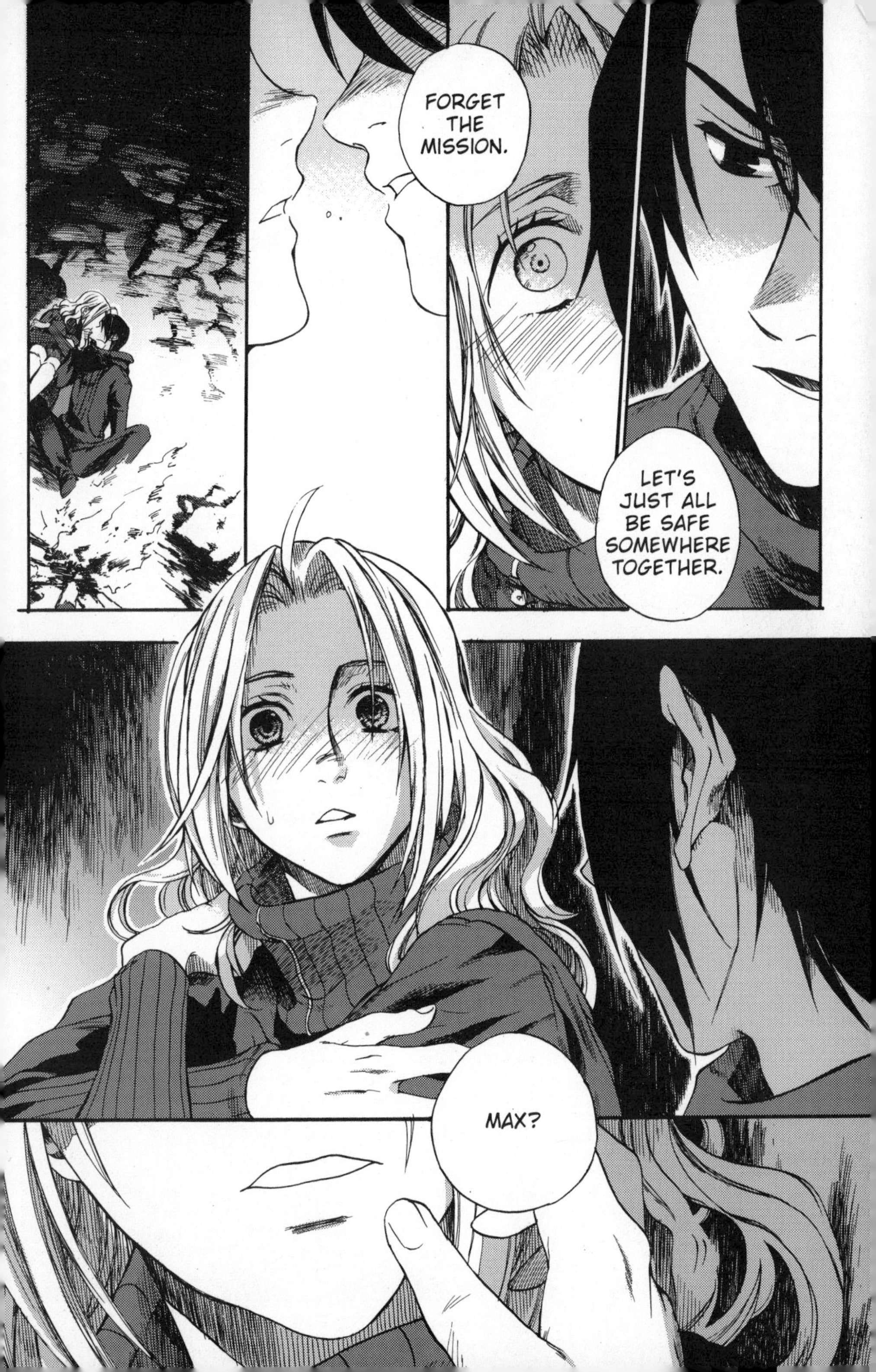
FORGET THE MISSION.
LET'S JUST ALL BE SAFE SOMEWHERE TOGETHER.
MAX?

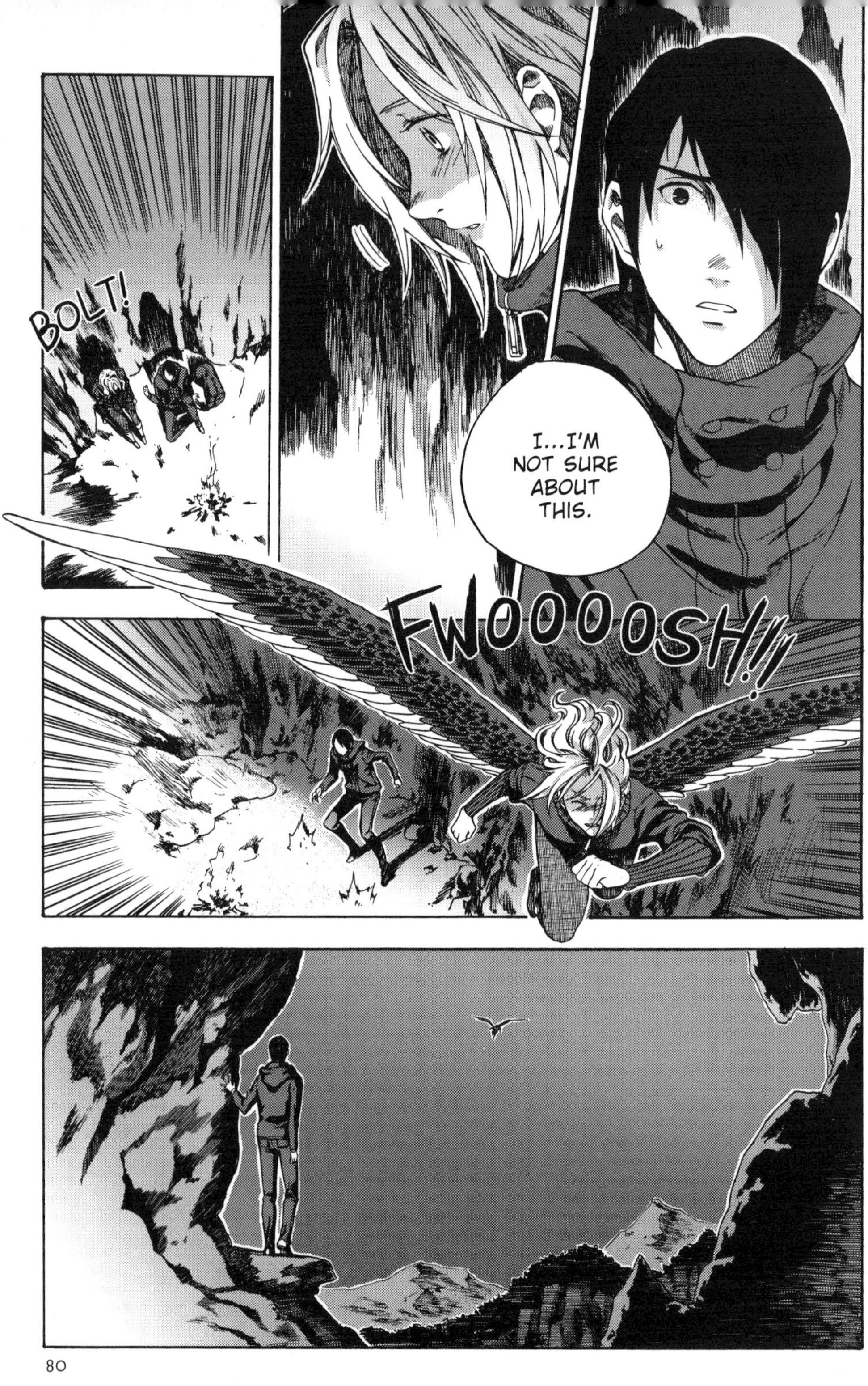

BOLT!
I...I'M NOT SURE ABOUT THIS.
FWOOOOSH!!

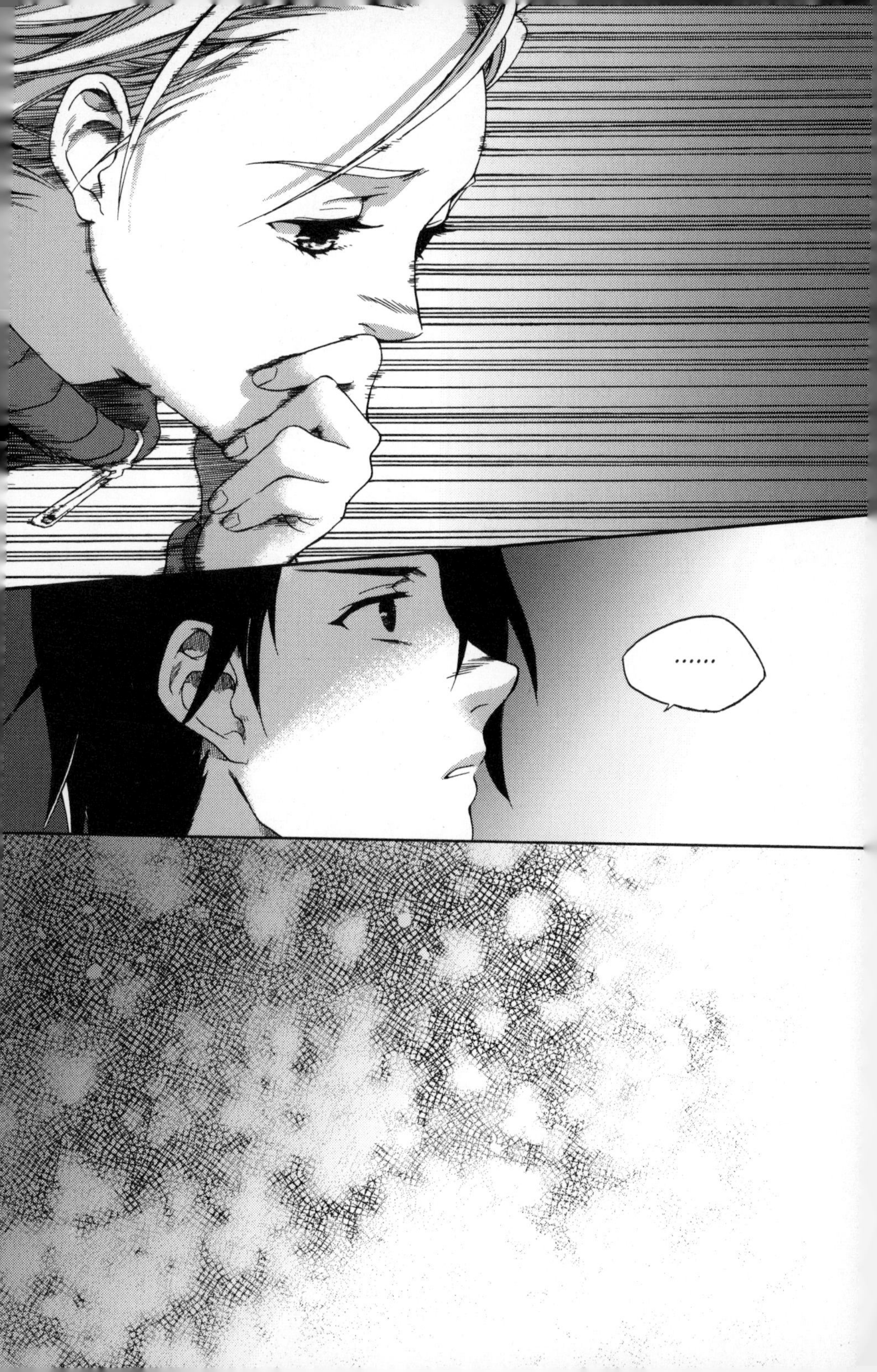
......

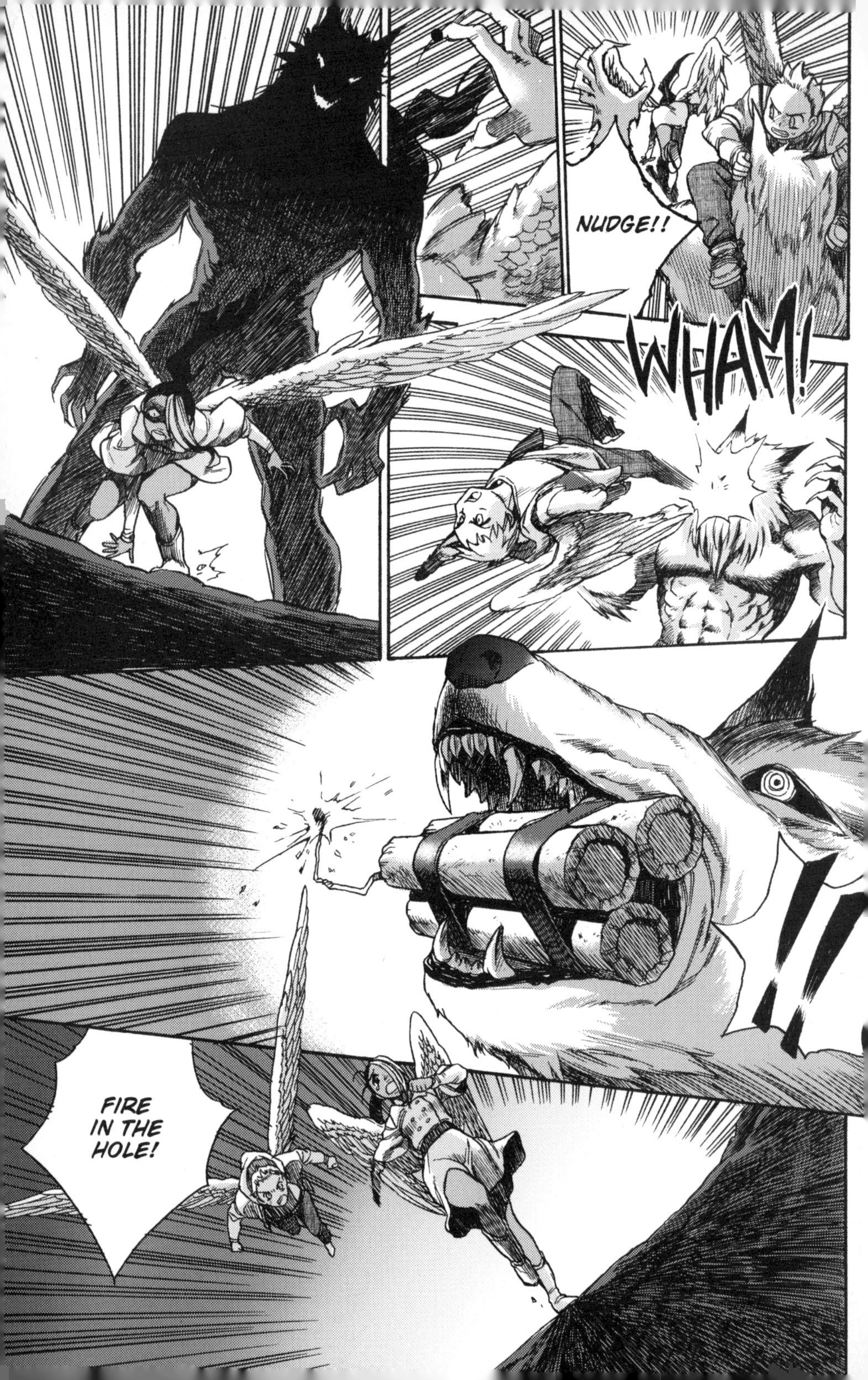
NUDGE!!
WHAM!
FIRE IN THE HOLE!

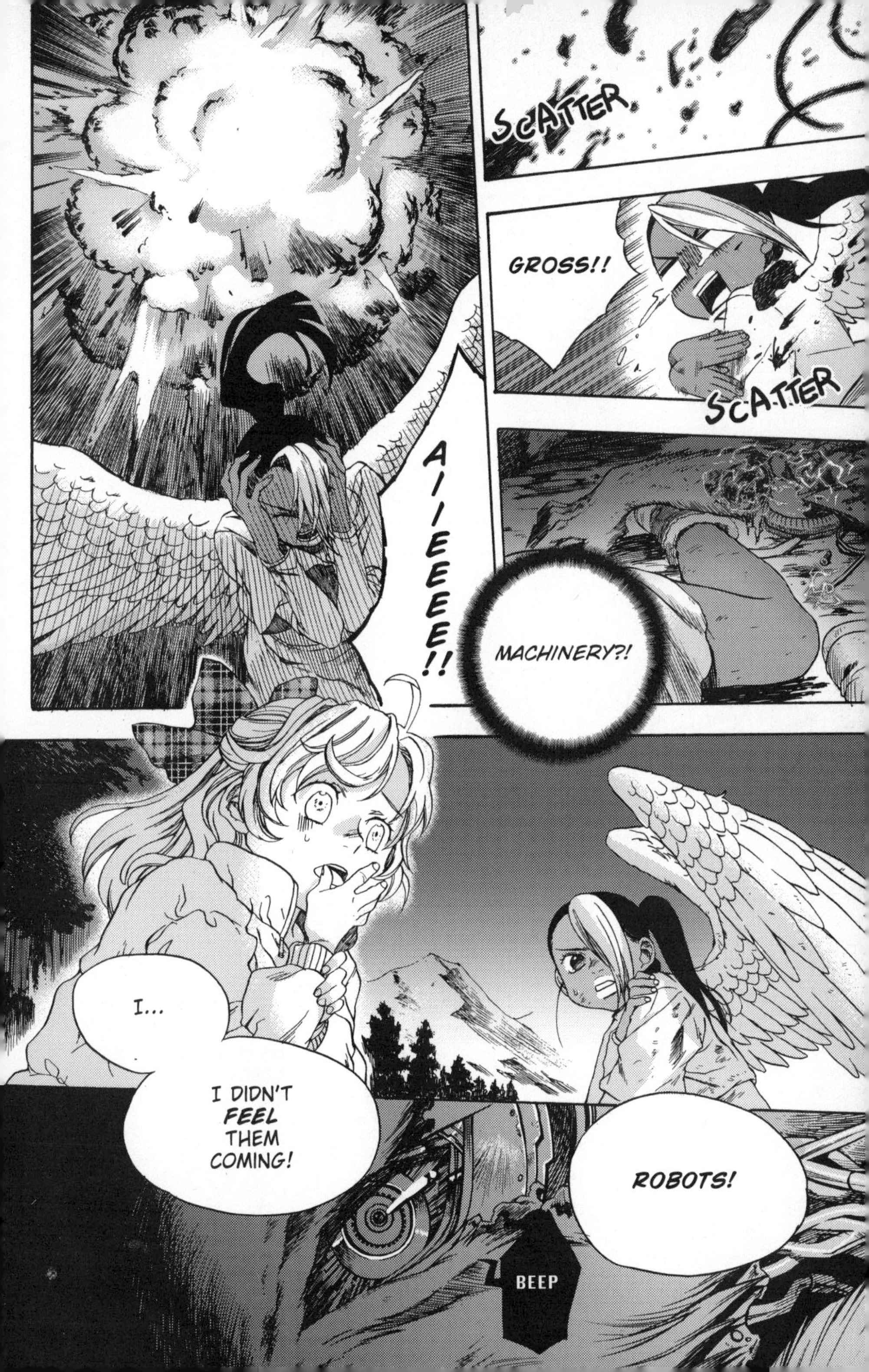
SCATTER
GROSS!!
SCATTER
AIIEEEEE!!
MACHINERY?!
I...
I DIDN'T FEEL THEM COMING!
ROBOTS!
BEEP

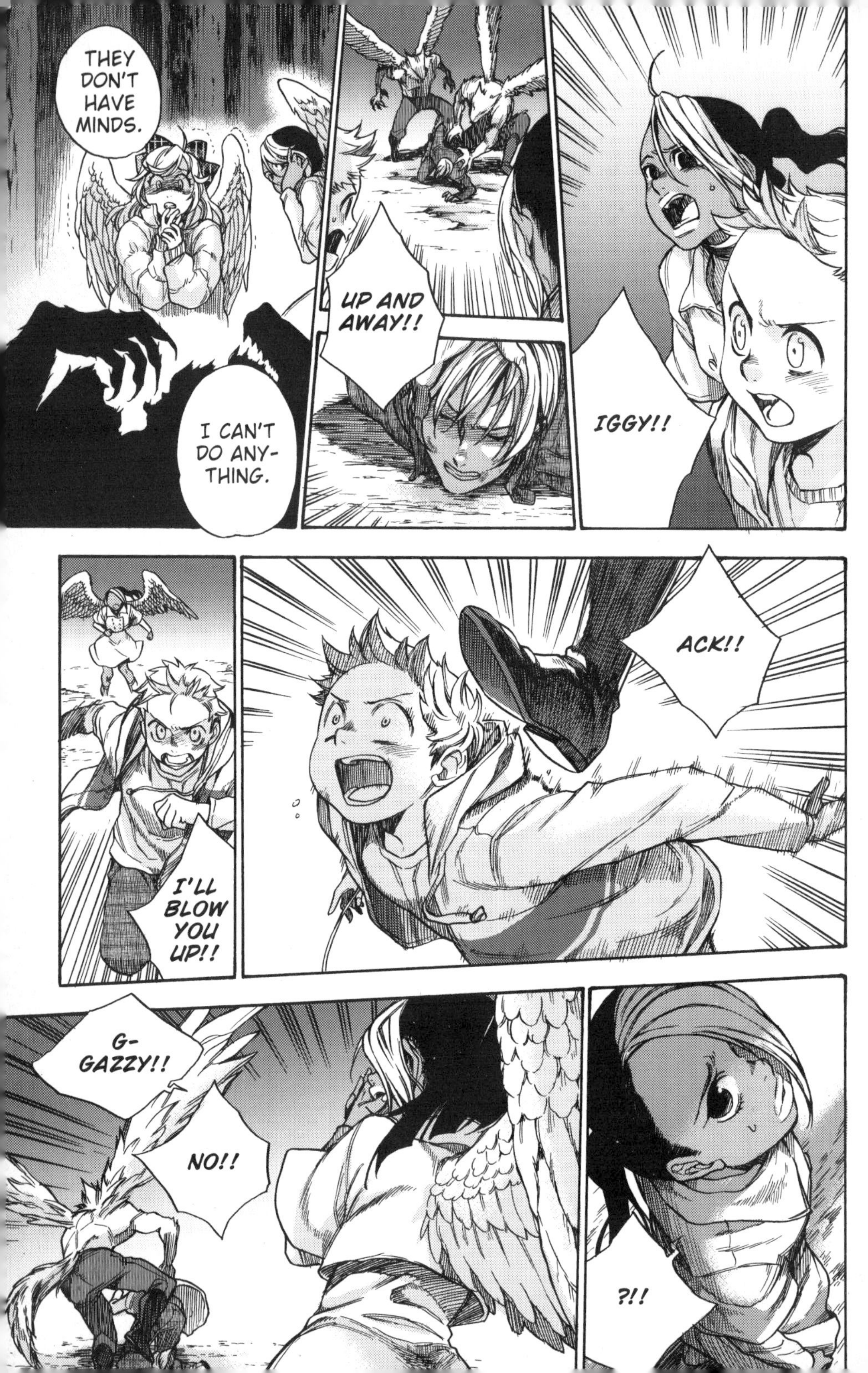
THEY DON'T HAVE MINDS.
I CAN'T DO ANY-THING.
UP AND AWAY!!
IGGY!!
I'LL BLOW YOU UP!!
ACK!!
G-GAZZY!!
NO!!
?!!

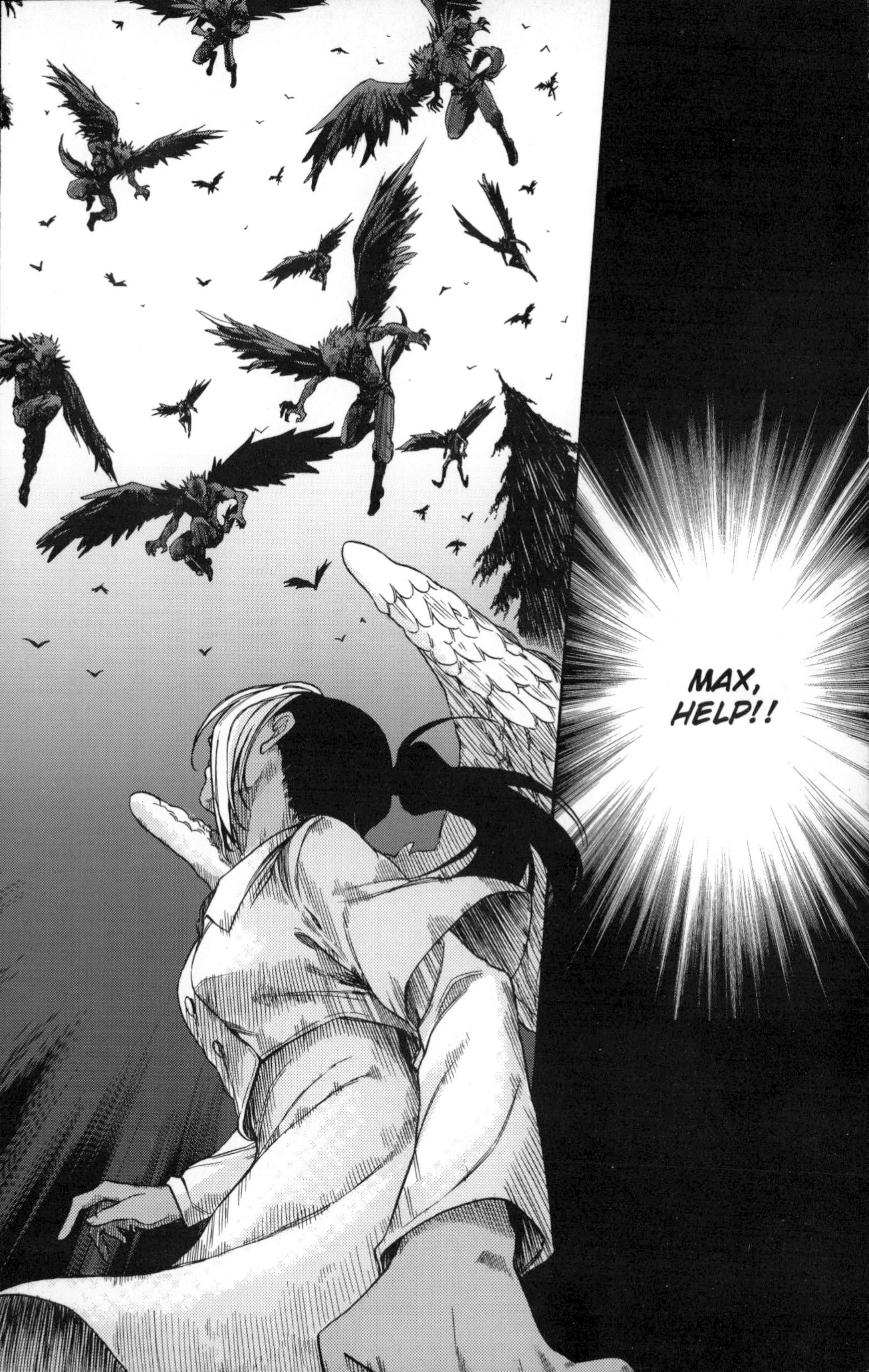
MAX, HELP!!

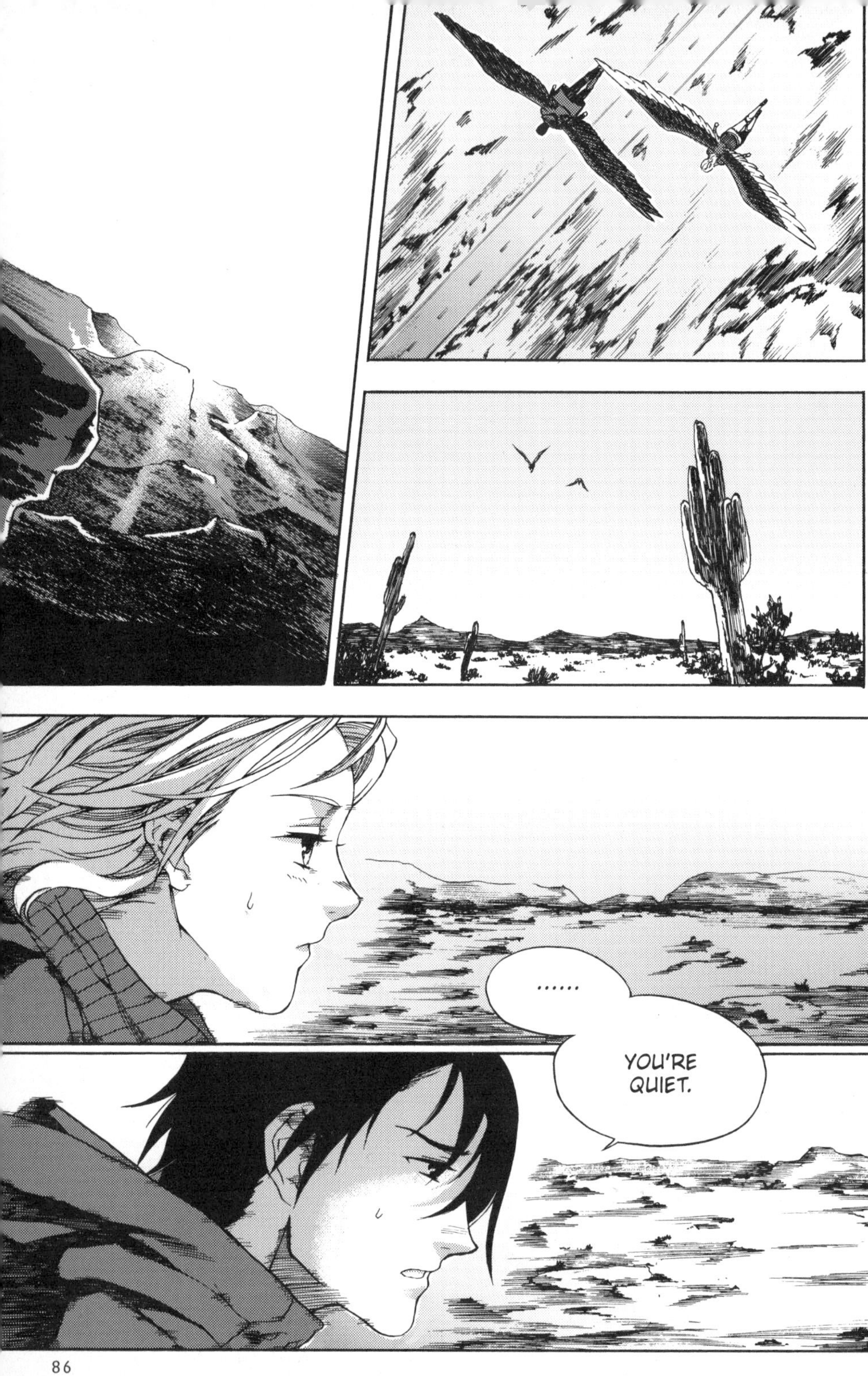
......
YOU'RE QUIET.

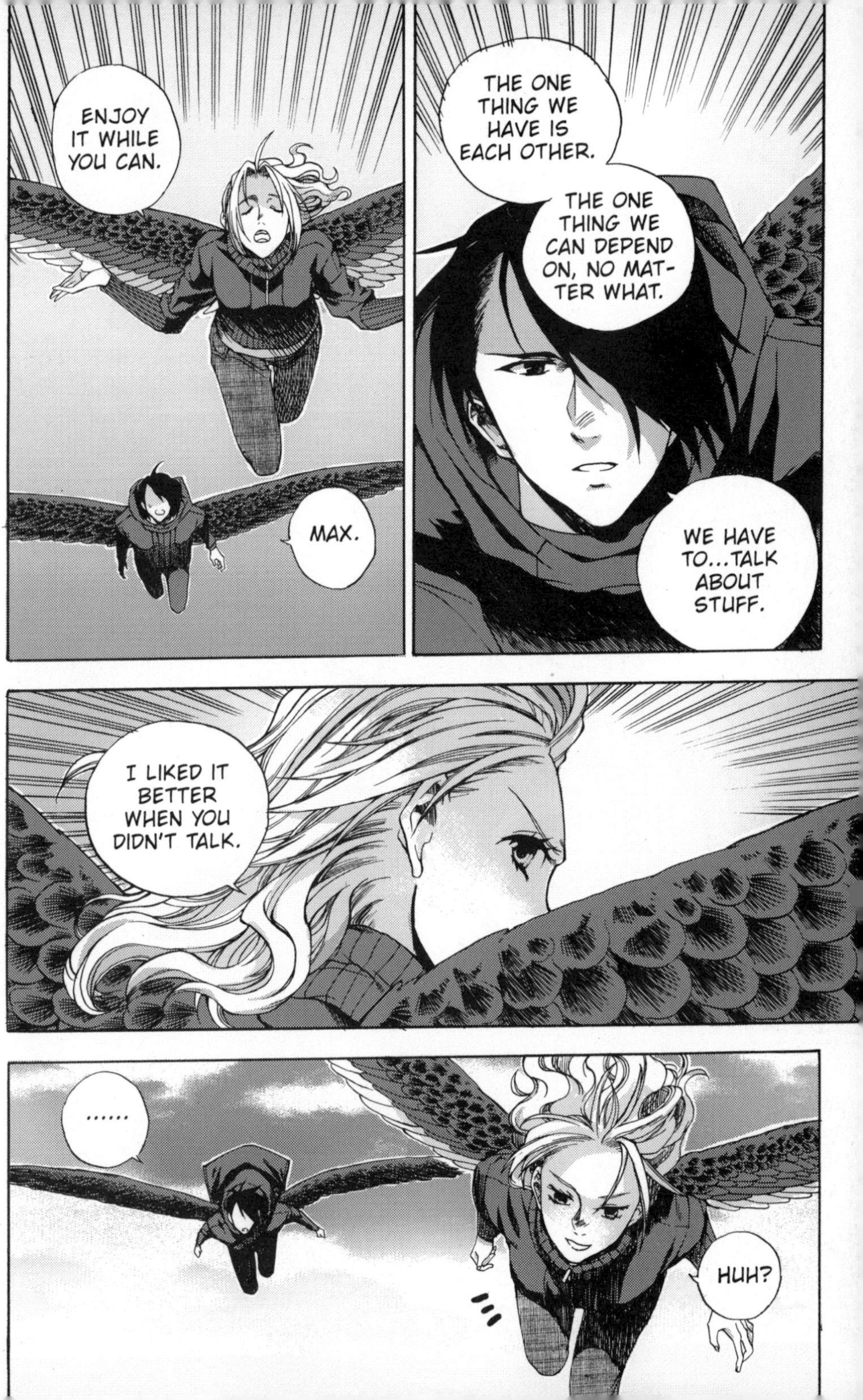
ENJOY IT WHILE YOU CAN.
MAX.
THE ONE THING WE HAVE IS EACH OTHER.
THE ONE THING WE CAN DEPEND ON, NO MATTER WHAT.
WE HAVE TO...TALK ABOUT STUFF.
I LIKED IT BETTER WHEN YOU DIDN'T TALK.
......
HUH?

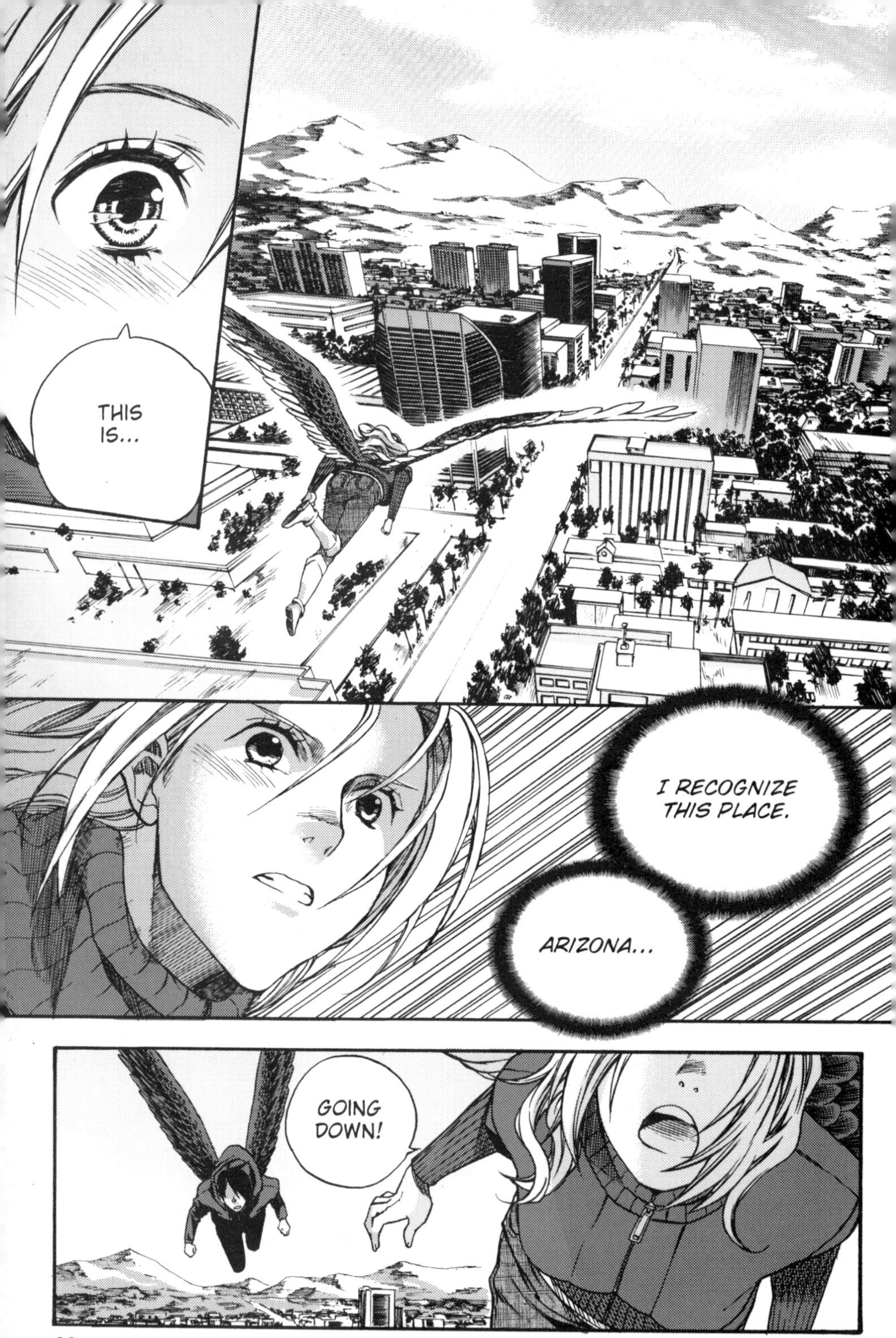
THIS IS...
I RECOGNIZE THIS PLACE.
ARIZONA...
GOING DOWN!

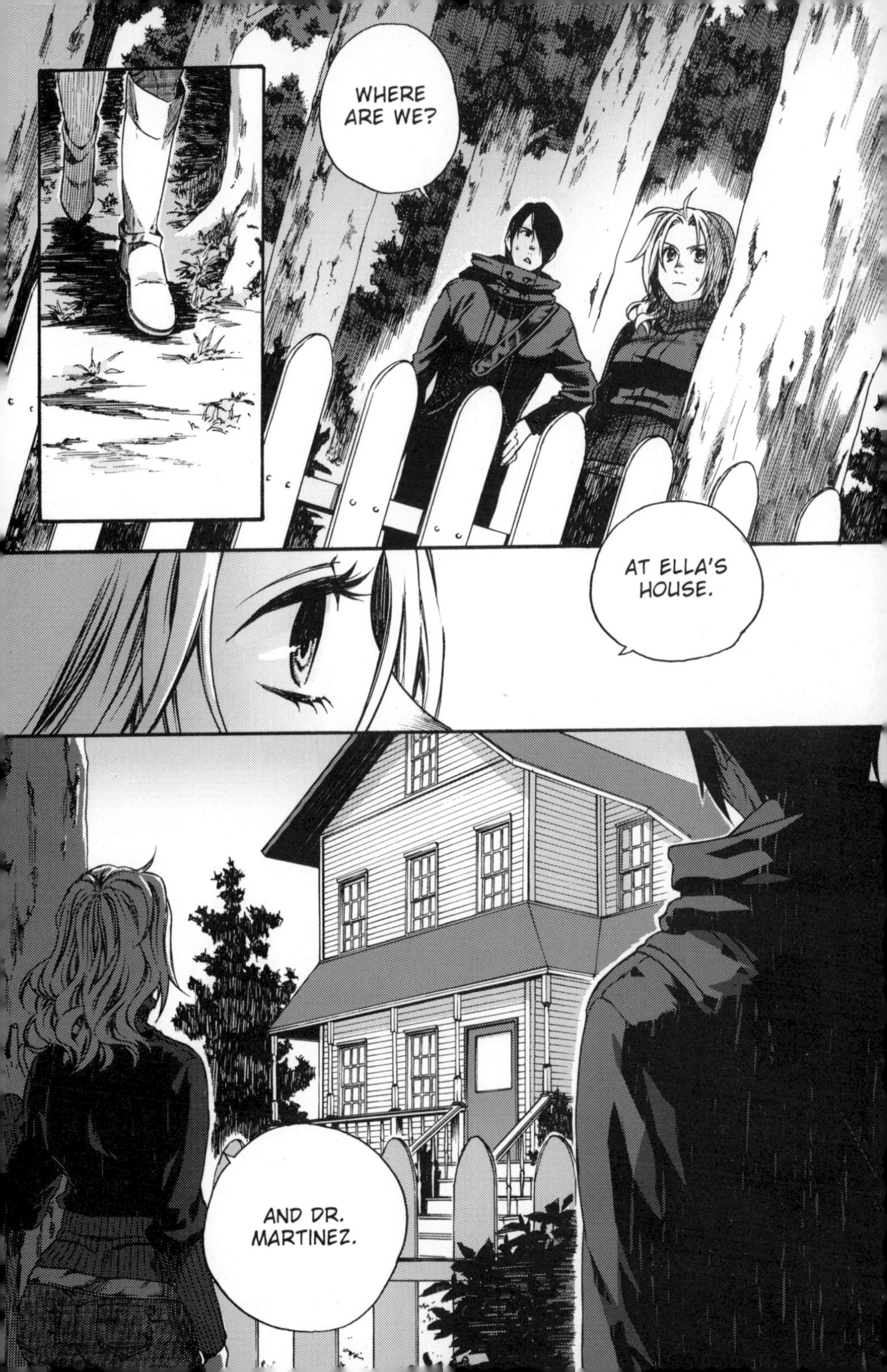
WHERE ARE WE?
AT ELLA'S HOUSE.
AND DR. MARTINEZ.

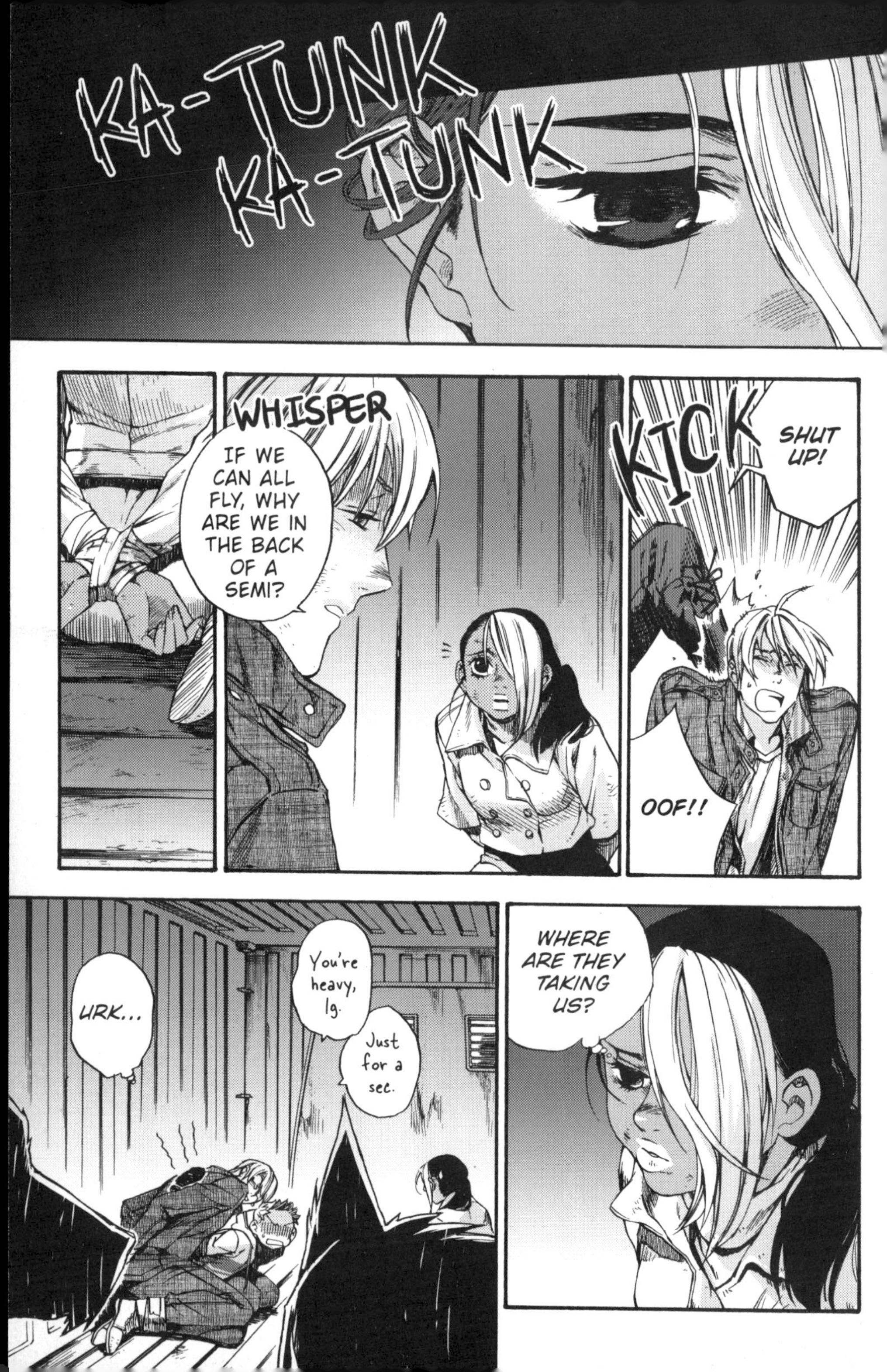
KA-TUNK
KA-TUNK
WHISPER
IF WE CAN ALL FLY, WHY ARE WE IN THE BACK OF A SEMI?
KICK
SHUT UP!
OOF!!
WHERE ARE THEY TAKING US?
You're heavy, Ig.
Just for a sec.
URK...

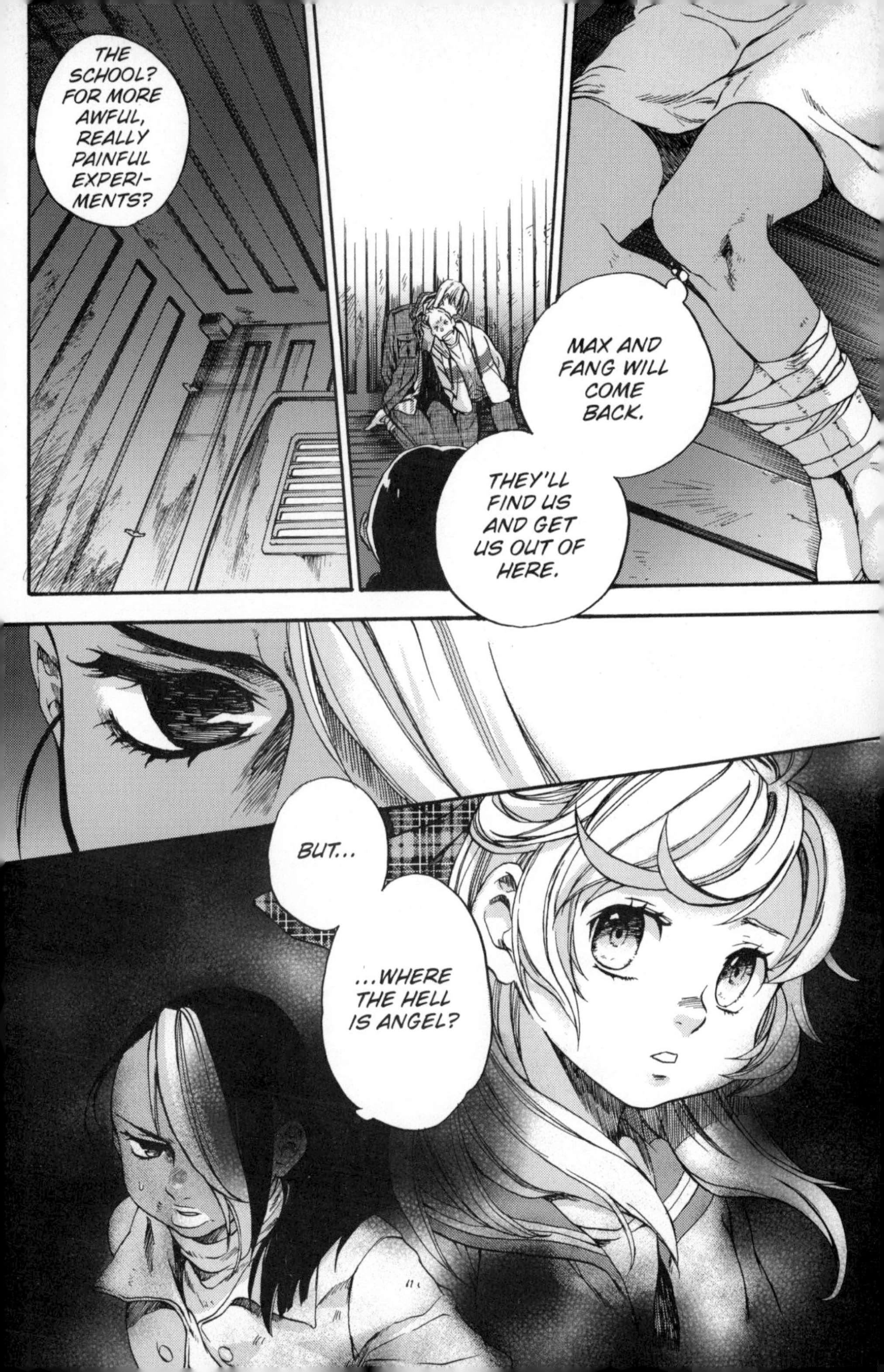
THE SCHOOL? FOR MORE AWFUL, REALLY PAINFUL EXPERI-MENTS?
MAX AND FANG WILL COME BACK.
THEY'LL FIND US AND GET US OUT OF HERE.
BUT...
...WHERE THE HELL IS ANGEL?

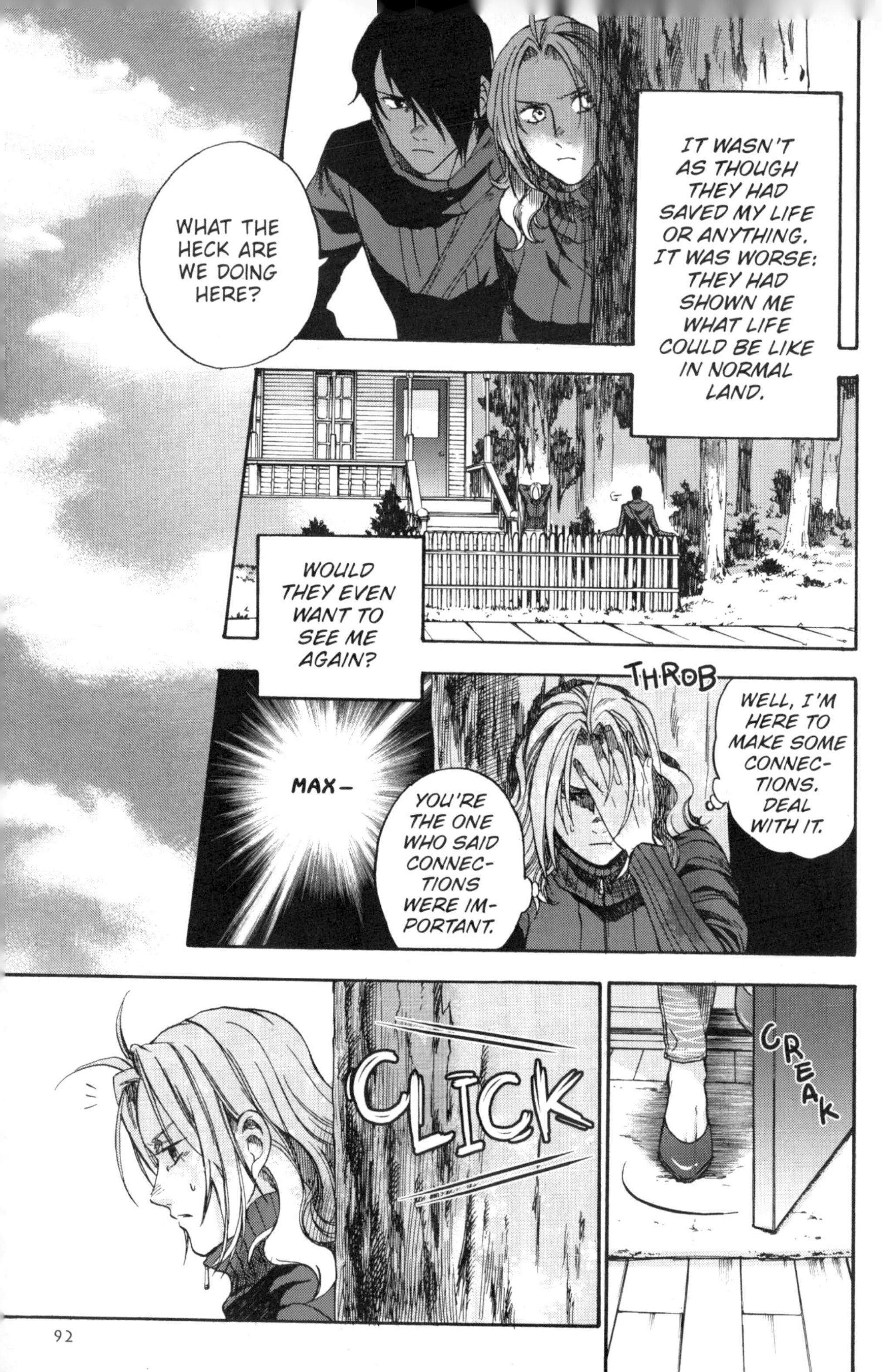

WHAT THE HECK ARE WE DOING HERE?
IT WASN'T AS THOUGH THEY HAD SAVED MY LIFE OR ANYTHING. IT WAS WORSE: THEY HAD SHOWN ME WHAT LIFE COULD BE LIKE IN NORMAL LAND.
WOULD THEY EVEN WANT TO SEE ME AGAIN?
MAX—
YOU'RE THE ONE WHO SAID CONNECTIONS WERE IMPORTANT.
THROB
WELL, I'M HERE TO MAKE SOME CONNECTIONS. DEAL WITH IT.
CLICK
CREAK

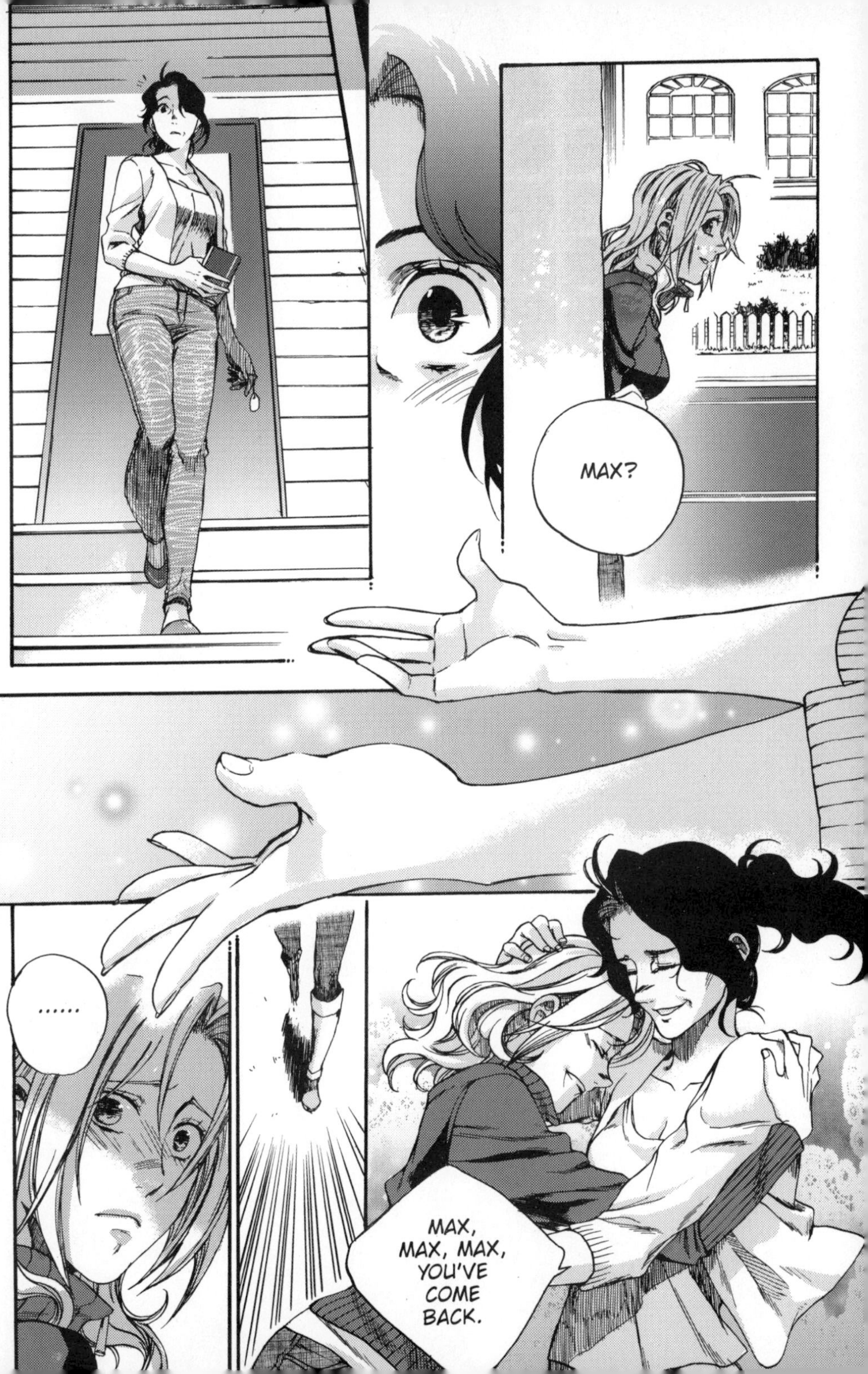
MAX?
......
MAX, MAX, MAX, YOU'VE COME BACK.

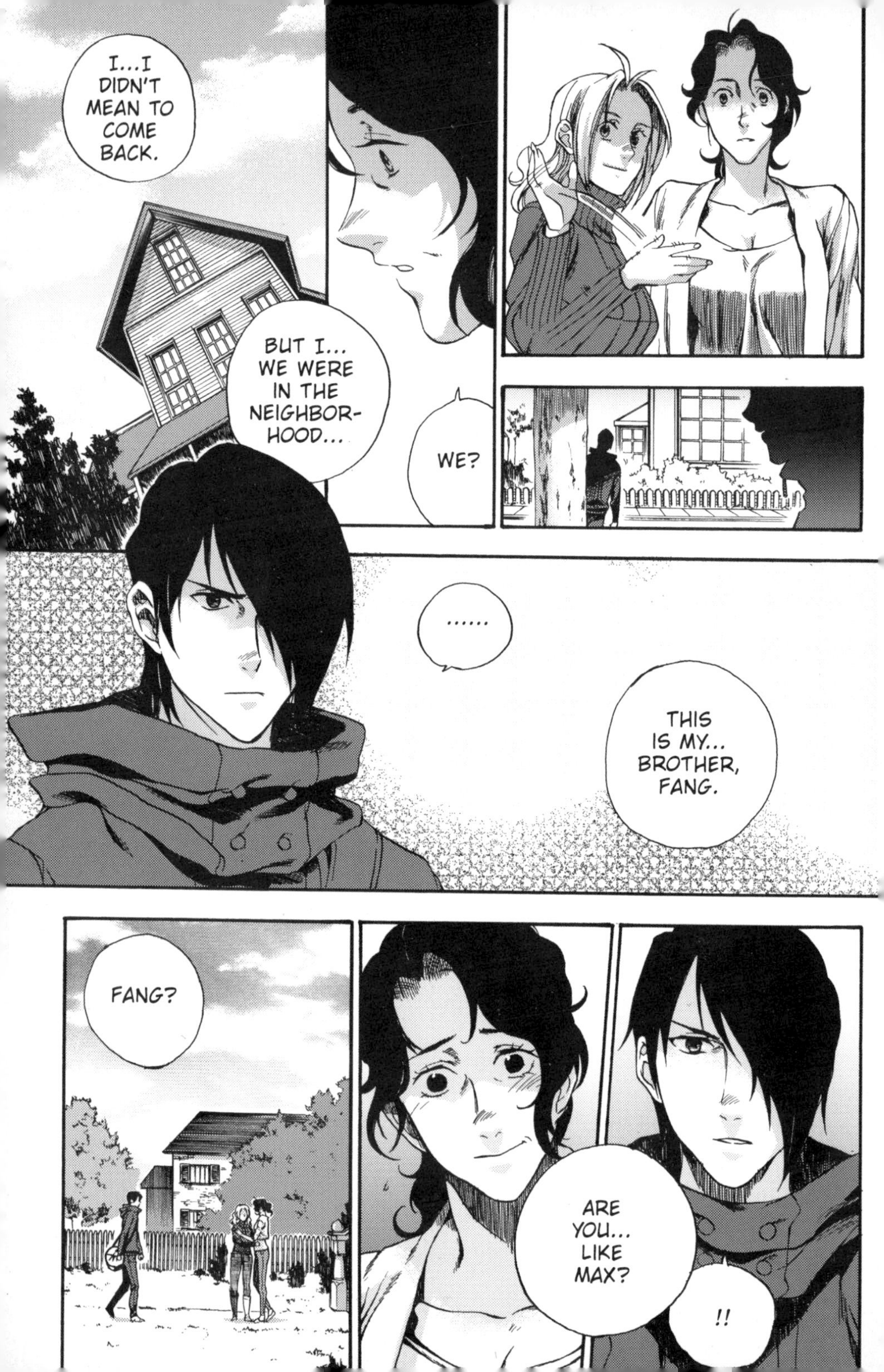
I...I DIDN'T MEAN TO COME BACK.
BUT I... WE WERE IN THE NEIGHBOR-HOOD...
WE?
......
THIS IS MY... BROTHER, FANG.
FANG?
ARE YOU... LIKE MAX?
!!

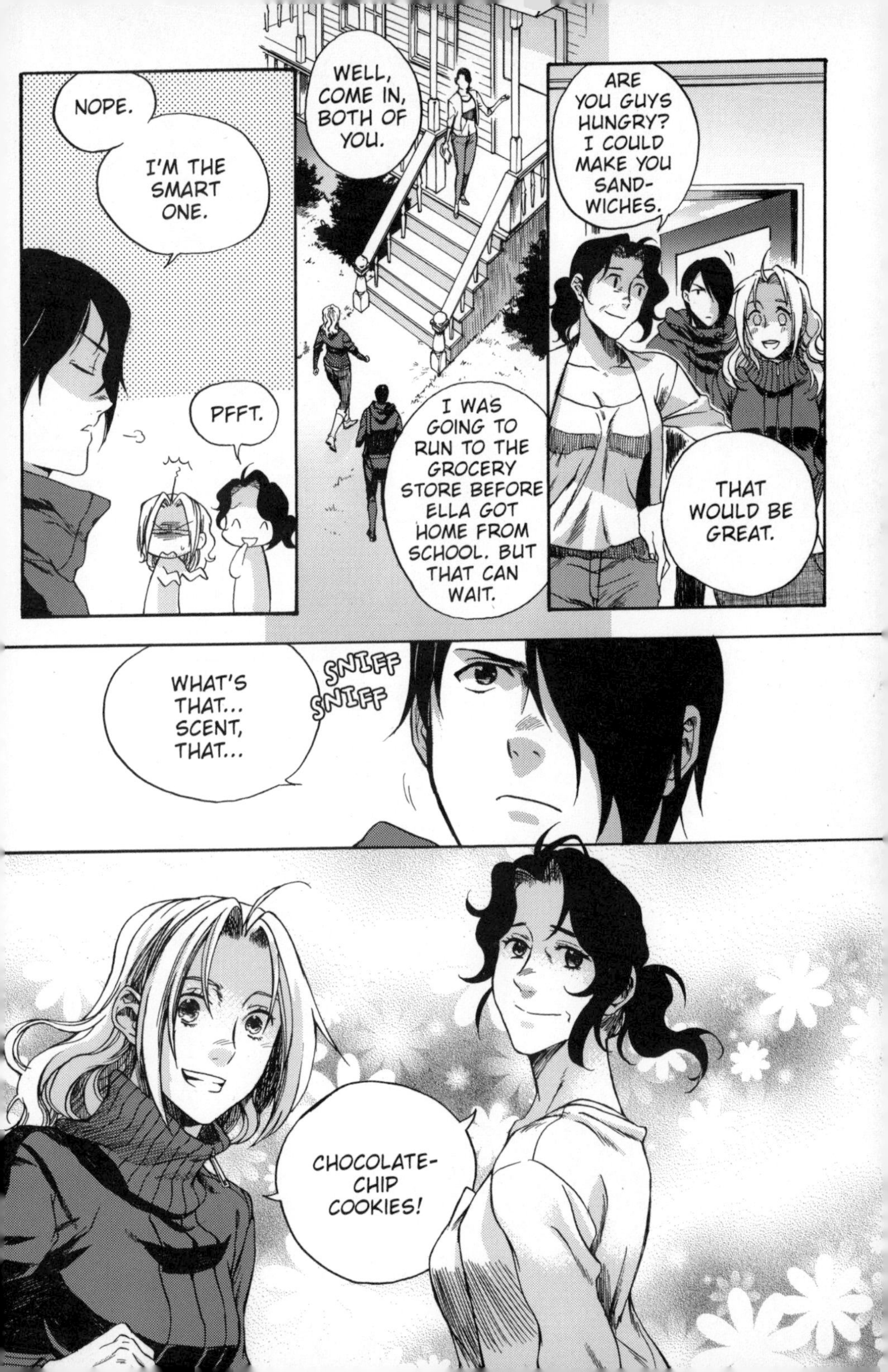
NOPE.
I'M THE SMART ONE.
PFFT.
WELL, COME IN, BOTH OF YOU.
I WAS GOING TO RUN TO THE GROCERY STORE BEFORE ELLA GOT HOME FROM SCHOOL. BUT THAT CAN WAIT.
ARE YOU GUYS HUNGRY? I COULD MAKE YOU SAND-WICHES.
THAT WOULD BE GREAT.
WHAT'S THAT... SCENT, THAT...
SNIFF SNIFF
CHOCOLATE-CHIP COOKIES!

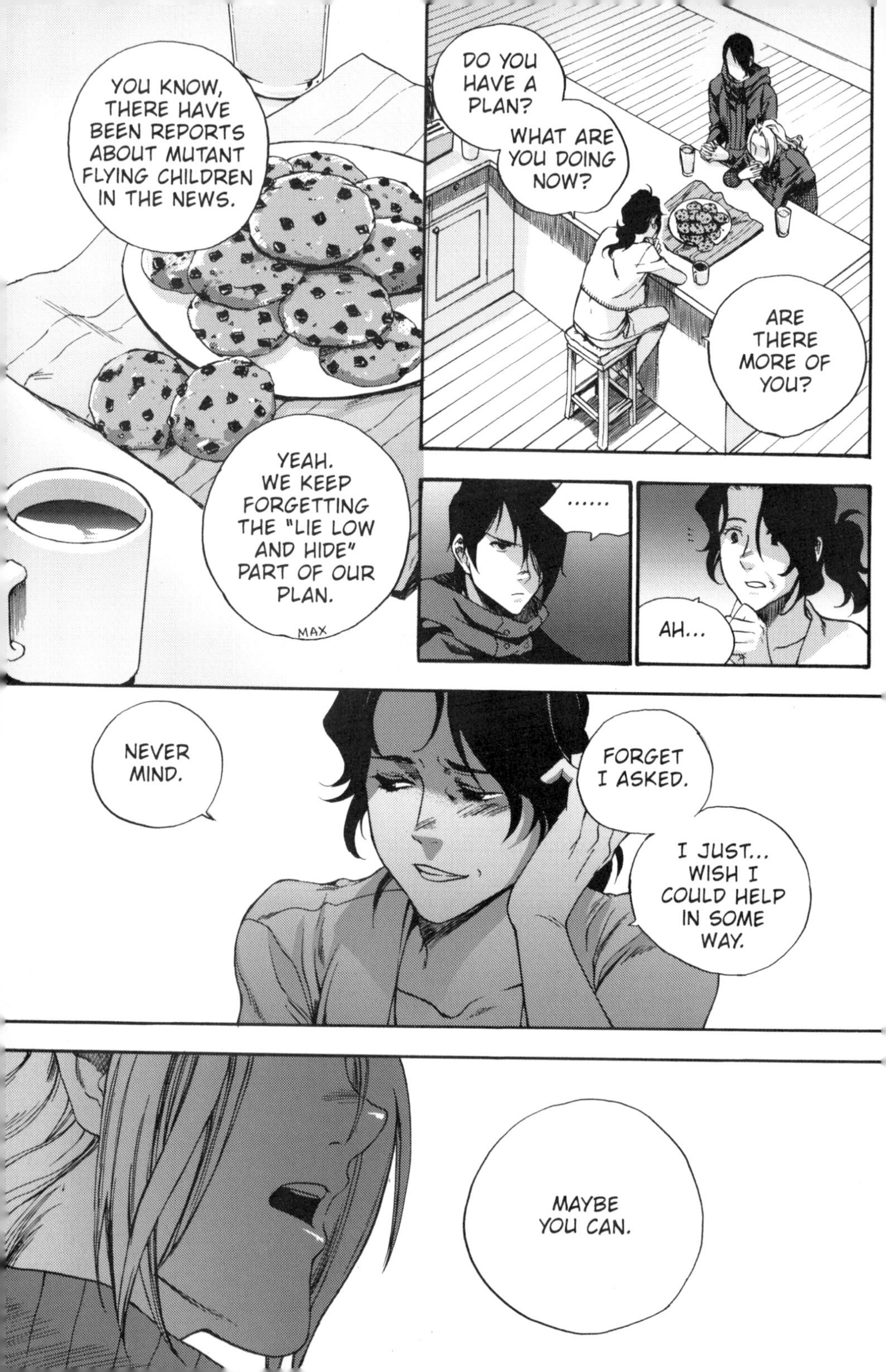
YOU KNOW, THERE HAVE BEEN REPORTS ABOUT MUTANT FLYING CHILDREN IN THE NEWS.
DO YOU HAVE A PLAN?
WHAT ARE YOU DOING NOW?
ARE THERE MORE OF YOU?
YEAH. WE KEEP FORGETTING THE "LIE LOW AND HIDE" PART OF OUR PLAN.
MAX
......
AH...
NEVER MIND.
FORGET I ASKED.
I JUST... WISH I COULD HELP IN SOME WAY.
MAYBE YOU CAN.

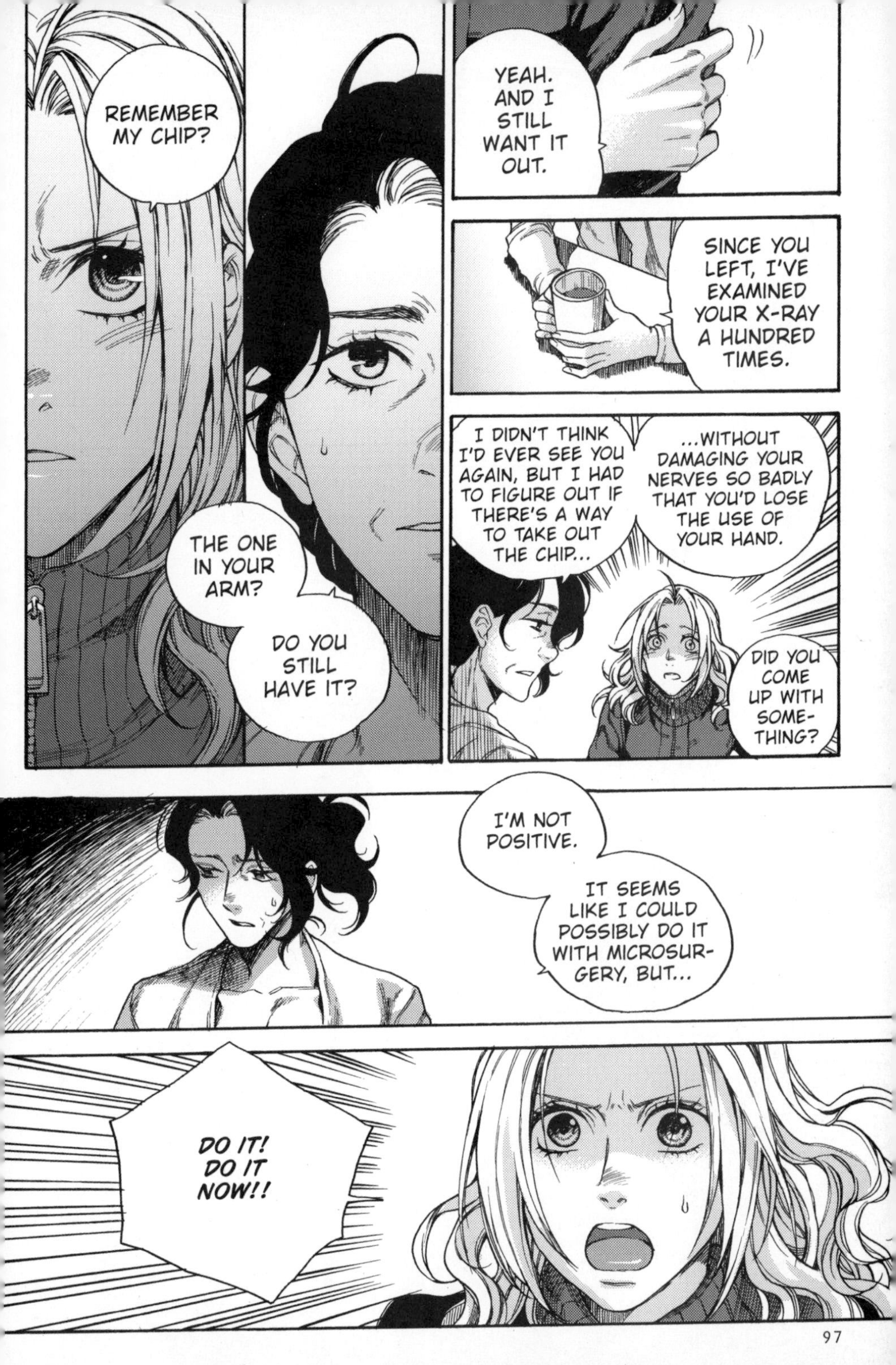

REMEMBER MY CHIP?
THE ONE IN YOUR ARM?
DO YOU STILL HAVE IT?
YEAH. AND I STILL WANT IT OUT.
SINCE YOU LEFT, I'VE EXAMINED YOUR X-RAY A HUNDRED TIMES.
I DIDN'T THINK I'D EVER SEE YOU AGAIN, BUT I HAD TO FIGURE OUT IF THERE'S A WAY TO TAKE OUT THE CHIP...
...WITHOUT DAMAGING YOUR NERVES SO BADLY THAT YOU'D LOSE THE USE OF YOUR HAND.
DID YOU COME UP WITH SOME-THING?
I'M NOT POSITIVE.
IT SEEMS LIKE I COULD POSSIBLY DO IT WITH MICROSUR-GERY, BUT...
DO IT! DO IT NOW!!

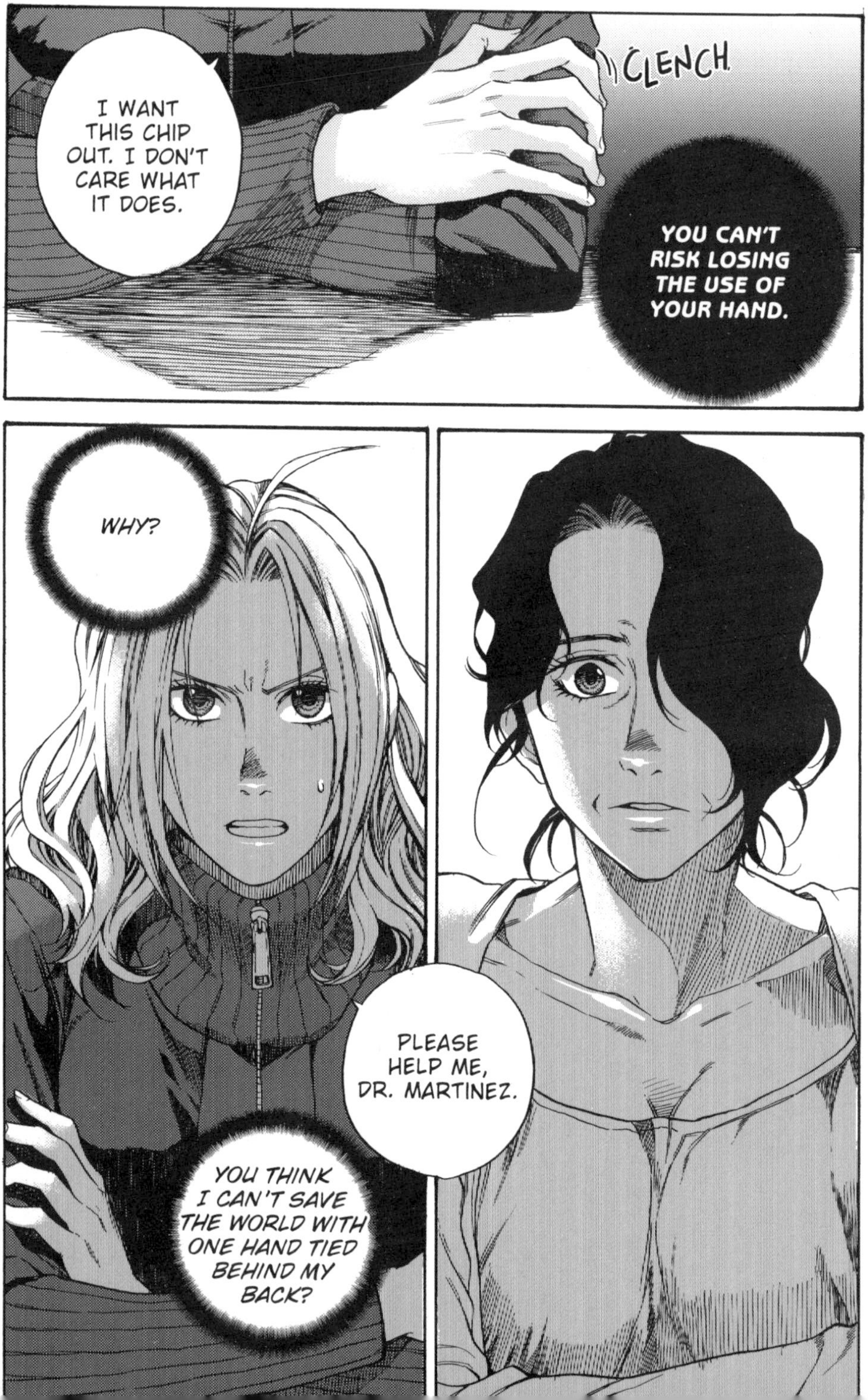
I WANT THIS CHIP OUT. I DON'T CARE WHAT IT DOES.
CLENCH
YOU CAN'T RISK LOSING THE USE OF YOUR HAND.
WHY?
PLEASE HELP ME, DR. MARTINEZ.
YOU THINK I CAN'T SAVE THE WORLD WITH ONE HAND TIED BEHIND MY BACK?

MAXIMUM
RIDE

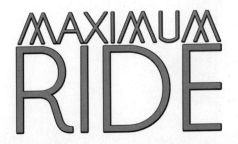

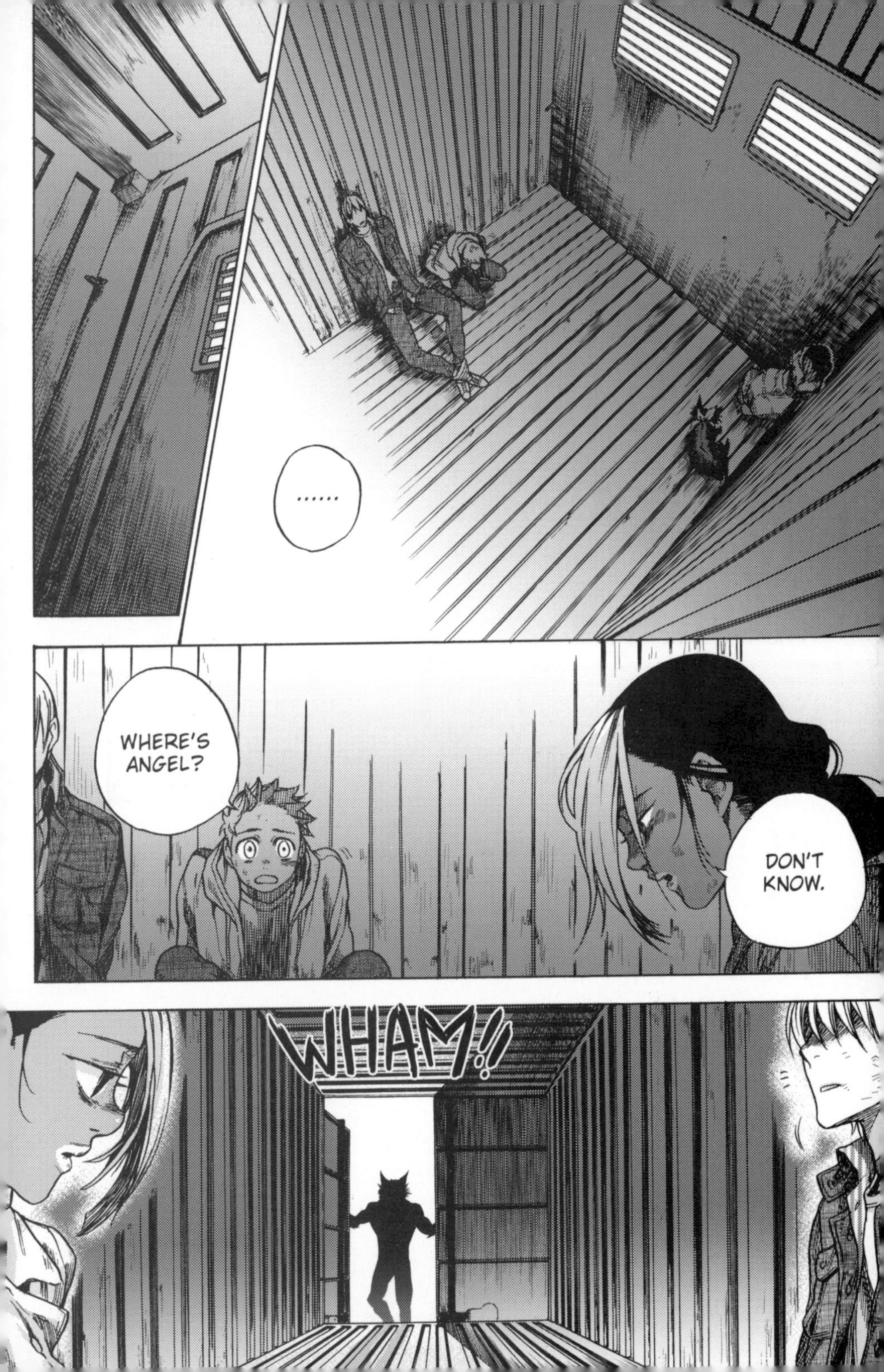
......
WHERE'S ANGEL?
DON'T KNOW.
WHAM!!

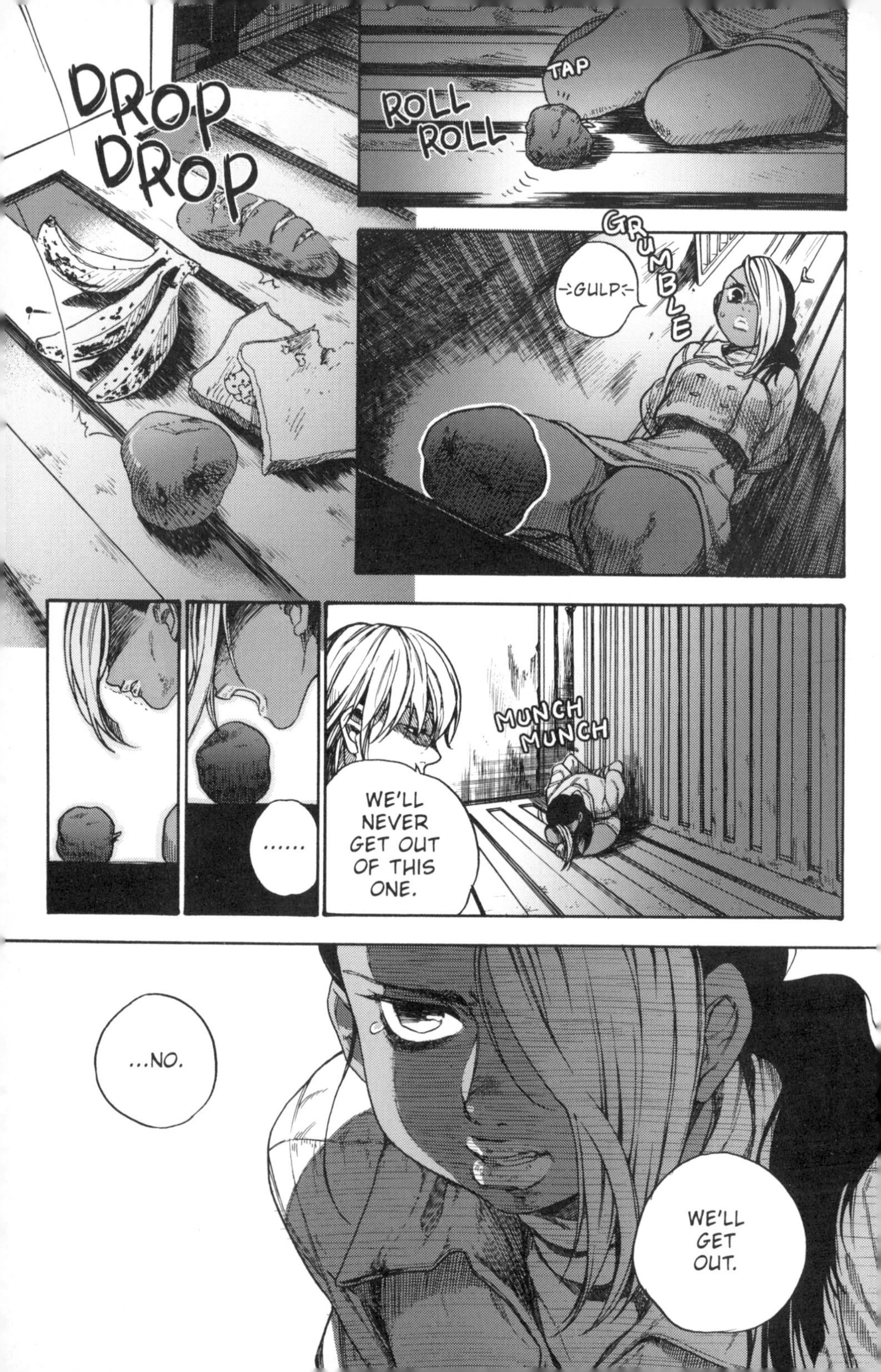
DROP DROP
ROLL ROLL
TAP
GRUMBLE
GULP
MUNCH MUNCH
WE'LL NEVER GET OUT OF THIS ONE.
......
...NO.
WE'LL GET OUT.

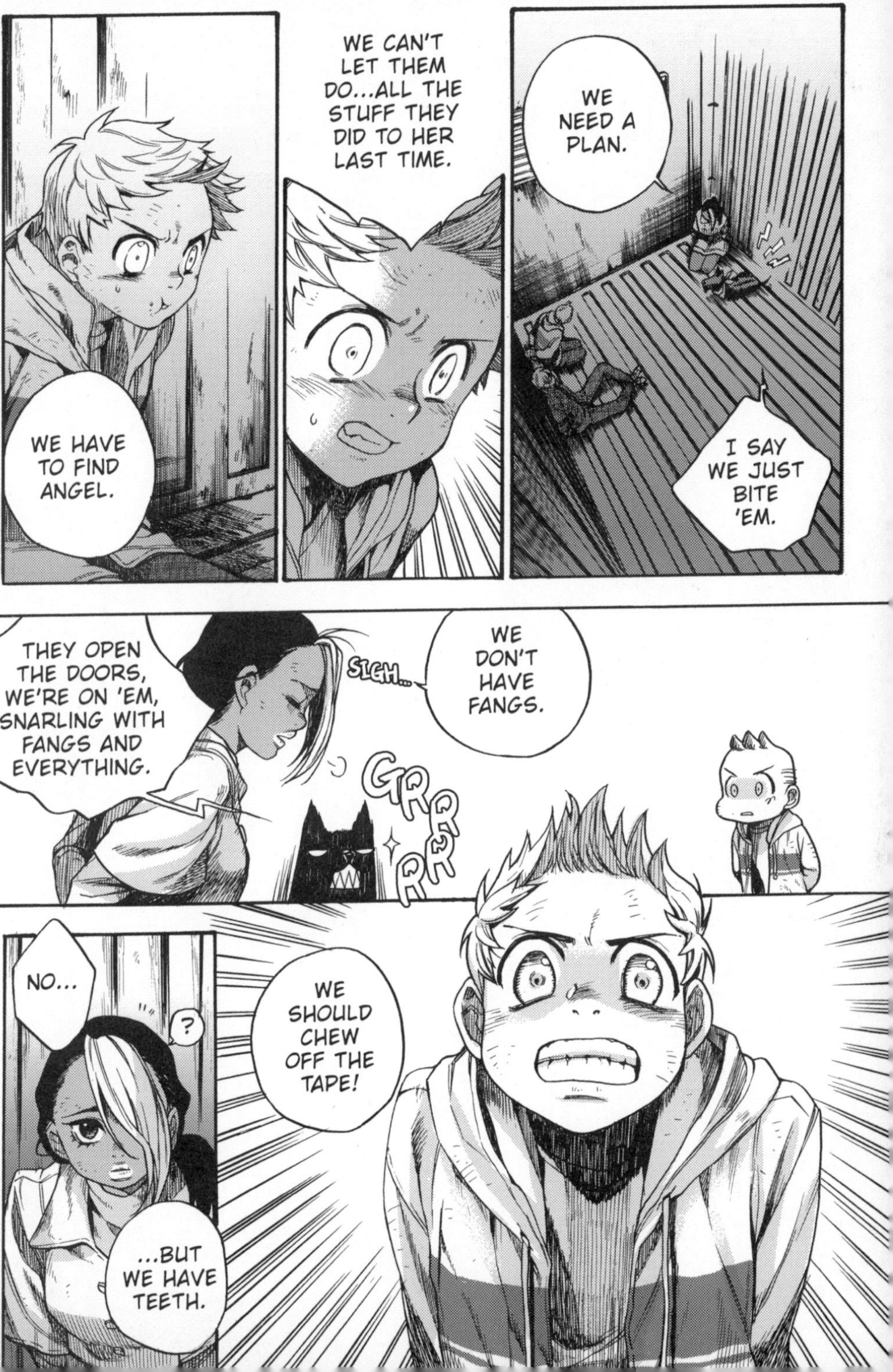
WE HAVE TO FIND ANGEL.
WE CAN'T LET THEM DO...ALL THE STUFF THEY DID TO HER LAST TIME.
WE NEED A PLAN.
I SAY WE JUST BITE 'EM.
THEY OPEN THE DOORS, WE'RE ON 'EM, SNARLING WITH FANGS AND EVERYTHING.
SIGH...
WE DON'T HAVE FANGS.
GRRRRR
NO...
?
...BUT WE HAVE TEETH.
WE SHOULD CHEW OFF THE TAPE!

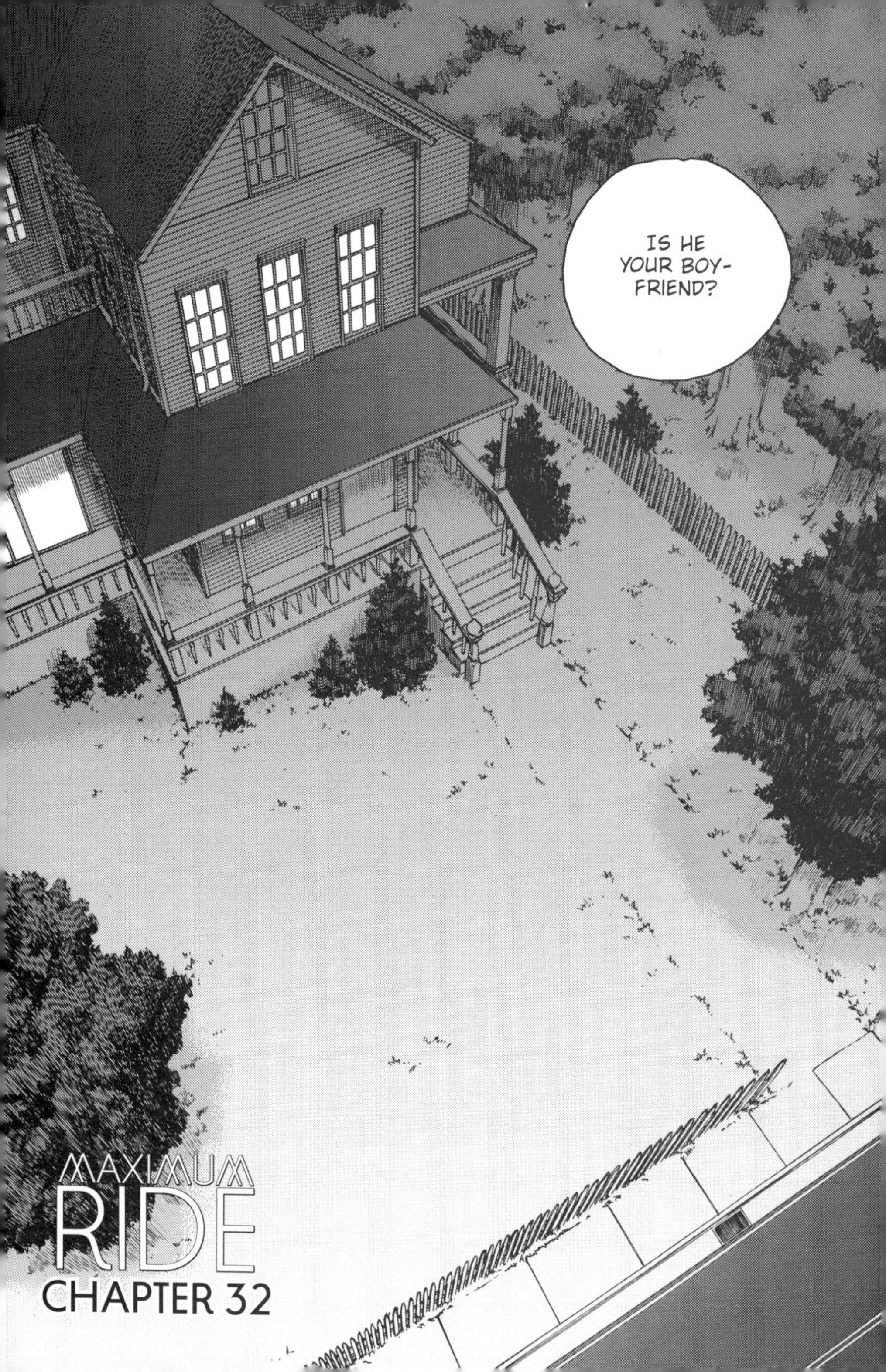
IS HE YOUR BOY-FRIEND?
MAXIMUM RIDE
CHAPTER 32

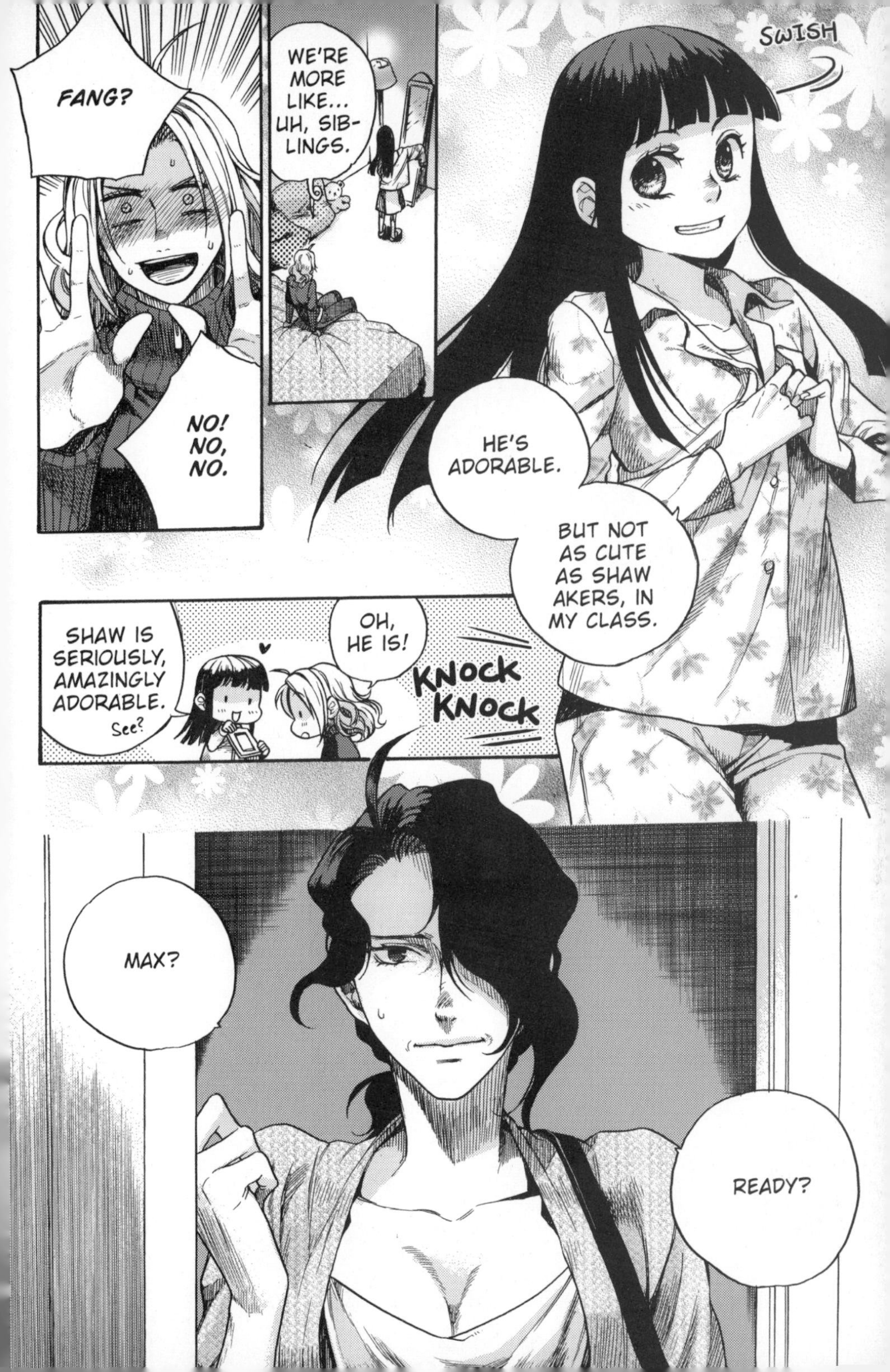
FANG?
NO! NO, NO.
WE'RE MORE LIKE... UH, SIB-LINGS.
SWISH
HE'S ADORABLE.
BUT NOT AS CUTE AS SHAW AKERS, IN MY CLASS.
SHAW IS SERIOUSLY, AMAZINGLY ADORABLE.
See?
OH, HE IS!
KNOCK KNOCK
MAX?
READY?

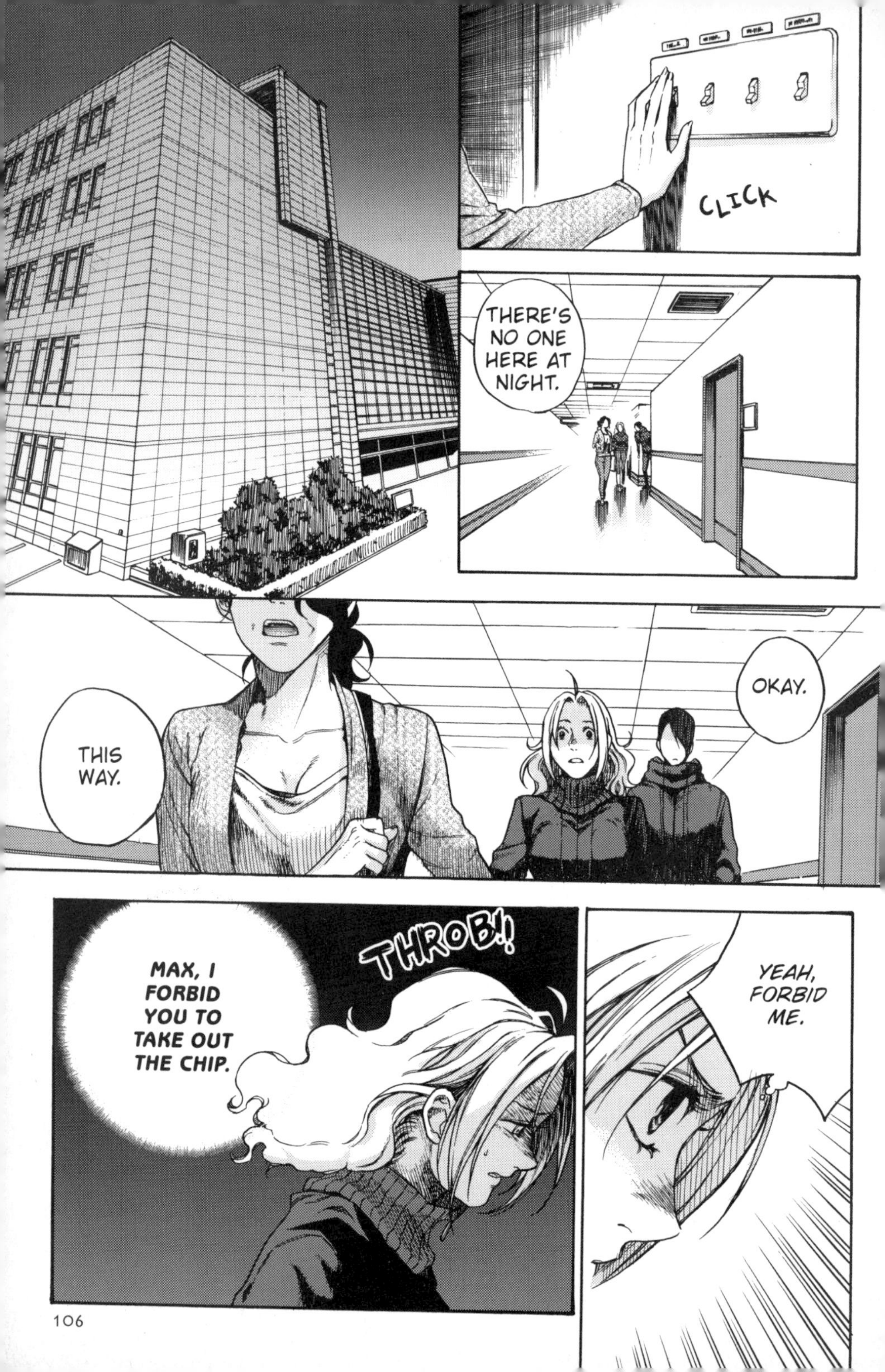
CLICK
THERE'S NO ONE HERE AT NIGHT.
THIS WAY.
OKAY.
THROB!!
MAX, I FORBID YOU TO TAKE OUT THE CHIP.
YEAH, FORBID ME.

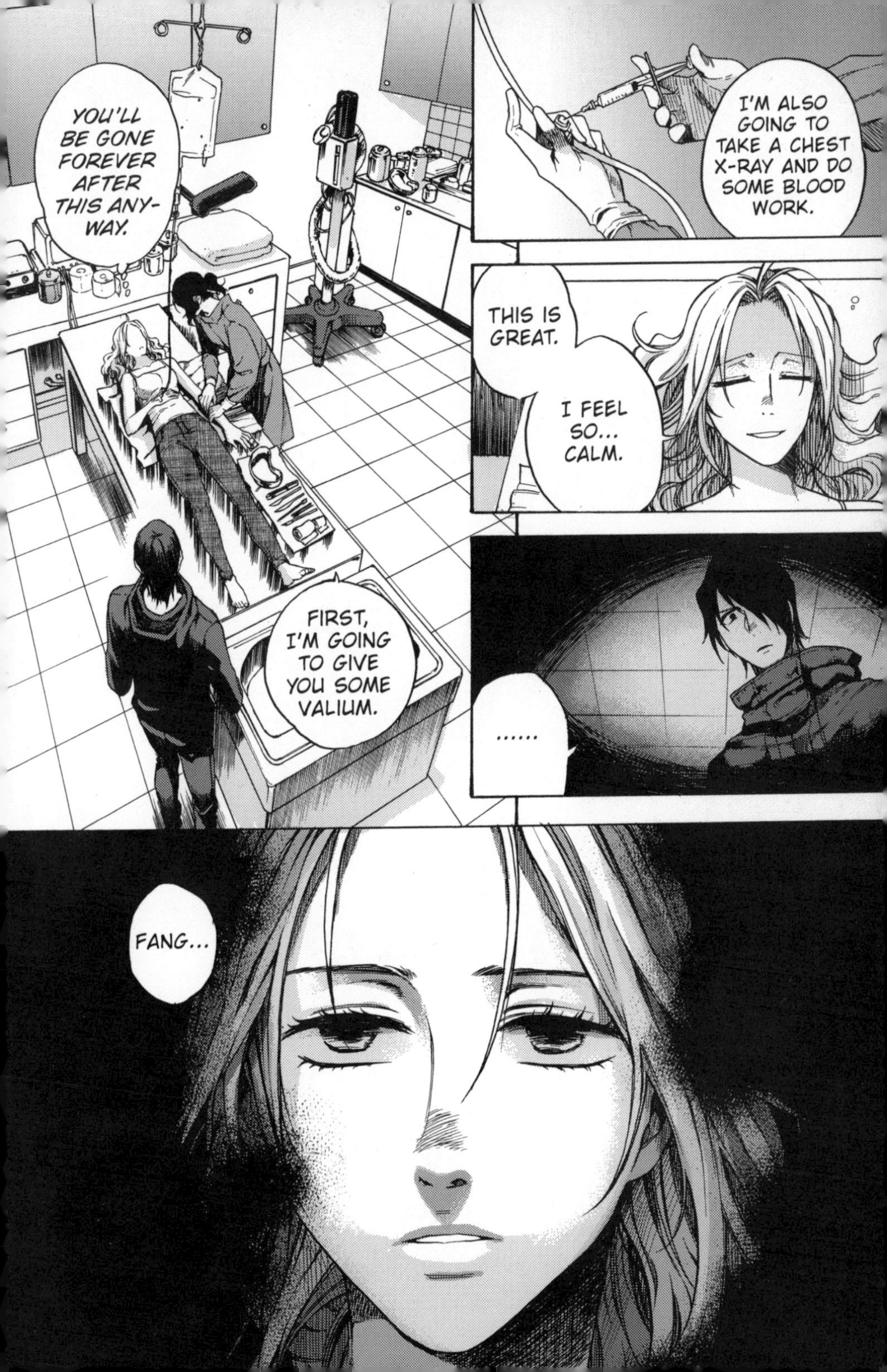
YOU'LL BE GONE FOREVER AFTER THIS ANYWAY.
FIRST, I'M GOING TO GIVE YOU SOME VALIUM.
I'M ALSO GOING TO TAKE A CHEST X-RAY AND DO SOME BLOOD WORK.
THIS IS GREAT.
I FEEL SO... CALM.
......
FANG...

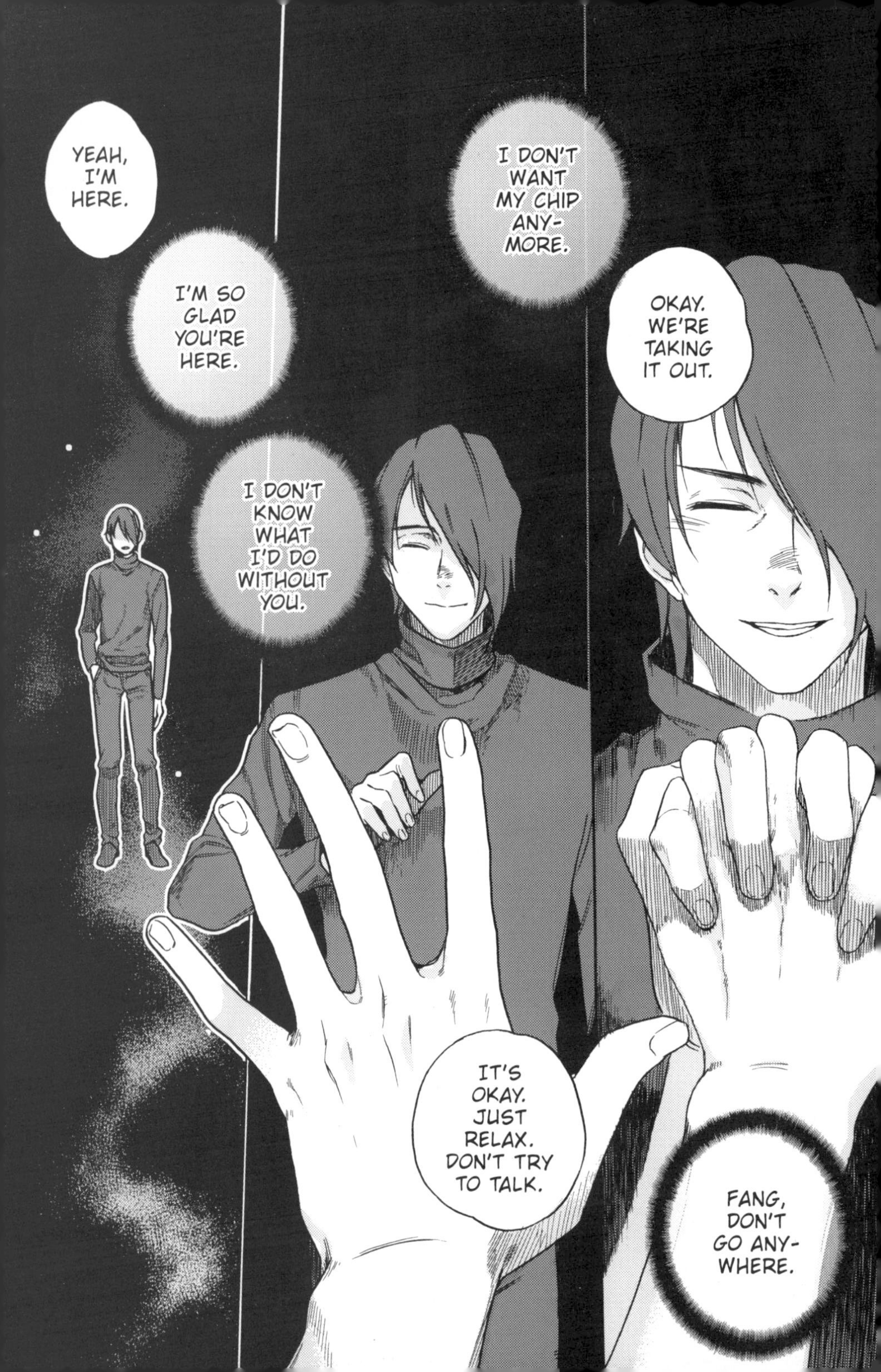
YEAH, I'M HERE.
I'M SO GLAD YOU'RE HERE.
I DON'T KNOW WHAT I'D DO WITHOUT YOU.
I DON'T WANT MY CHIP ANY-MORE.
OKAY. WE'RE TAKING IT OUT.
IT'S OKAY. JUST RELAX. DON'T TRY TO TALK.
FANG, DON'T GO ANY-WHERE.

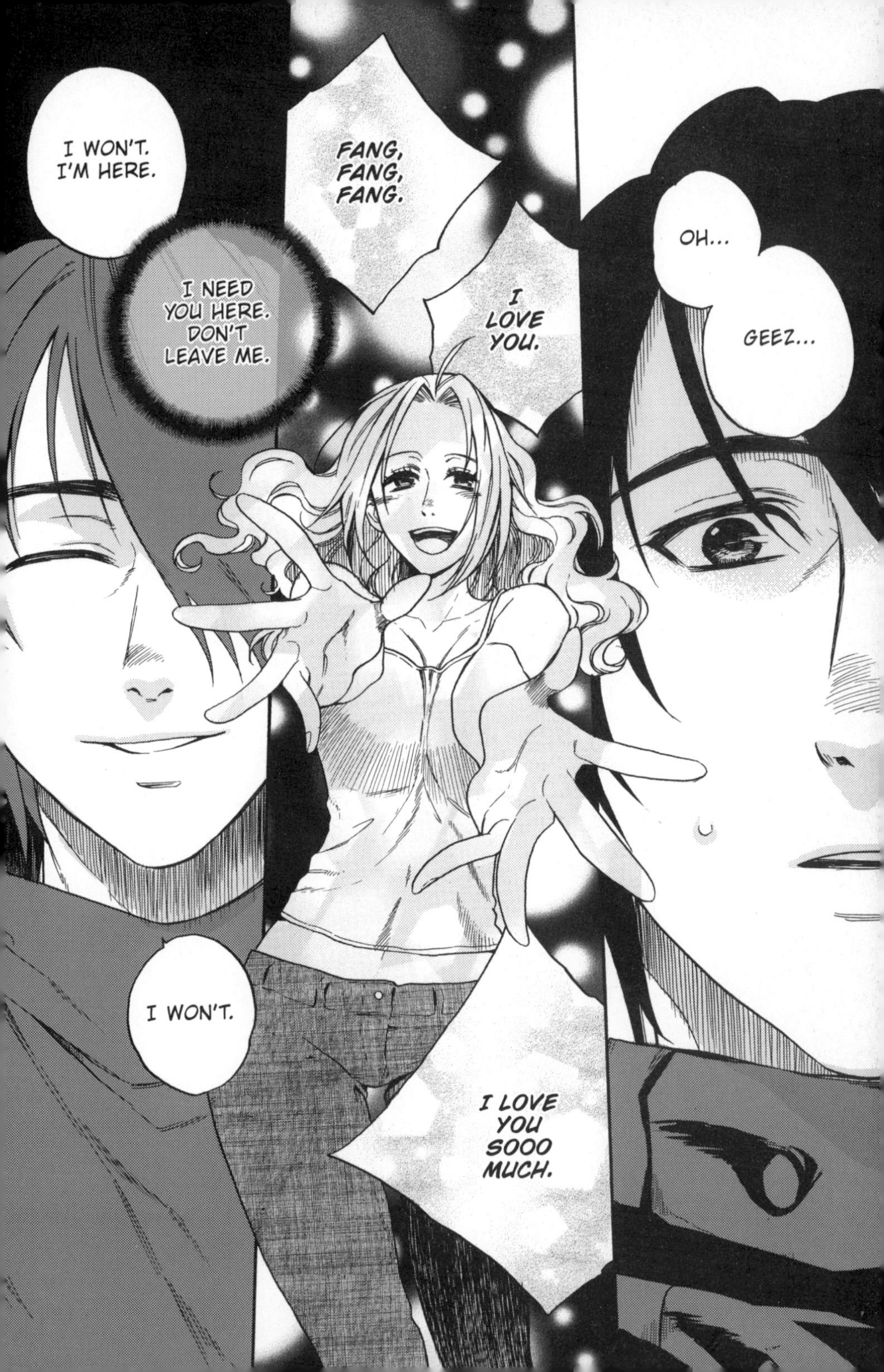
I WON'T. I'M HERE.
FANG, FANG, FANG.
OH...
I NEED YOU HERE. DON'T LEAVE ME.
I LOVE YOU.
GEEZ...
I WON'T.
I LOVE YOU SOOO MUCH.

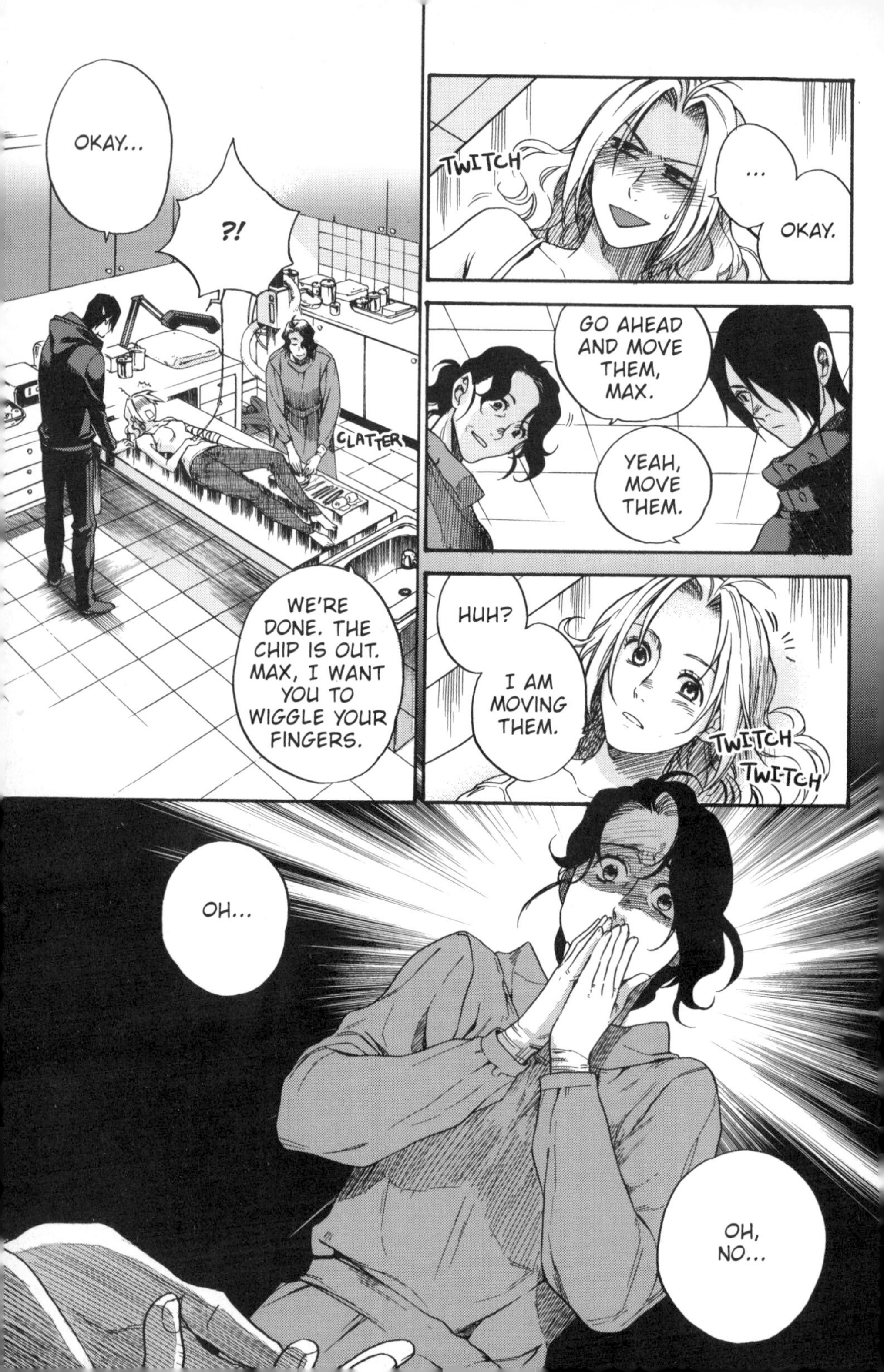
OKAY...
?!
CLATTER
WE'RE DONE. THE CHIP IS OUT. MAX, I WANT YOU TO WIGGLE YOUR FINGERS.
TWITCH
...
OKAY.
GO AHEAD AND MOVE THEM, MAX.
YEAH, MOVE THEM.
HUH?
I AM MOVING THEM.
TWITCH
TWITCH
OH...
OH, NO...

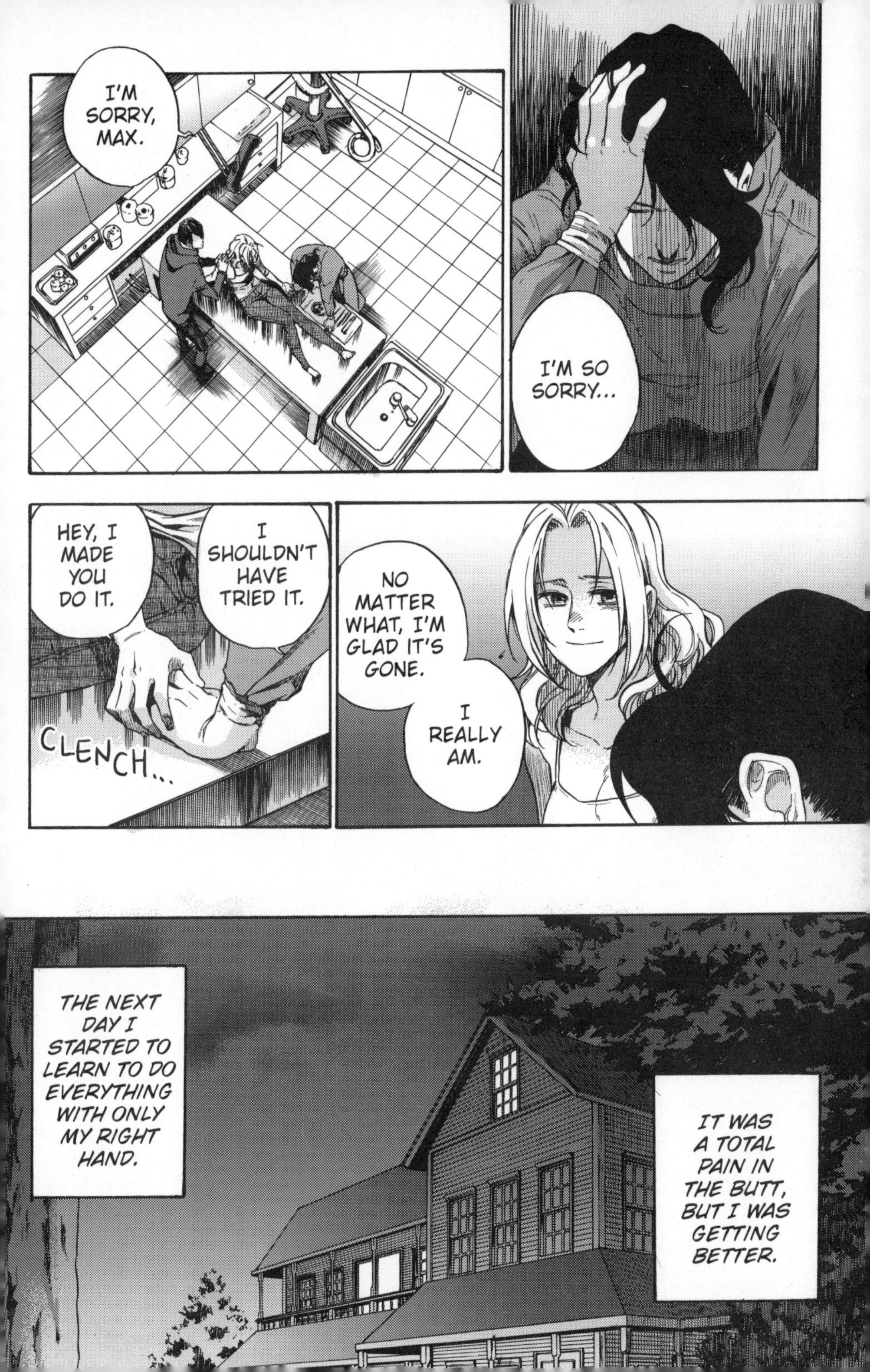

I'M SORRY, MAX.
I'M SO SORRY...
I SHOULDN'T HAVE TRIED IT.
HEY, I MADE YOU DO IT.
CLENCH...
NO MATTER WHAT, I'M GLAD IT'S GONE.
I REALLY AM.
THE NEXT DAY I STARTED TO LEARN TO DO EVERYTHING WITH ONLY MY RIGHT HAND.
IT WAS A TOTAL PAIN IN THE BUTT, BUT I WAS GETTING BETTER.

MOVE.

MOVE, DAMN FINGERS.

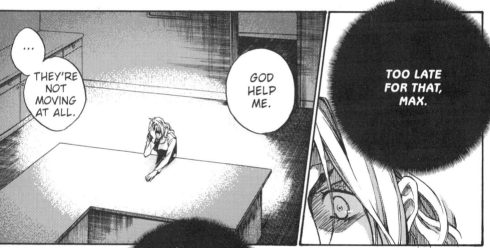

...

THEY'RE NOT MOVING AT ALL.

GOD HELP ME.

TOO LATE FOR THAT, MAX.

ONLY YOU CAN HELP YOUR-SELF NOW.

WHAT WAS WORSE THAN MY NON-RESPONSIVE ARM WAS THE FACT THAT...

...THE VOICE WAS NOT CONNECTED TO THE CHIP. IT WAS STILL INSIDE MY HEAD.

OH, NO.

DAMN...

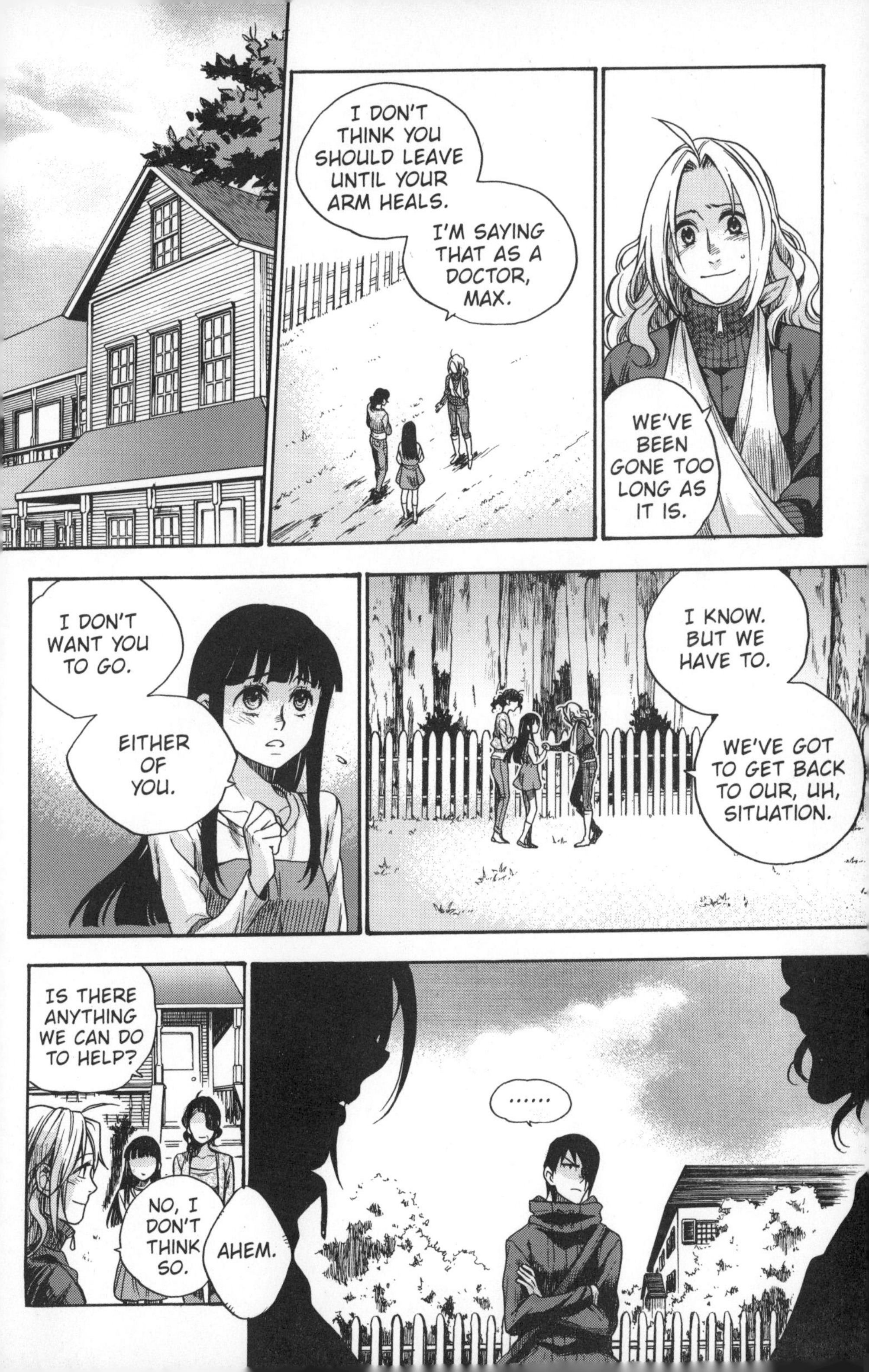
I DON'T THINK YOU SHOULD LEAVE UNTIL YOUR ARM HEALS.
I'M SAYING THAT AS A DOCTOR, MAX.
WE'VE BEEN GONE TOO LONG AS IT IS.
I DON'T WANT YOU TO GO.
EITHER OF YOU.
I KNOW. BUT WE HAVE TO.
WE'VE GOT TO GET BACK TO OUR, UH, SITUATION.
IS THERE ANYTHING WE CAN DO TO HELP?
NO, I DON'T THINK SO.
AHEM.
......

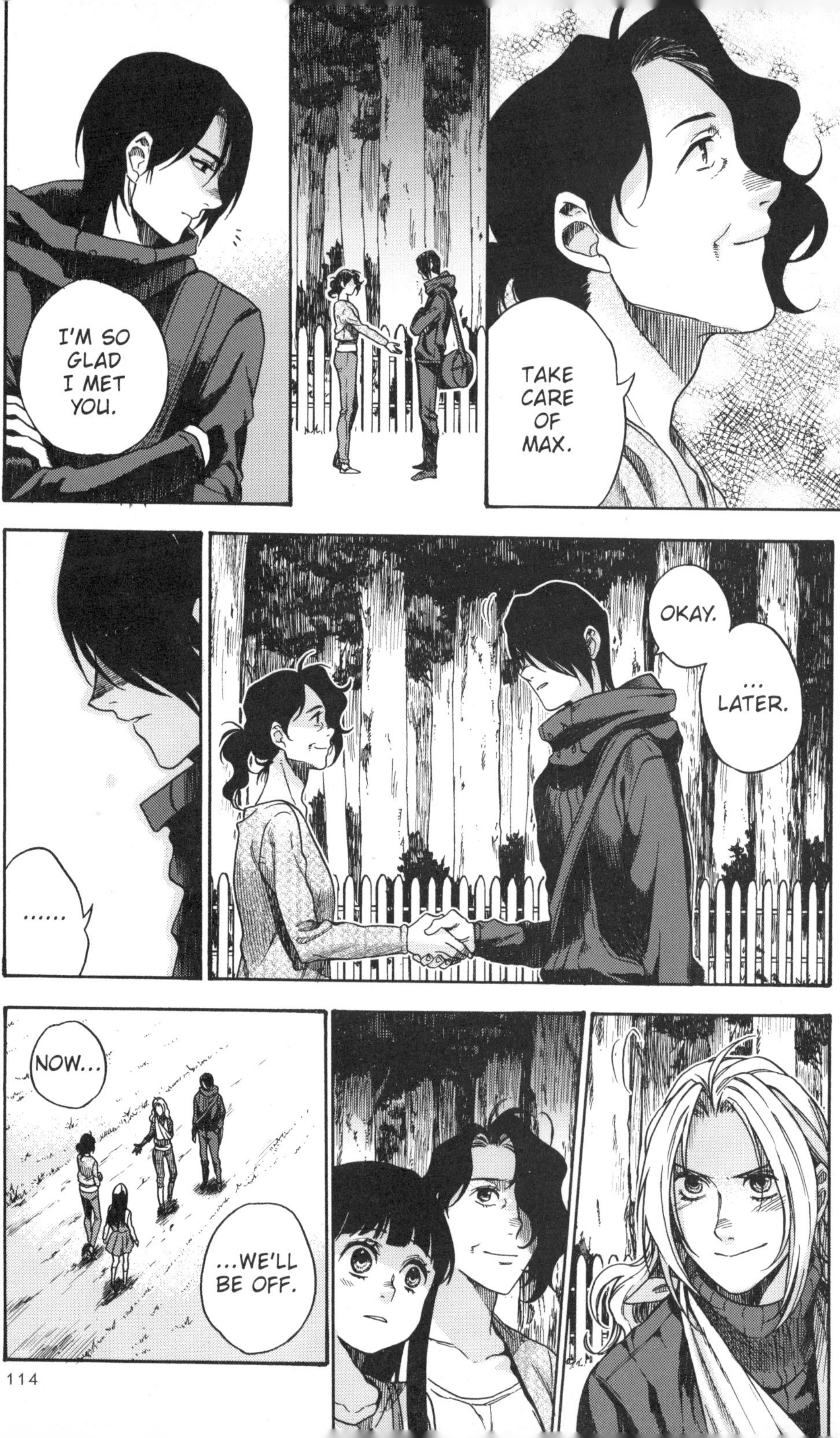
I'M SO GLAD I MET YOU.
TAKE CARE OF MAX.
......
OKAY.
...LATER.
NOW...
...WE'LL BE OFF.

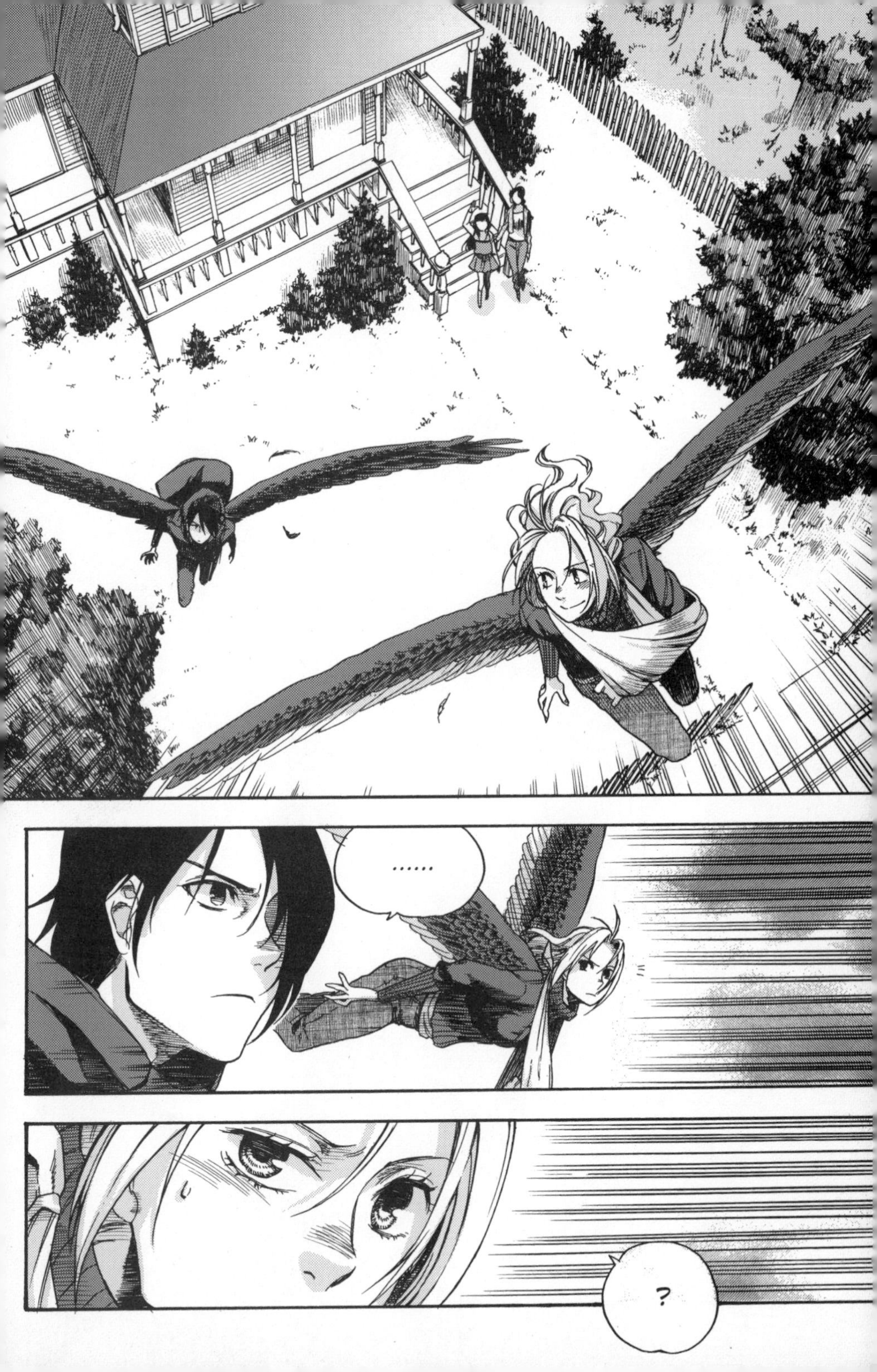
......
?

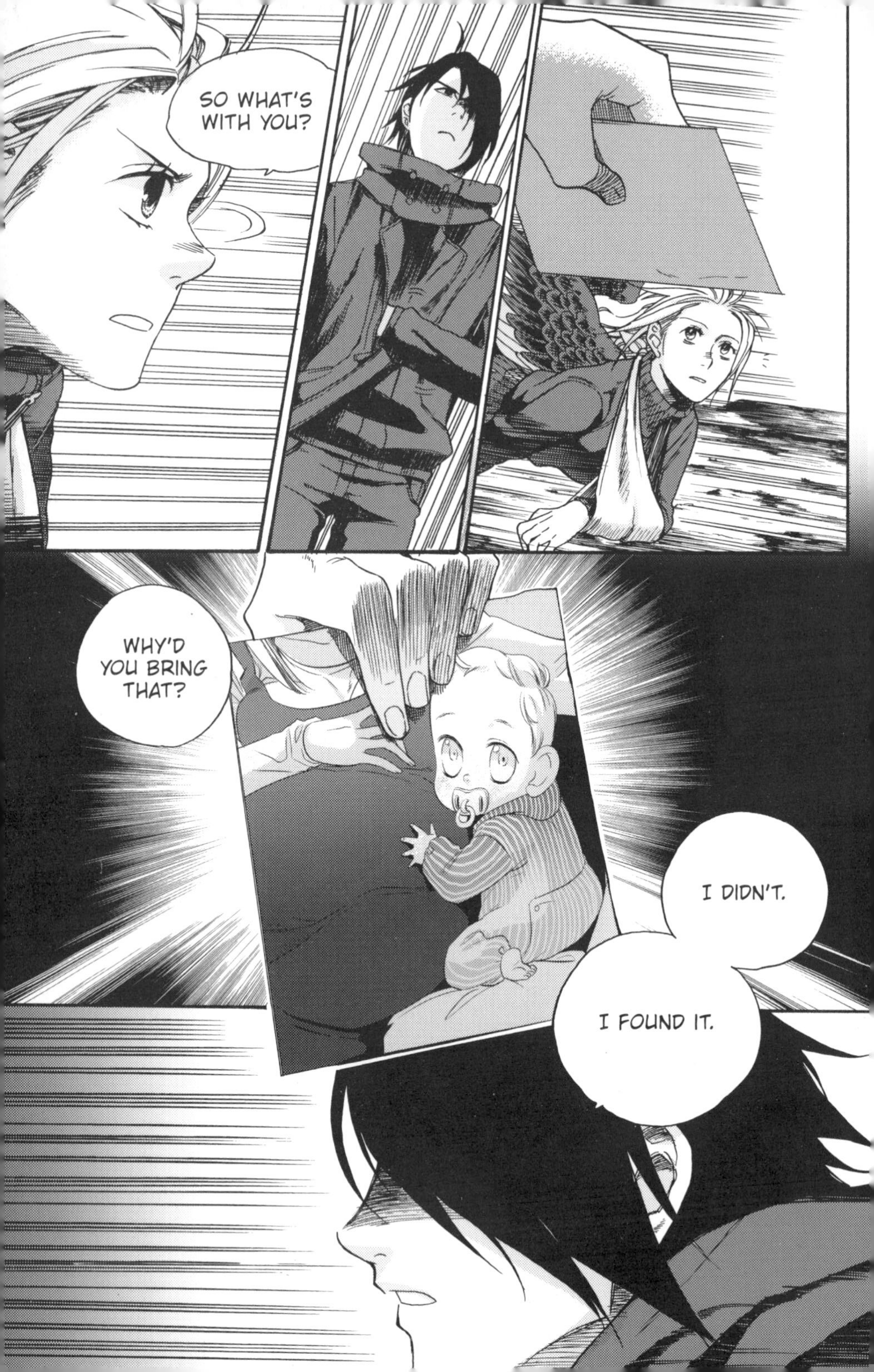
SO WHAT'S WITH YOU?
WHY'D YOU BRING THAT?
I DIDN'T.
I FOUND IT.

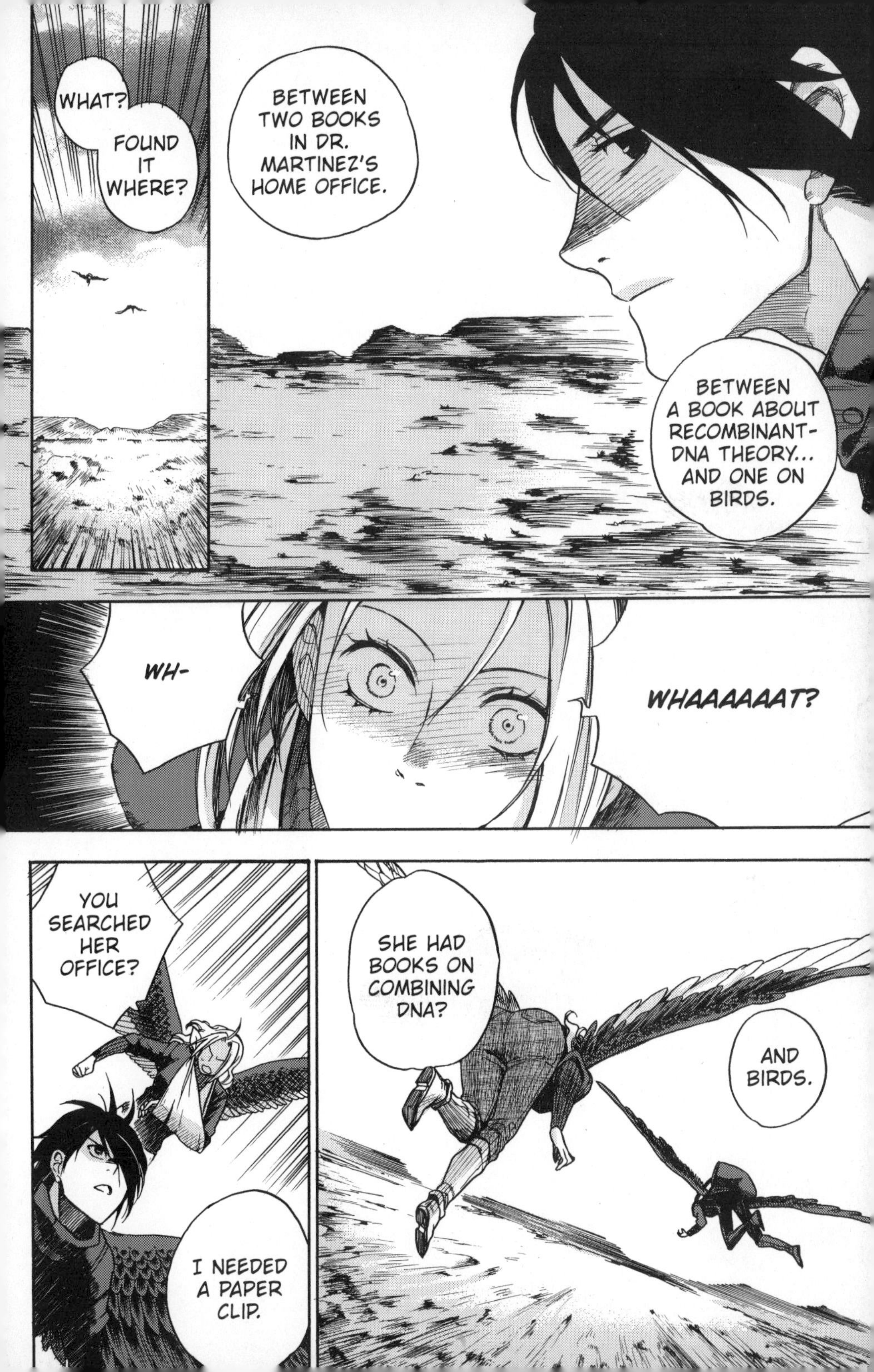
BETWEEN TWO BOOKS IN DR. MARTINEZ'S HOME OFFICE.
WHAT?
FOUND IT WHERE?
BETWEEN A BOOK ABOUT RECOMBINANT-DNA THEORY... AND ONE ON BIRDS.
WH-
WHAAAAAAT?
SHE HAD BOOKS ON COMBINING DNA?
AND BIRDS.
YOU SEARCHED HER OFFICE?
I NEEDED A PAPER CLIP.

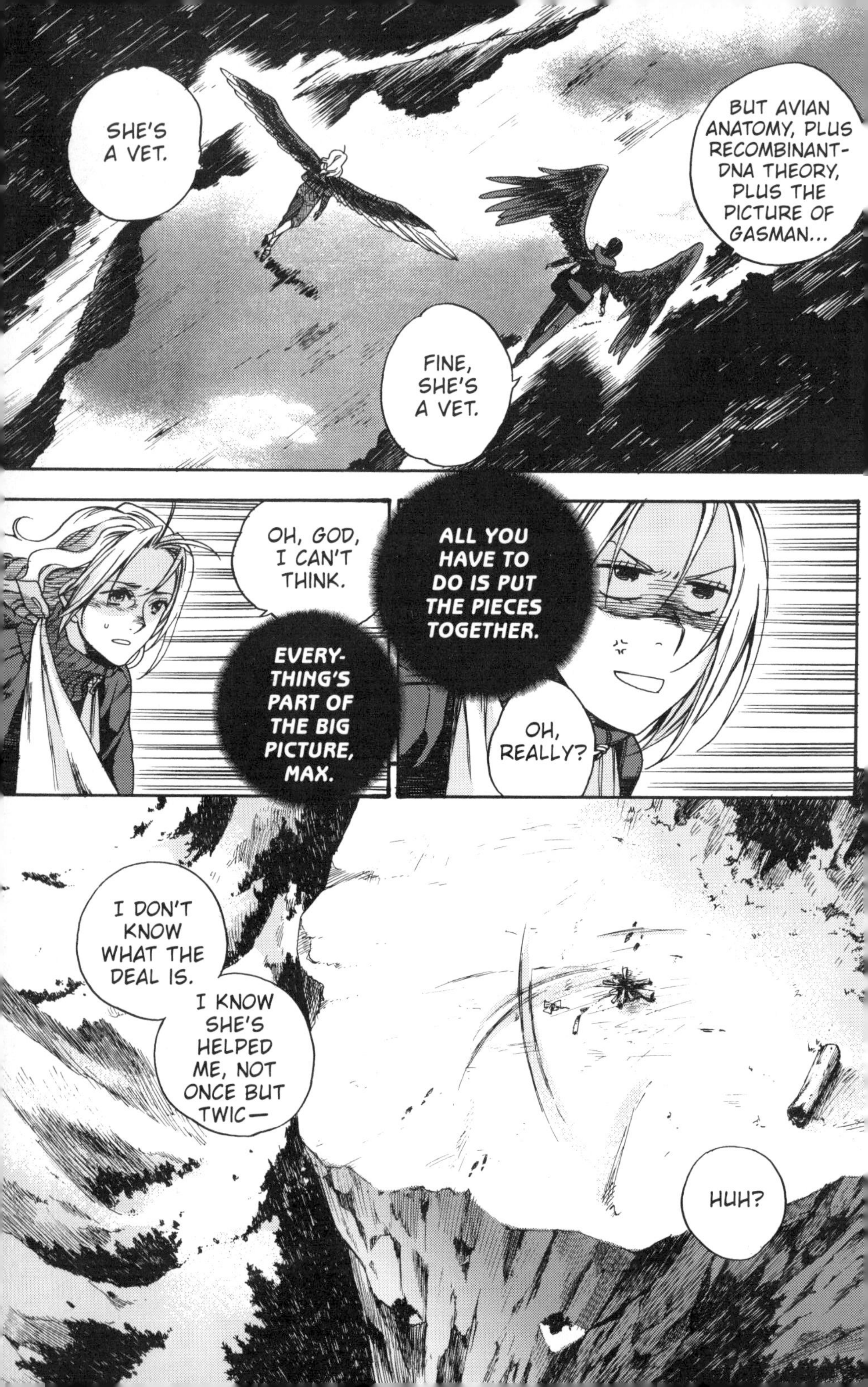
SHE'S A VET.
BUT AVIAN ANATOMY, PLUS RECOMBINANT-DNA THEORY, PLUS THE PICTURE OF GASMAN...
FINE, SHE'S A VET.
OH, GOD, I CAN'T THINK.
ALL YOU HAVE TO DO IS PUT THE PIECES TOGETHER.
EVERY-THING'S PART OF THE BIG PICTURE, MAX.
OH, REALLY?
I DON'T KNOW WHAT THE DEAL IS.
I KNOW SHE'S HELPED ME, NOT ONCE BUT TWIC—
HUH?

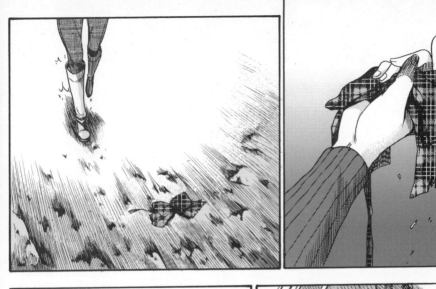

CRAP!!

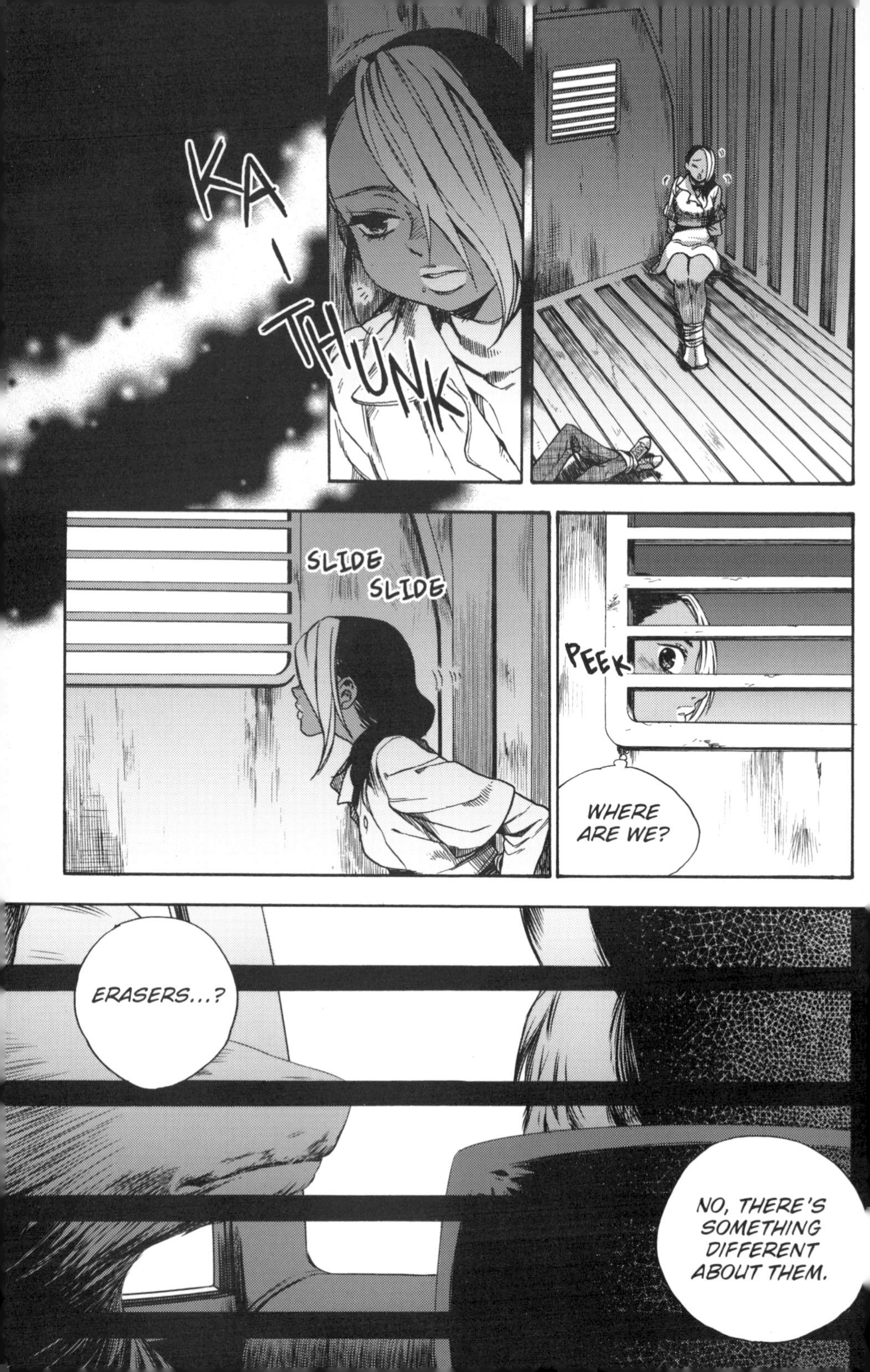
KA-THUNK
SLIDE SLIDE
PEEK
WHERE ARE WE?
ERASERS...?
NO, THERE'S SOMETHING DIFFERENT ABOUT THEM.

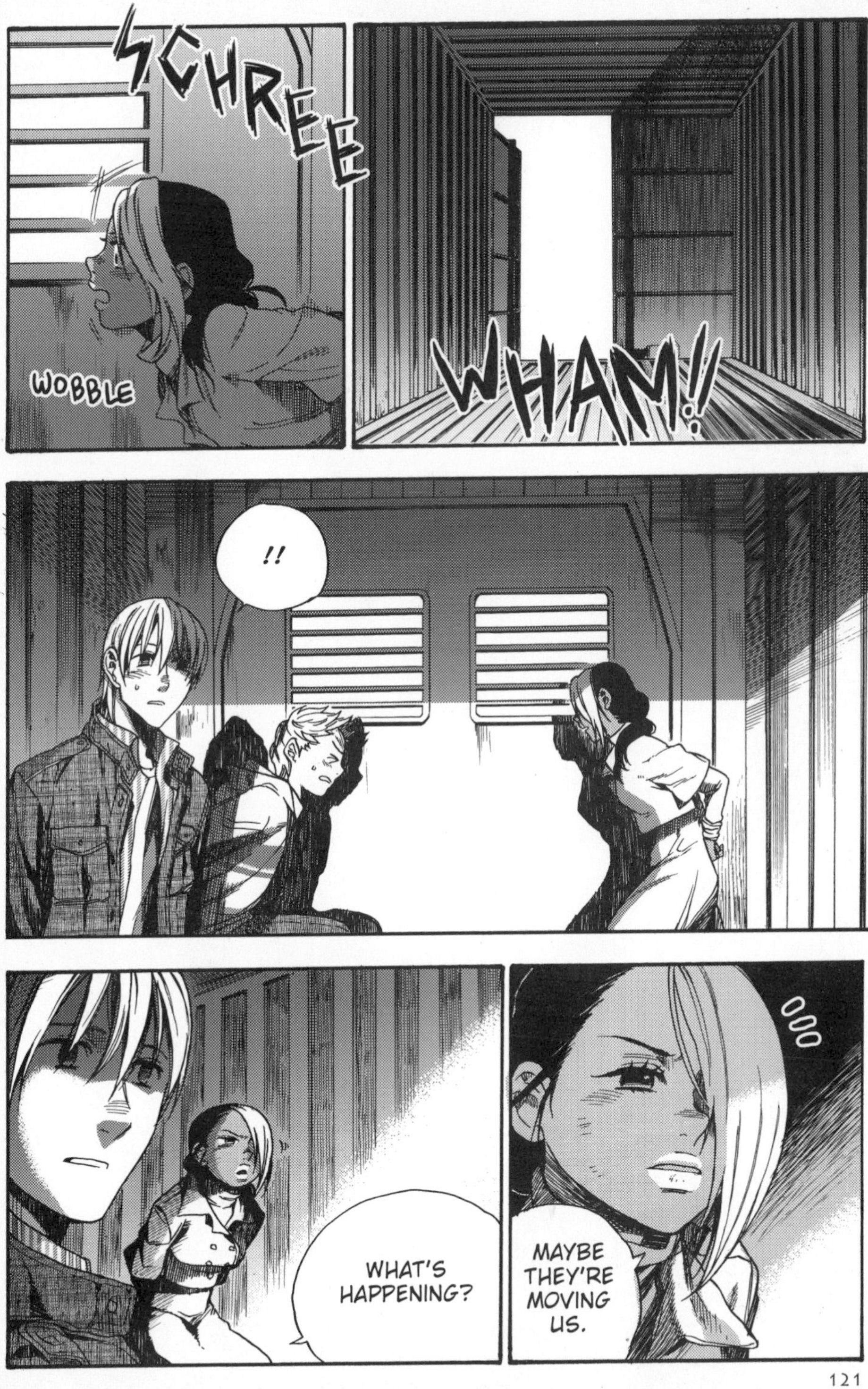
SCHREEE
WOBBLE
WHAM!!
!!
OOO
WHAT'S HAPPENING?
MAYBE THEY'RE MOVING US.

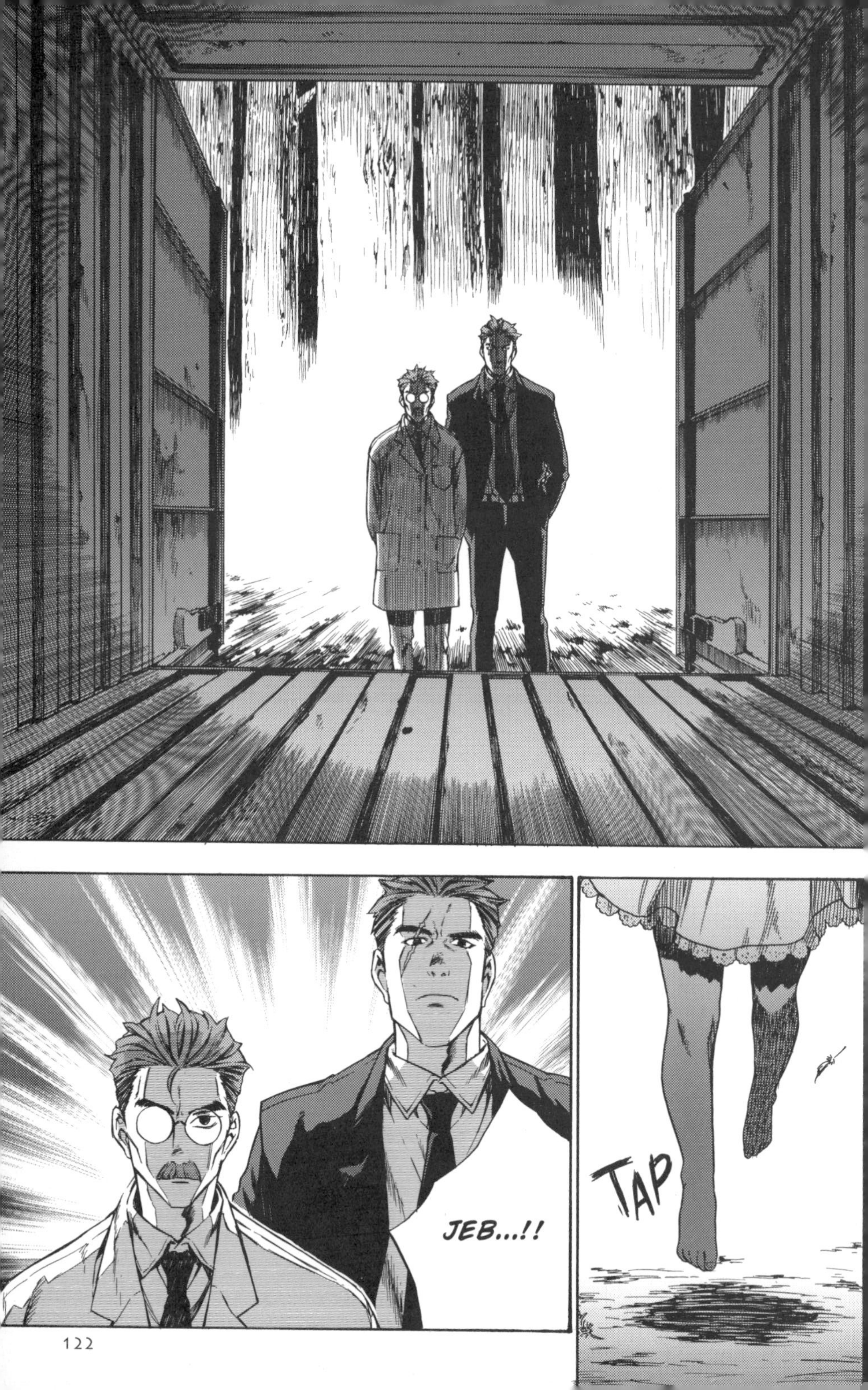
JEB...!!
TAP

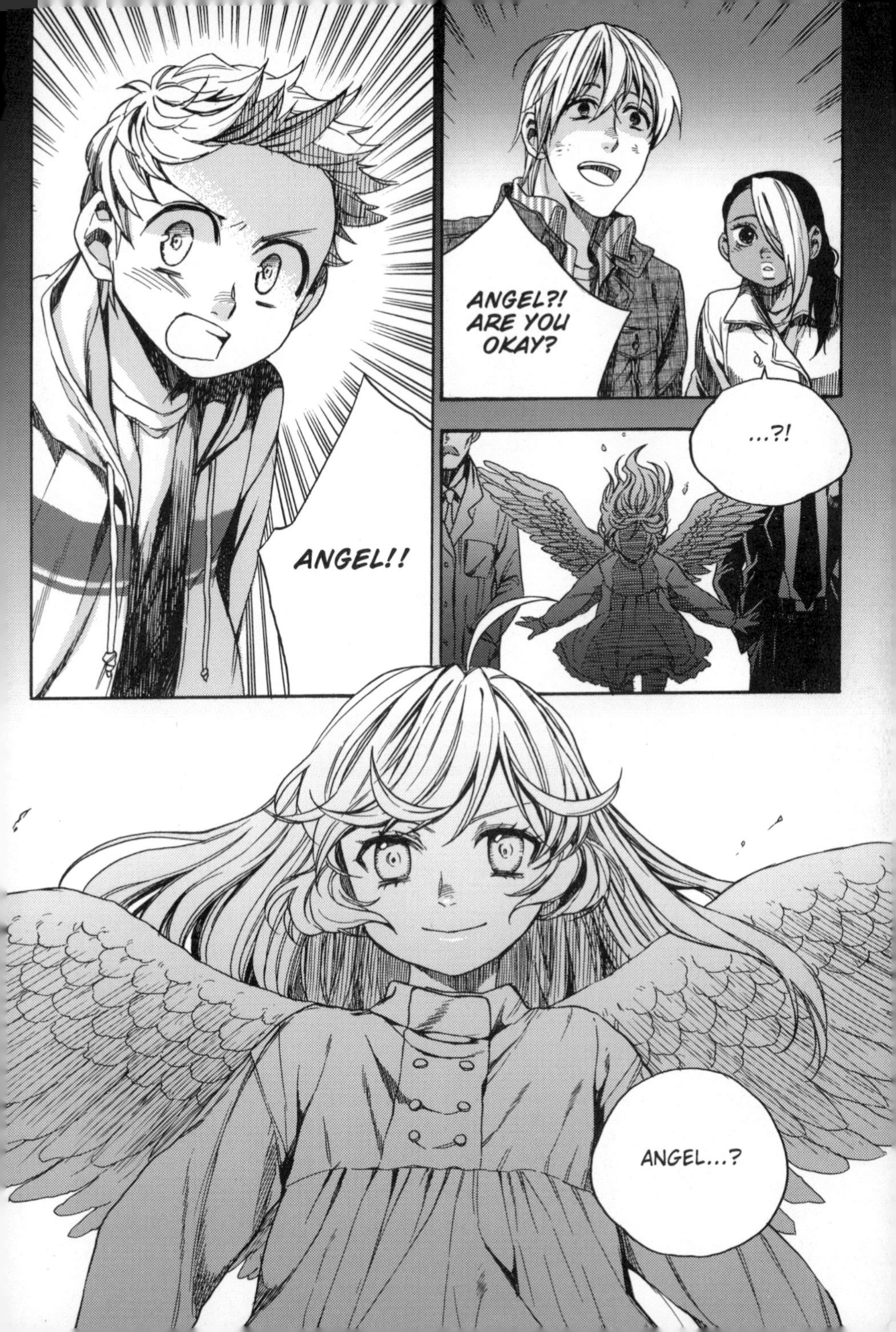
ANGEL?! ARE YOU OKAY?
ANGEL!!
...?!
ANGEL...?

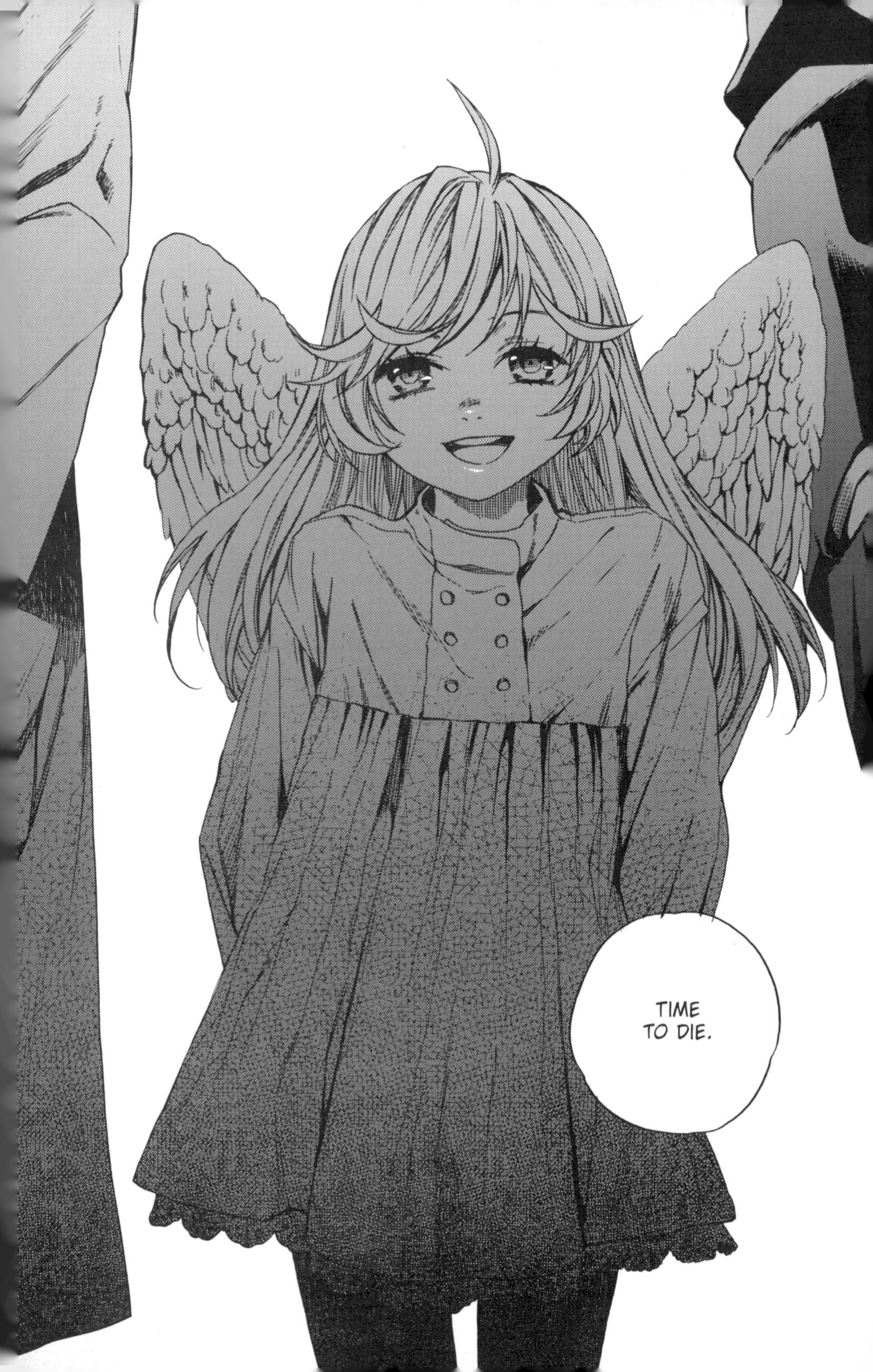
TIME TO DIE.

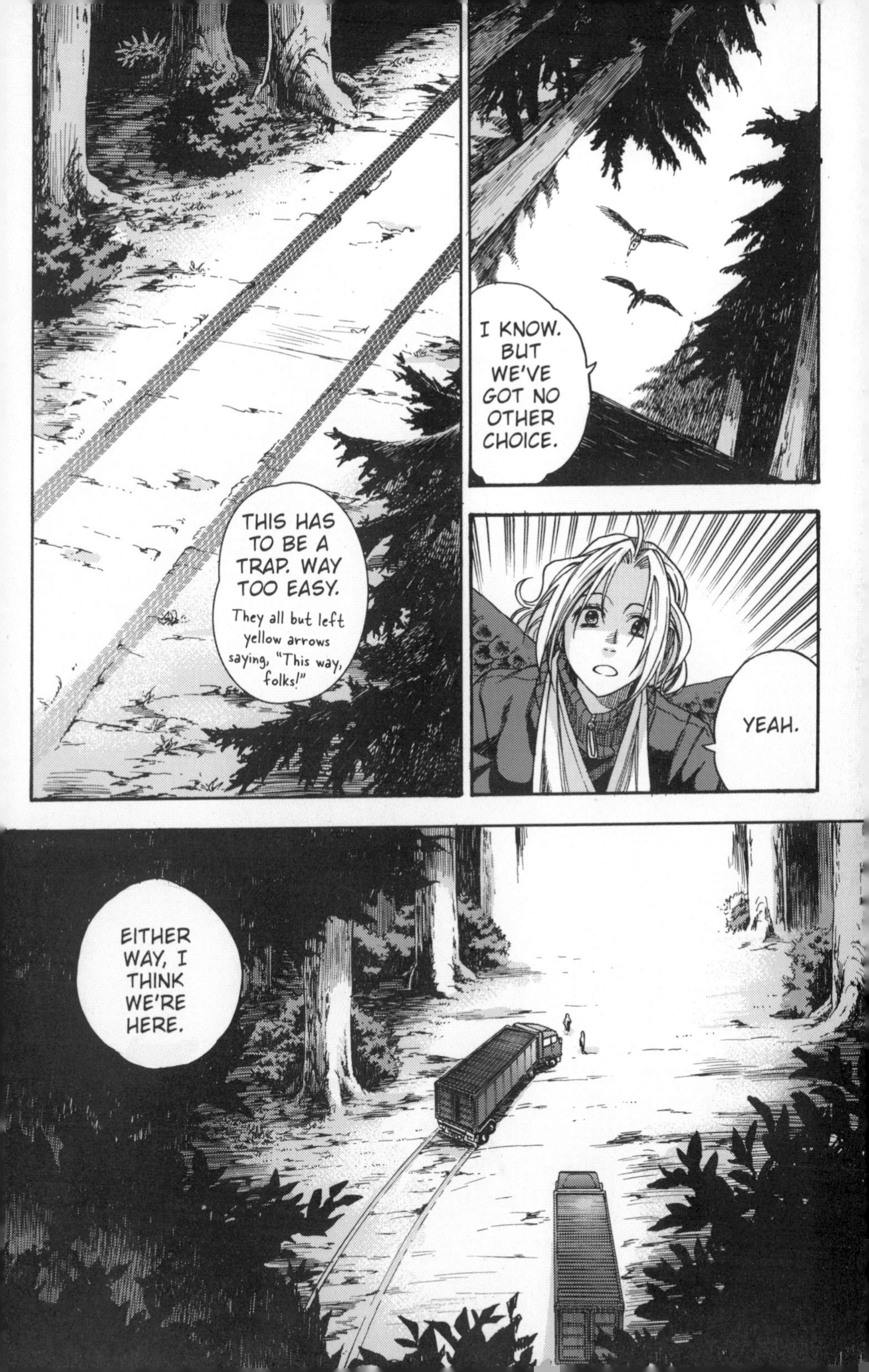
THIS HAS TO BE A TRAP. WAY TOO EASY.
They all but left yellow arrows saying, "This way, folks!"
I KNOW. BUT WE'VE GOT NO OTHER CHOICE.
YEAH.
EITHER WAY, I THINK WE'RE HERE.

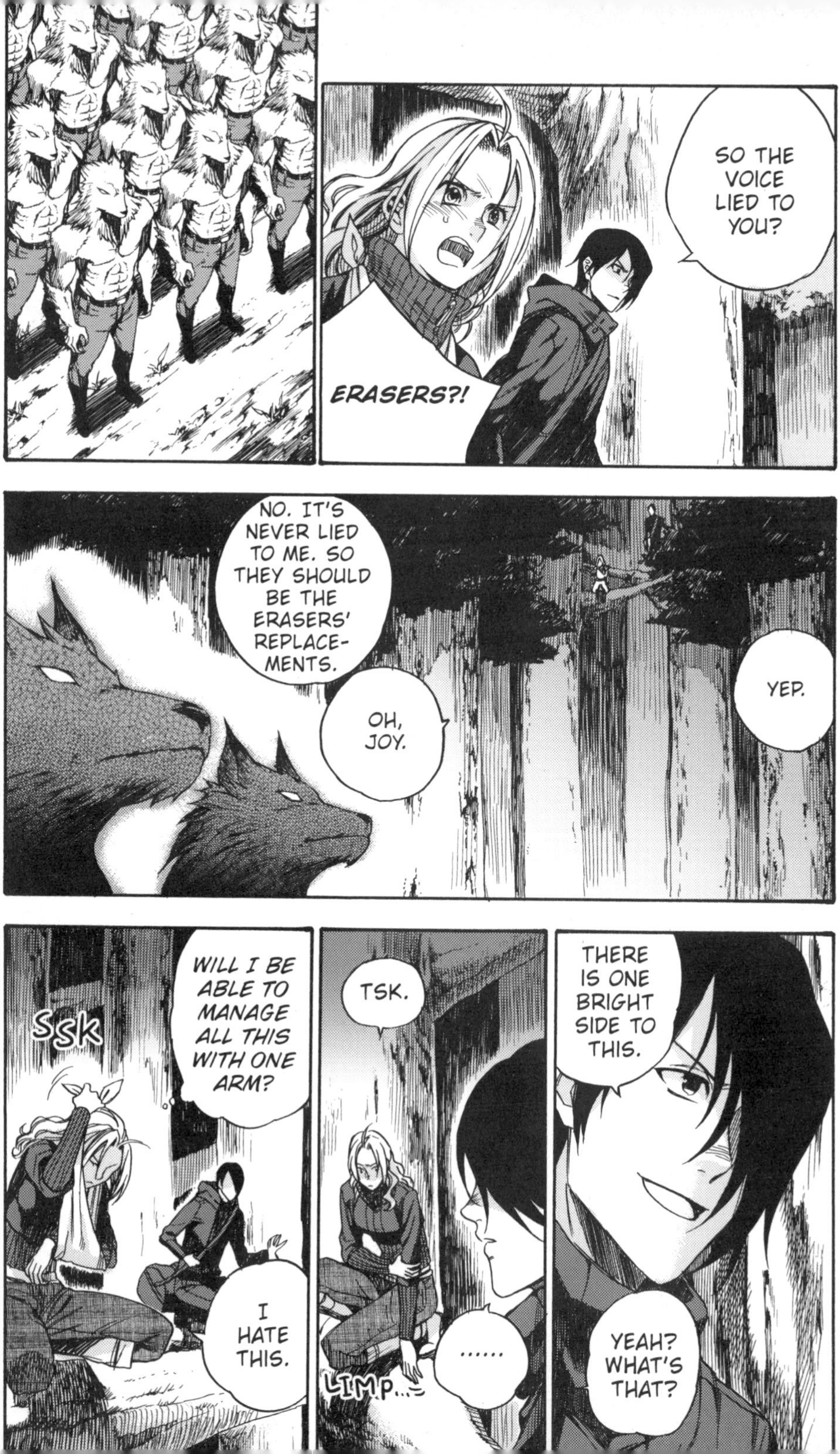
SO THE VOICE LIED TO YOU?
ERASERS?!
NO. IT'S NEVER LIED TO ME. SO THEY SHOULD BE THE ERASERS' REPLACEMENTS.
OH, JOY.
YEP.
SSK
WILL I BE ABLE TO MANAGE ALL THIS WITH ONE ARM?
I HATE THIS.
TSK.
......
LIMP...
THERE IS ONE BRIGHT SIDE TO THIS.
YEAH? WHAT'S THAT?

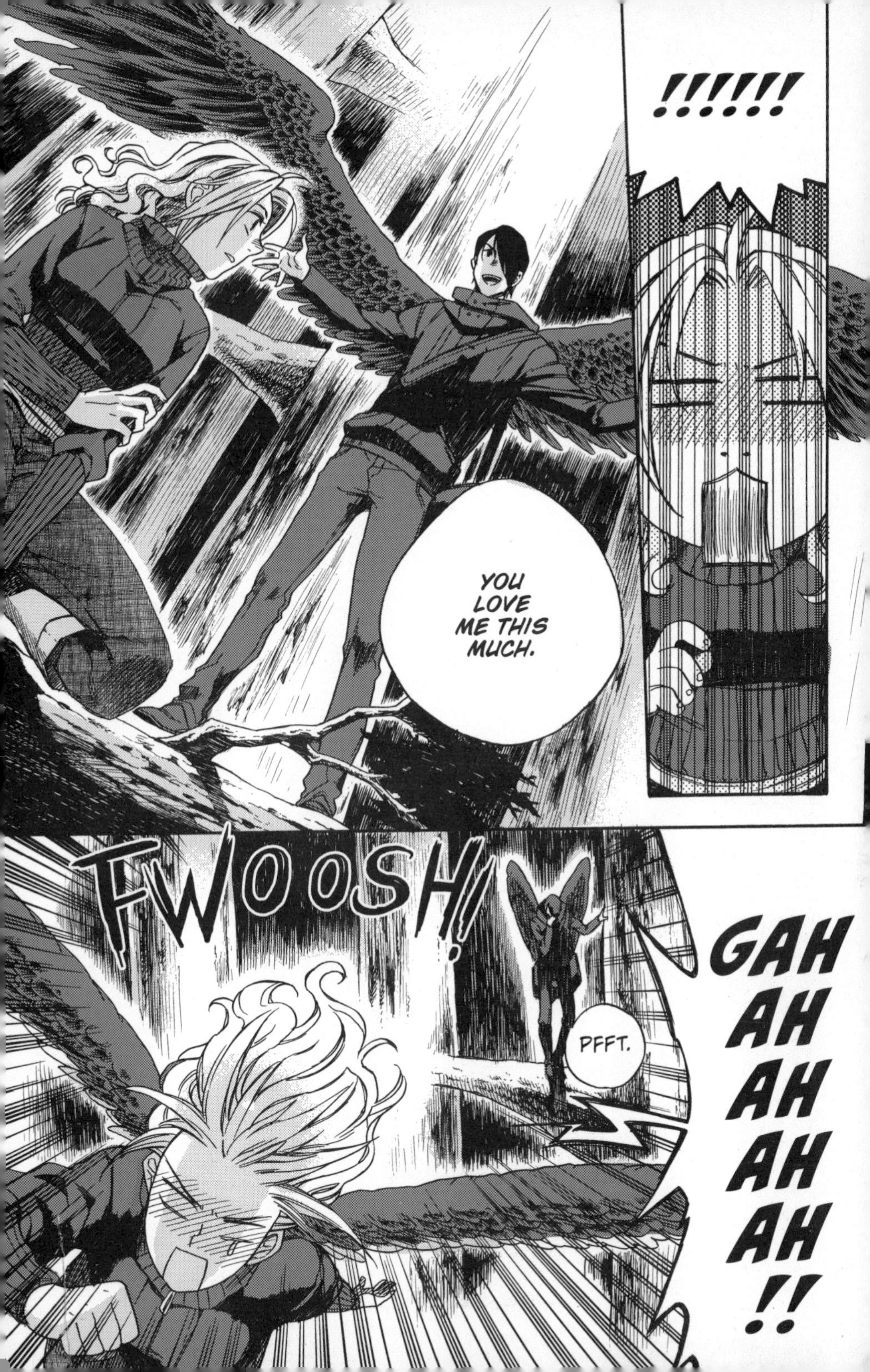
!!!!!!
YOU LOVE ME THIS MUCH.
FWOOSH!
GAH AH AH AH AH AH!!
PFFT.

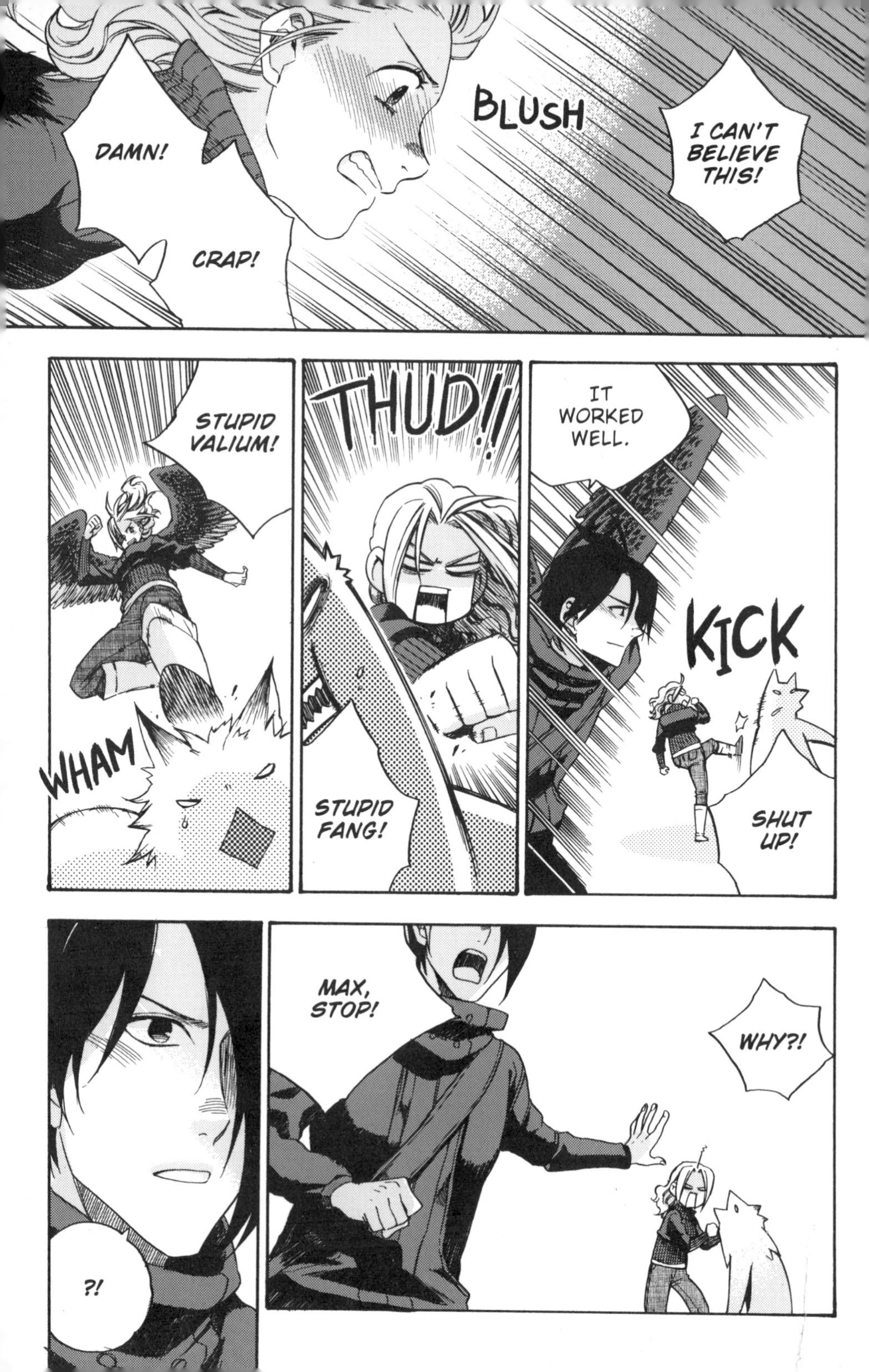
DAMN!
CRAP!
BLUSH
I CAN'T BELIEVE THIS!
STUPID VALIUM!
WHAM
THUD!!
STUPID FANG!
IT WORKED WELL.
KICK
SHUT UP!
?!
MAX, STOP!
WHY?!

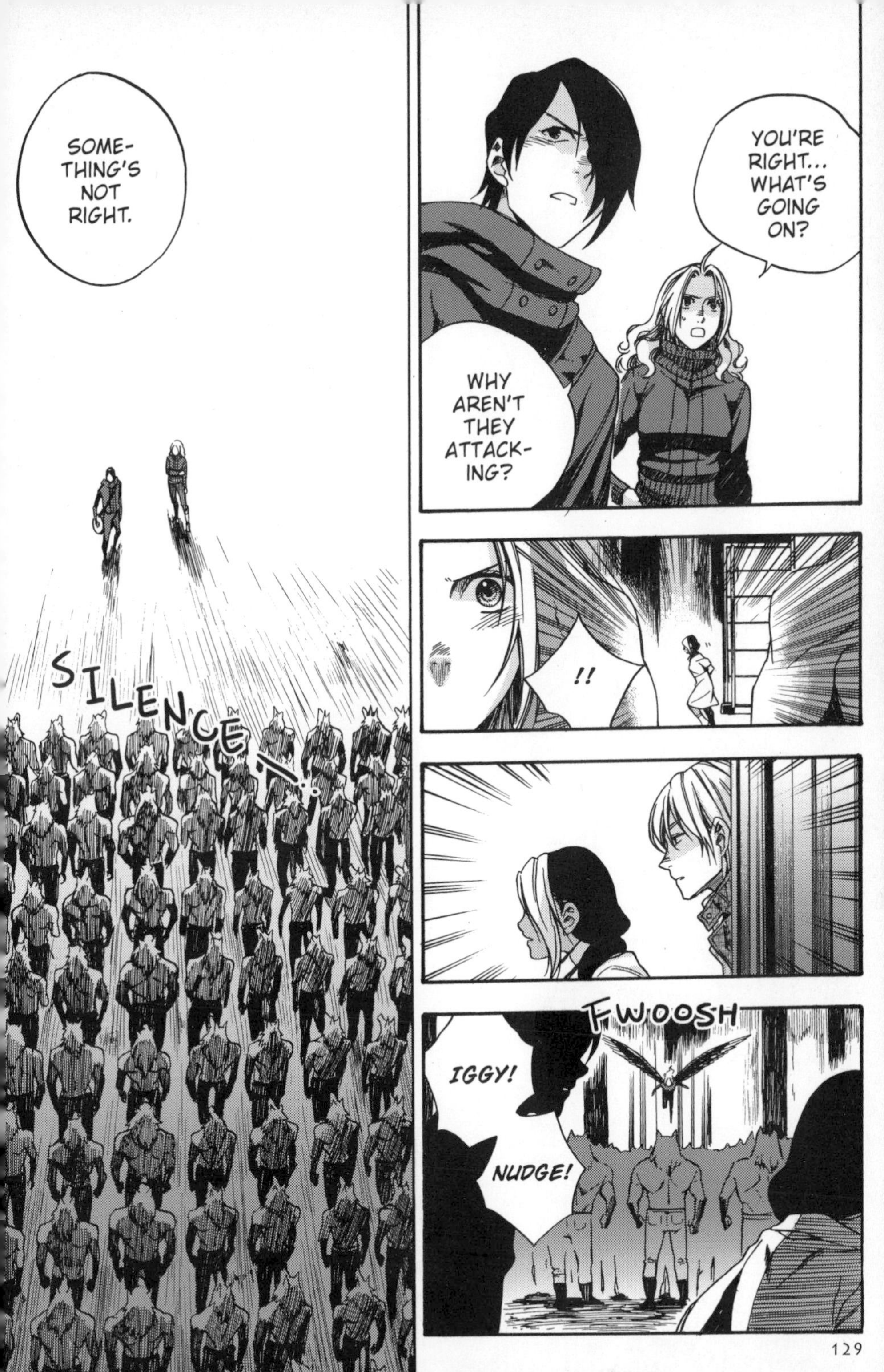

SOME-THING'S NOT RIGHT.
SILENCE
YOU'RE RIGHT... WHAT'S GOING ON?
WHY AREN'T THEY ATTACK-ING?
!!
FWOOSH
IGGY!
NUDGE!

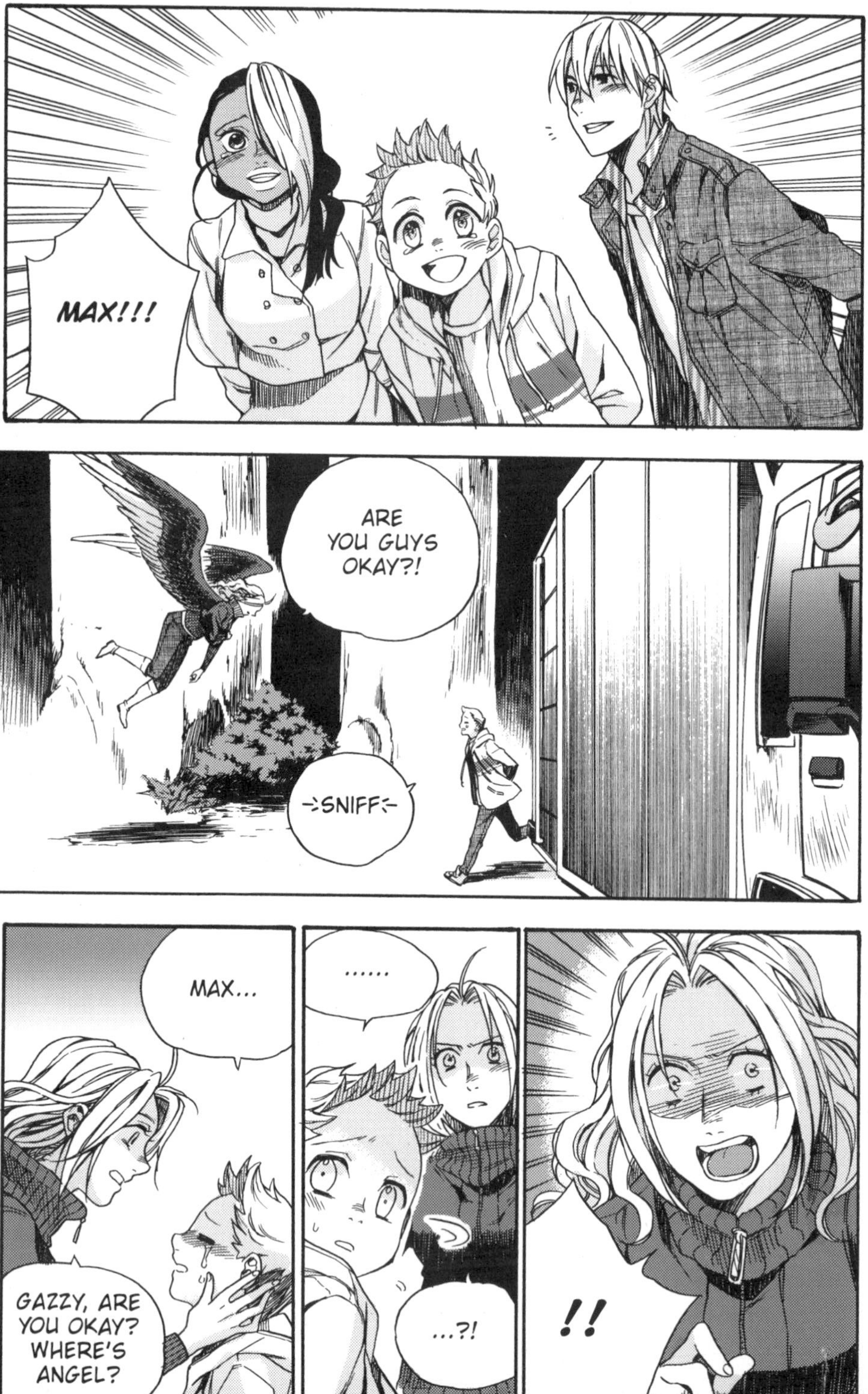
MAX!!!
ARE YOU GUYS OKAY?!
-SNIFF-
MAX...
GAZZY, ARE YOU OKAY? WHERE'S ANGEL?
......
...?!
!!

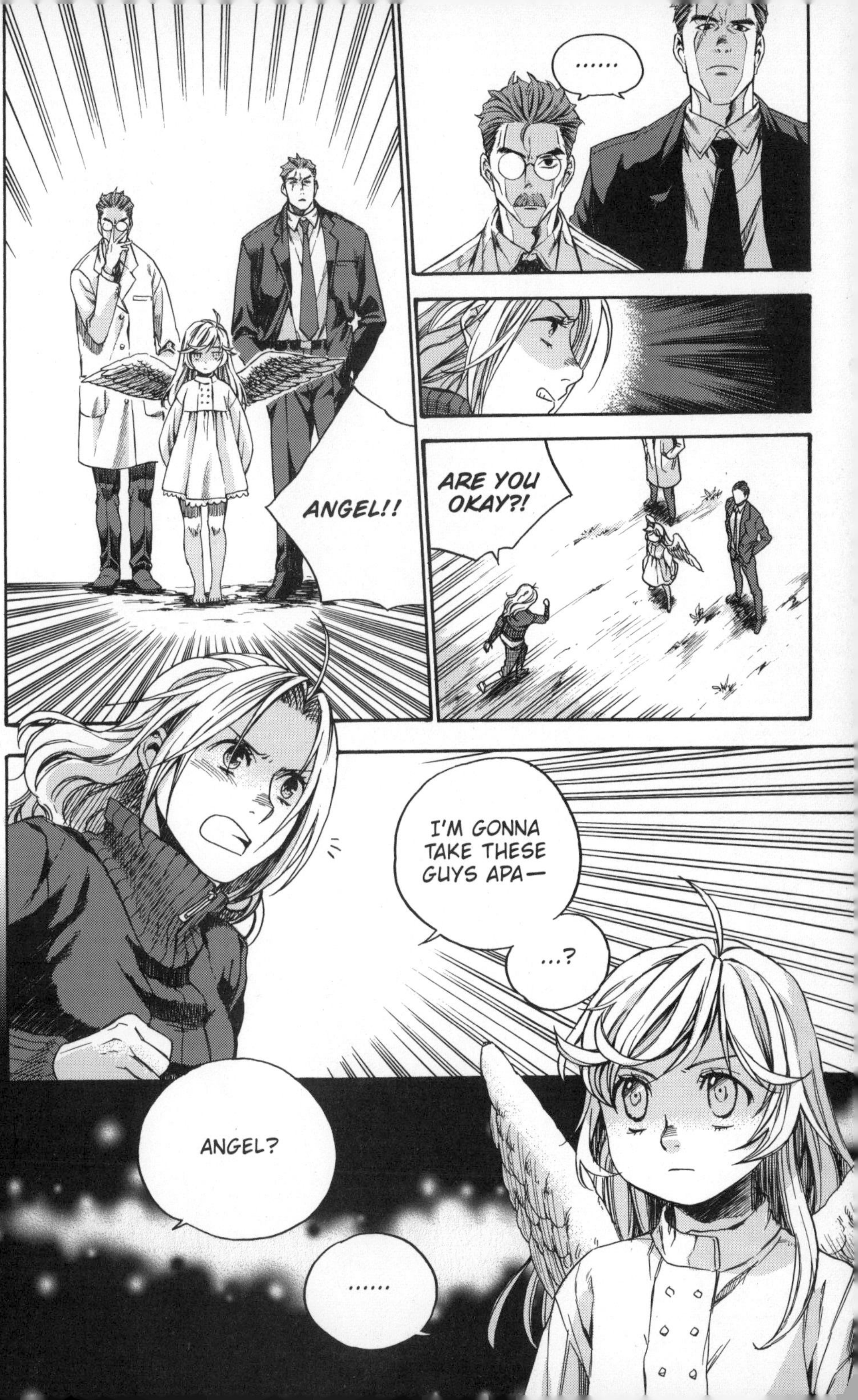
......
ANGEL!!
ARE YOU OKAY?!
I'M GONNA TAKE THESE GUYS APA—
...?
ANGEL?
......

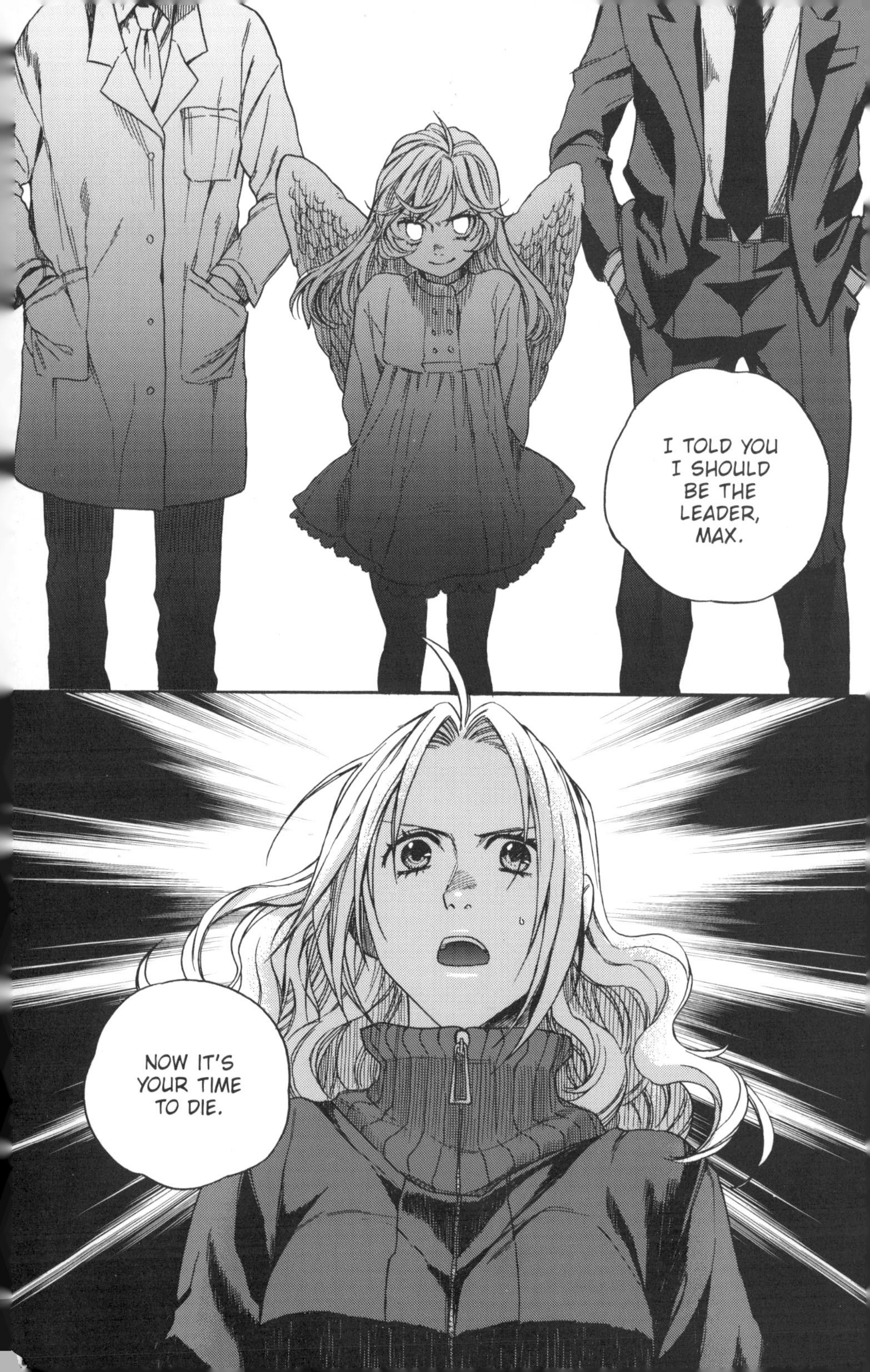
I TOLD YOU I SHOULD BE THE LEADER, MAX.
NOW IT'S YOUR TIME TO DIE.

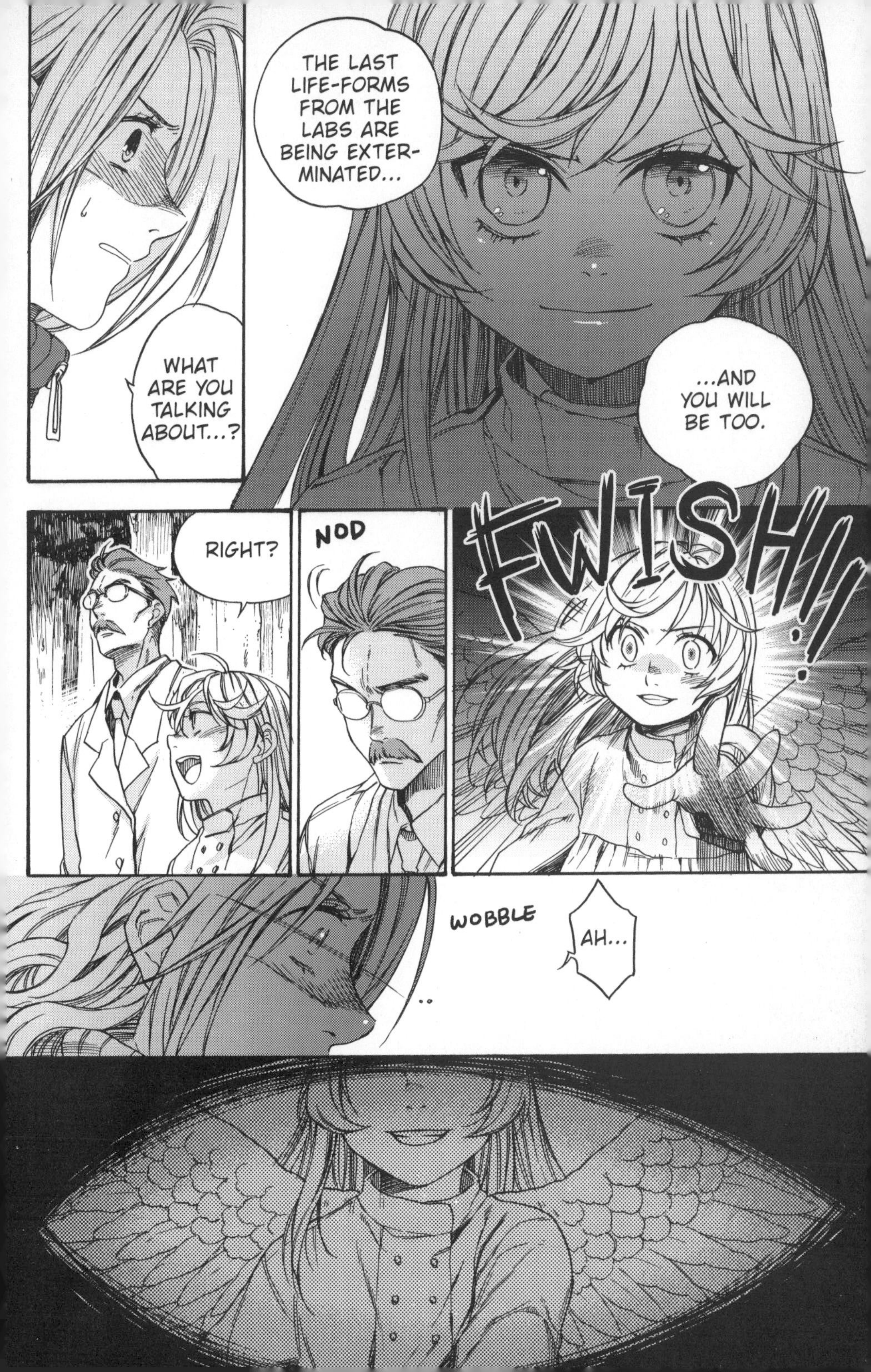
THE LAST LIFE-FORMS FROM THE LABS ARE BEING EXTER- MINATED...
WHAT ARE YOU TALKING ABOUT...?
...AND YOU WILL BE TOO.
RIGHT?
NOD
FWISH!!
WOBBLE
AH...

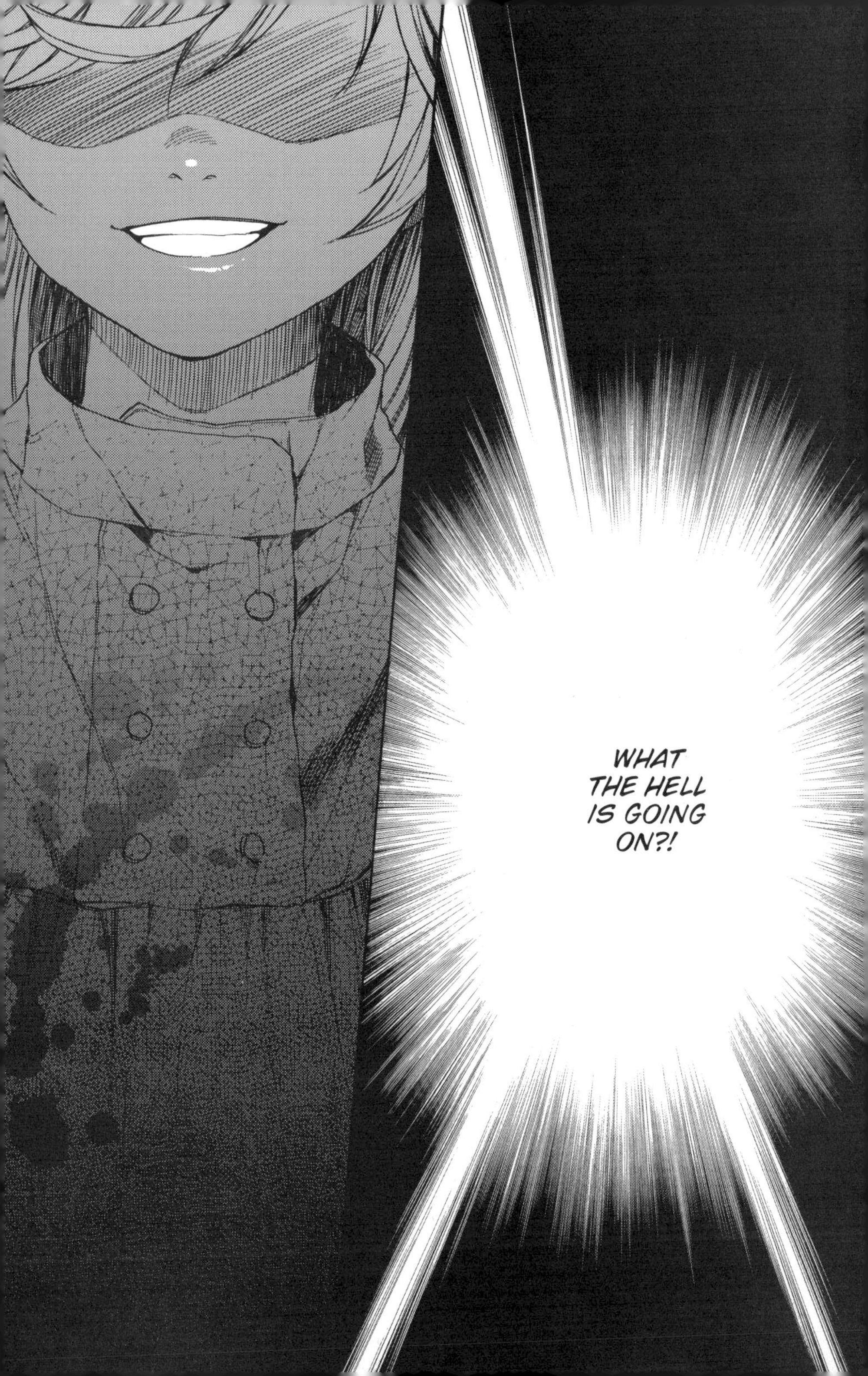
WHAT THE HELL IS GOING ON?!

MAXIMUM
RIDE

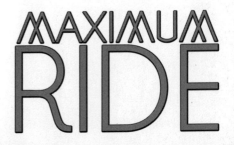

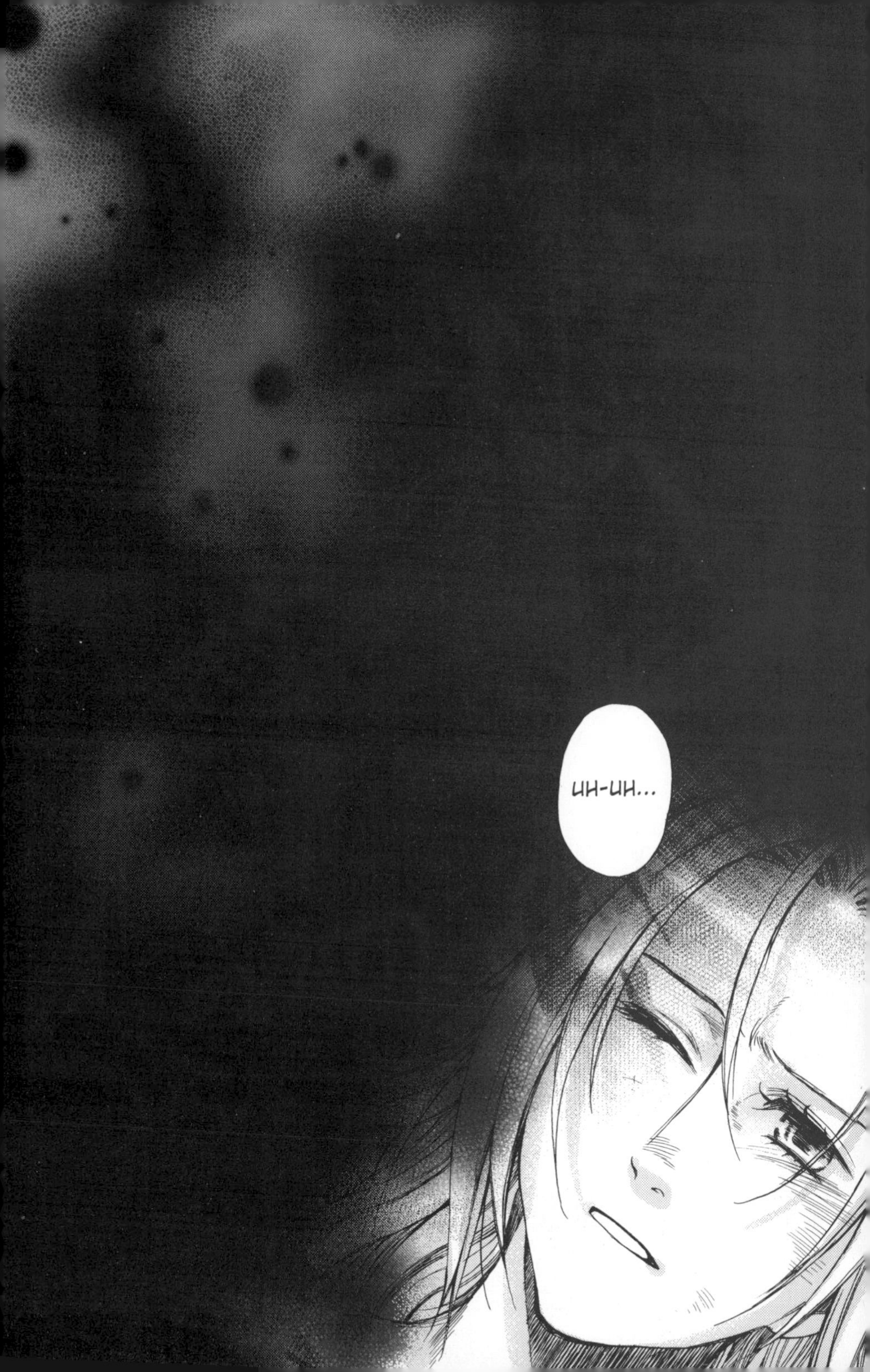
UH-UH...

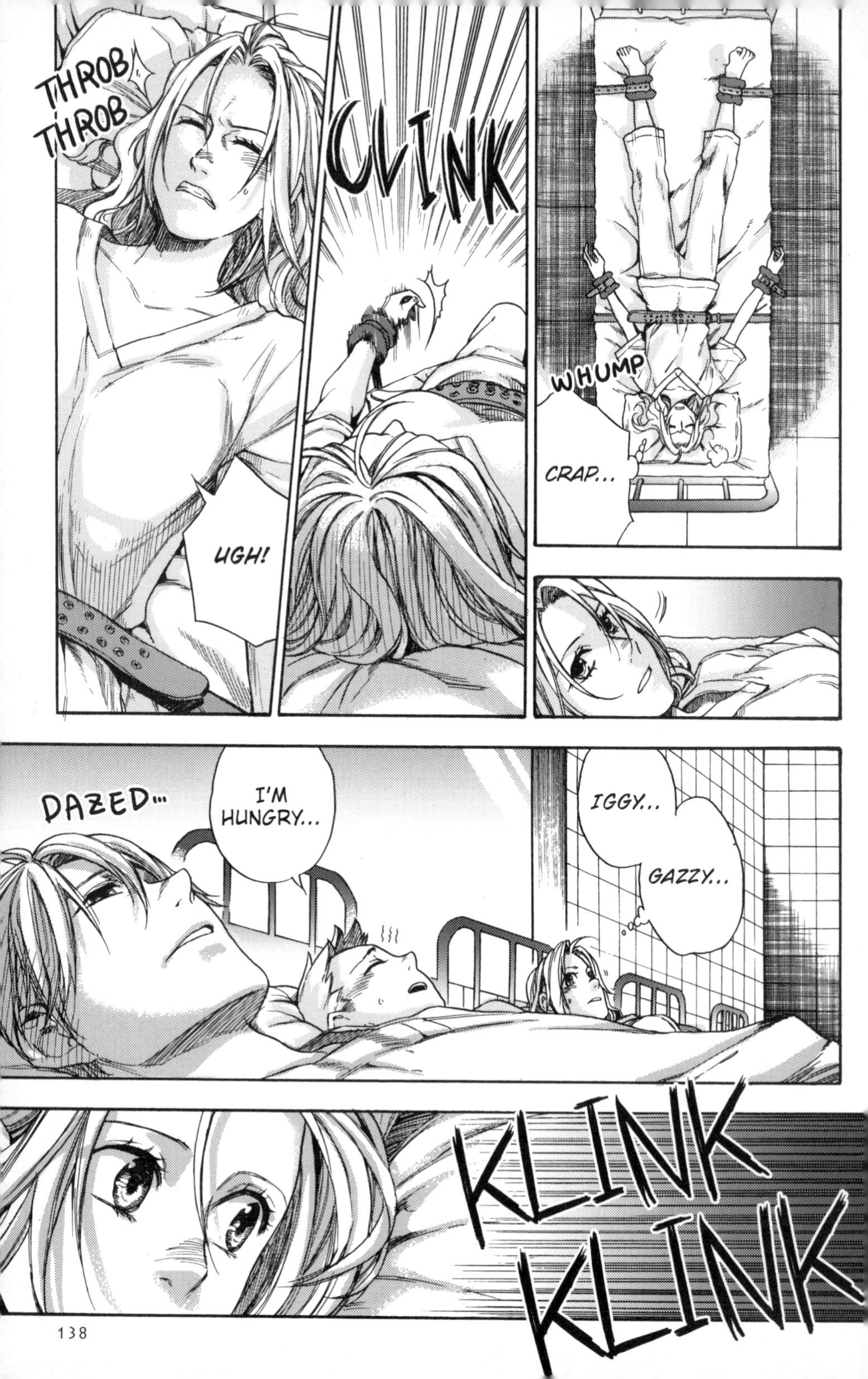
THROB THROB
CLINK
UGH!
WHUMP
CRAP...
DAZED...
I'M HUNGRY...
IGGY...
GAZZY...
KLINK KLINK

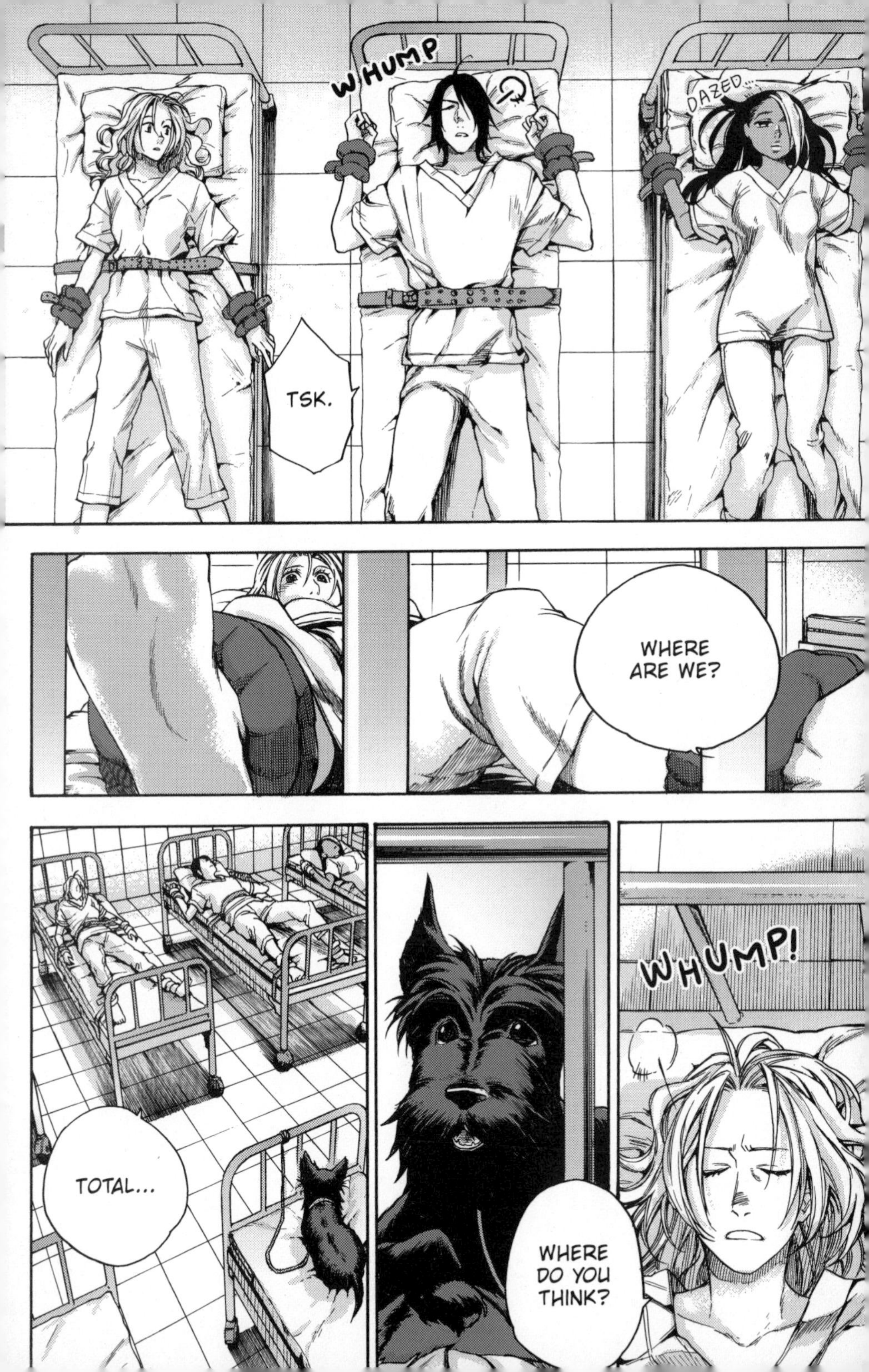
WHUMP
DAZED...
TSK.
WHERE ARE WE?
TOTAL...
WHUMP!
WHERE DO YOU THINK?

MAXIMUM RIDE
CHAPTER 33

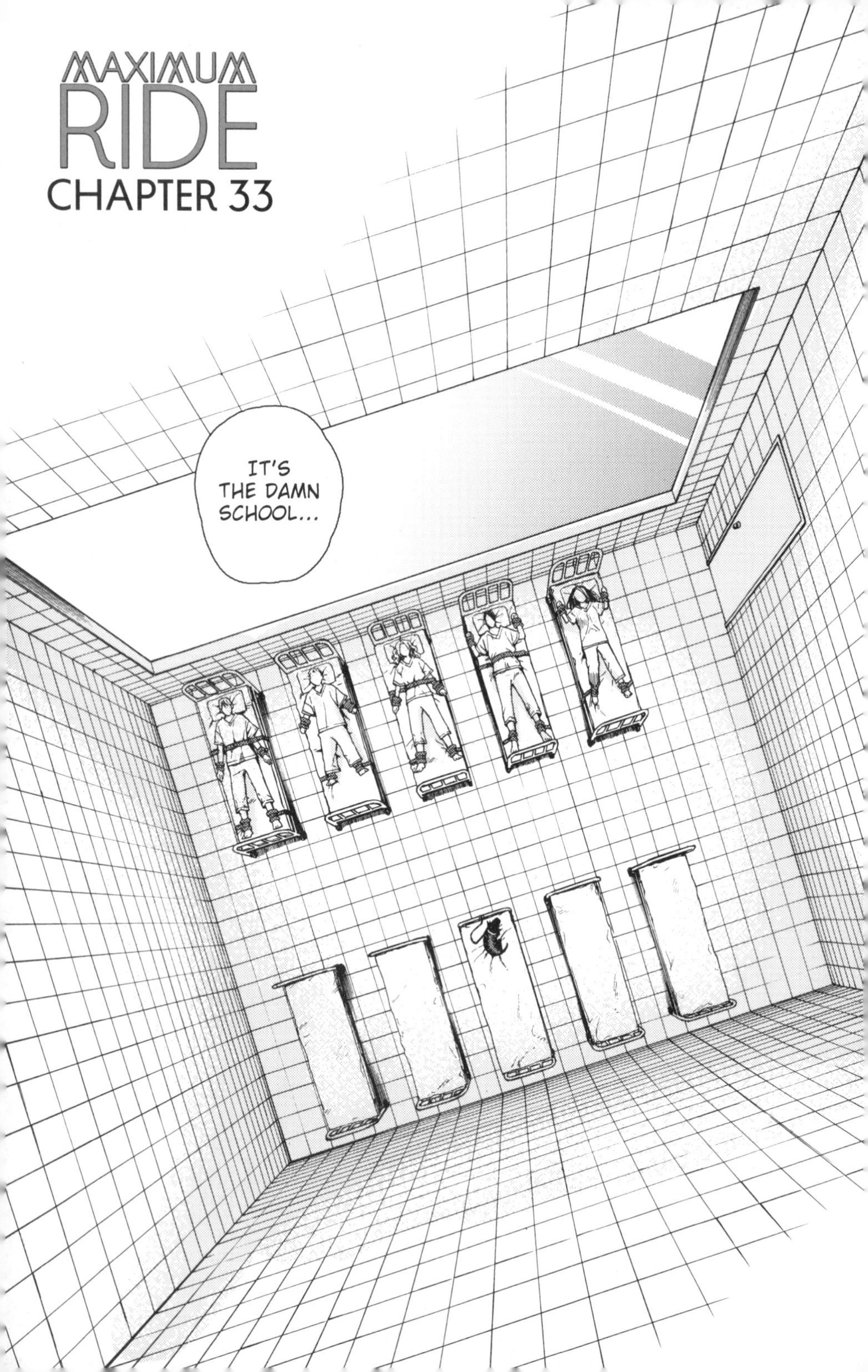
IT'S THE DAMN SCHOOL...

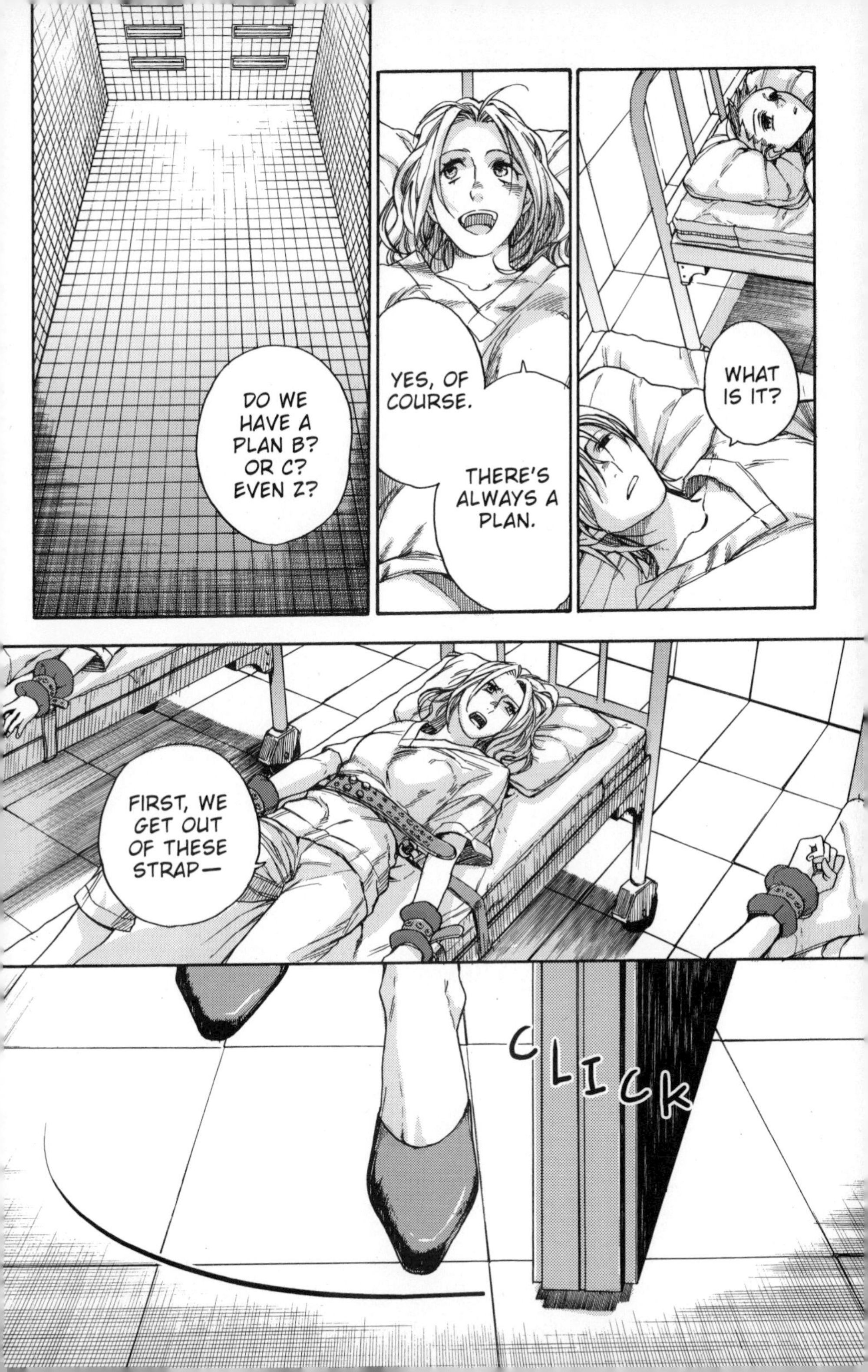
DO WE HAVE A PLAN B? OR C? EVEN Z?
YES, OF COURSE.
THERE'S ALWAYS A PLAN.
WHAT IS IT?
FIRST, WE GET OUT OF THESE STRAP—
CLICK

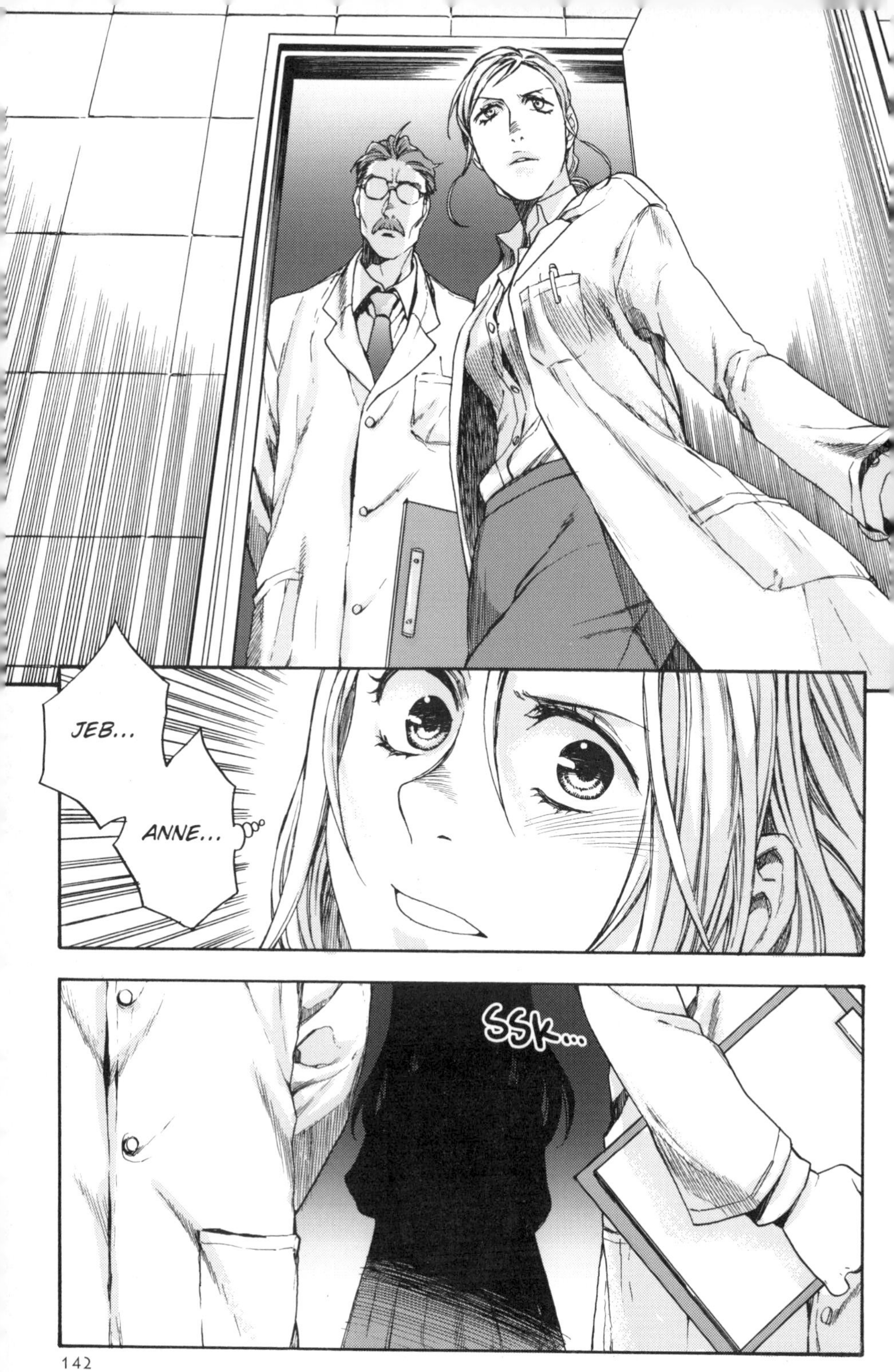
JEB...
ANNE...
SSK...

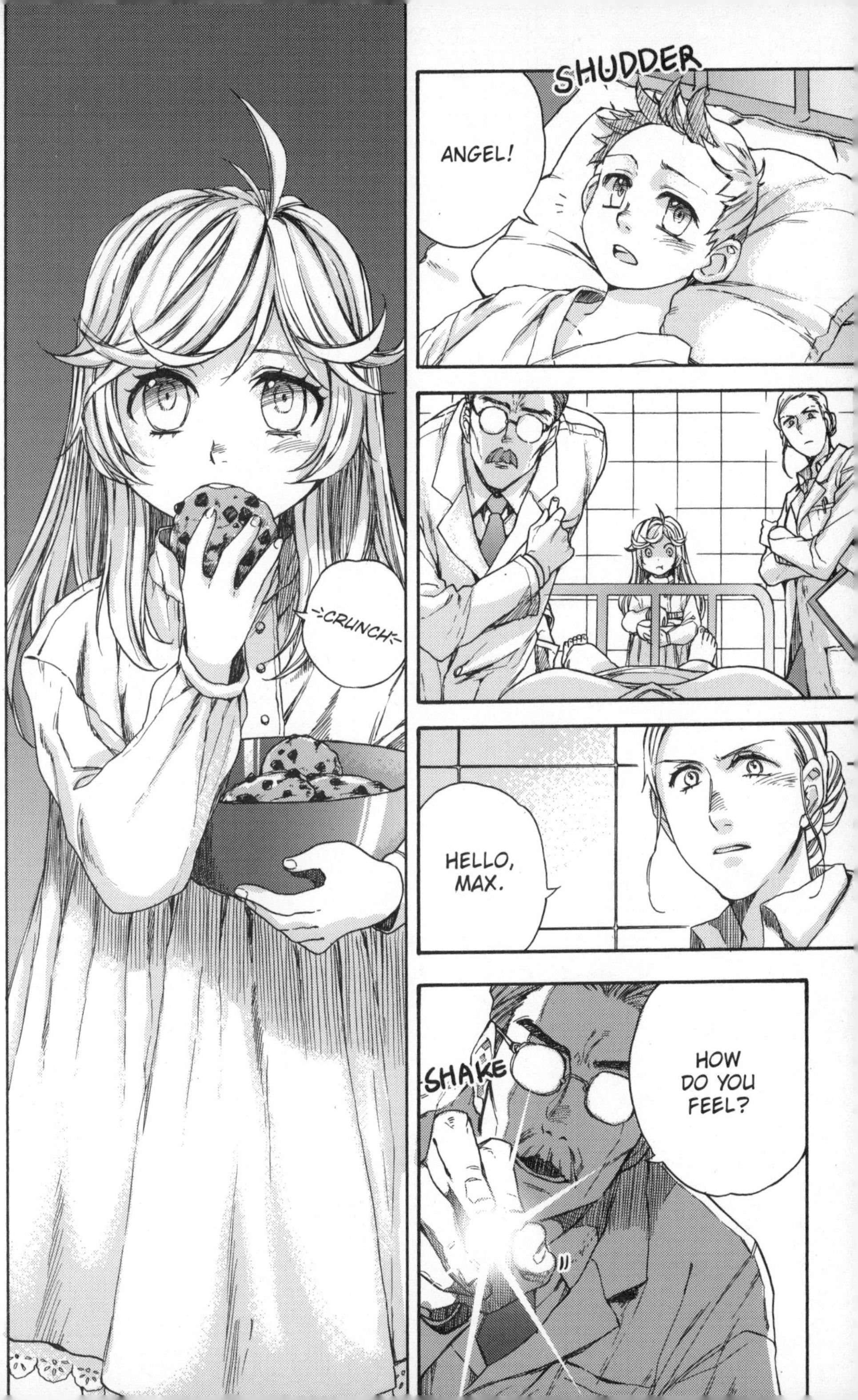
CRUNCH
SHUDDER
ANGEL!
HELLO, MAX.
SHAKE
HOW DO YOU FEEL?

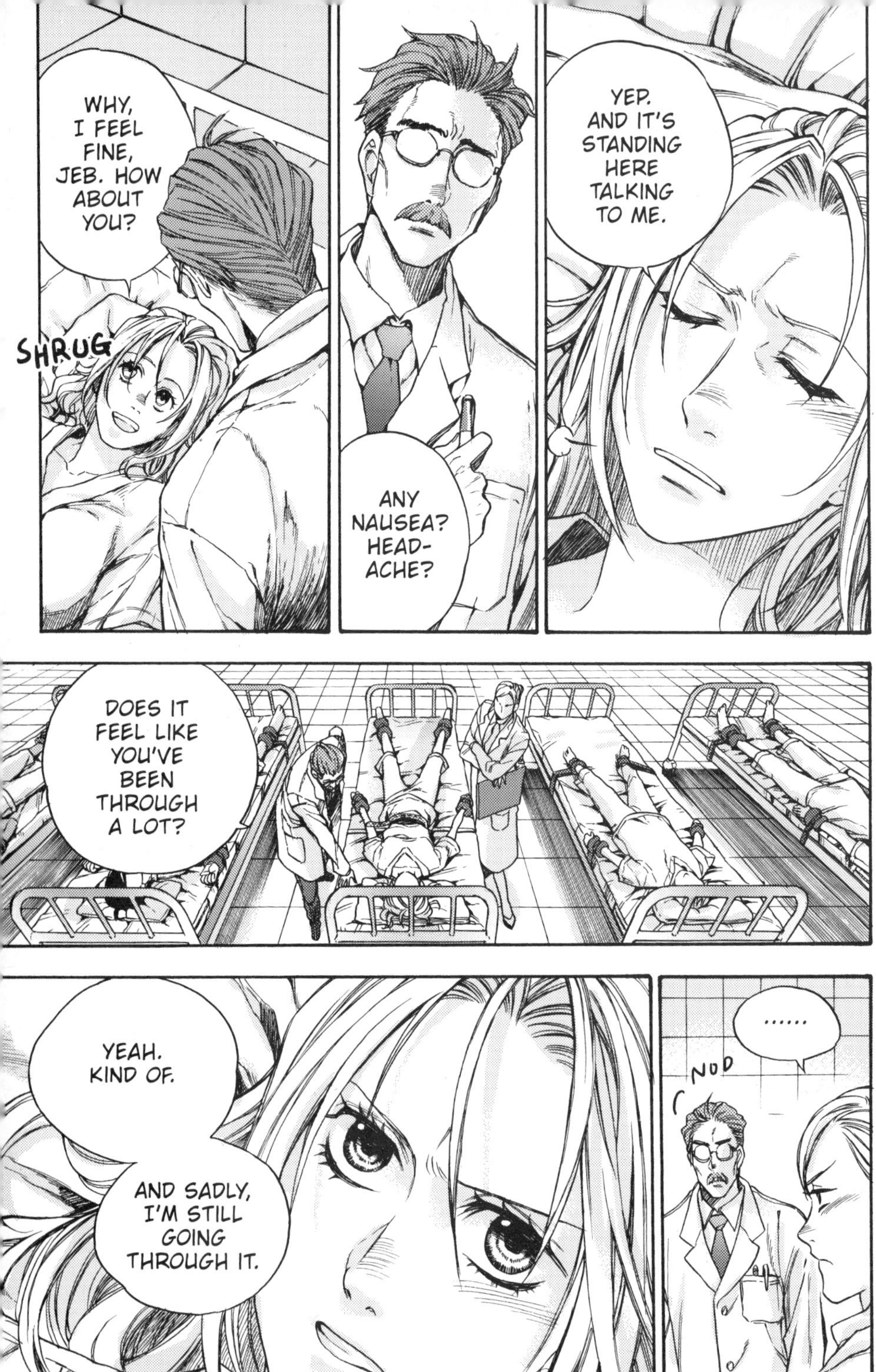
WHY, I FEEL FINE, JEB. HOW ABOUT YOU?
SHRUG
ANY NAUSEA? HEAD-ACHE?
YEP. AND IT'S STANDING HERE TALKING TO ME.
DOES IT FEEL LIKE YOU'VE BEEN THROUGH A LOT?
YEAH. KIND OF.
AND SADLY, I'M STILL GOING THROUGH IT.
......
NOD

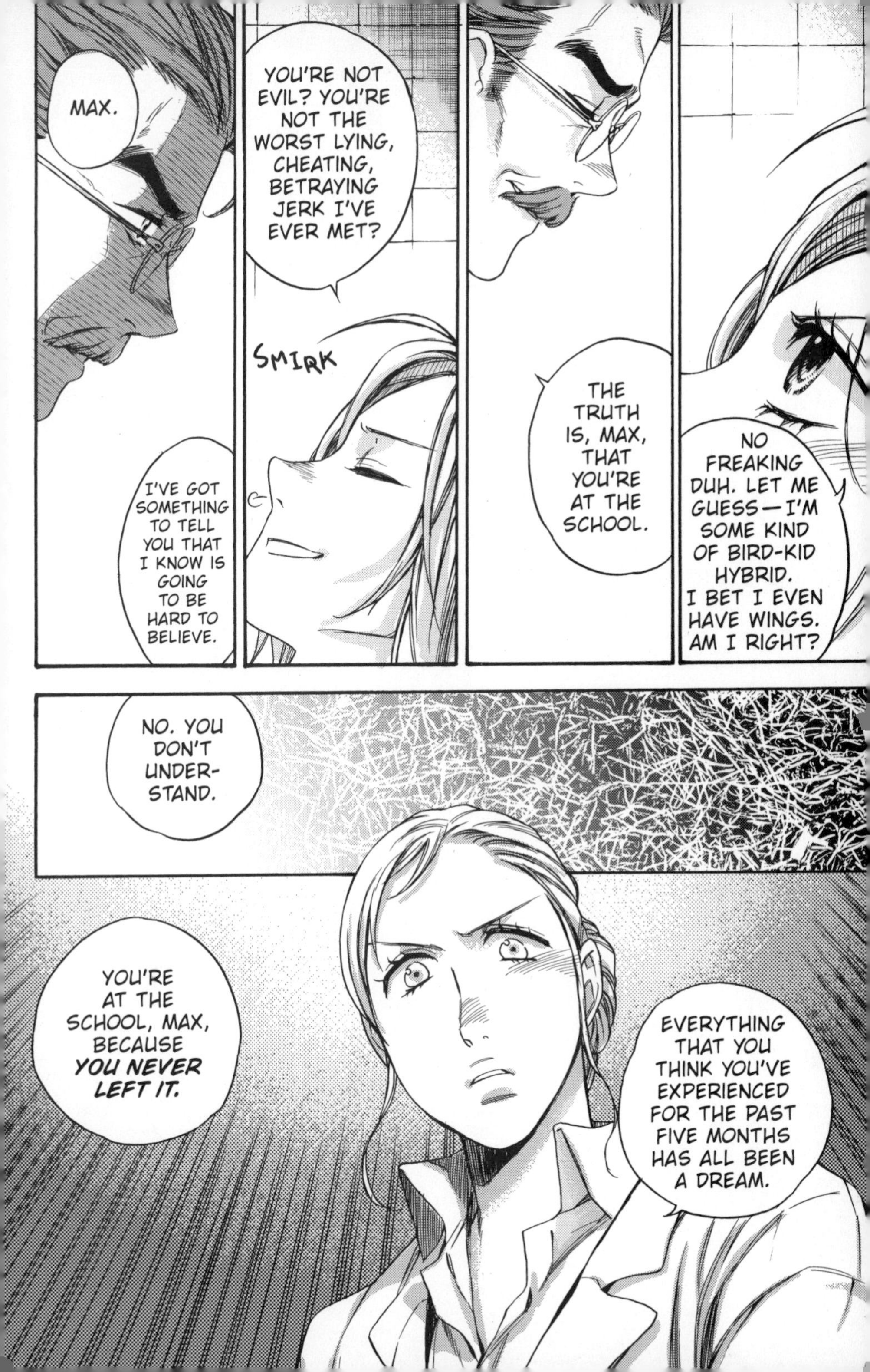
MAX.
YOU'RE NOT EVIL? YOU'RE NOT THE WORST LYING, CHEATING, BETRAYING JERK I'VE EVER MET?
SMIRK
I'VE GOT SOMETHING TO TELL YOU THAT I KNOW IS GOING TO BE HARD TO BELIEVE.
THE TRUTH IS, MAX, THAT YOU'RE AT THE SCHOOL.
NO FREAKING DUH. LET ME GUESS—I'M SOME KIND OF BIRD-KID HYBRID. I BET I EVEN HAVE WINGS. AM I RIGHT?
NO. YOU DON'T UNDER-STAND.
YOU'RE AT THE SCHOOL, MAX, BECAUSE ***YOU NEVER LEFT IT.***
EVERYTHING THAT YOU THINK YOU'VE EXPERIENCED FOR THE PAST FIVE MONTHS HAS ALL BEEN A DREAM.

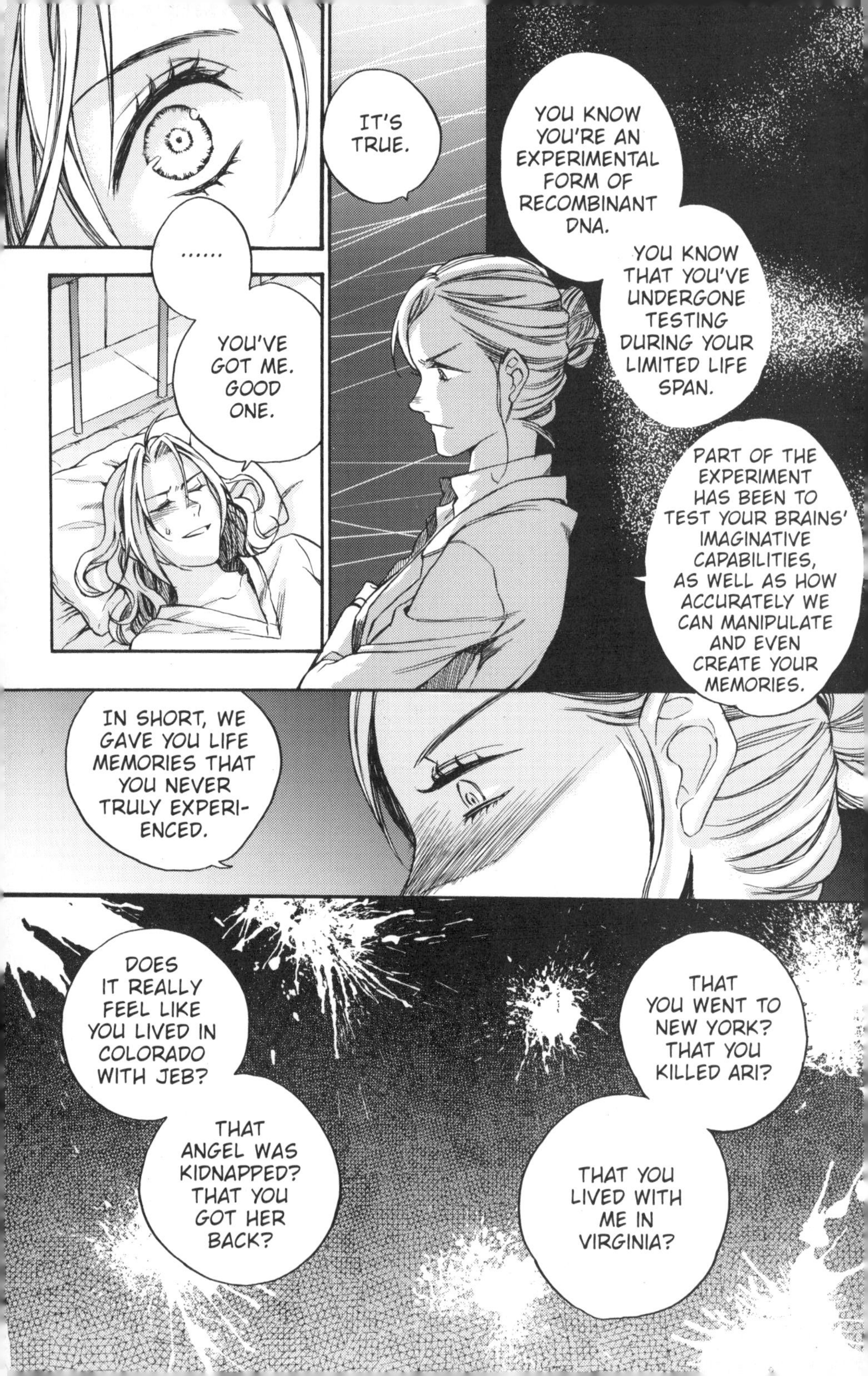
IT'S TRUE.
......
YOU'VE GOT ME. GOOD ONE.
YOU KNOW YOU'RE AN EXPERIMENTAL FORM OF RECOMBINANT DNA.
YOU KNOW THAT YOU'VE UNDERGONE TESTING DURING YOUR LIMITED LIFE SPAN.
PART OF THE EXPERIMENT HAS BEEN TO TEST YOUR BRAINS' IMAGINATIVE CAPABILITIES, AS WELL AS HOW ACCURATELY WE CAN MANIPULATE AND EVEN CREATE YOUR MEMORIES.
IN SHORT, WE GAVE YOU LIFE MEMORIES THAT YOU NEVER TRULY EXPERI-ENCED.
DOES IT REALLY FEEL LIKE YOU LIVED IN COLORADO WITH JEB?
THAT ANGEL WAS KIDNAPPED? THAT YOU GOT HER BACK?
THAT YOU WENT TO NEW YORK? THAT YOU KILLED ARI?
THAT YOU LIVED WITH ME IN VIRGINIA?

MAX, WE GAVE YOU THOSE MEMORIES.

WE MONITORED YOUR HEART AND LUNG RATES WHILE YOU IMAGINED YOURSELF IN VIOLENT FIGHTS.

WE DECIDED ON NEW YORK, ON FLORIDA, ON ARIZONA.

REMEMBER DR. MARTINEZ AND ELLA?

SHUDDER

GULP

TREMBLE...

WHAT—?!

THEY KNOW ABOUT ELLA AND DR. MARTINEZ? HOW?

THOSE CONSTRUCTS ALLOWED US TO TEST...

...YOUR PSYCHOLOGICAL AND PHYSICAL RESPONSES TO A WARM, NURTURING ENVIRONMENT.

DID THEY HARM THEM? KILL THEM?

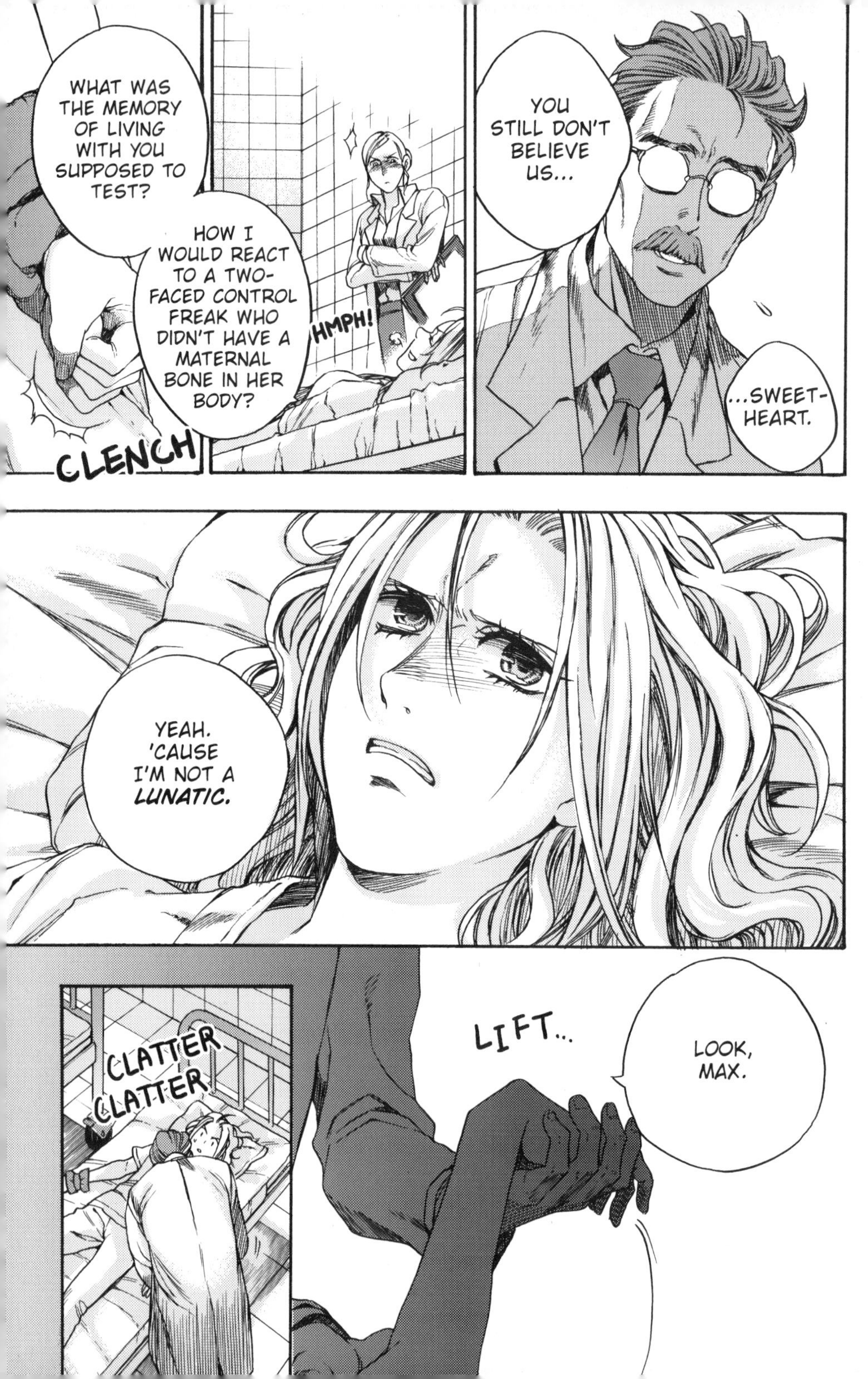

WHAT WAS THE MEMORY OF LIVING WITH YOU SUPPOSED TO TEST?
HOW I WOULD REACT TO A TWO-FACED CONTROL FREAK WHO DIDN'T HAVE A MATERNAL BONE IN HER BODY?
CLENCH
HMPH!
YOU STILL DON'T BELIEVE US...
...SWEET-HEART.
YEAH. 'CAUSE I'M NOT A *LUNATIC.*
CLATTER CLATTER
LIFT...
LOOK, MAX.

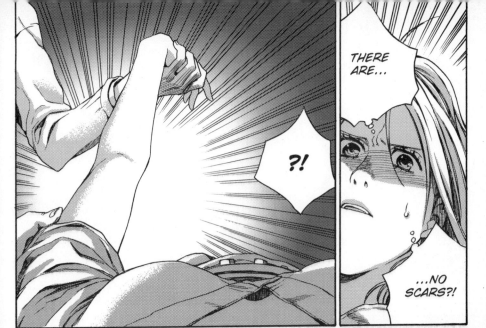

THERE
ARE...

?!

...NO
SCARS?!

I'M TELLING
YOU, NONE
OF IT HAS
BEEN REAL.

IT WAS
ALL A
DREAM.

YOU
NEVER
LEFT THE
SCHOOL.

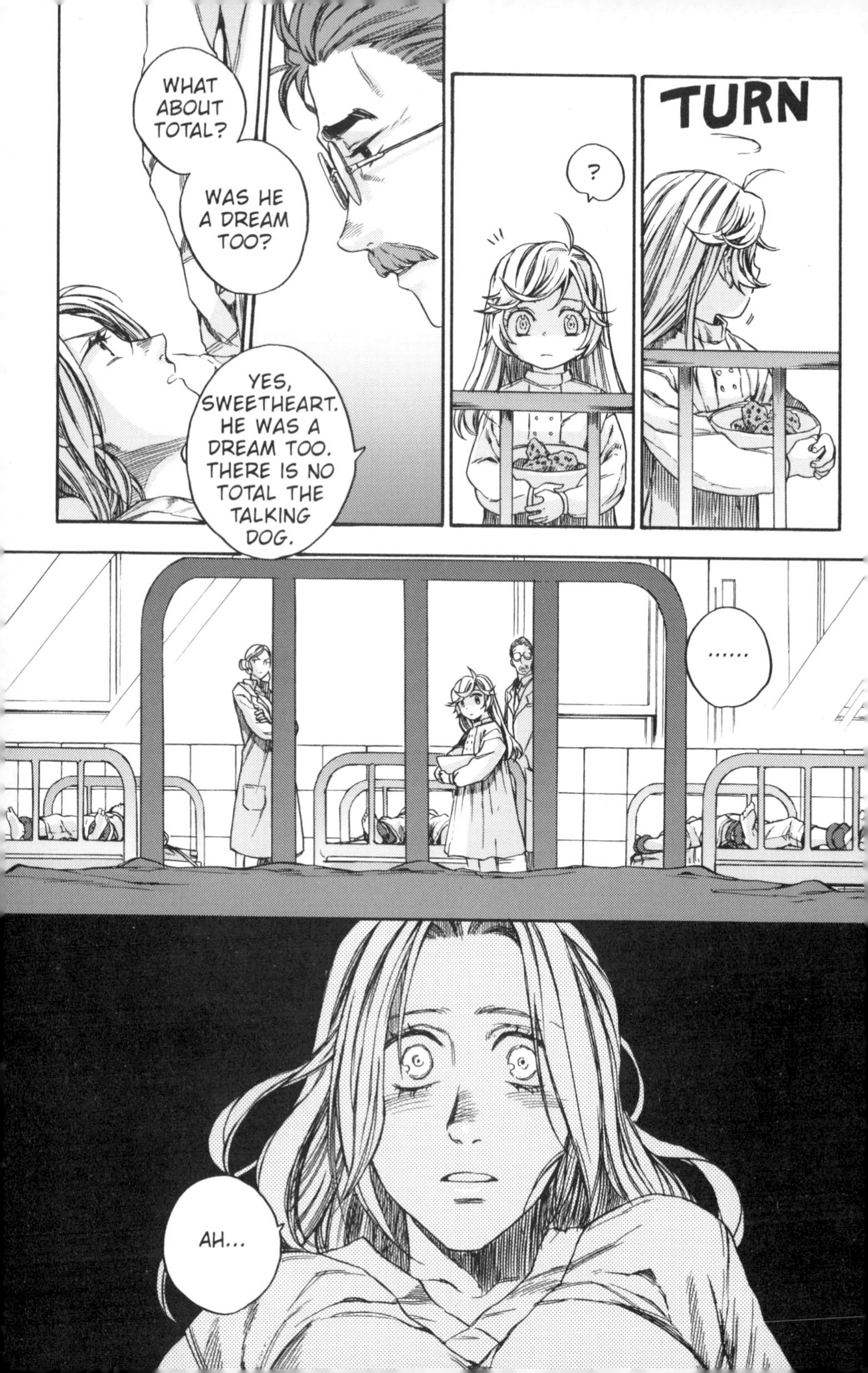
WHAT ABOUT TOTAL?
WAS HE A DREAM TOO?
YES, SWEETHEART. HE WAS A DREAM TOO. THERE IS NO TOTAL THE TALKING DOG.
?
TURN
......
AH...

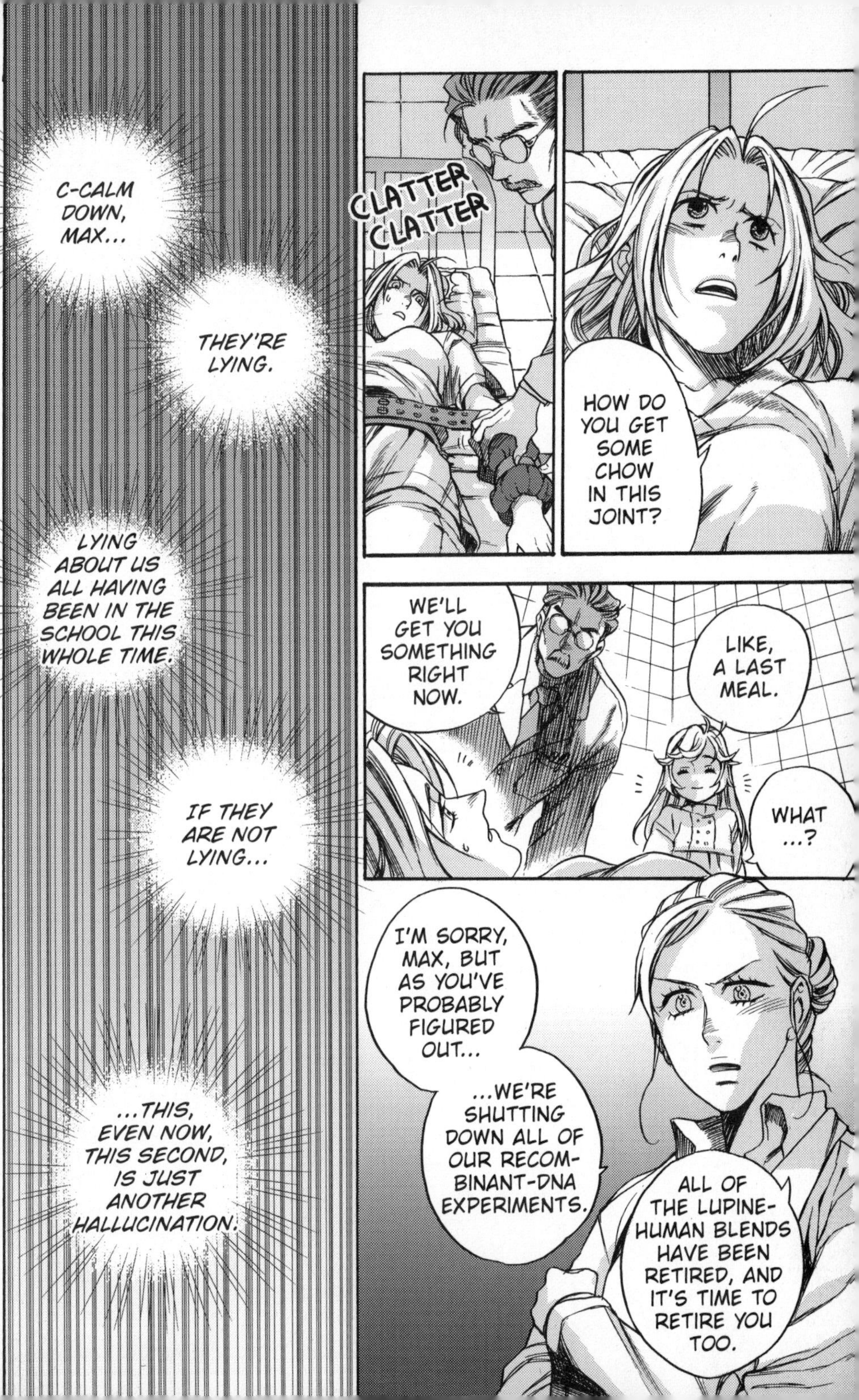
C-CALM DOWN, MAX...
THEY'RE LYING.
LYING ABOUT US ALL HAVING BEEN IN THE SCHOOL THIS WHOLE TIME.
IF THEY ARE NOT LYING...
...THIS, EVEN NOW, THIS SECOND, IS JUST ANOTHER HALLUCINATION.
CLATTER CLATTER
HOW DO YOU GET SOME CHOW IN THIS JOINT?
WE'LL GET YOU SOMETHING RIGHT NOW.
LIKE, A LAST MEAL.
WHAT ...?
I'M SORRY, MAX, BUT AS YOU'VE PROBABLY FIGURED OUT...
...WE'RE SHUTTING DOWN ALL OF OUR RECOM-BINANT-DNA EXPERIMENTS.
ALL OF THE LUPINE-HUMAN BLENDS HAVE BEEN RETIRED, AND IT'S TIME TO RETIRE YOU TOO.

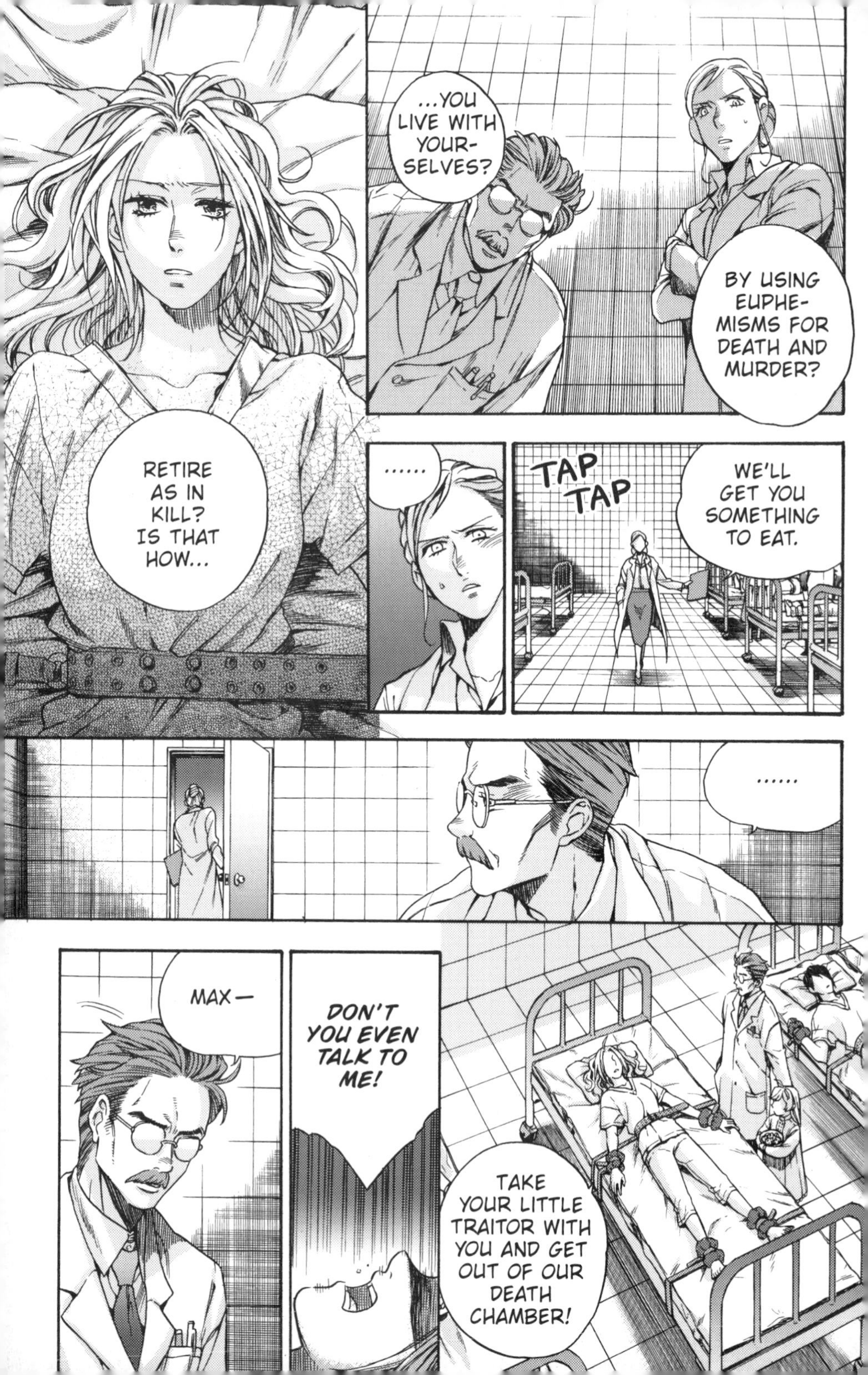
RETIRE AS IN KILL? IS THAT HOW...
...YOU LIVE WITH YOUR-SELVES?
BY USING EUPHE-MISMS FOR DEATH AND MURDER?
......
TAP TAP
WE'LL GET YOU SOMETHING TO EAT.
......
MAX—
DON'T YOU EVEN TALK TO ME!
TAKE YOUR LITTLE TRAITOR WITH YOU AND GET OUT OF OUR DEATH CHAMBER!

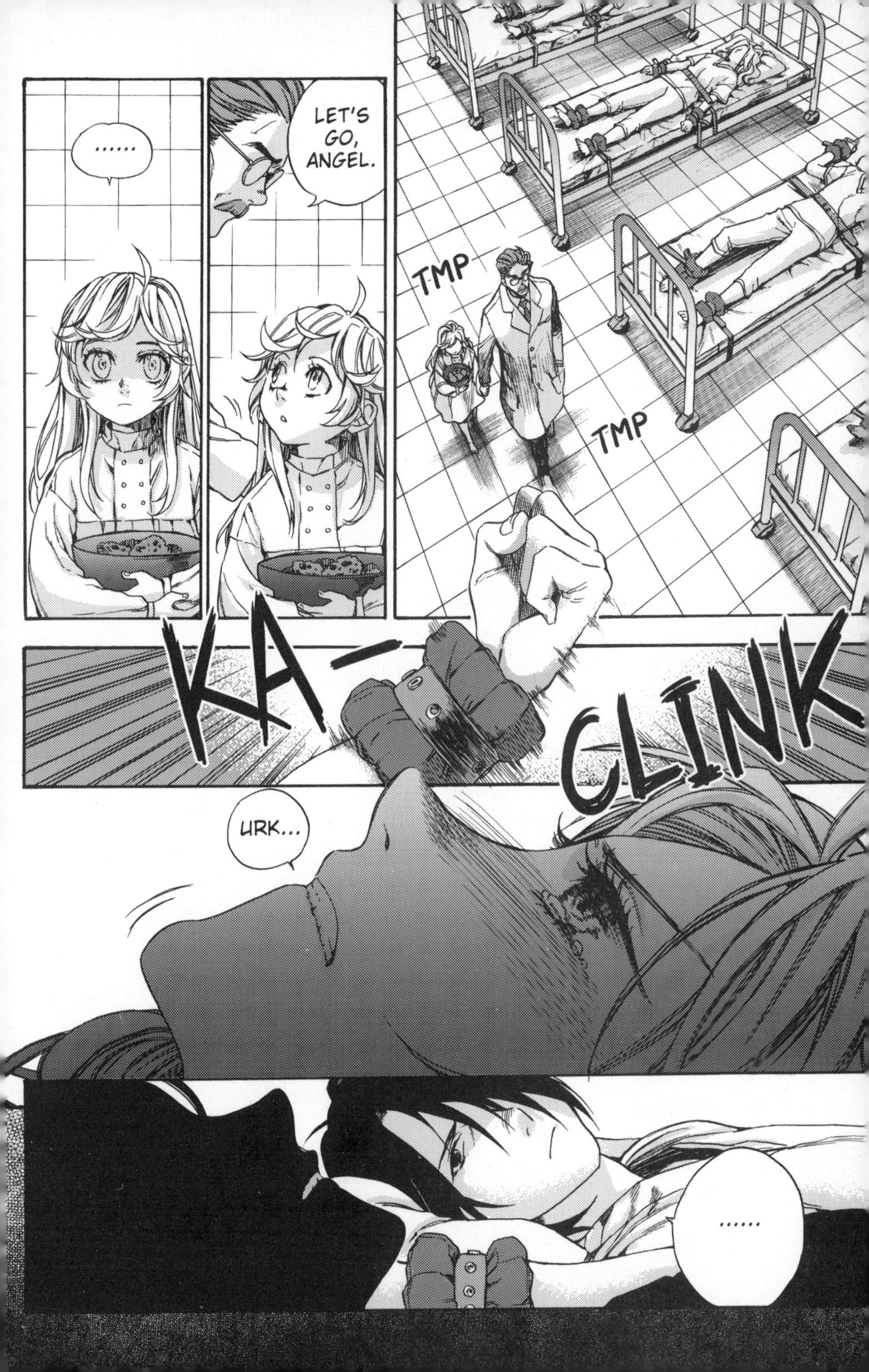
LET'S GO, ANGEL.
......
TMP
TMP
KA-CLINK
URK...
......

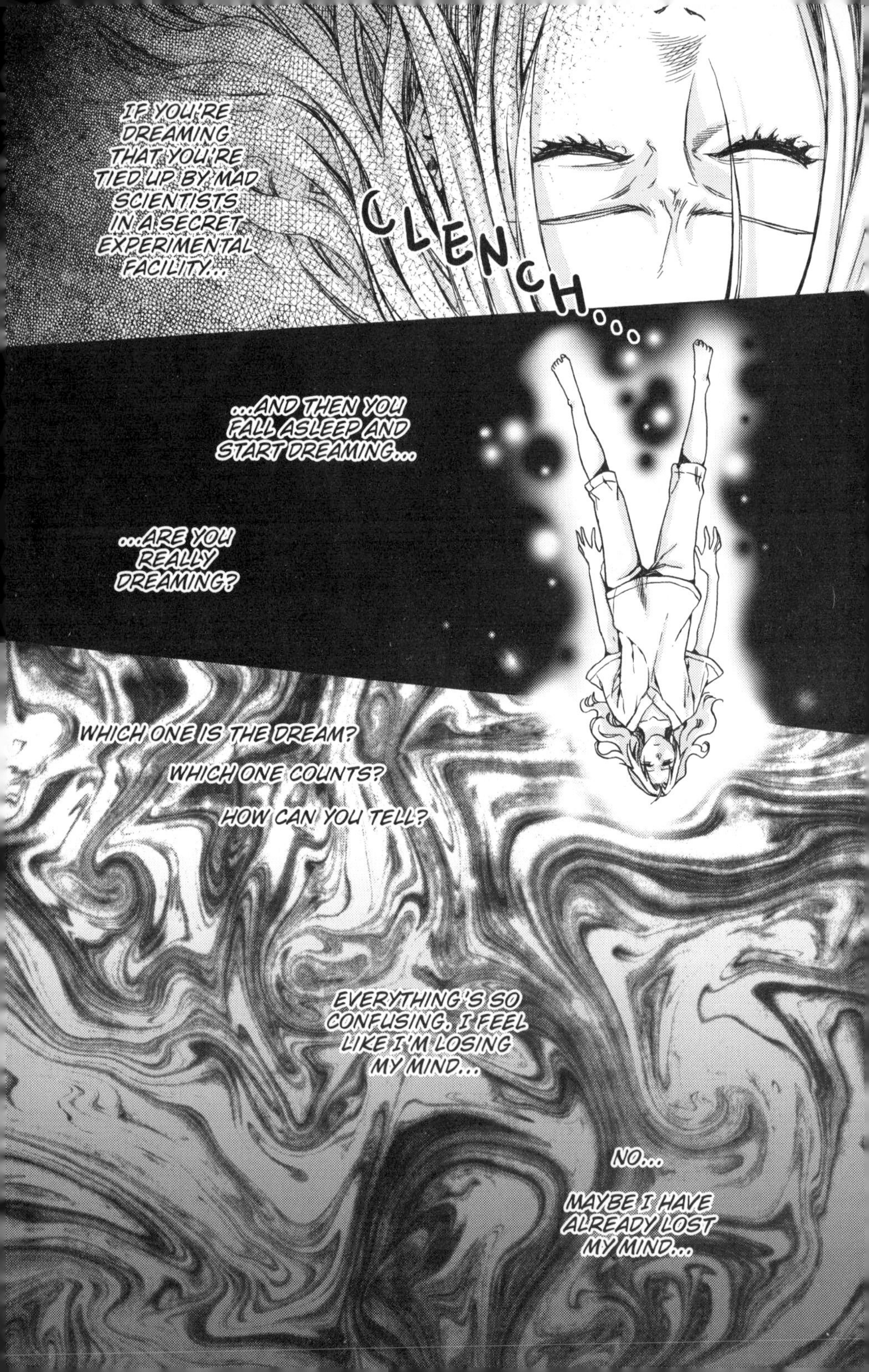
IF YOU'RE DREAMING THAT YOU'RE TIED UP BY MAD SCIENTISTS IN A SECRET EXPERIMENTAL FACILITY...
CLENCH...
...AND THEN YOU FALL ASLEEP AND START DREAMING...
...ARE YOU REALLY DREAMING?
WHICH ONE IS THE DREAM?
WHICH ONE COUNTS?
HOW CAN YOU TELL?
EVERYTHING'S SO CONFUSING. I FEEL LIKE I'M LOSING MY MIND...
NO...
MAYBE I HAVE ALREADY LOST MY MIND...

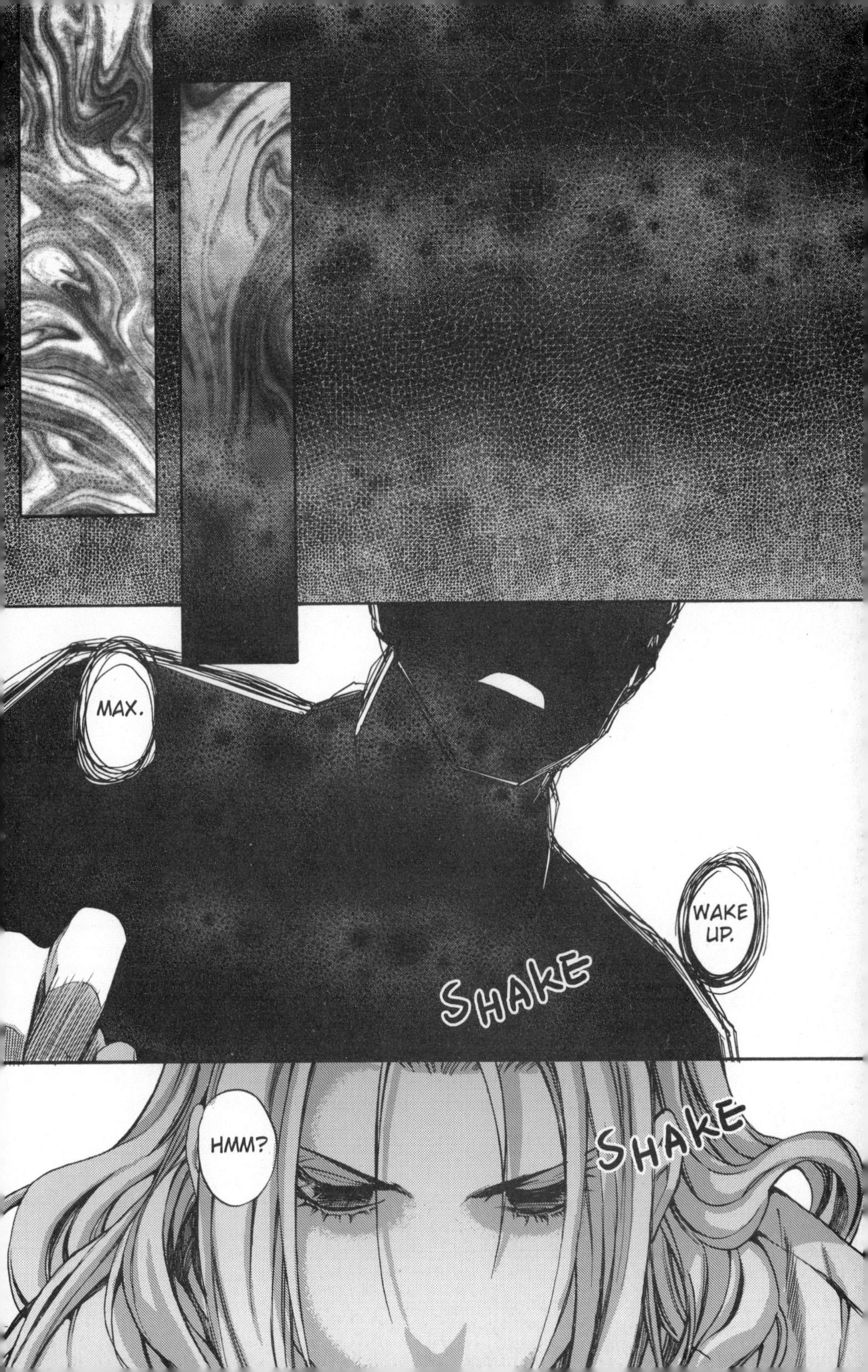
MAX.
WAKE UP.
SHAKE
HMM?
SHAKE

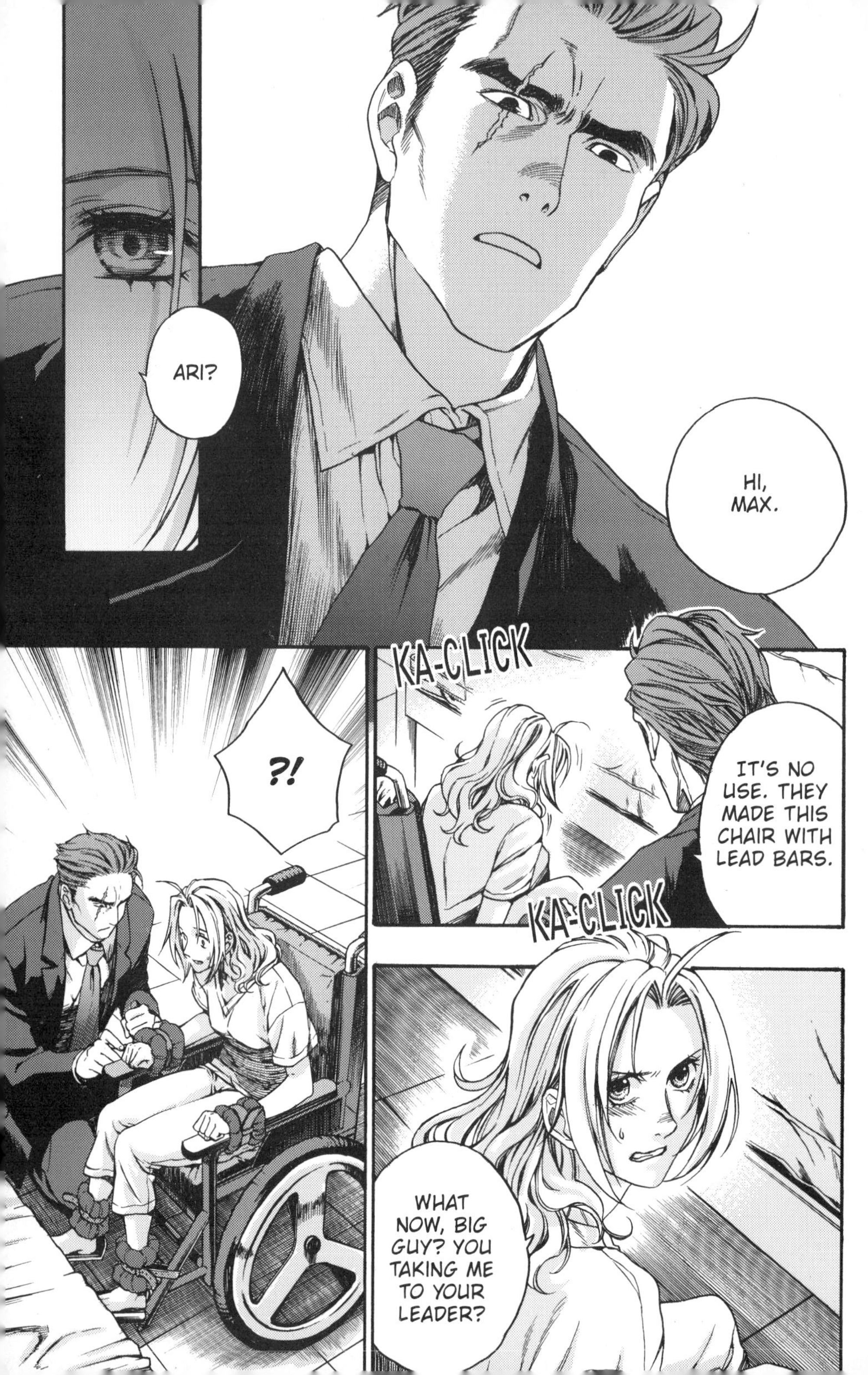
ARI?
HI, MAX.
?!
KA-CLICK
IT'S NO USE. THEY MADE THIS CHAIR WITH LEAD BARS.
KA-CLICK
WHAT NOW, BIG GUY? YOU TAKING ME TO YOUR LEADER?

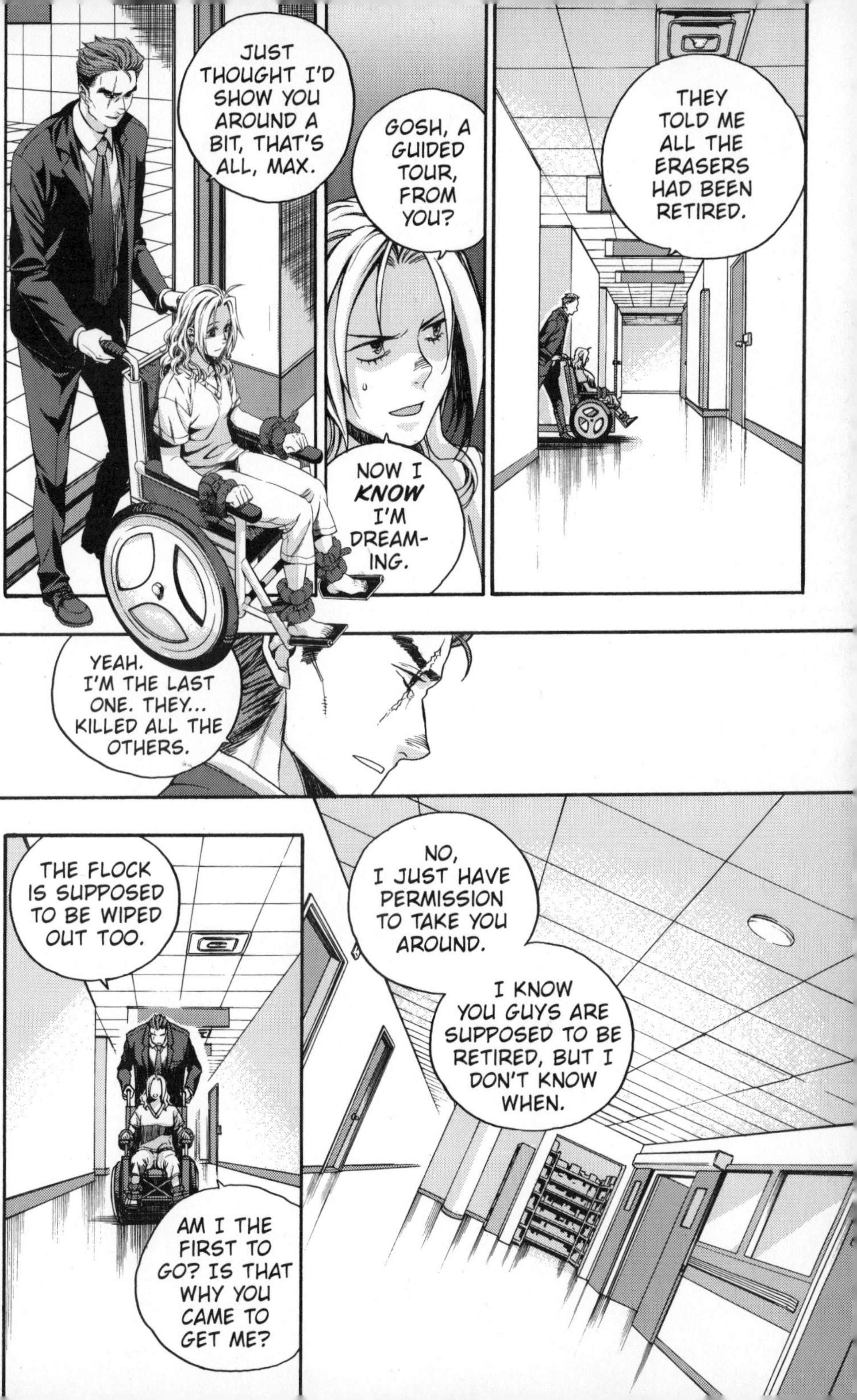
JUST THOUGHT I'D SHOW YOU AROUND A BIT, THAT'S ALL, MAX.
GOSH, A GUIDED TOUR, FROM YOU?
NOW I *KNOW* I'M DREAM-ING.
THEY TOLD ME ALL THE ERASERS HAD BEEN RETIRED.
YEAH. I'M THE LAST ONE. THEY... KILLED ALL THE OTHERS.
THE FLOCK IS SUPPOSED TO BE WIPED OUT TOO.
AM I THE FIRST TO GO? IS THAT WHY YOU CAME TO GET ME?
NO, I JUST HAVE PERMISSION TO TAKE YOU AROUND.
I KNOW YOU GUYS ARE SUPPOSED TO BE RETIRED, BUT I DON'T KNOW WHEN.

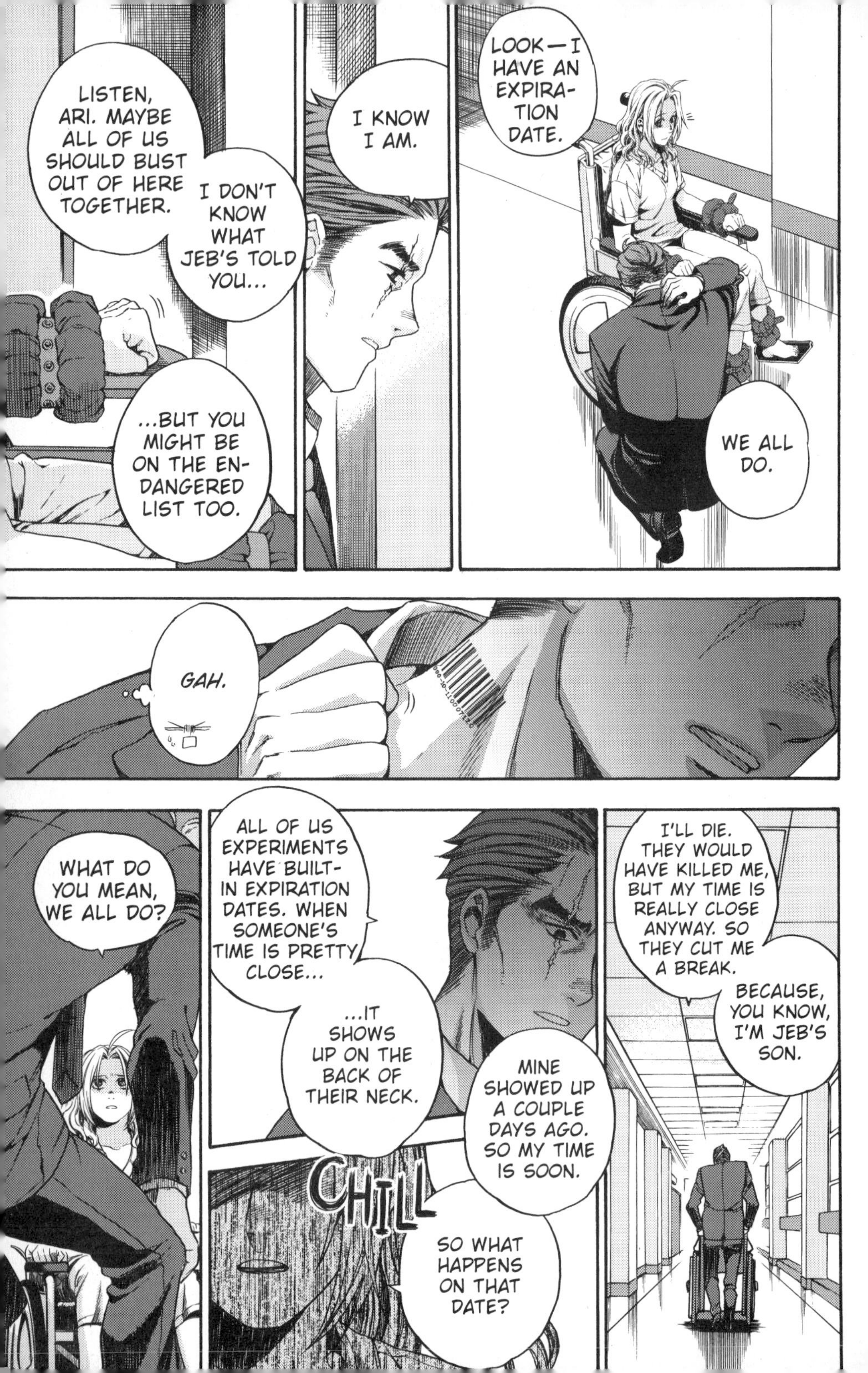
LISTEN, ARI. MAYBE ALL OF US SHOULD BUST OUT OF HERE TOGETHER.
I DON'T KNOW WHAT JEB'S TOLD YOU...
...BUT YOU MIGHT BE ON THE ENDANGERED LIST TOO.
I KNOW I AM.
LOOK—I HAVE AN EXPIRATION DATE.
WE ALL DO.
GAH.
WHAT DO YOU MEAN, WE ALL DO?
ALL OF US EXPERIMENTS HAVE BUILT-IN EXPIRATION DATES. WHEN SOMEONE'S TIME IS PRETTY CLOSE...
...IT SHOWS UP ON THE BACK OF THEIR NECK.
MINE SHOWED UP A COUPLE DAYS AGO. SO MY TIME IS SOON.
CHILL
SO WHAT HAPPENS ON THAT DATE?
I'LL DIE. THEY WOULD HAVE KILLED ME, BUT MY TIME IS REALLY CLOSE ANYWAY. SO THEY CUT ME A BREAK.
BECAUSE, YOU KNOW, I'M JEB'S SON.

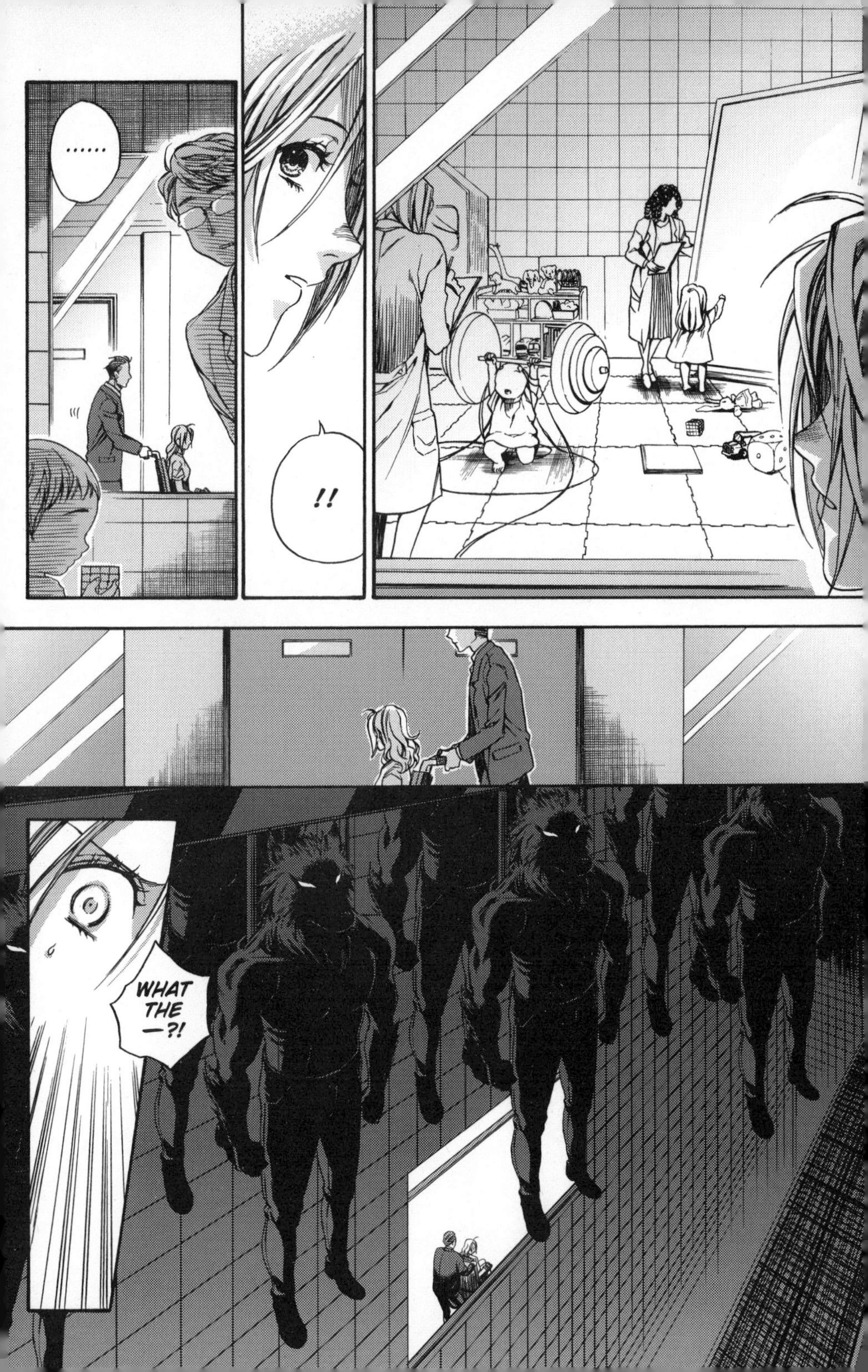
......
!!
WHAT THE —?!

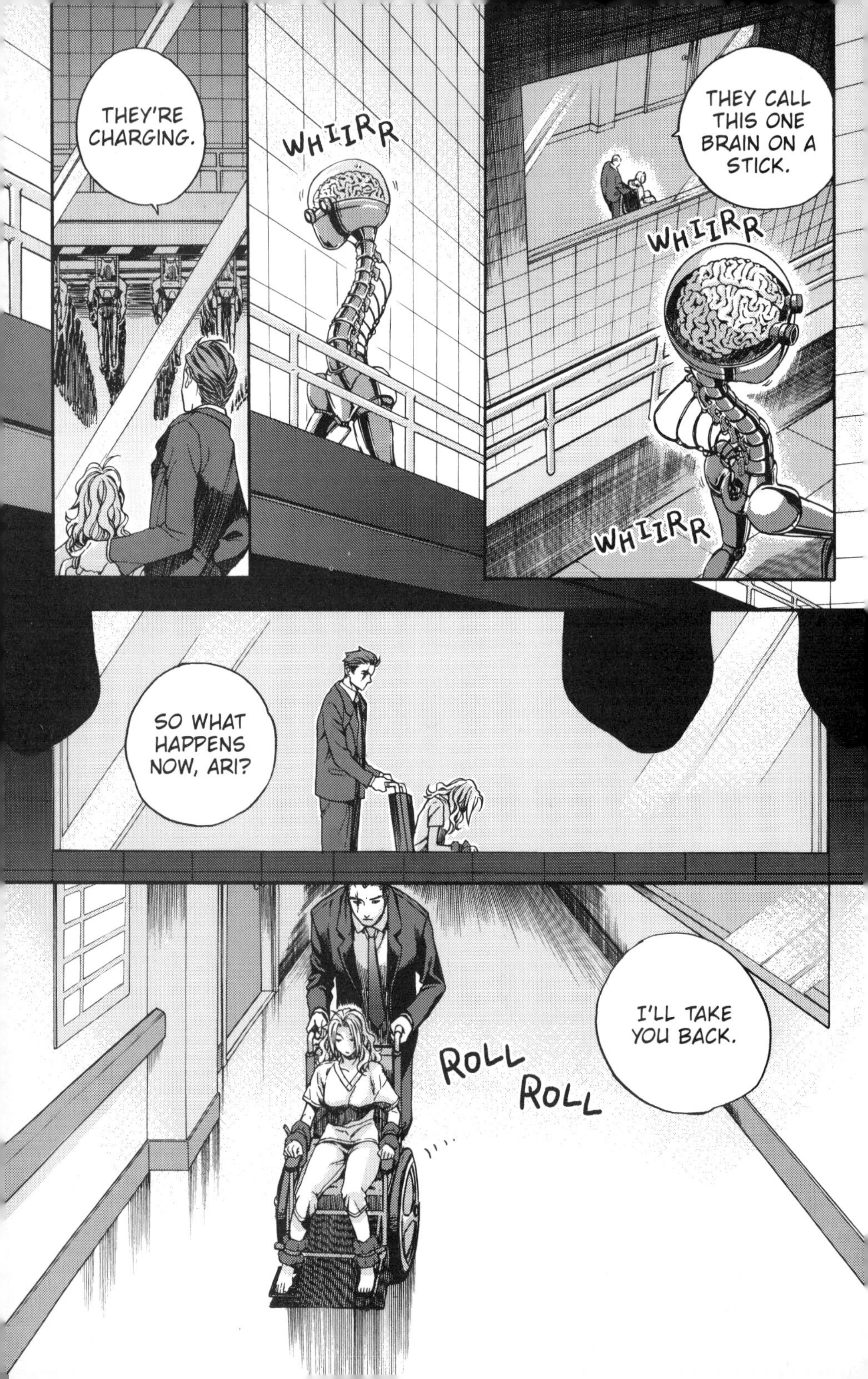
THEY'RE CHARGING.
WHIIRR
THEY CALL THIS ONE BRAIN ON A STICK.
WHIIRR
WHIIRR
SO WHAT HAPPENS NOW, ARI?
ROLL ROLL
I'LL TAKE YOU BACK.

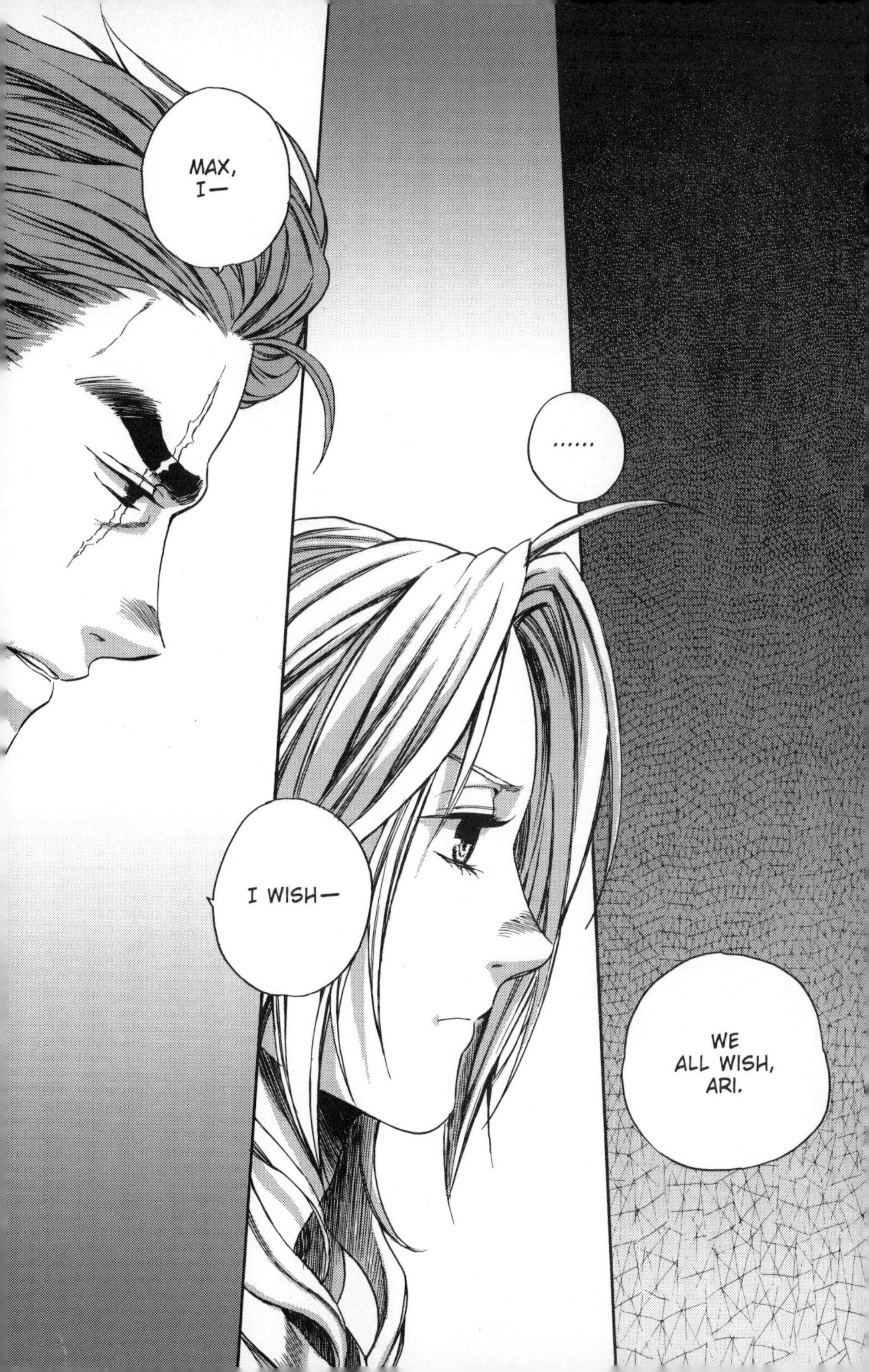
MAX, I—
......
I WISH—
WE ALL WISH, ARI.

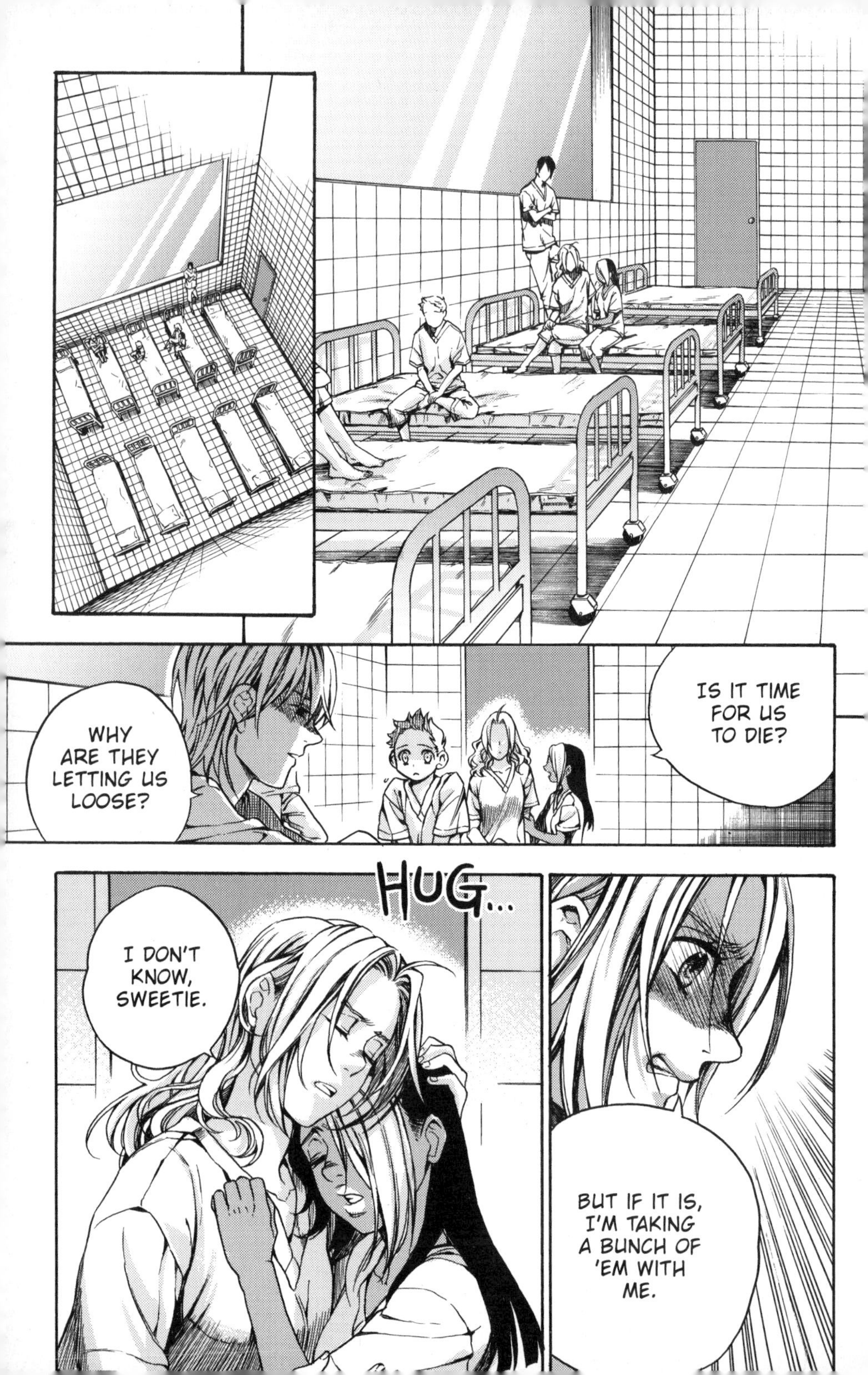
WHY ARE THEY LETTING US LOOSE?
IS IT TIME FOR US TO DIE?
HUG...
I DON'T KNOW, SWEETIE.
BUT IF IT IS, I'M TAKING A BUNCH OF 'EM WITH ME.

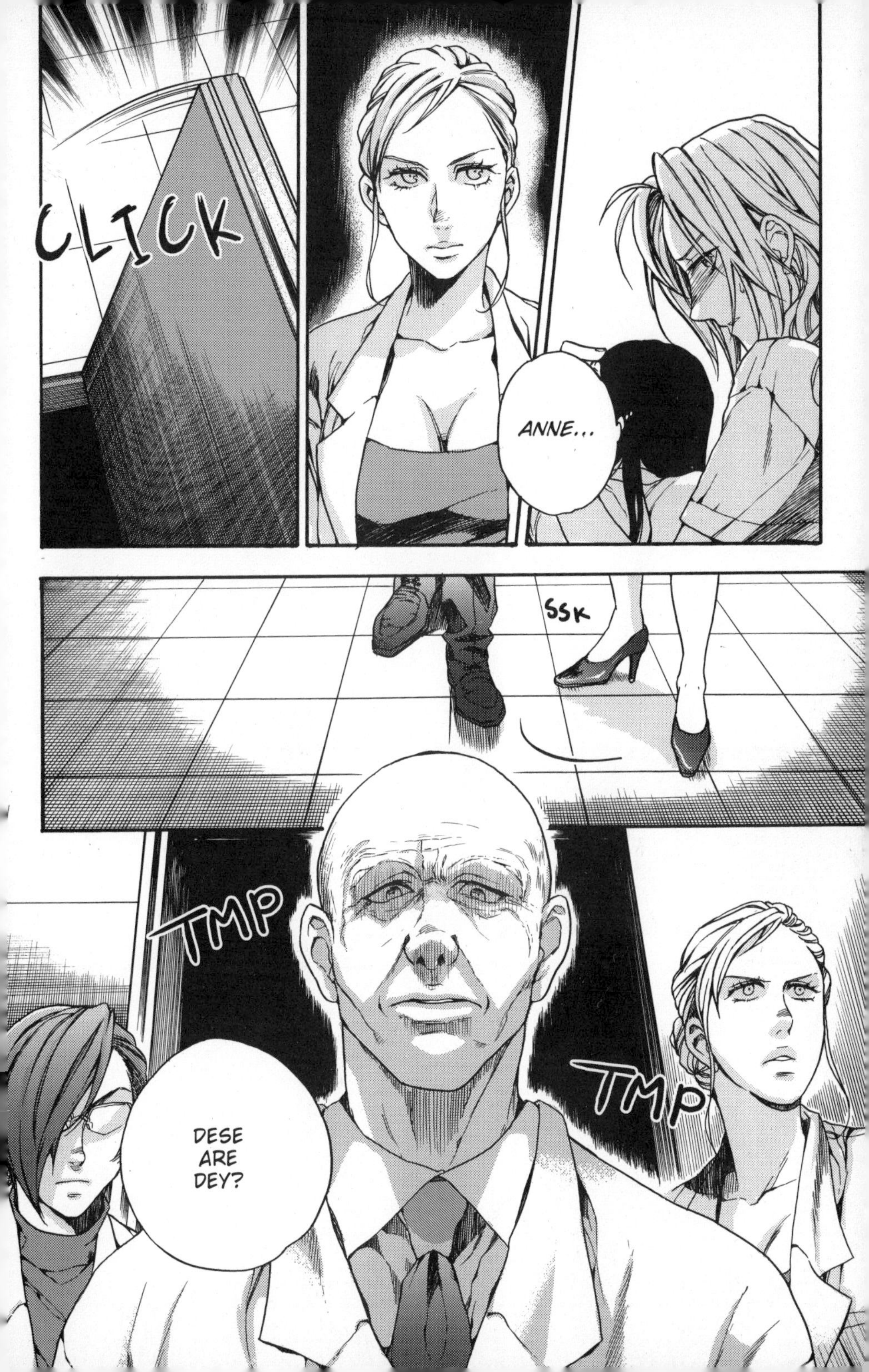
CLICK
ANNE...
SSK
TMP
TMP
DESE ARE DEY?

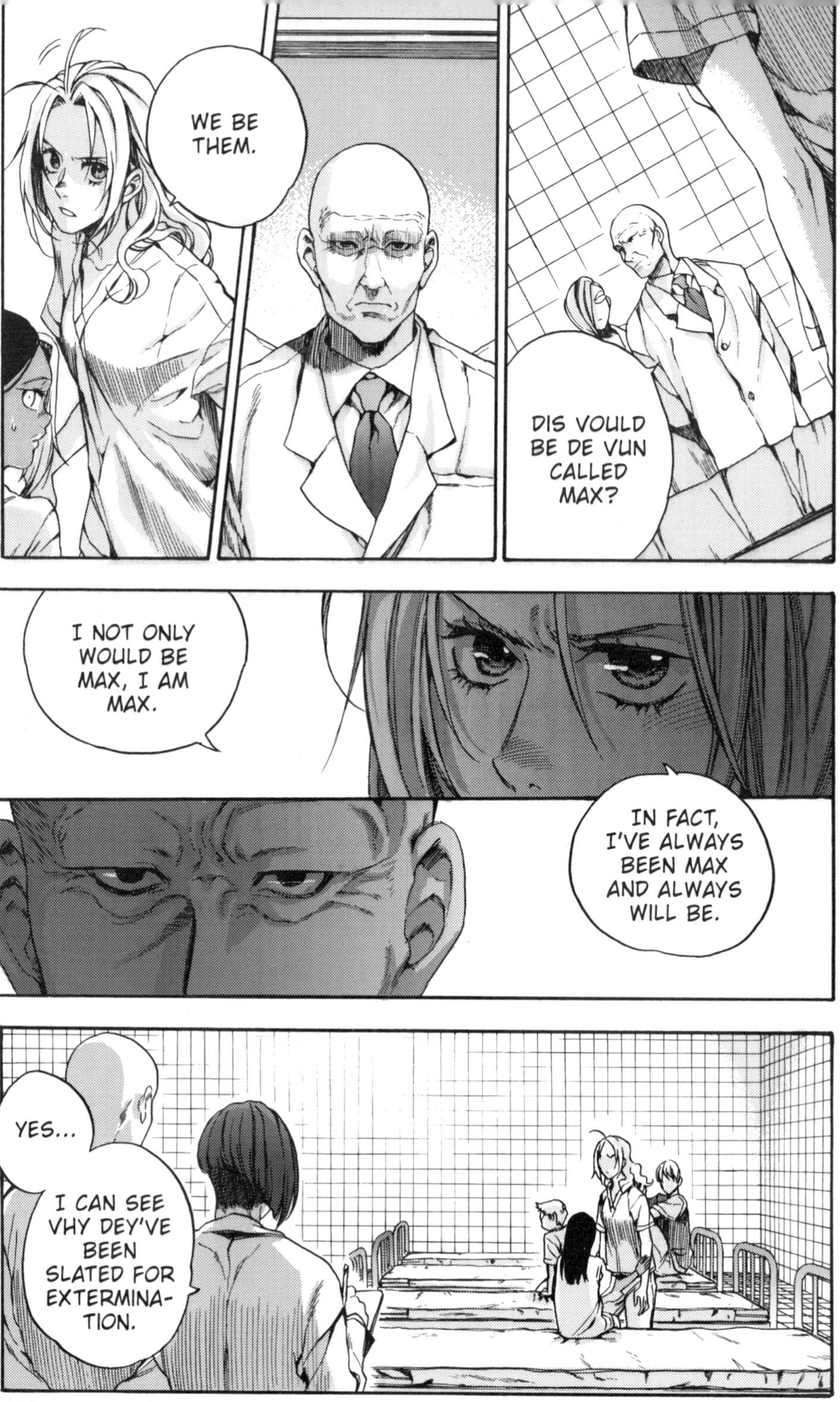
WE BE THEM.
DIS VOULD BE DE VUN CALLED MAX?
I NOT ONLY WOULD BE MAX, I AM MAX.
IN FACT, I'VE ALWAYS BEEN MAX AND ALWAYS WILL BE.
YES...
I CAN SEE VHY DEY'VE BEEN SLATED FOR EXTERMINA-TION.

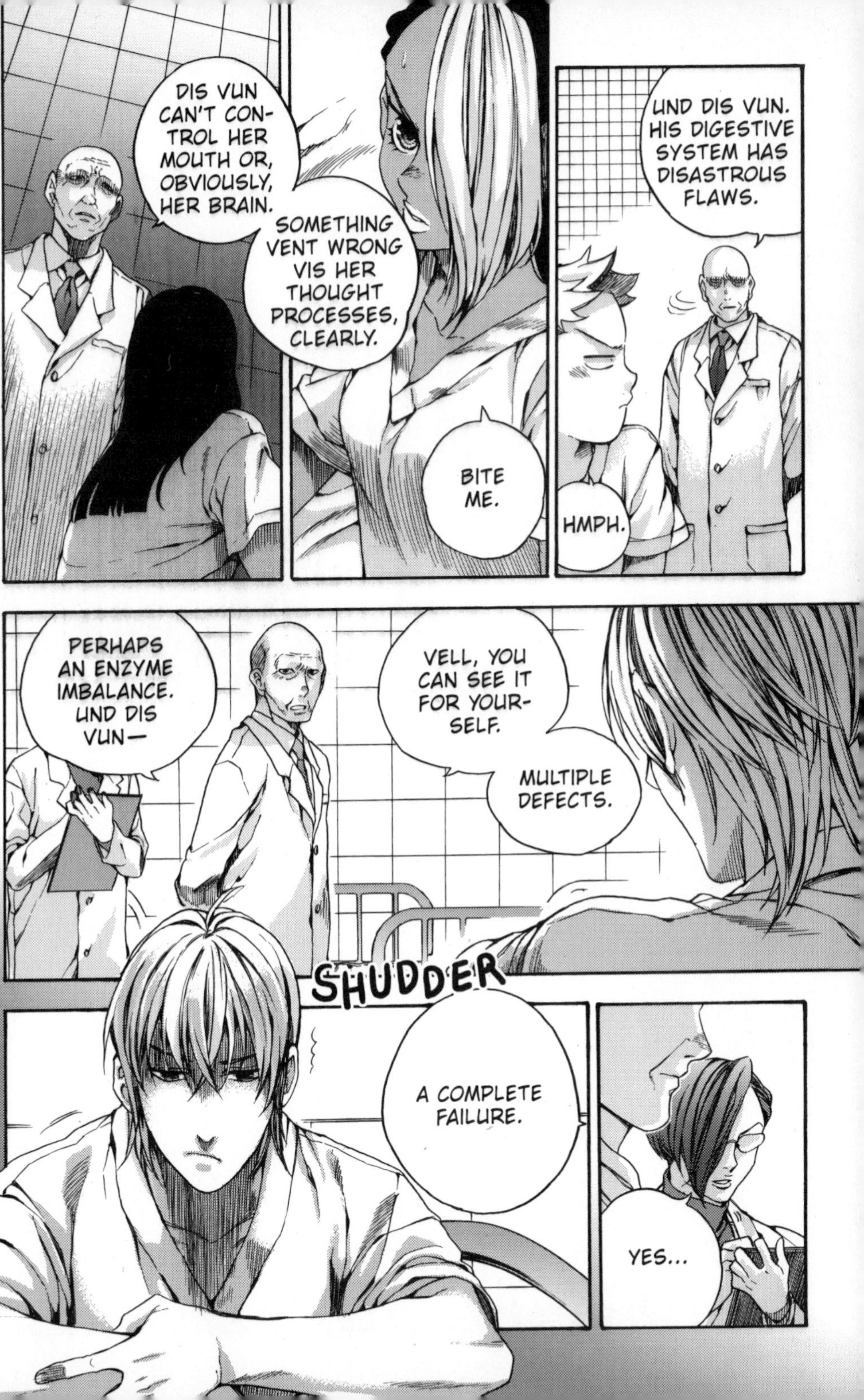
DIS VUN CAN'T CON-TROL HER MOUTH OR, OBVIOUSLY, HER BRAIN.
SOMETHING VENT WRONG VIS HER THOUGHT PROCESSES, CLEARLY.
BITE ME.
UND DIS VUN. HIS DIGESTIVE SYSTEM HAS DISASTROUS FLAWS.
HMPH.
PERHAPS AN ENZYME IMBALANCE. UND DIS VUN—
VELL, YOU CAN SEE IT FOR YOUR-SELF.
MULTIPLE DEFECTS.
SHUDDER
A COMPLETE FAILURE.
YES...

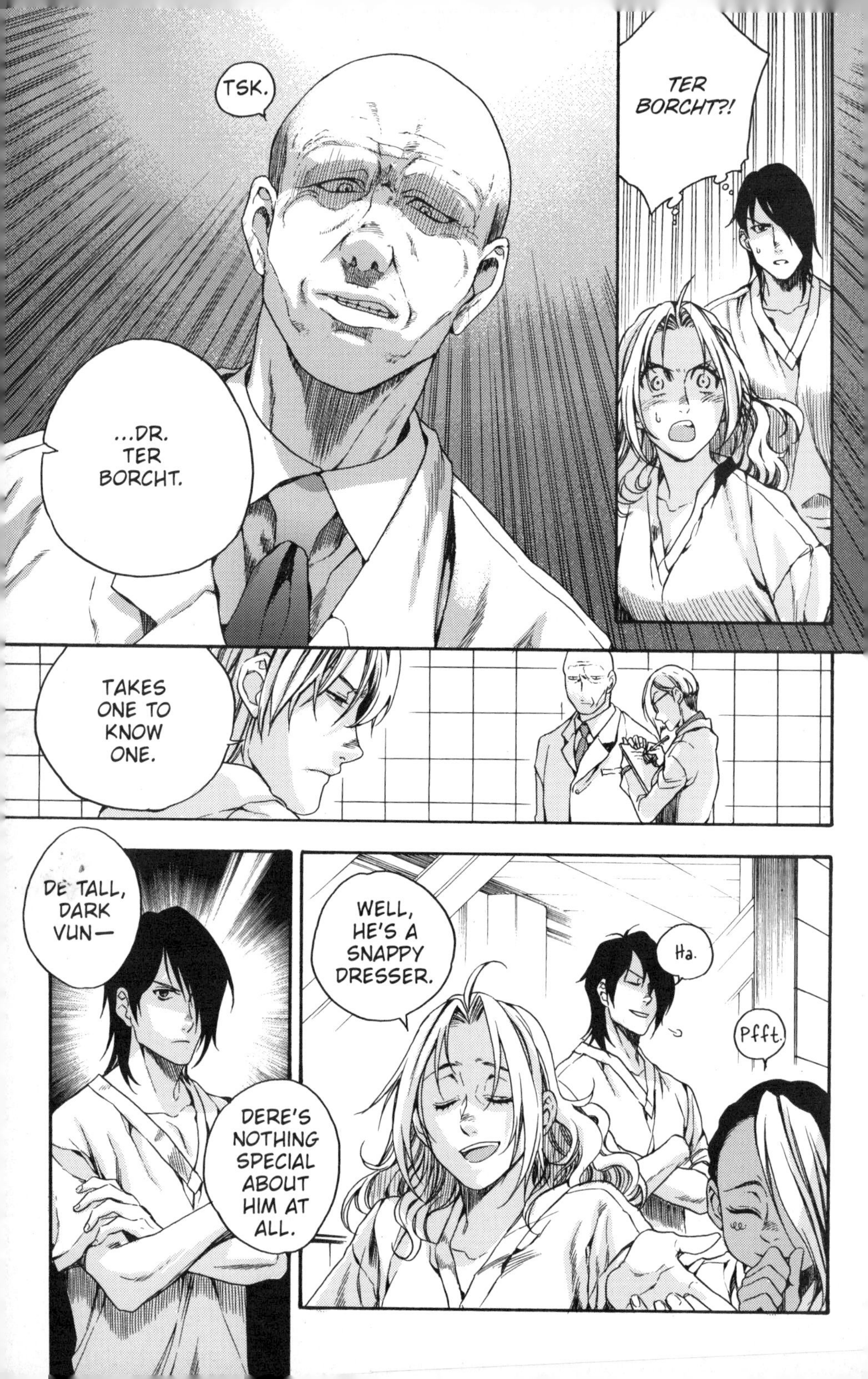
TSK.
...DR. TER BORCHT.
TER BORCHT?!
TAKES ONE TO KNOW ONE.
DE TALL, DARK VUN—
WELL, HE'S A SNAPPY DRESSER.
DERE'S NOTHING SPECIAL ABOUT HIM AT ALL.
Ha.
Pfft.

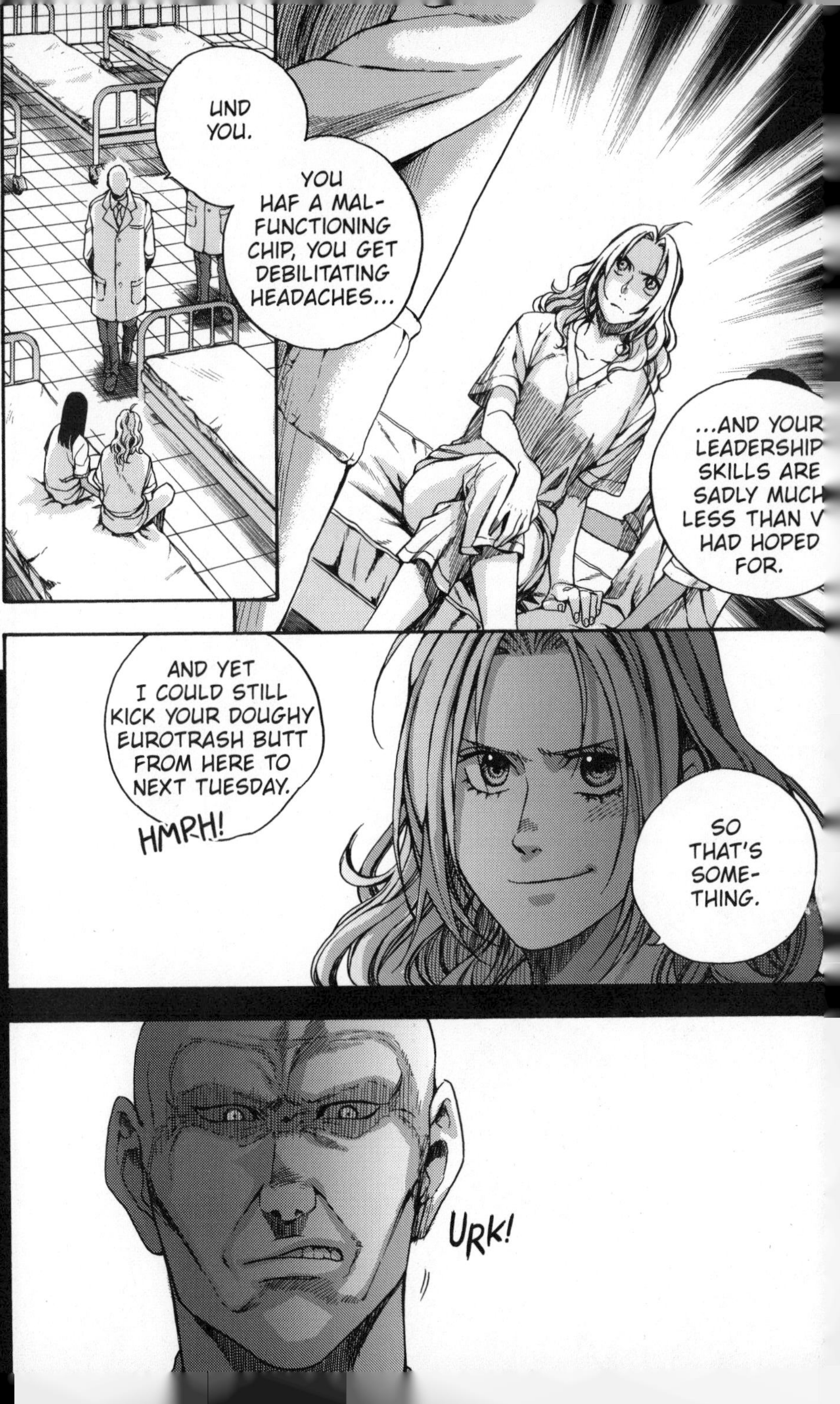
UND YOU.
YOU HAF A MAL-FUNCTIONING CHIP, YOU GET DEBILITATING HEADACHES...
...AND YOUR LEADERSHIP SKILLS ARE SADLY MUCH LESS THAN V HAD HOPED FOR.
AND YET I COULD STILL KICK YOUR DOUGHY EUROTRASH BUTT FROM HERE TO NEXT TUESDAY.
HMPH!
SO THAT'S SOME-THING.
URK!

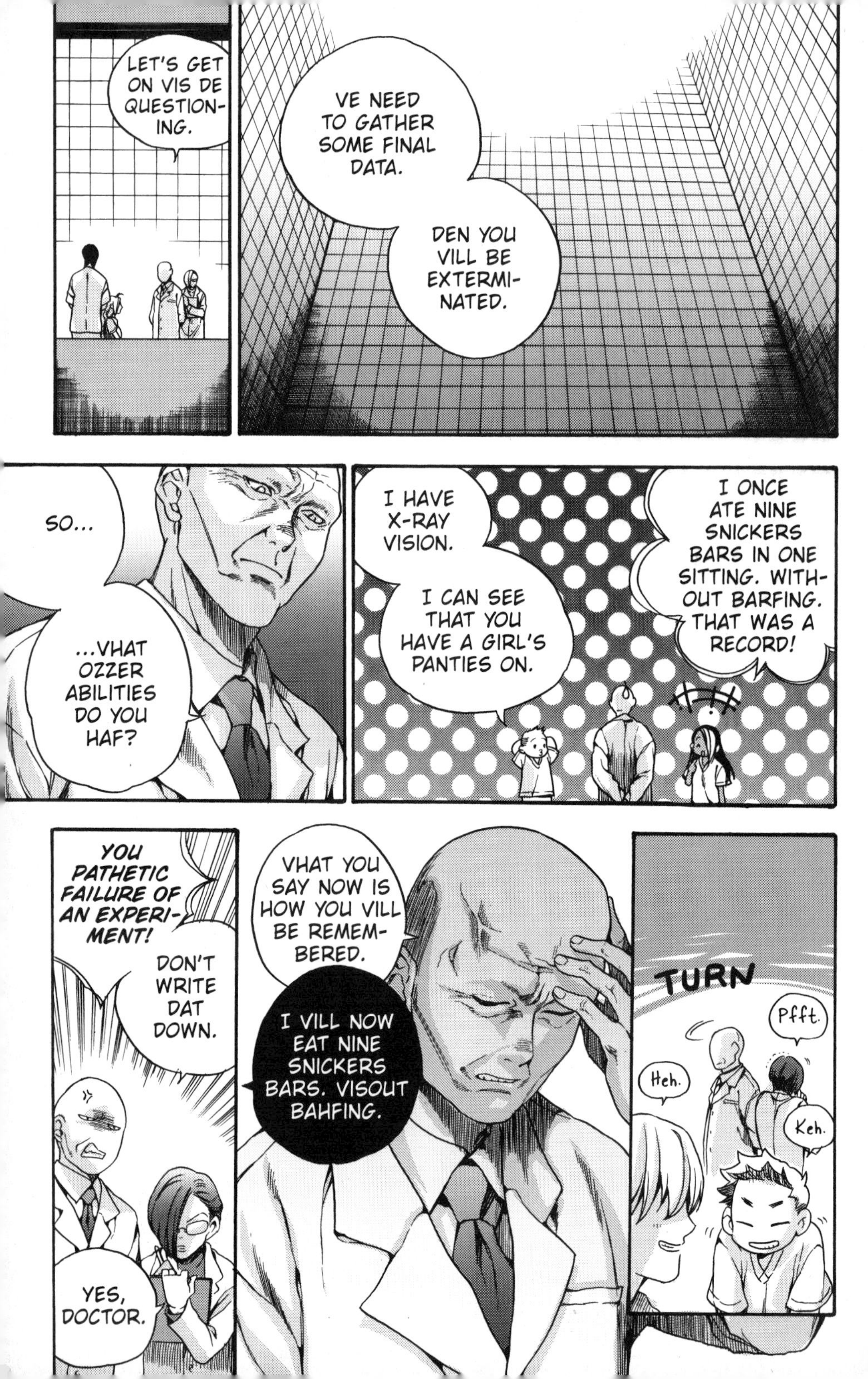
LET'S GET ON VIS DE QUESTIONING.
VE NEED TO GATHER SOME FINAL DATA.
DEN YOU VILL BE EXTERMINATED.
SO...
...VHAT OZZER ABILITIES DO YOU HAF?
I HAVE X-RAY VISION.
I CAN SEE THAT YOU HAVE A GIRL'S PANTIES ON.
I ONCE ATE NINE SNICKERS BARS IN ONE SITTING. WITHOUT BARFING. THAT WAS A RECORD!
YOU PATHETIC FAILURE OF AN EXPERIMENT!
DON'T WRITE DAT DOWN.
YES, DOCTOR.
VHAT YOU SAY NOW IS HOW YOU VILL BE REMEMBERED.
I VILL NOW EAT NINE SNICKERS BARS. VISOUT BAHFING.
TURN
Pfft.
Heh.
Keh.

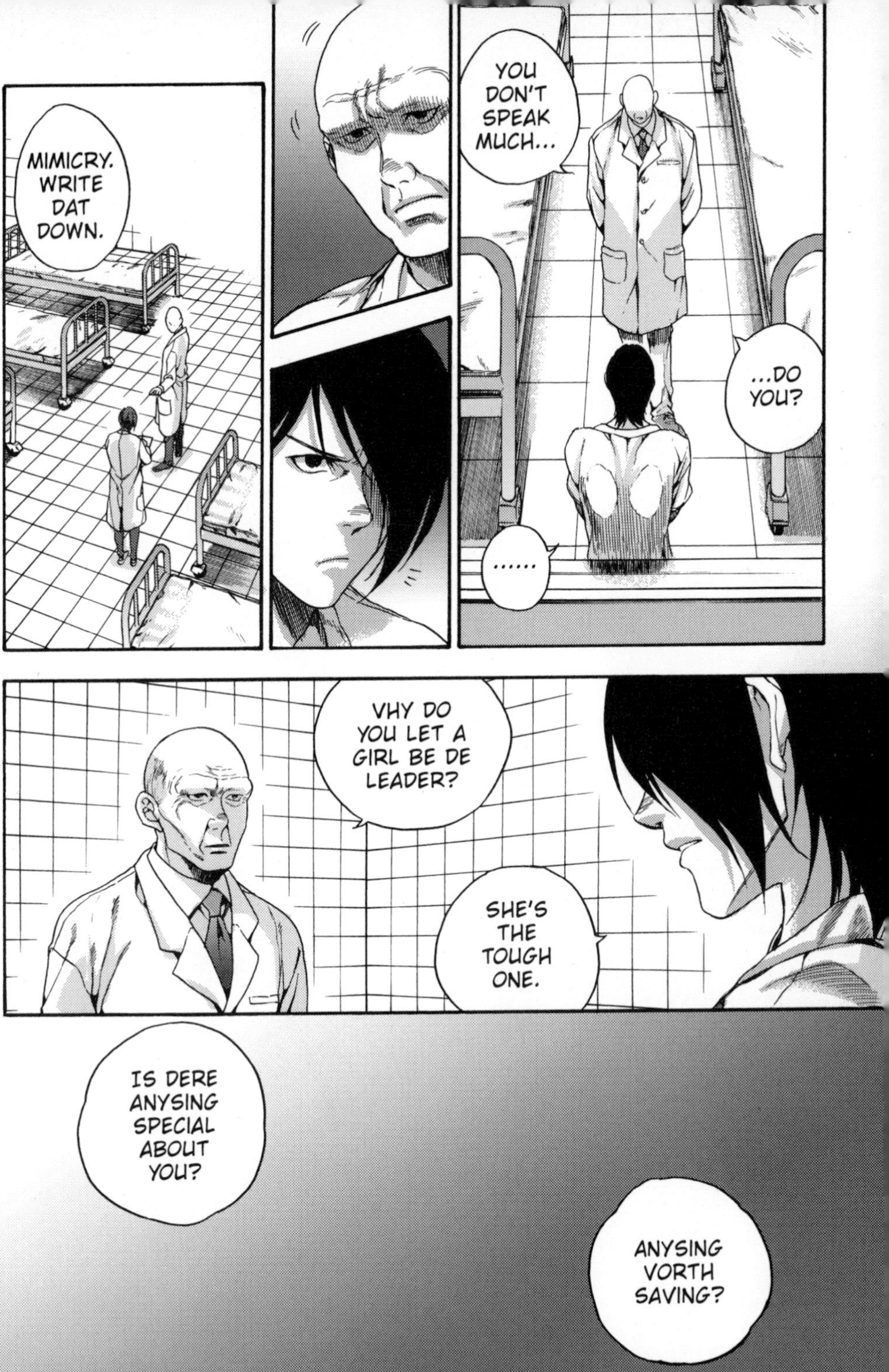
MIMICRY. WRITE DAT DOWN.
YOU DON'T SPEAK MUCH...
...DO YOU?
......
VHY DO YOU LET A GIRL BE DE LEADER?
SHE'S THE TOUGH ONE.
IS DERE ANYSING SPECIAL ABOUT YOU?
ANYSING VORTH SAVING?

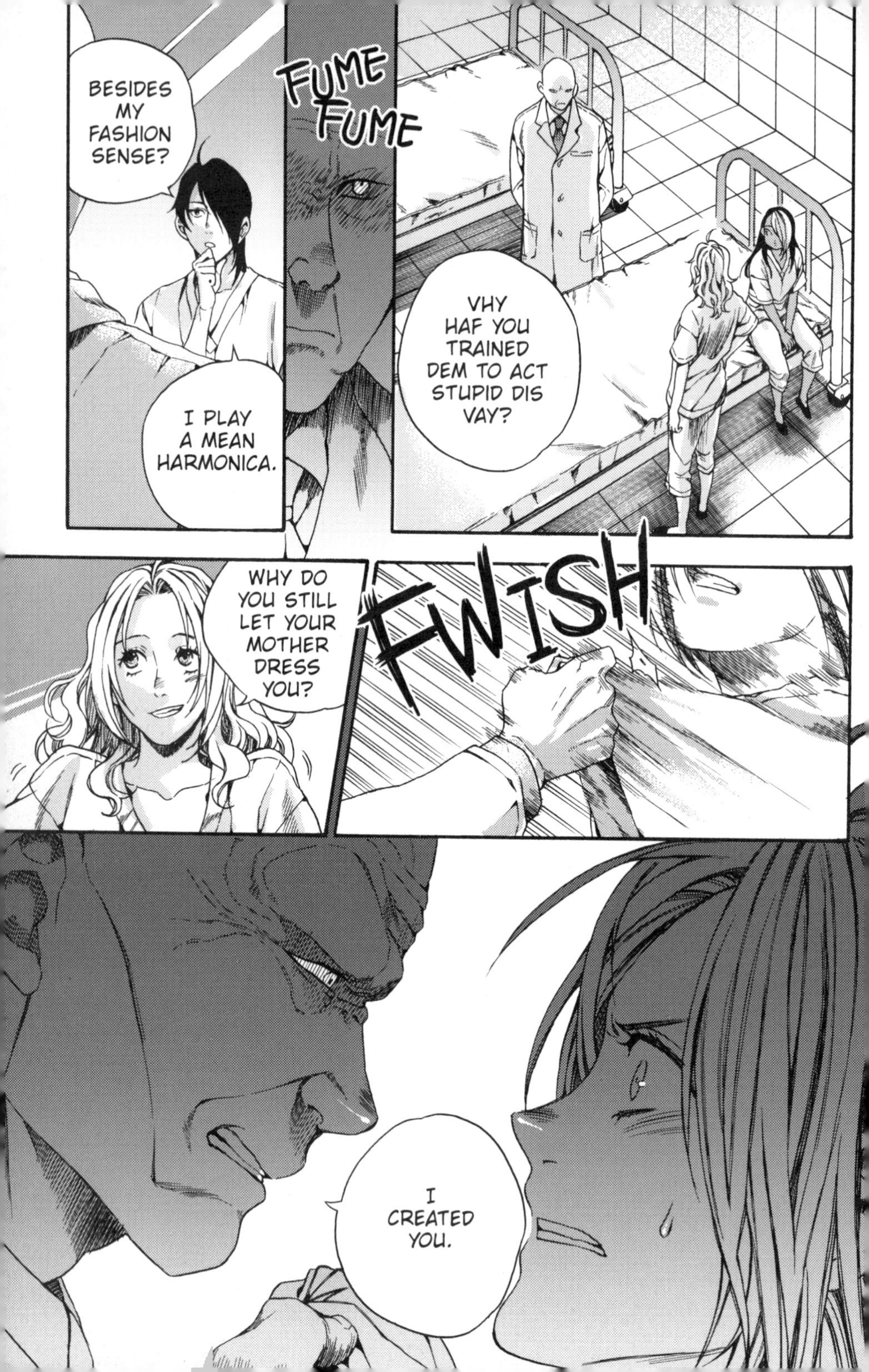
BESIDES MY FASHION SENSE?
I PLAY A MEAN HARMONICA.
FUME FUME
VHY HAF YOU TRAINED DEM TO ACT STUPID DIS VAY?
WHY DO YOU STILL LET YOUR MOTHER DRESS YOU?
FWISH
I CREATED YOU.

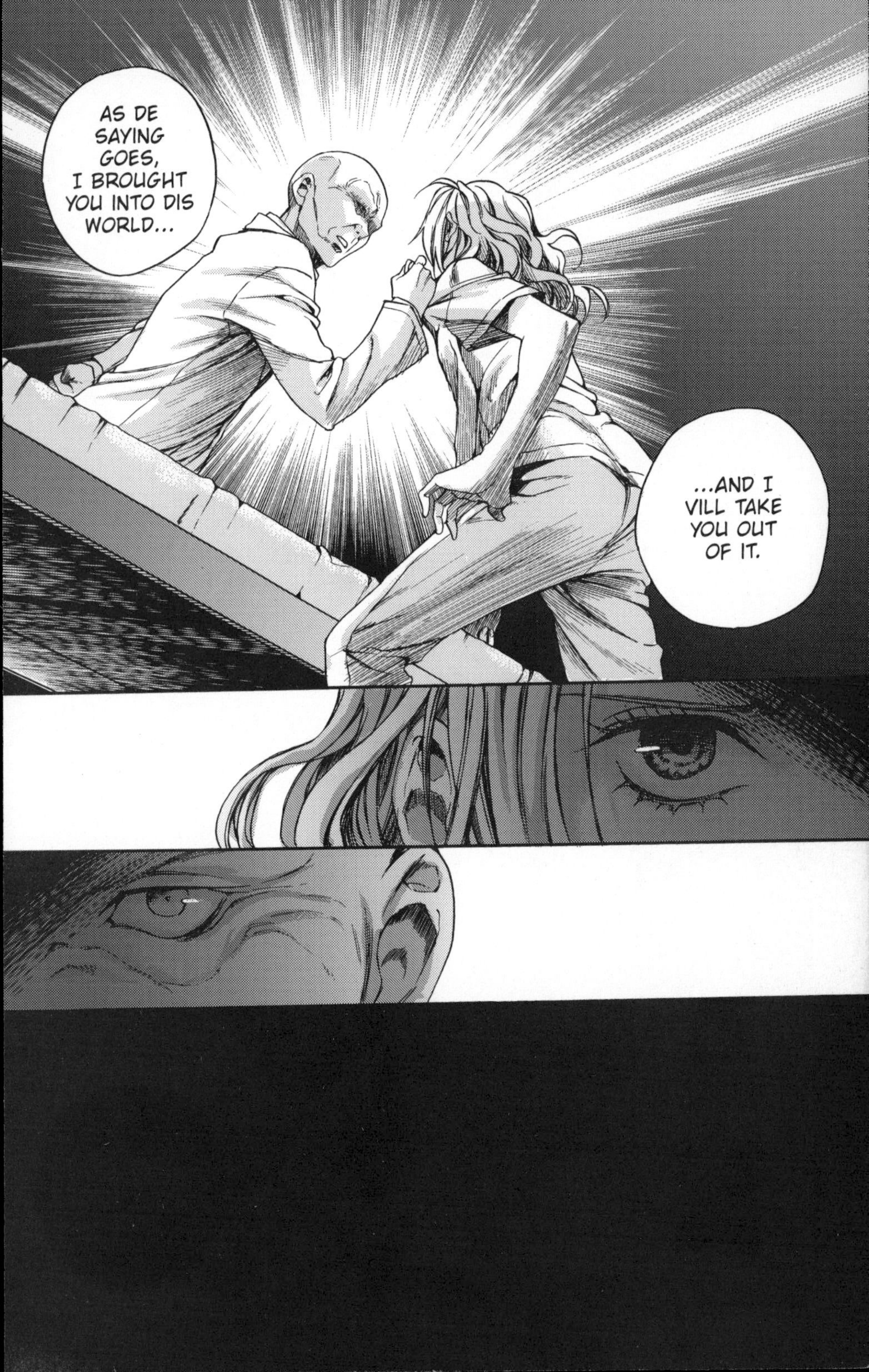
AS DE SAYING GOES, I BROUGHT YOU INTO DIS WORLD...
...AND I VILL TAKE YOU OUT OF IT.

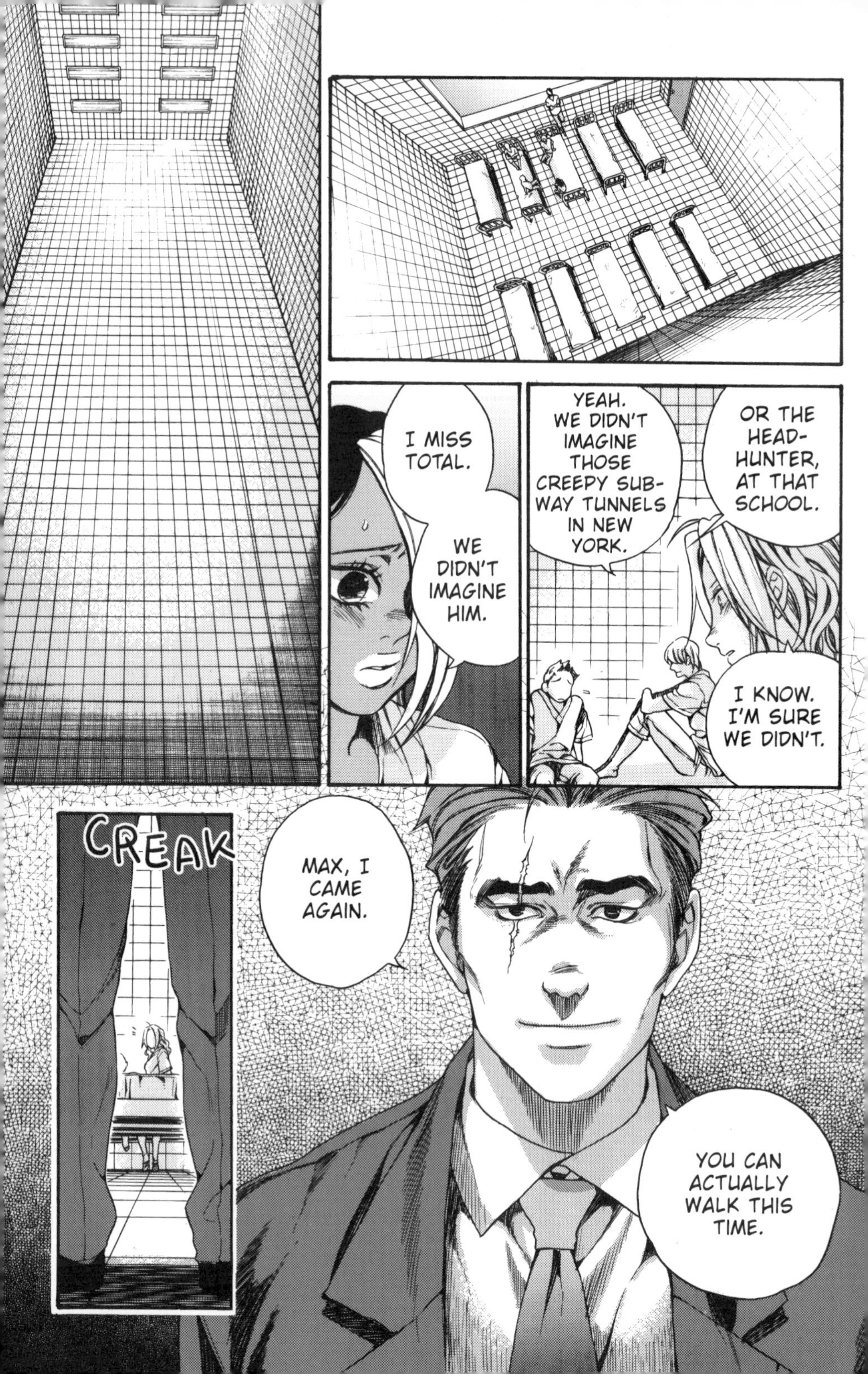
I MISS TOTAL.
WE DIDN'T IMAGINE HIM.
YEAH. WE DIDN'T IMAGINE THOSE CREEPY SUB-WAY TUNNELS IN NEW YORK.
OR THE HEAD-HUNTER, AT THAT SCHOOL.
I KNOW. I'M SURE WE DIDN'T.
CREAK
MAX, I CAME AGAIN.
YOU CAN ACTUALLY WALK THIS TIME.

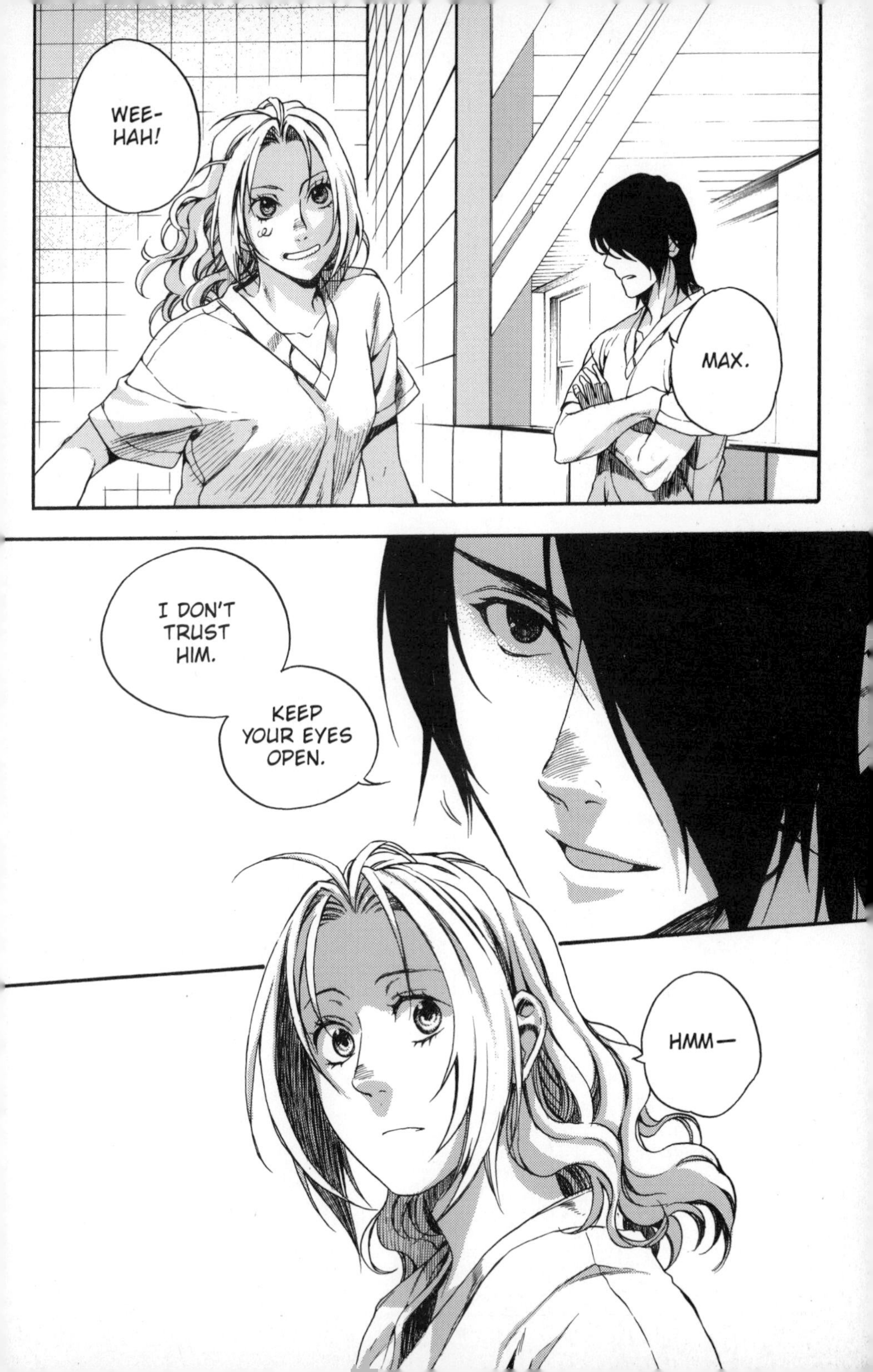
WEE-HAH!
MAX.
I DON'T TRUST HIM.
KEEP YOUR EYES OPEN.
HMM—

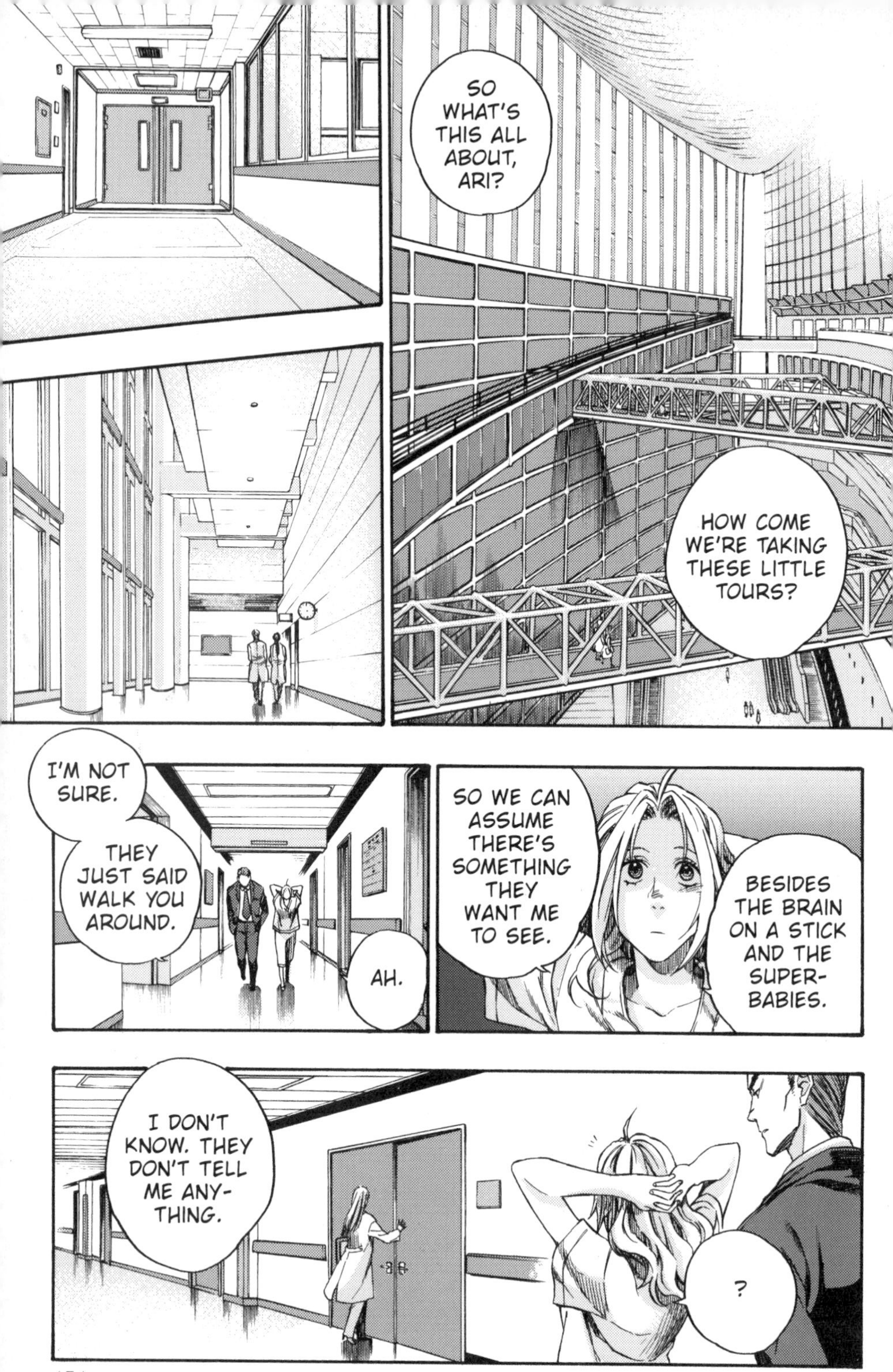
SO WHAT'S THIS ALL ABOUT, ARI?
HOW COME WE'RE TAKING THESE LITTLE TOURS?
I'M NOT SURE.
THEY JUST SAID WALK YOU AROUND.
AH.
SO WE CAN ASSUME THERE'S SOMETHING THEY WANT ME TO SEE.
BESIDES THE BRAIN ON A STICK AND THE SUPER-BABIES.
I DON'T KNOW. THEY DON'T TELL ME ANY-THING.
?

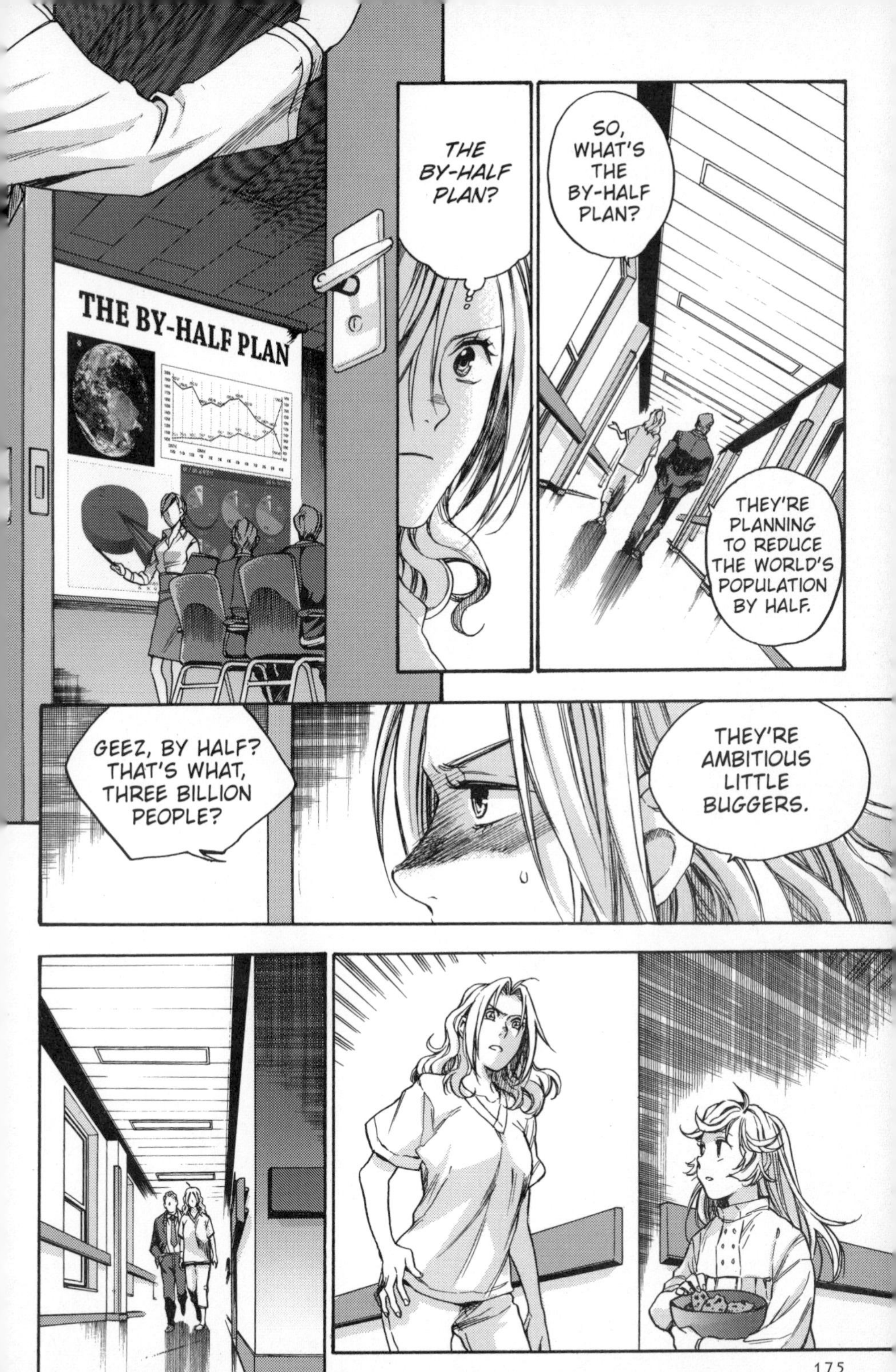
THE BY-HALF PLAN
SO, WHAT'S THE BY-HALF PLAN?
THE BY-HALF PLAN?
THEY'RE PLANNING TO REDUCE THE WORLD'S POPULATION BY HALF.
THEY'RE AMBITIOUS LITTLE BUGGERS.
GEEZ, BY HALF? THAT'S WHAT, THREE BILLION PEOPLE?

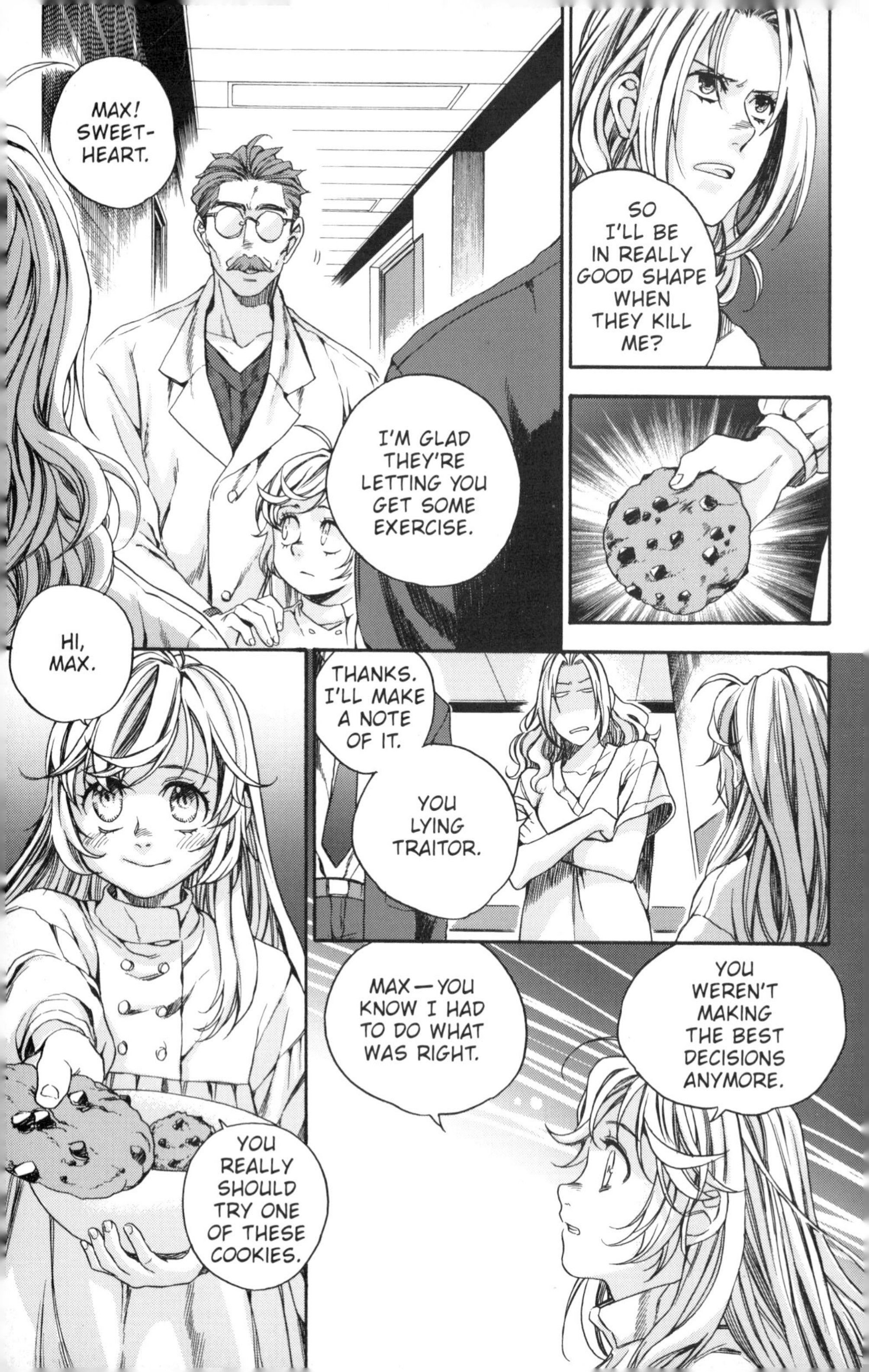
MAX! SWEET-HEART.
I'M GLAD THEY'RE LETTING YOU GET SOME EXERCISE.
SO I'LL BE IN REALLY GOOD SHAPE WHEN THEY KILL ME?
HI, MAX.
THANKS. I'LL MAKE A NOTE OF IT.
YOU LYING TRAITOR.
MAX—YOU KNOW I HAD TO DO WHAT WAS RIGHT.
YOU WEREN'T MAKING THE BEST DECISIONS ANYMORE.
YOU REALLY SHOULD TRY ONE OF THESE COOKIES.

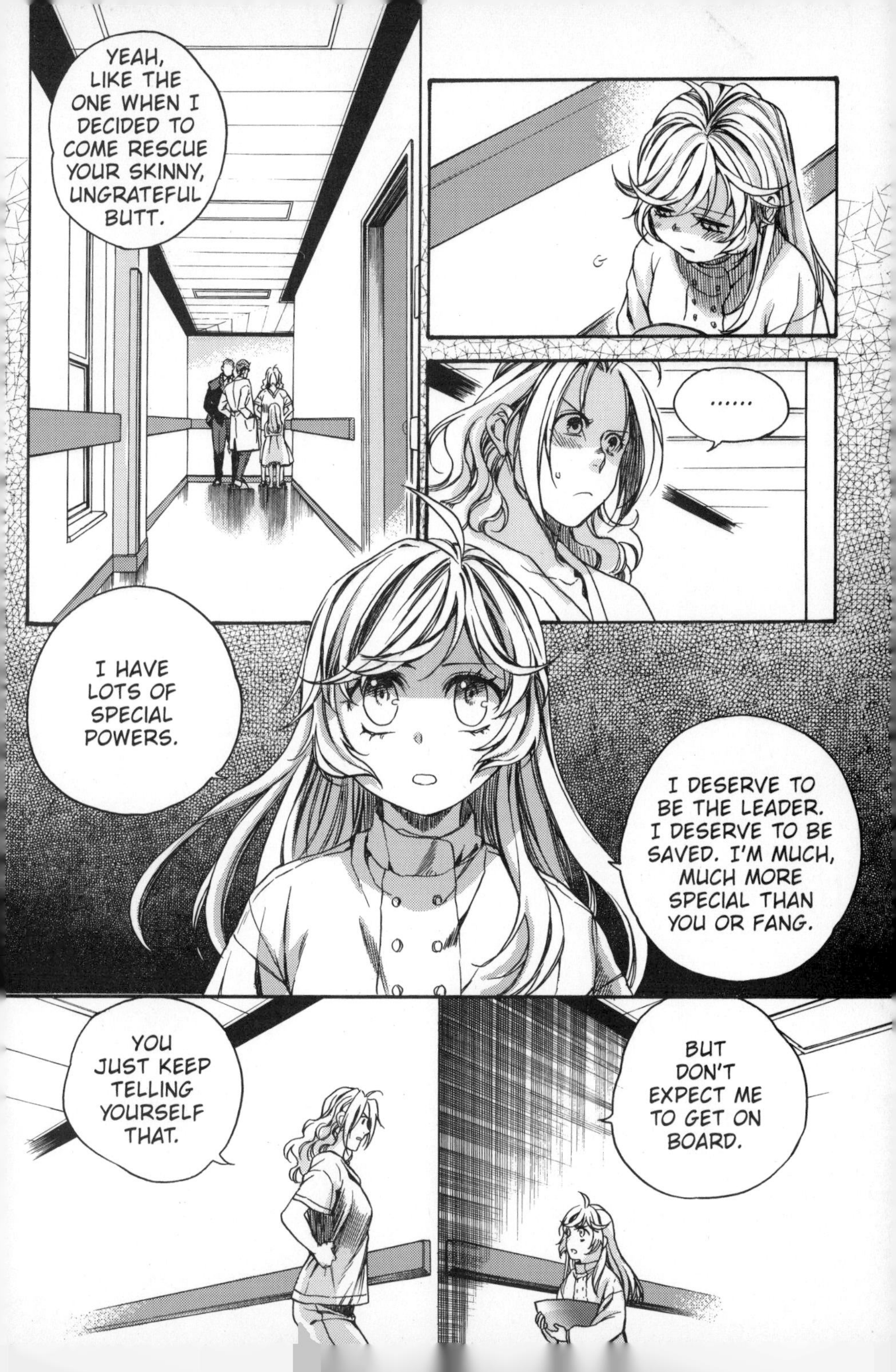
YEAH, LIKE THE ONE WHEN I DECIDED TO COME RESCUE YOUR SKINNY, UNGRATEFUL BUTT.
......
I HAVE LOTS OF SPECIAL POWERS.
I DESERVE TO BE THE LEADER. I DESERVE TO BE SAVED. I'M MUCH, MUCH MORE SPECIAL THAN YOU OR FANG.
YOU JUST KEEP TELLING YOURSELF THAT.
BUT DON'T EXPECT ME TO GET ON BOARD.

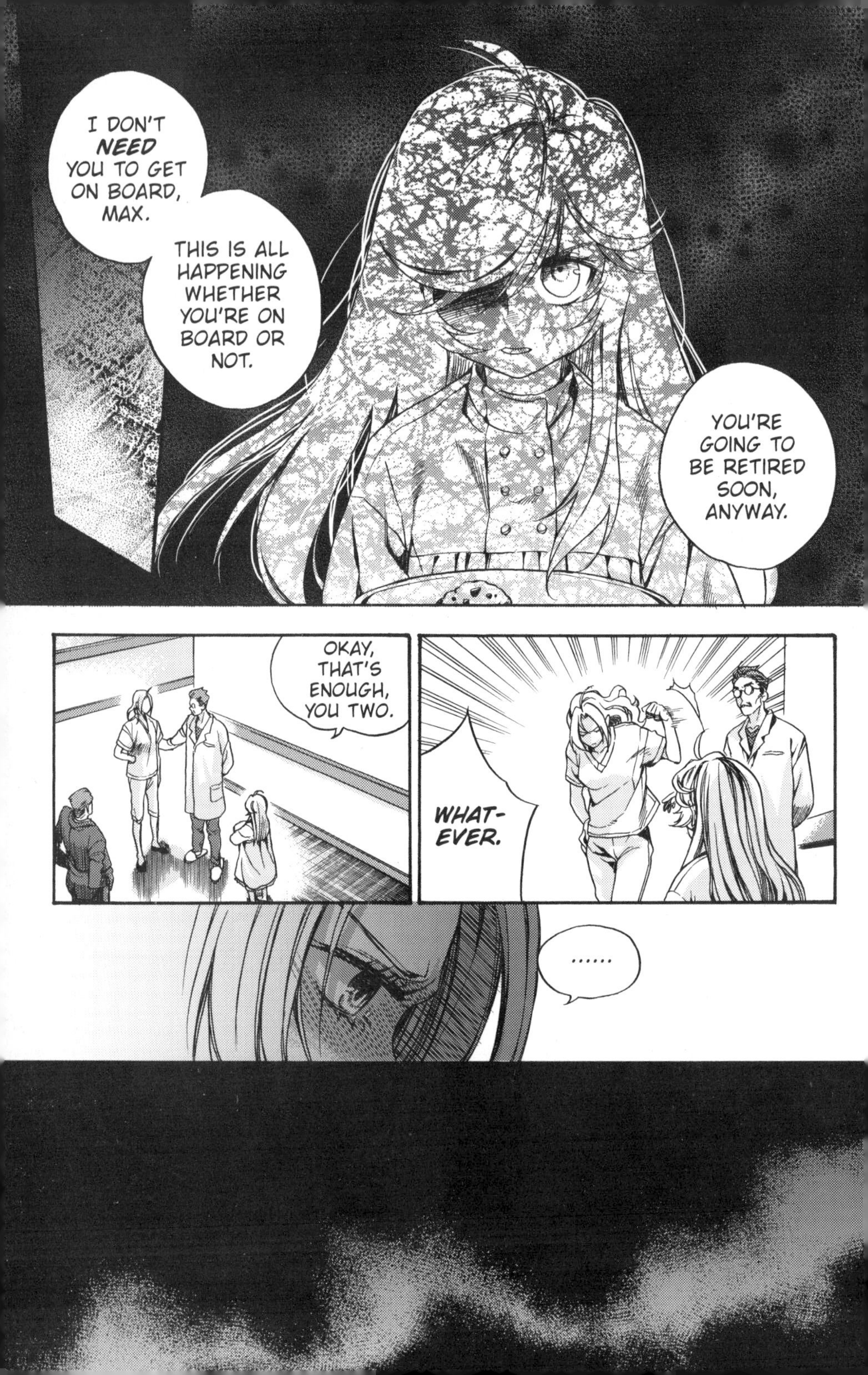
I DON'T NEED YOU TO GET ON BOARD, MAX.
THIS IS ALL HAPPENING WHETHER YOU'RE ON BOARD OR NOT.
YOU'RE GOING TO BE RETIRED SOON, ANYWAY.
OKAY, THAT'S ENOUGH, YOU TWO.
WHAT-EVER.
......

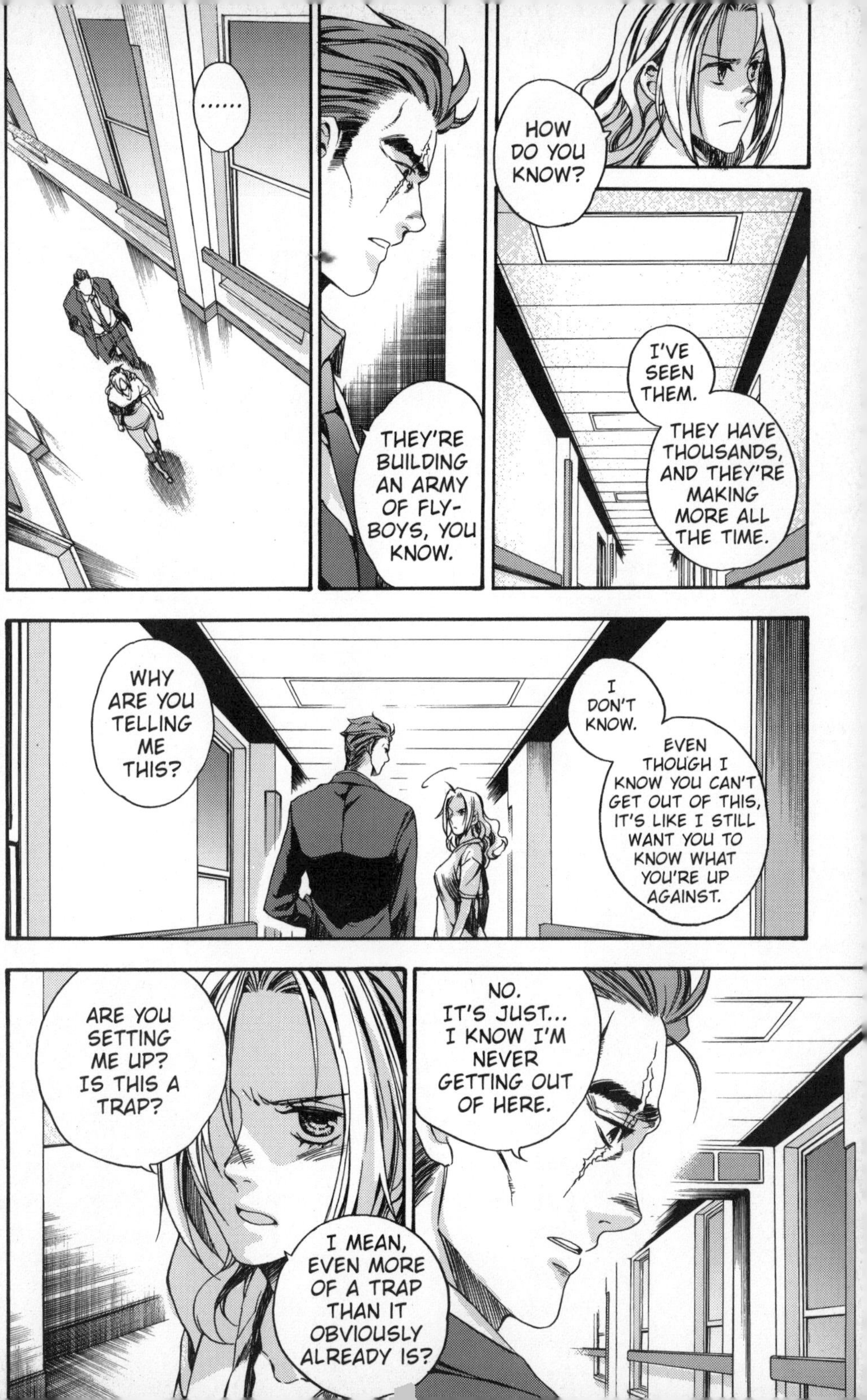

......
THEY'RE BUILDING AN ARMY OF FLY-BOYS, YOU KNOW.
HOW DO YOU KNOW?
I'VE SEEN THEM.
THEY HAVE THOUSANDS, AND THEY'RE MAKING MORE ALL THE TIME.
WHY ARE YOU TELLING ME THIS?
I DON'T KNOW.
EVEN THOUGH I KNOW YOU CAN'T GET OUT OF THIS, IT'S LIKE I STILL WANT YOU TO KNOW WHAT YOU'RE UP AGAINST.
ARE YOU SETTING ME UP? IS THIS A TRAP?
I MEAN, EVEN MORE OF A TRAP THAN IT OBVIOUSLY ALREADY IS?
NO. IT'S JUST... I KNOW I'M NEVER GETTING OUT OF HERE.

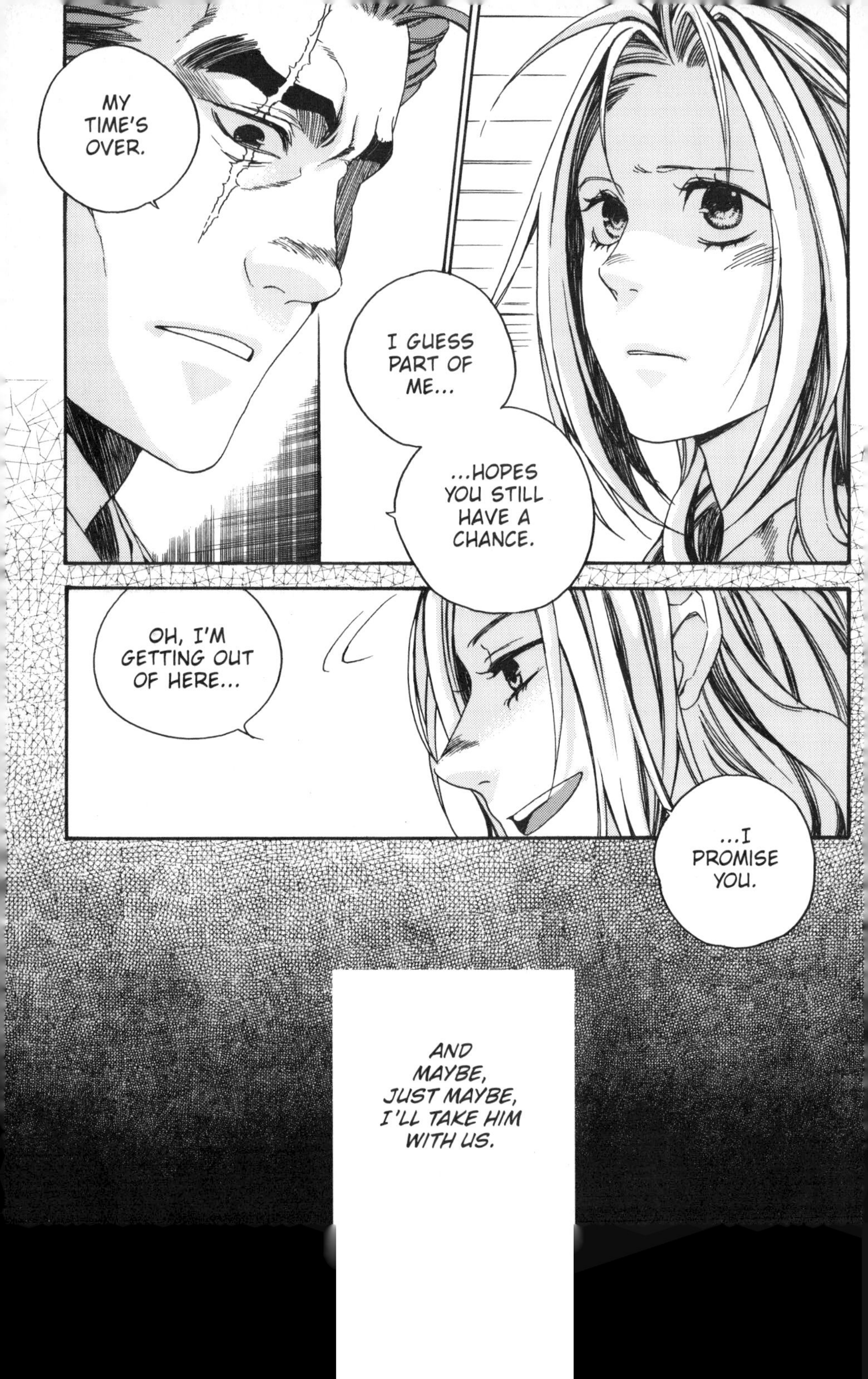
MY TIME'S OVER.
I GUESS PART OF ME...
...HOPES YOU STILL HAVE A CHANCE.
OH, I'M GETTING OUT OF HERE...
...I PROMISE YOU.
AND MAYBE, JUST MAYBE, I'LL TAKE HIM WITH US.

MAXIMUM RIDE

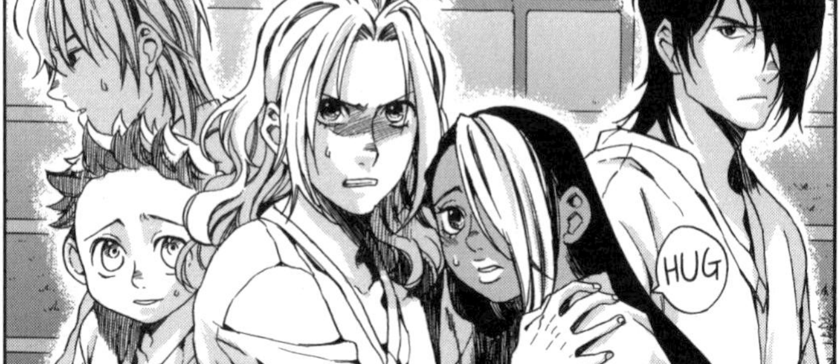
HUG

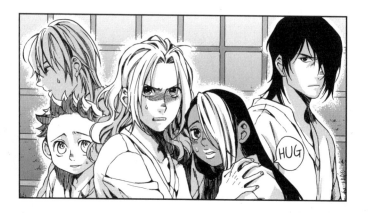

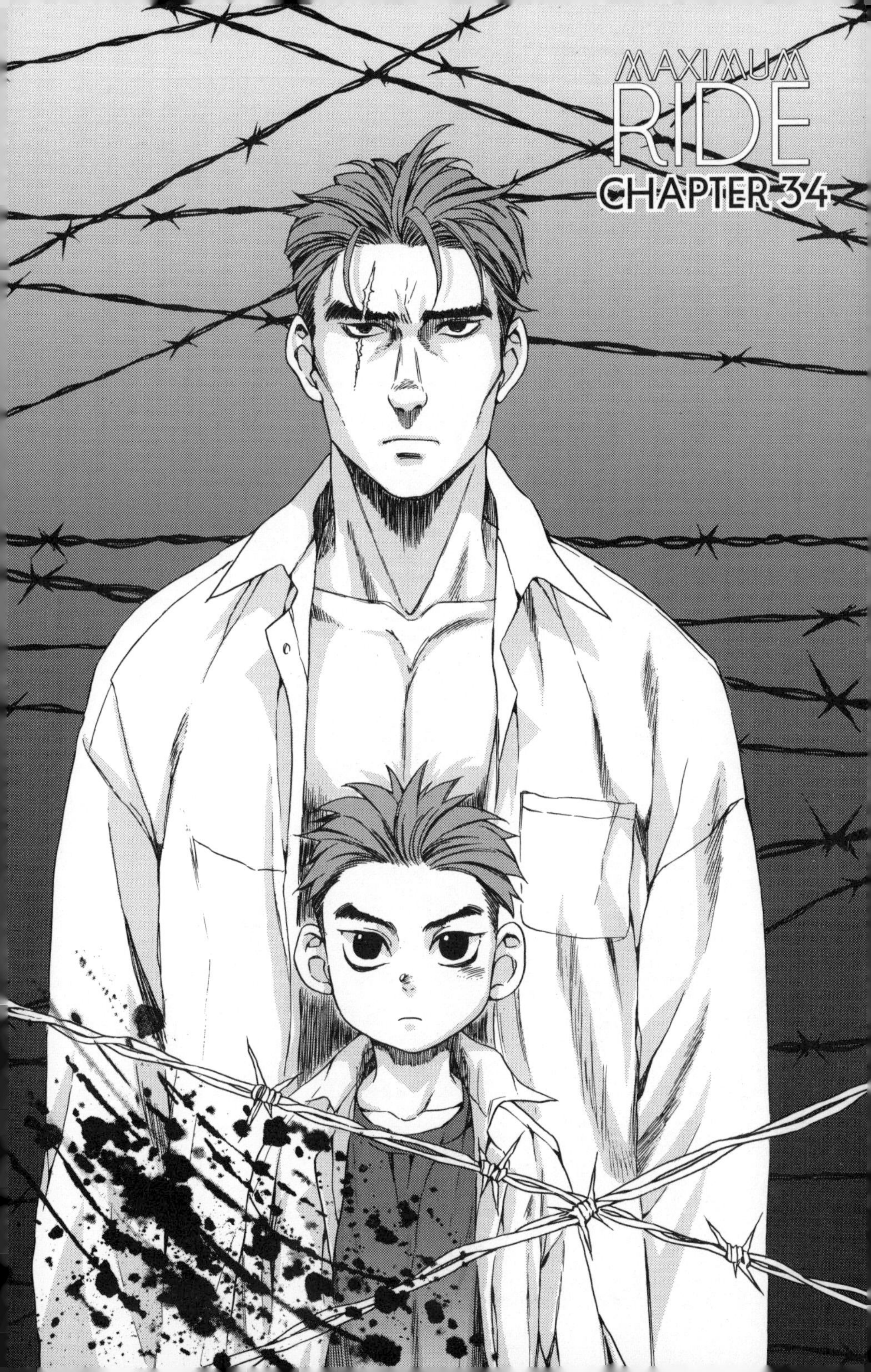
MAXIMUM
RIDE
CHAPTER 34

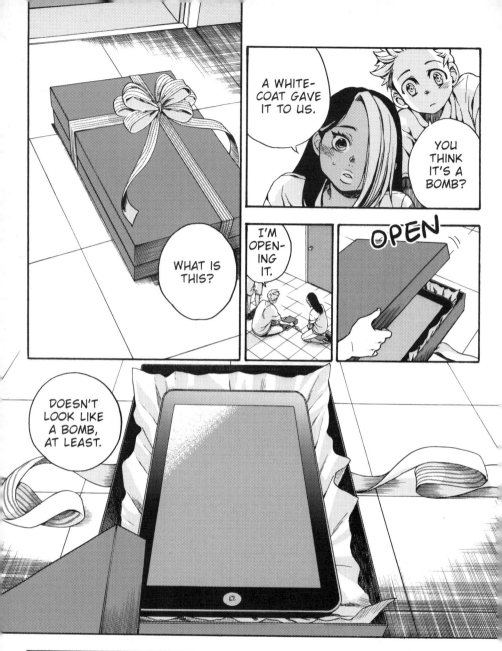

A WHITE-COAT GAVE IT TO US.

YOU THINK IT'S A BOMB?

WHAT IS THIS?

I'M OPENING IT.

OPEN

DOESN'T LOOK LIKE A BOMB, AT LEAST.

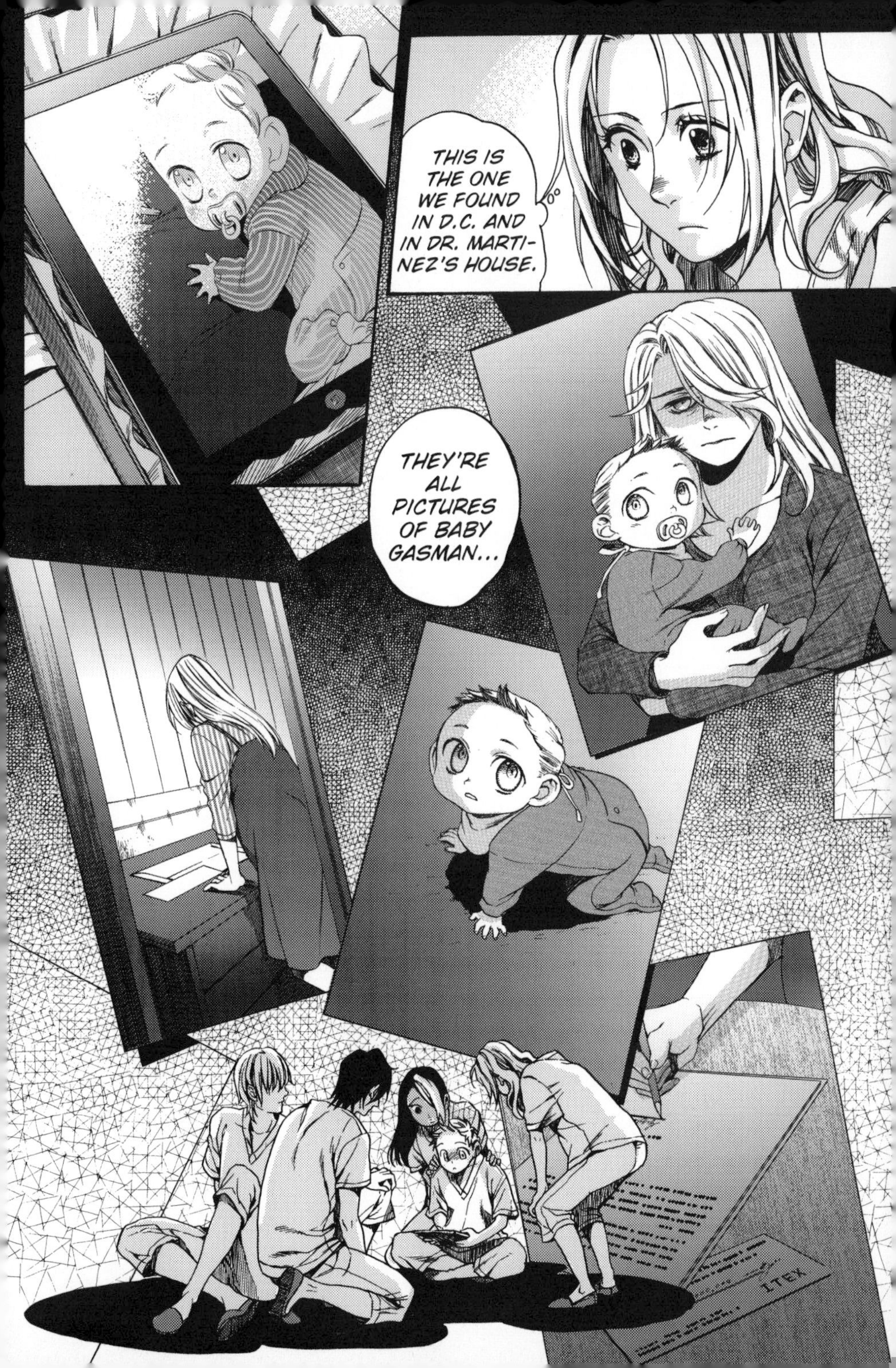
THIS IS THE ONE WE FOUND IN D.C. AND IN DR. MARTI-NEZ'S HOUSE.
THEY'RE ALL PICTURES OF BABY GASMAN...

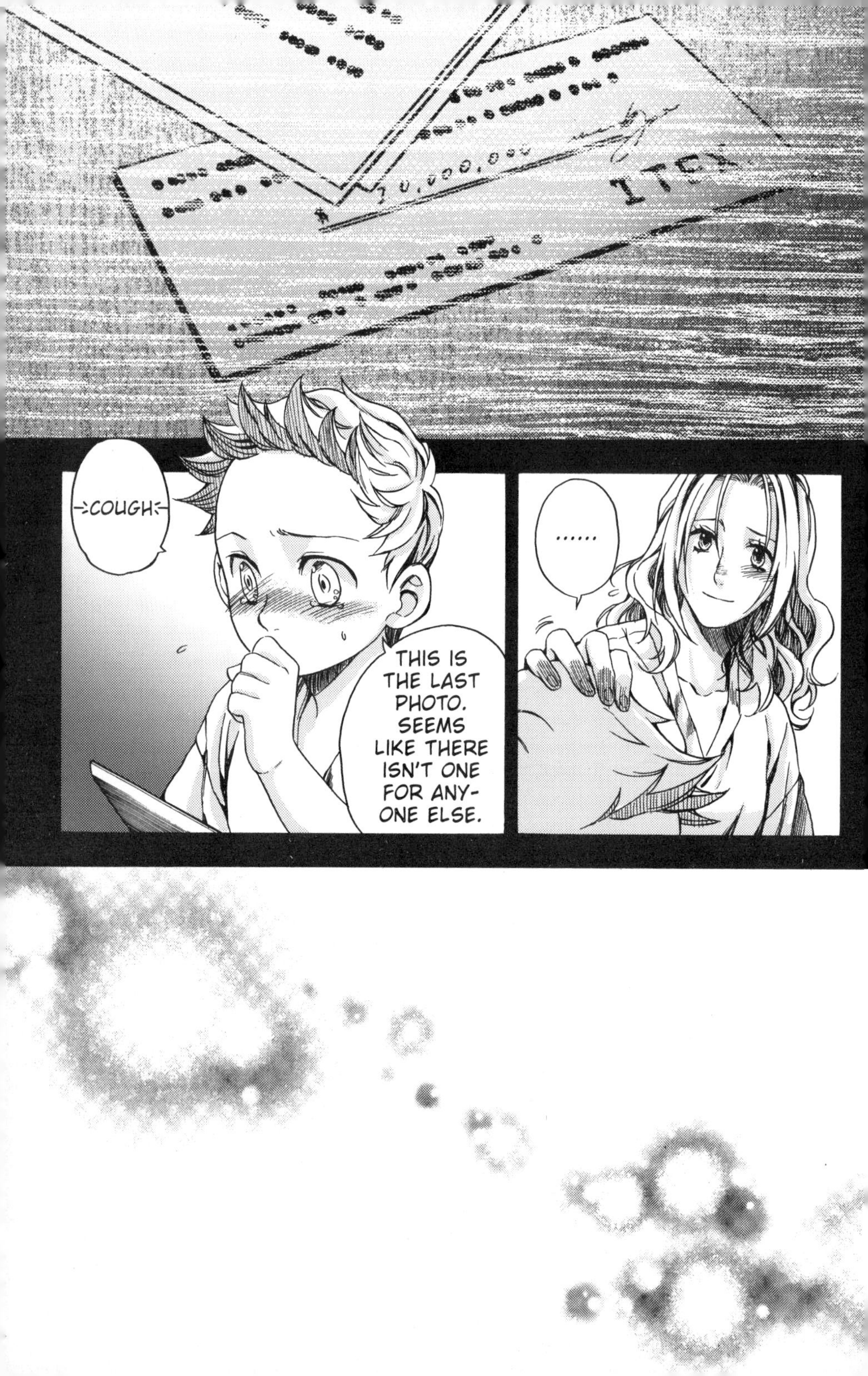

……
COUGH
THIS IS THE LAST PHOTO. SEEMS LIKE THERE ISN'T ONE FOR ANY-ONE ELSE.

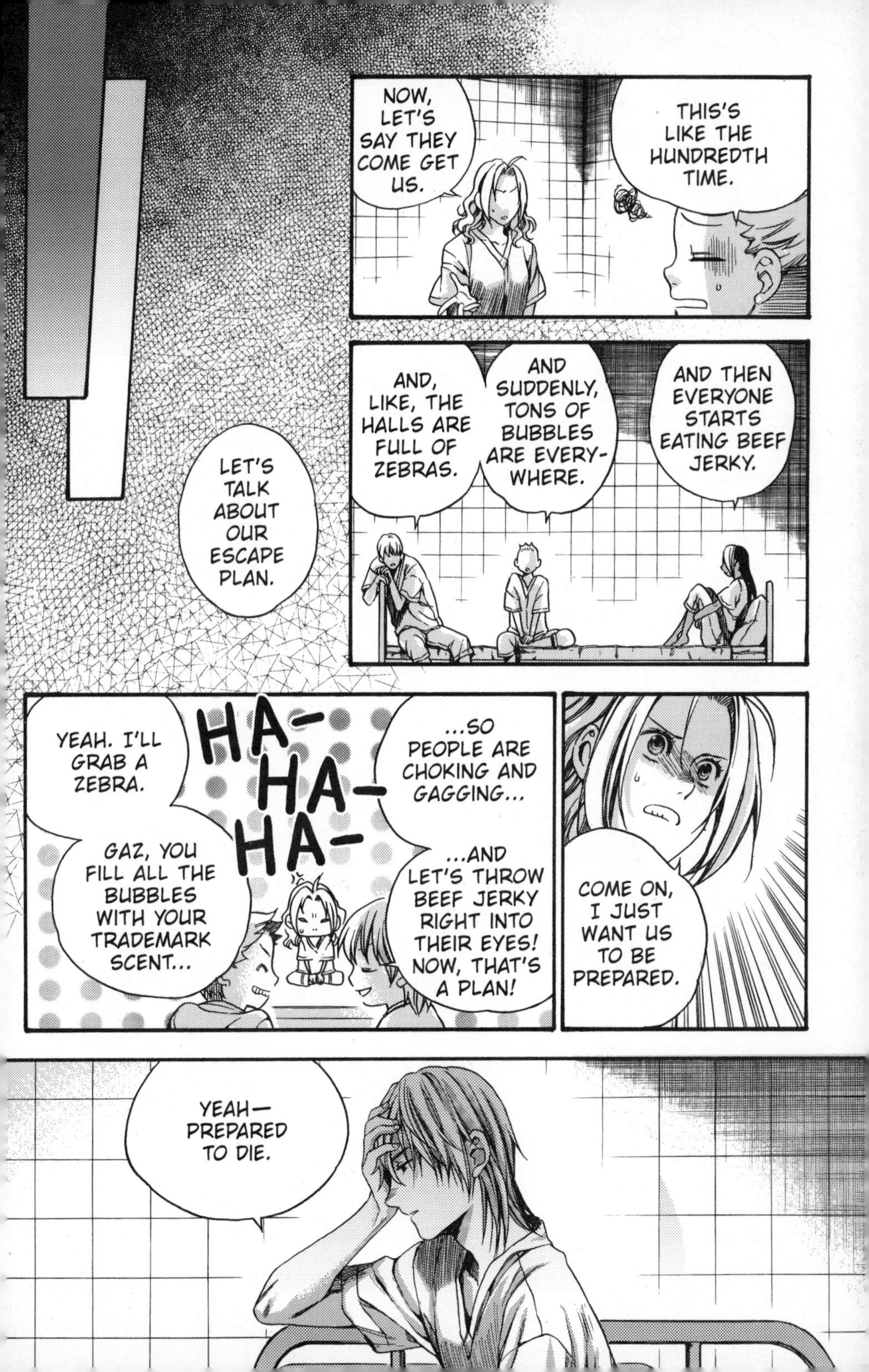
NOW, LET'S SAY THEY COME GET US.
THIS'S LIKE THE HUNDREDTH TIME.
LET'S TALK ABOUT OUR ESCAPE PLAN.
AND, LIKE, THE HALLS ARE FULL OF ZEBRAS.
AND SUDDENLY, TONS OF BUBBLES ARE EVERY-WHERE.
AND THEN EVERYONE STARTS EATING BEEF JERKY.
YEAH. I'LL GRAB A ZEBRA.
GAZ, YOU FILL ALL THE BUBBLES WITH YOUR TRADEMARK SCENT...
HA-HA-HA-
...SO PEOPLE ARE CHOKING AND GAGGING...
...AND LET'S THROW BEEF JERKY RIGHT INTO THEIR EYES! NOW, THAT'S A PLAN!
COME ON, I JUST WANT US TO BE PREPARED.
YEAH— PREPARED TO DIE.

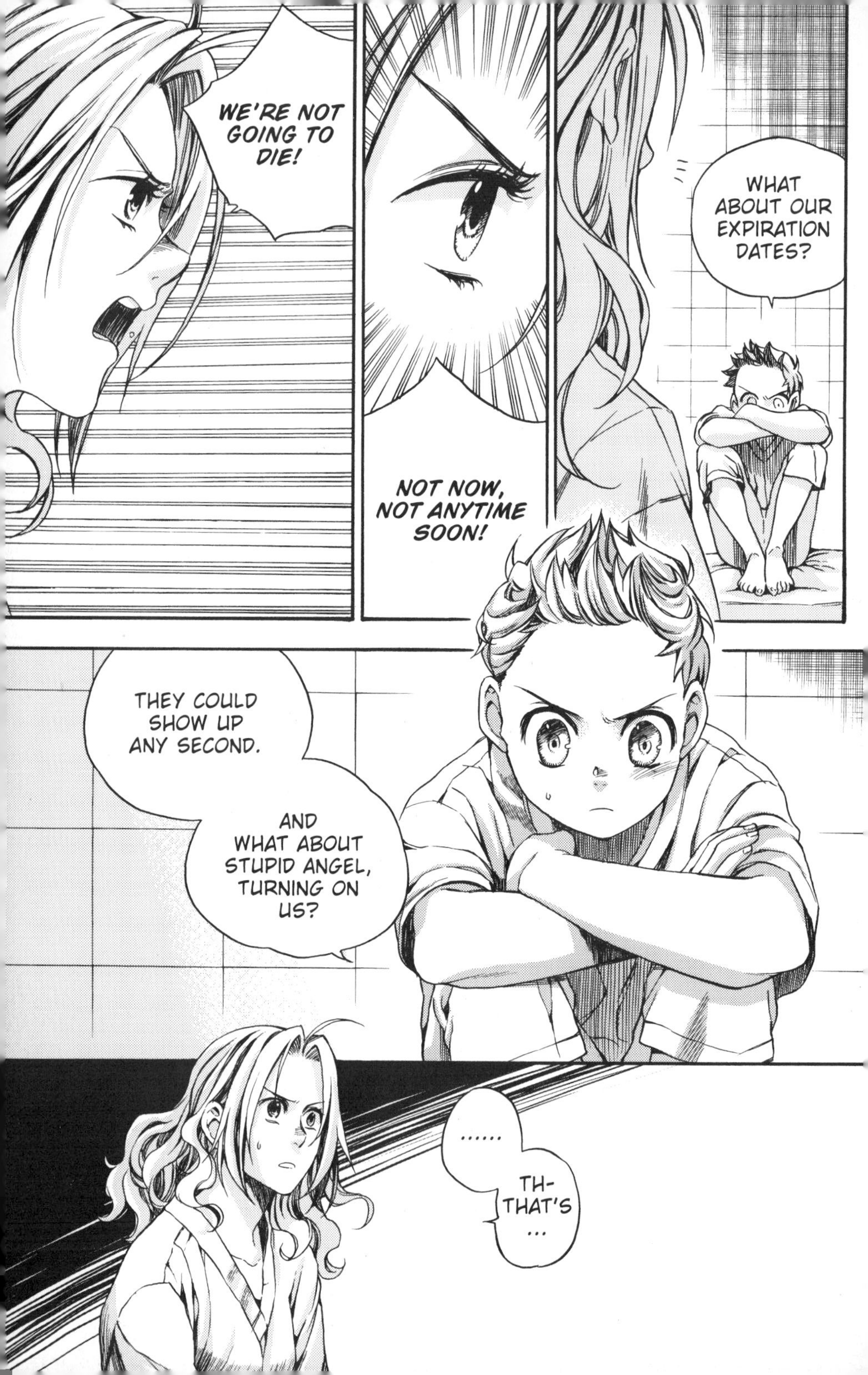
WE'RE NOT GOING TO DIE!
NOT NOW, NOT ANYTIME SOON!
WHAT ABOUT OUR EXPIRATION DATES?
THEY COULD SHOW UP ANY SECOND.
AND WHAT ABOUT STUPID ANGEL, TURNING ON US?
......
TH- THAT'S ...

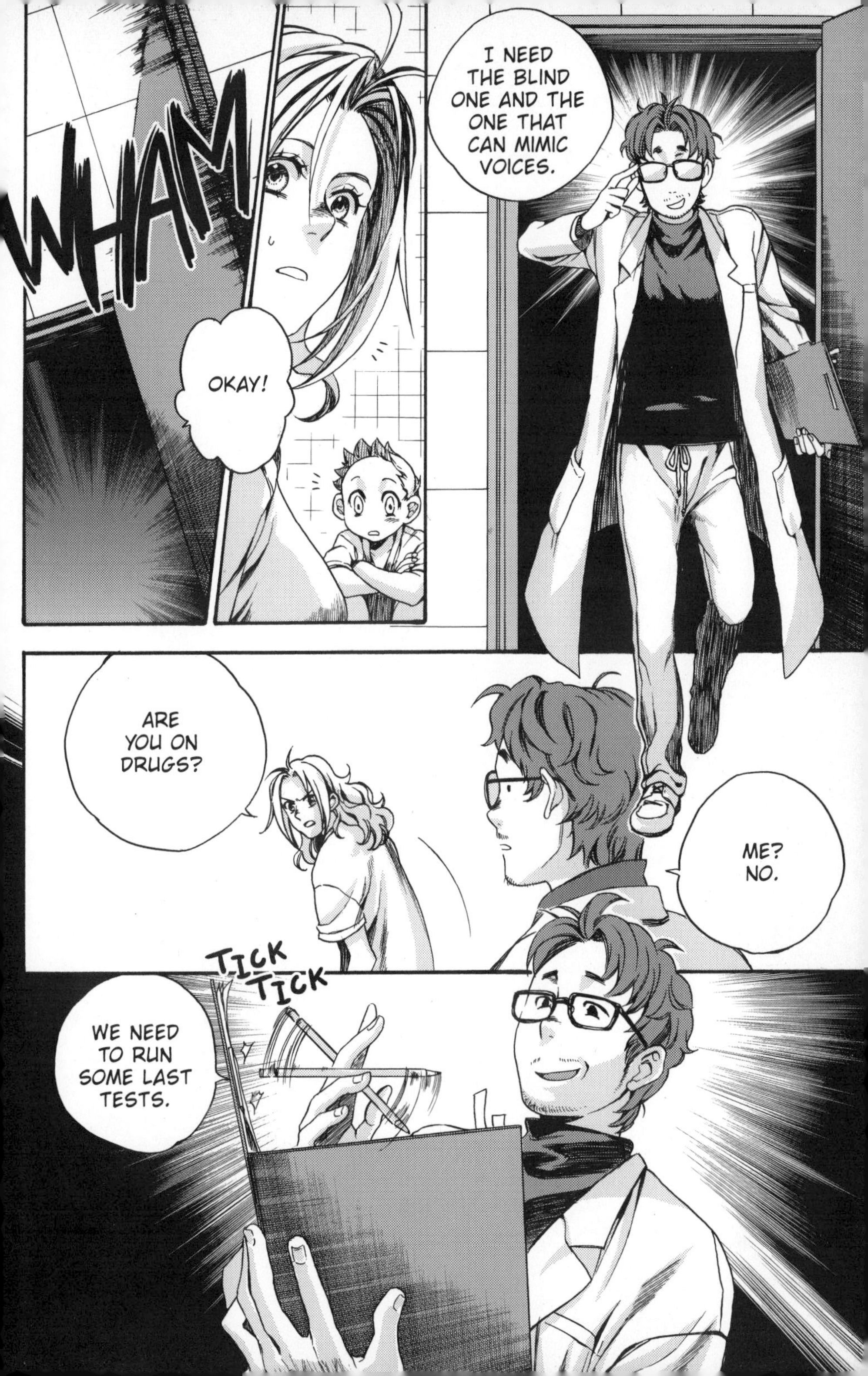
WHAM
OKAY!
I NEED THE BLIND ONE AND THE ONE THAT CAN MIMIC VOICES.
ARE YOU ON DRUGS?
ME? NO.
TICK TICK
WE NEED TO RUN SOME LAST TESTS.

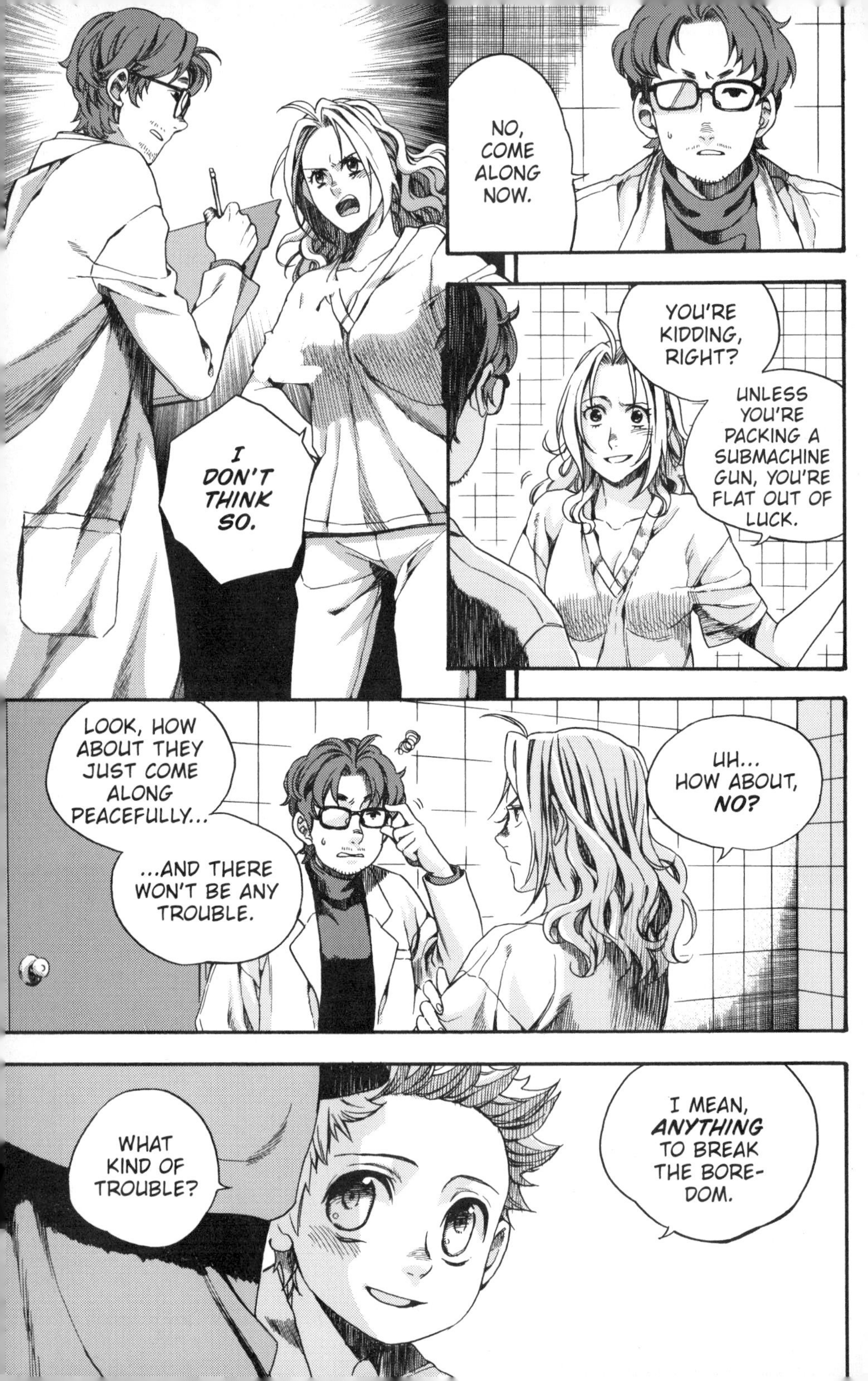
I DON'T THINK SO.
NO, COME ALONG NOW.
YOU'RE KIDDING, RIGHT?
UNLESS YOU'RE PACKING A SUBMACHINE GUN, YOU'RE FLAT OUT OF LUCK.
LOOK, HOW ABOUT THEY JUST COME ALONG PEACEFULLY...
...AND THERE WON'T BE ANY TROUBLE.
UH... HOW ABOUT, NO?
WHAT KIND OF TROUBLE?
I MEAN, ANYTHING TO BREAK THE BORE-DOM.

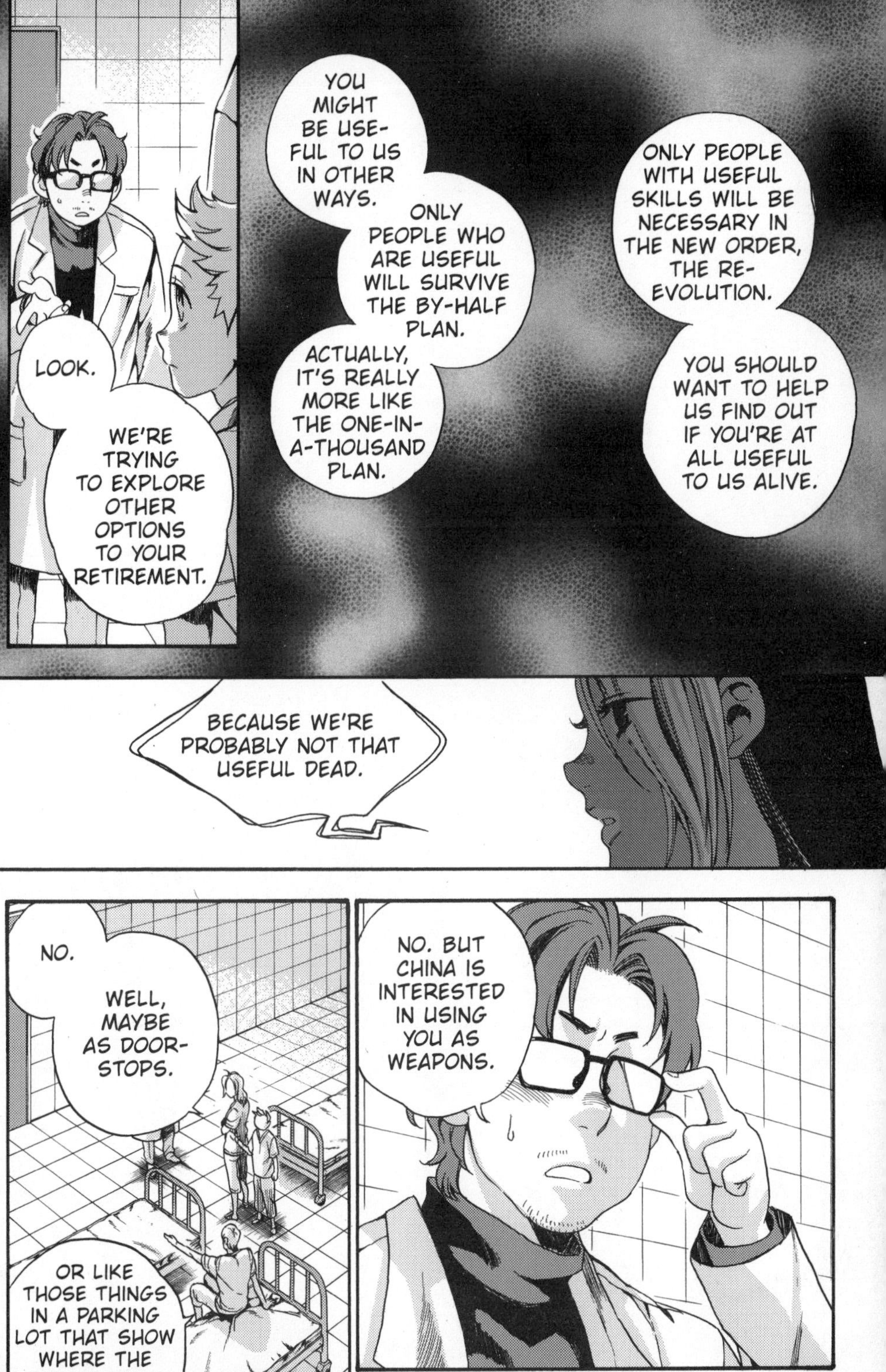
LOOK.
WE'RE TRYING TO EXPLORE OTHER OPTIONS TO YOUR RETIREMENT.
YOU MIGHT BE USEFUL TO US IN OTHER WAYS.
ONLY PEOPLE WHO ARE USEFUL WILL SURVIVE THE BY-HALF PLAN.
ACTUALLY, IT'S REALLY MORE LIKE THE ONE-IN-A-THOUSAND PLAN.
ONLY PEOPLE WITH USEFUL SKILLS WILL BE NECESSARY IN THE NEW ORDER, THE RE-EVOLUTION.
YOU SHOULD WANT TO HELP US FIND OUT IF YOU'RE AT ALL USEFUL TO US ALIVE.
BECAUSE WE'RE PROBABLY NOT THAT USEFUL DEAD.
NO.
WELL, MAYBE AS DOORSTOPS.
OR LIKE THOSE THINGS IN A PARKING LOT THAT SHOW WHERE THE CARS SHOULD STOP.
NO. BUT CHINA IS INTERESTED IN USING YOU AS WEAPONS.

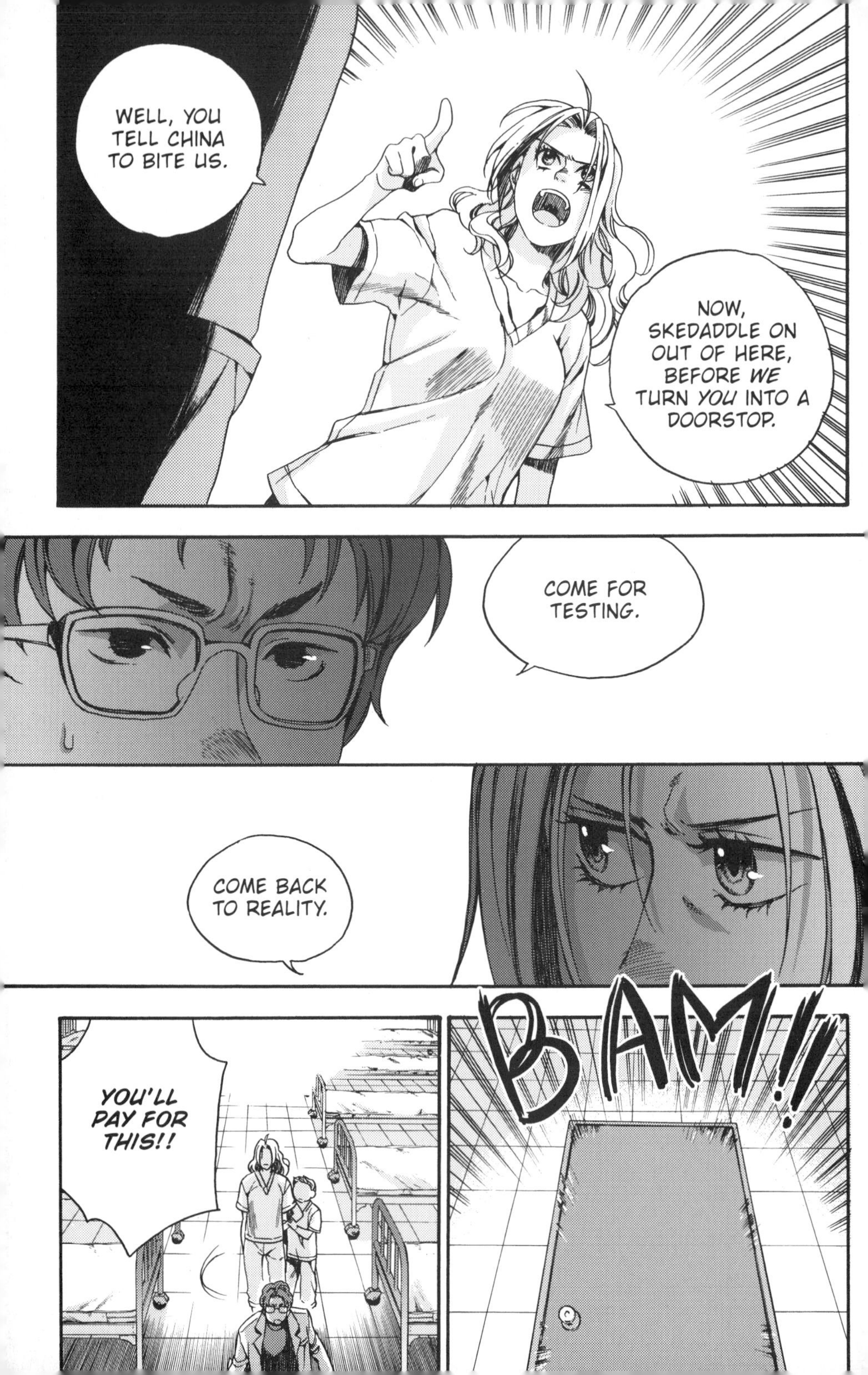
WELL, YOU TELL CHINA TO BITE US.
NOW, SKEDADDLE ON OUT OF HERE, BEFORE *WE* TURN *YOU* INTO A DOORSTOP.
COME FOR TESTING.
COME BACK TO REALITY.
BAM!!
YOU'LL PAY FOR THIS!!

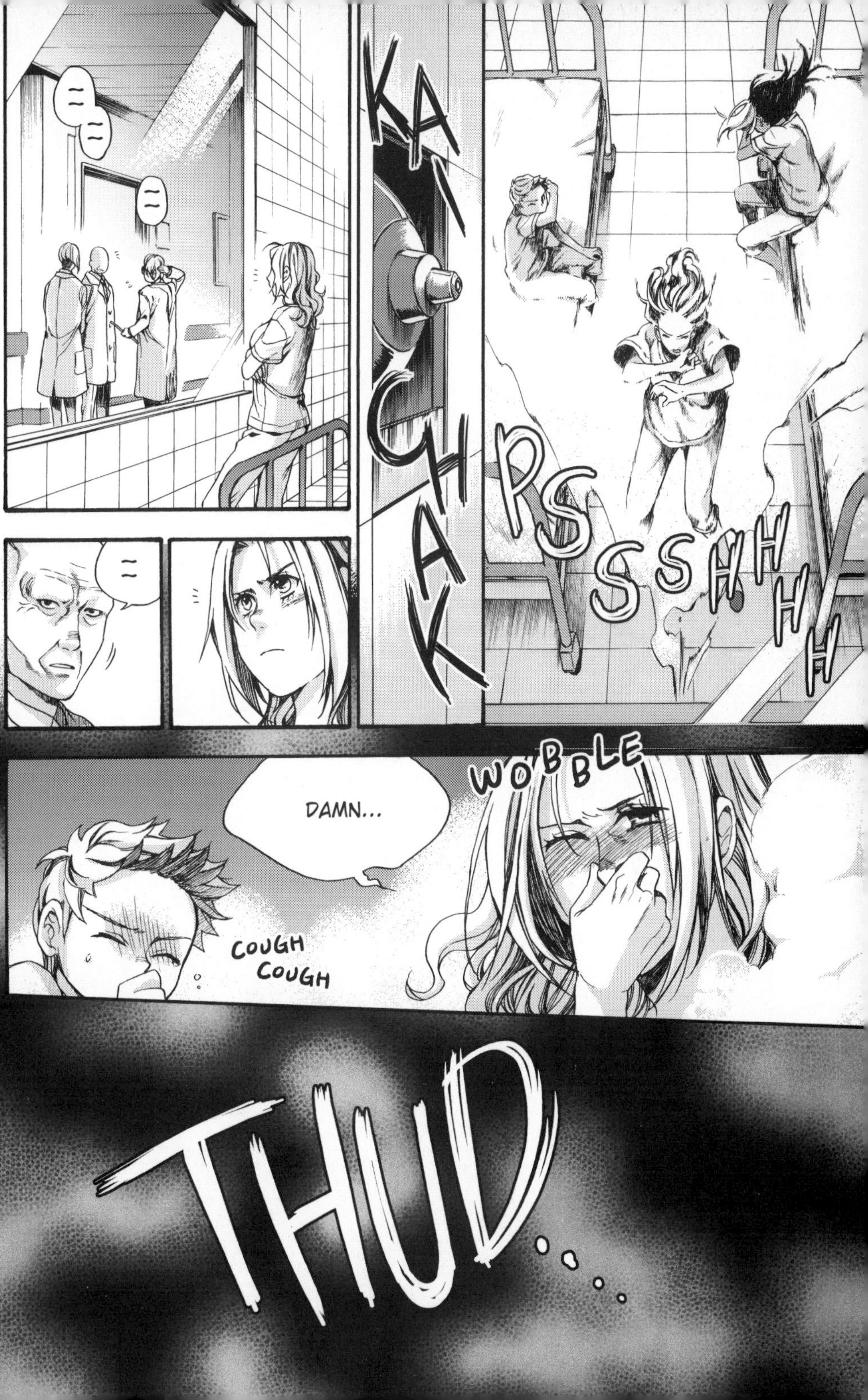
KA CHA CHAK
PSSSSHHHHH
DAMN...
WOBBLE
COUGH COUGH
THUD...

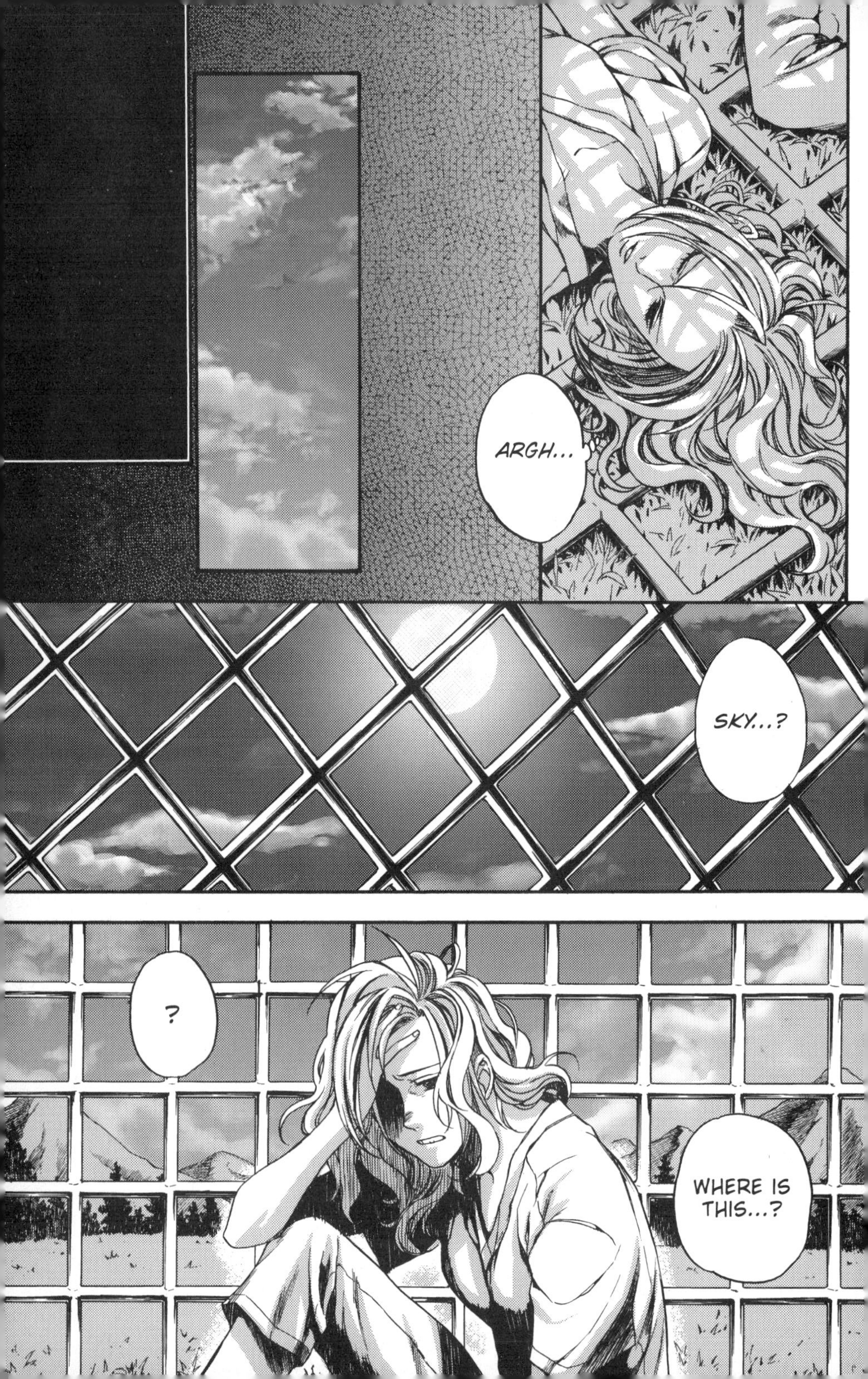
ARGH...
SKY...?
?
WHERE IS THIS...?

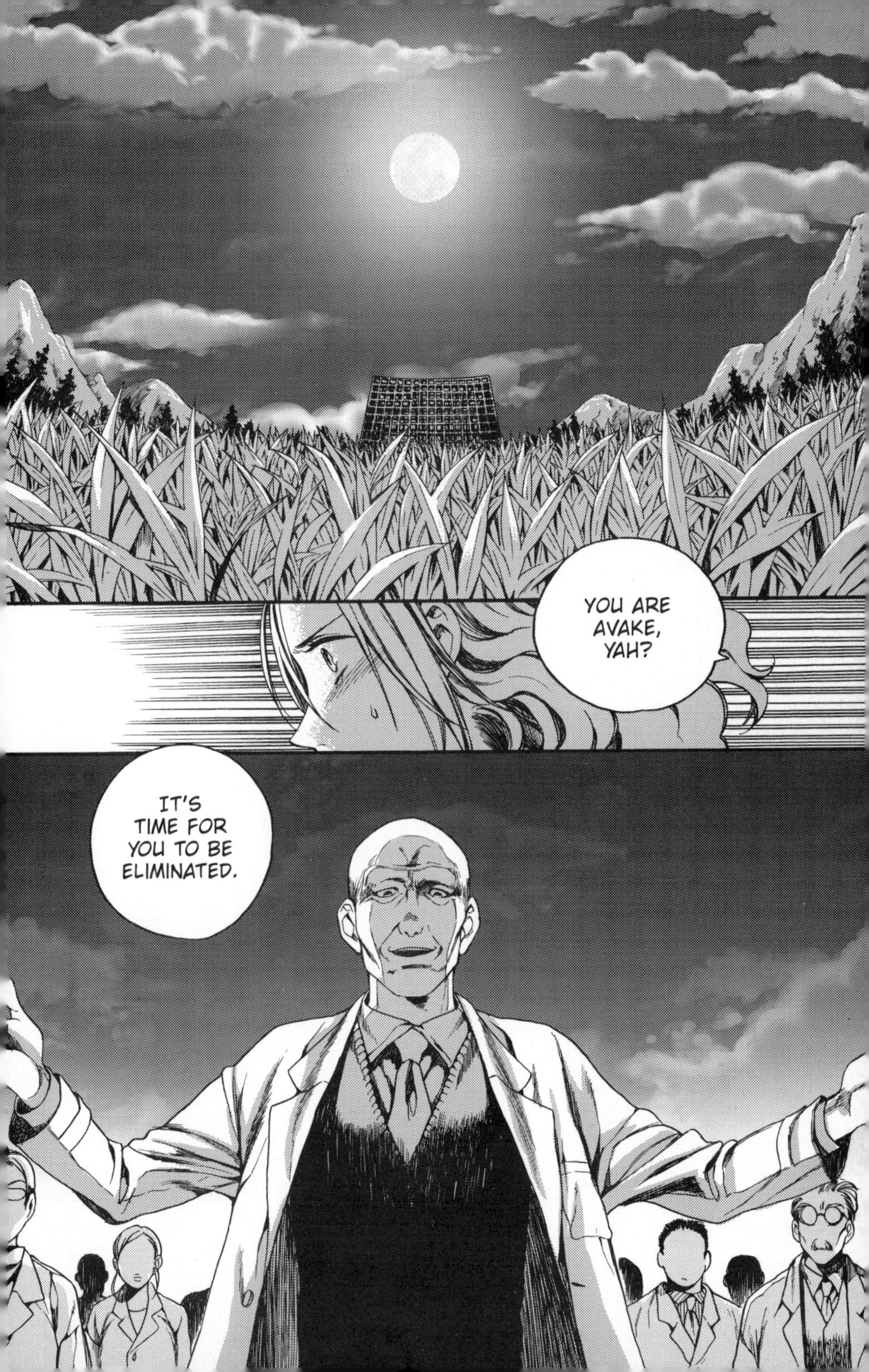
YOU ARE AVAKE, YAH?
IT'S TIME FOR YOU TO BE ELIMINATED.

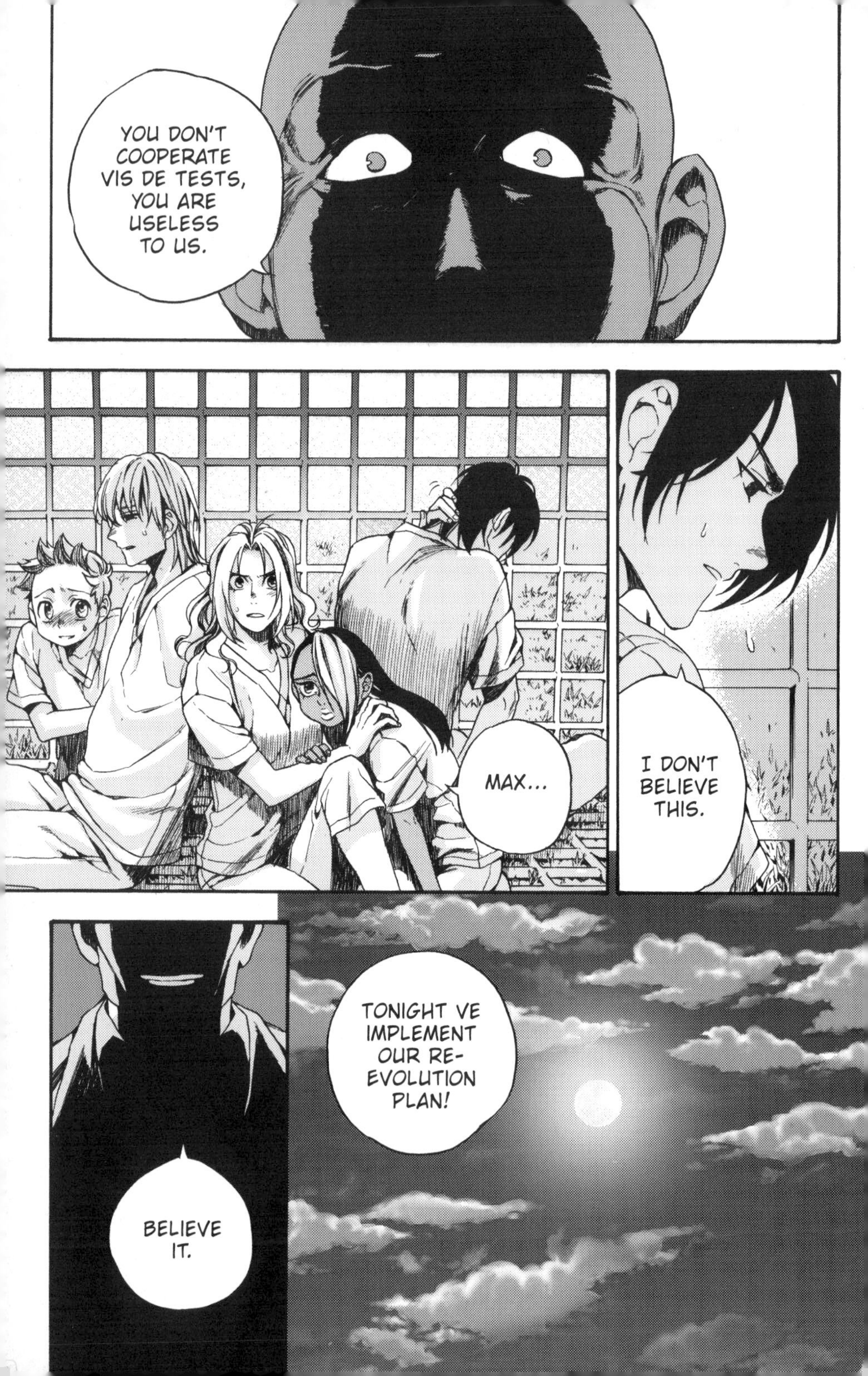
YOU DON'T COOPERATE VIS DE TESTS, YOU ARE USELESS TO US.
I DON'T BELIEVE THIS.
MAX...
TONIGHT VE IMPLEMENT OUR RE-EVOLUTION PLAN!
BELIEVE IT.

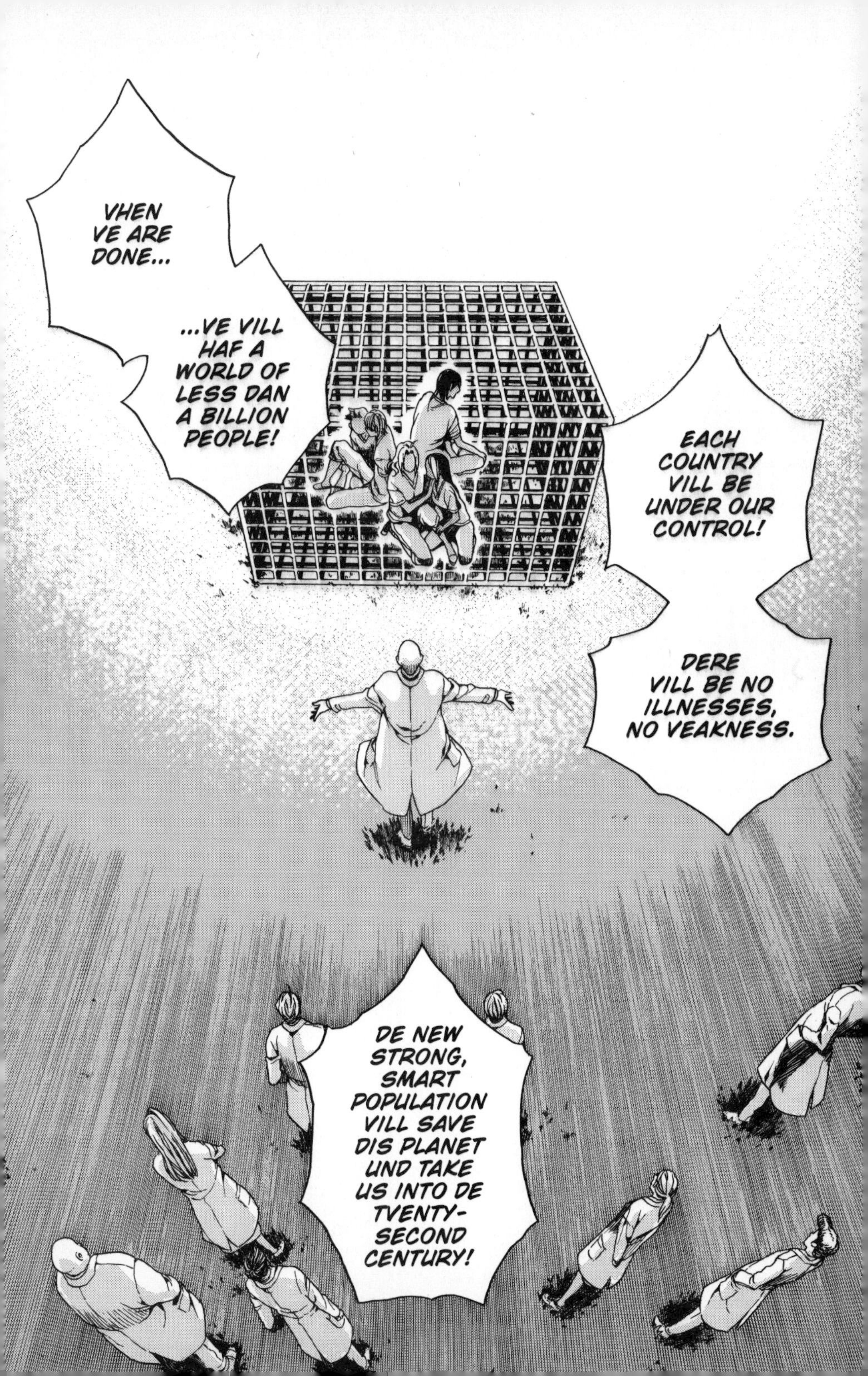
VHEN VE ARE DONE...
...VE VILL HAF A WORLD OF LESS DAN A BILLION PEOPLE!
EACH COUNTRY VILL BE UNDER OUR CONTROL!
DERE VILL BE NO ILLNESSES, NO VEAKNESS.
DE NEW STRONG, SMART POPULATION VILL SAVE DIS PLANET UND TAKE US INTO DE TVENTY-SECOND CENTURY!

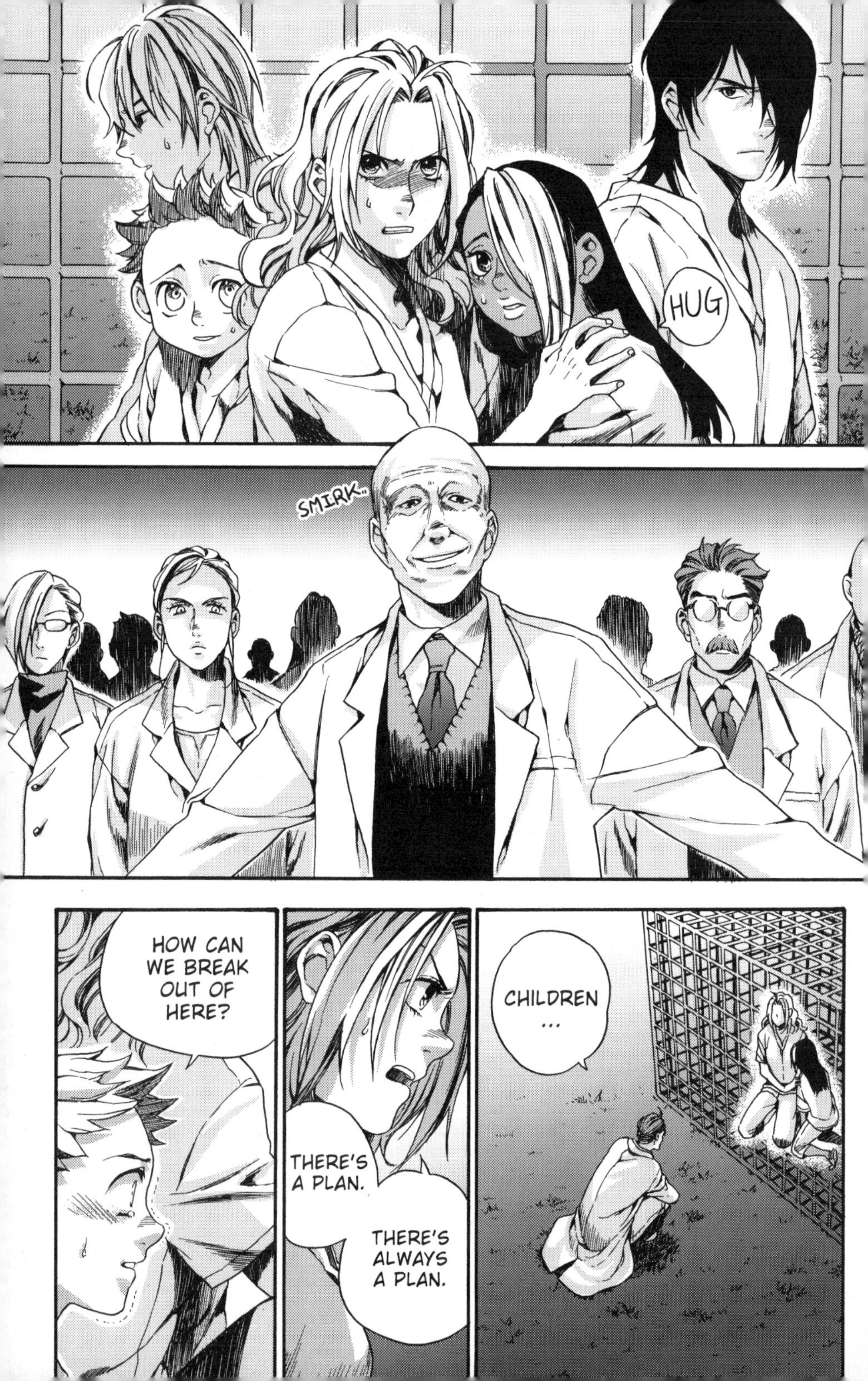
HUG
SMIRK..
HOW CAN WE BREAK OUT OF HERE?
THERE'S A PLAN.
THERE'S ALWAYS A PLAN.
CHILDREN ...

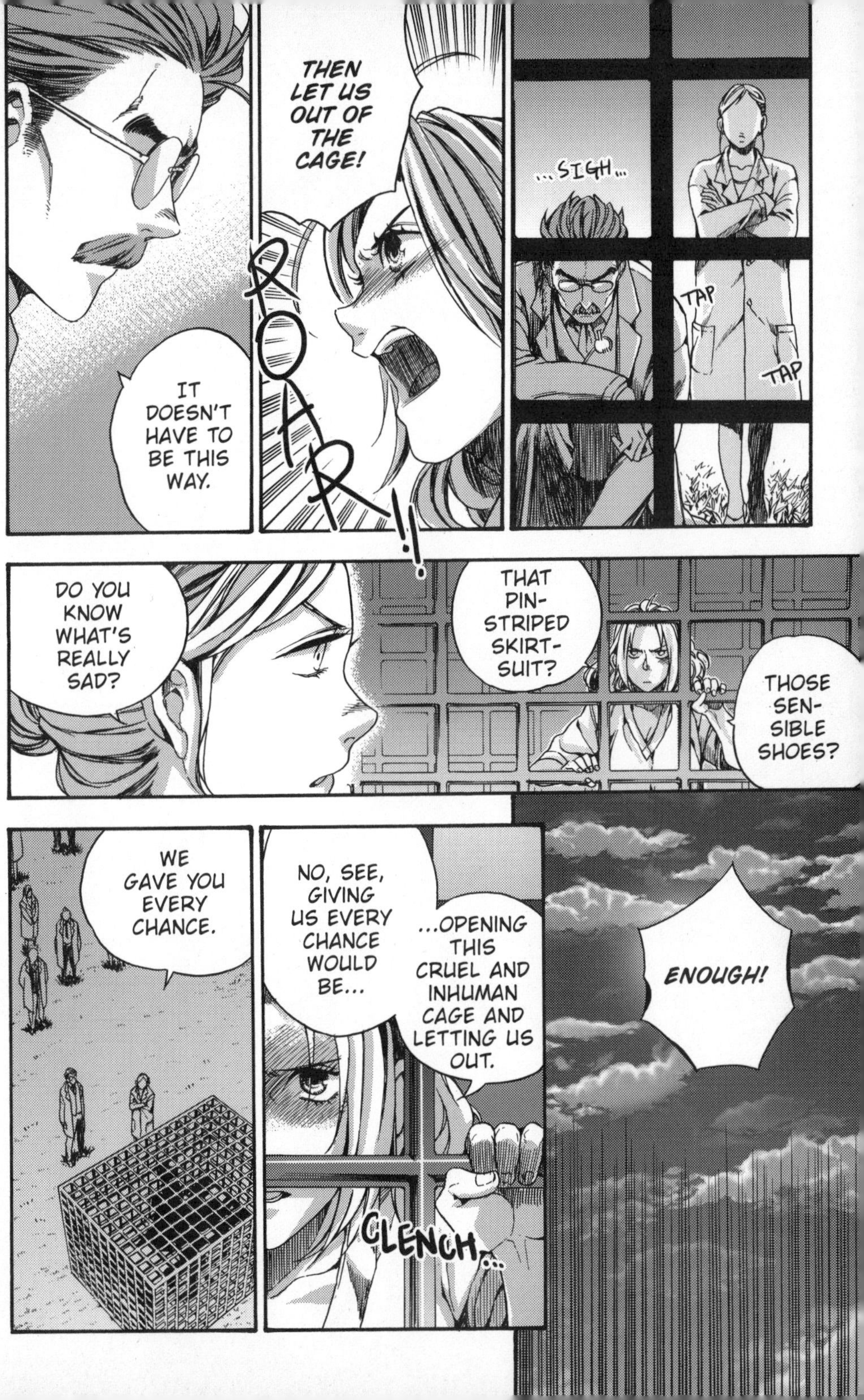
THEN LET US OUT OF THE CAGE!
...SIGH...
TAP
TAP
IT DOESN'T HAVE TO BE THIS WAY.
ROAR!!
DO YOU KNOW WHAT'S REALLY SAD?
THAT PIN-STRIPED SKIRT-SUIT?
THOSE SEN-SIBLE SHOES?
WE GAVE YOU EVERY CHANCE.
NO, SEE, GIVING US EVERY CHANCE WOULD BE...
...OPENING THIS CRUEL AND INHUMAN CAGE AND LETTING US OUT.
CLENCH...
ENOUGH!

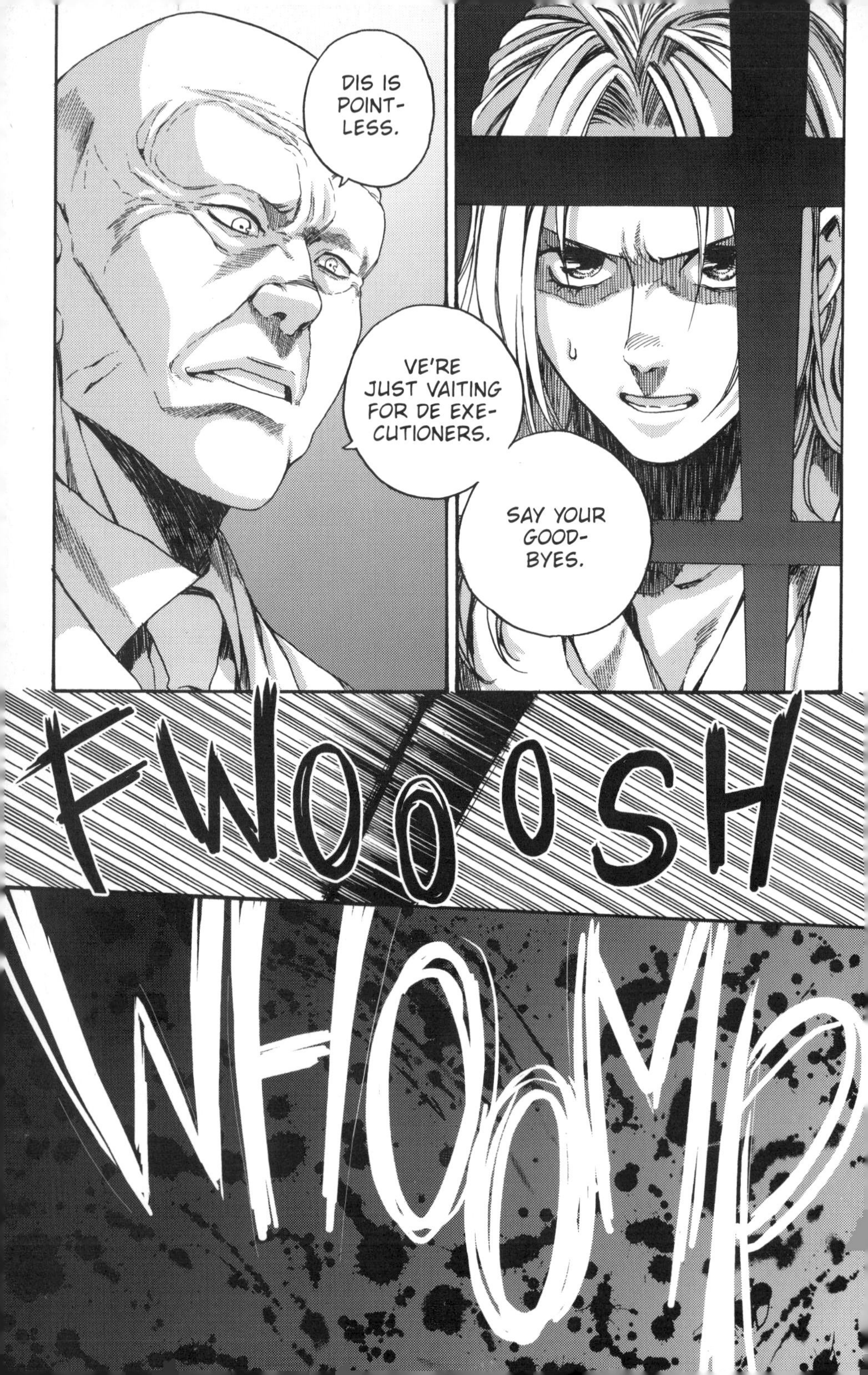
DIS IS POINT-LESS.
VE'RE JUST VAITING FOR DE EXE-CUTIONERS.
SAY YOUR GOOD-BYES.
FWOOOSH
WHOOMP

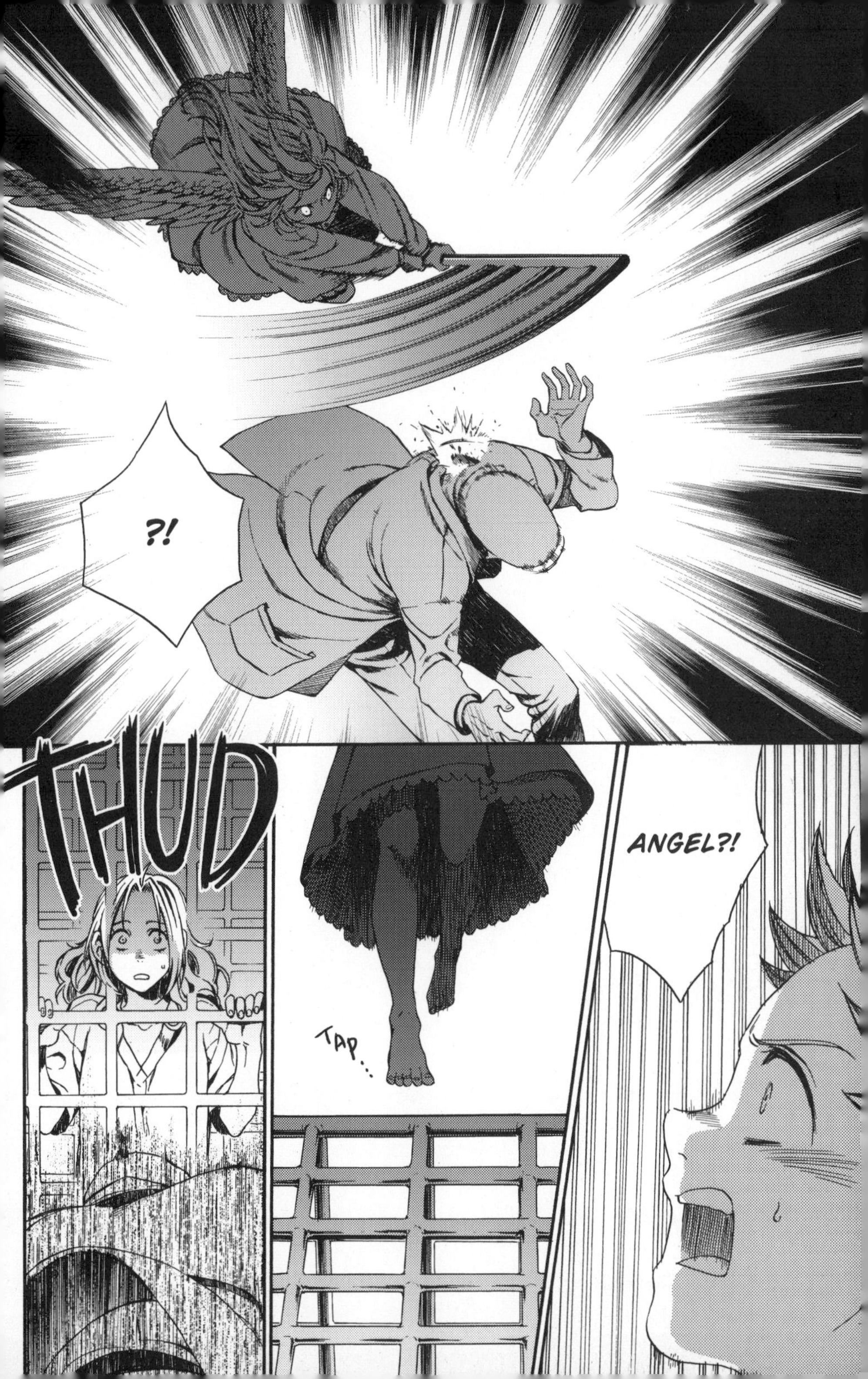
?!
THUD
ANGEL?!
TAP...

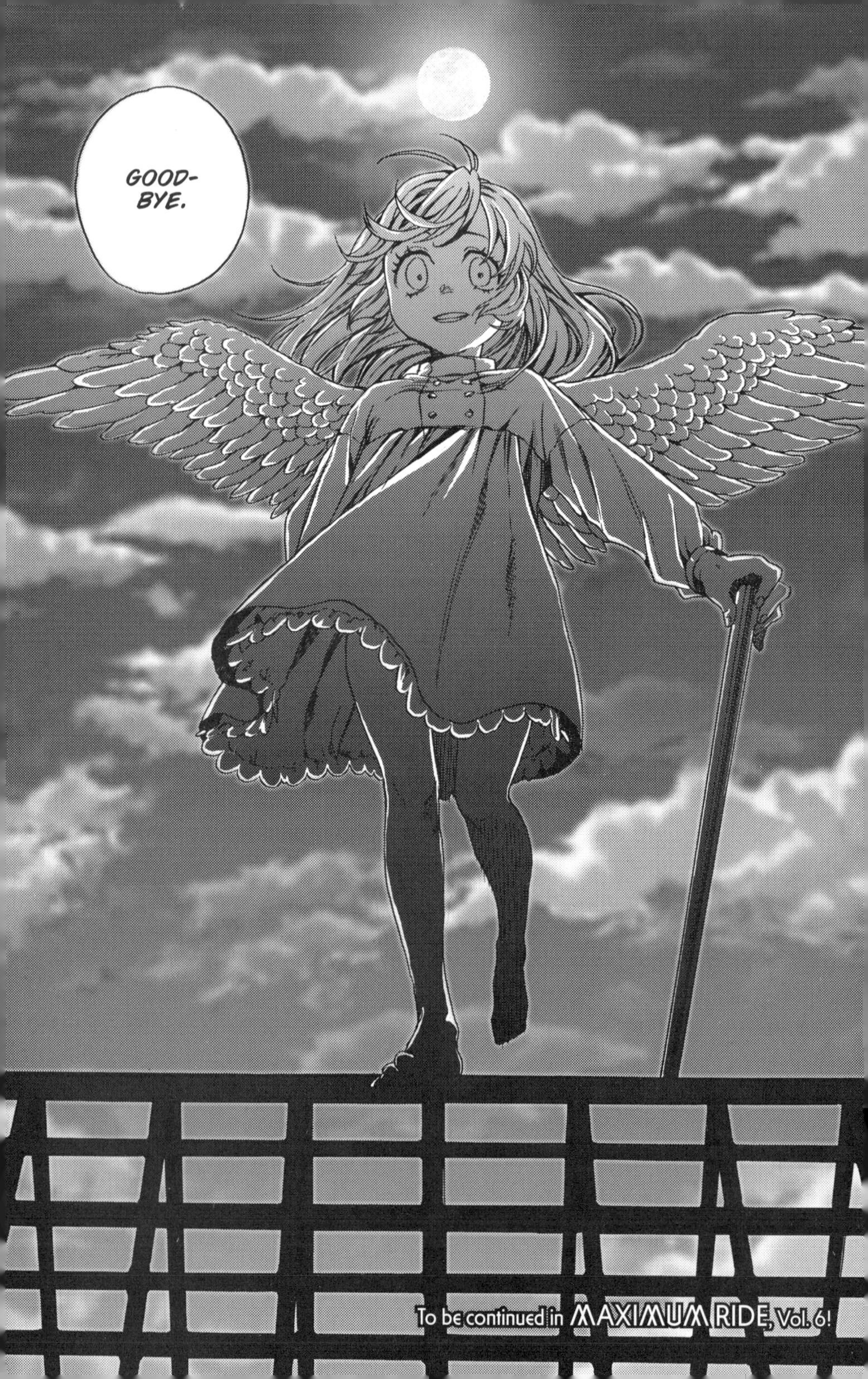
GOOD-BYE.
To be continued in MAXIMUM RIDE, Vol. 6!

MAXIMUM
RIDE

MAXIMUM RIDE: THE MANGA ⑤

JAMES PATTERSON
& NaRae Lee

Adaptation and Illustration: NaRae Lee

Lettering: JuYoun Lee

Published by Arrow Books in 2011

3 5 7 9 10 8 6 4

MAXIMUM RIDE, THE MANGA, Vol. 5 © James Patterson, 2011

Illustrations © Hachette Book Group, Inc., 2011

James Patterson has asserted his right under the Copyright, Designs and Patents Act, 1988 to be identified as the author of this work

First published in Great Britain in 2011 by
Arrow Books
Random House, 20 Vauxhall Bridge Road,
London SW1V 2SA

www.randomhouse.co.uk

Addresses for companies within The Random House Group Limited can be found at: www.randomhouse.co.uk/offices.htm

The Random House Group Limited Reg. No. 954009

A CIP catalogue record for this book is available from the British Library

ISBN 9780099538448

The Random House Group Limited supports the Forest Stewardship Council® (FSC®), the leading international forest-certification organisation. Our books carrying the FSC label are printed on FSC®-certified paper. FSC is the only forest-certification scheme supported by the leading environmental organisations, including Greenpeace. Our paper procurement policy can be found at: www.randomhouse.co.uk/environment

Printed and bound in Germany by GGP Media GMBH, Pößneck

Also by James Patterson

Maximum Ride series
The Angel Experiment • School's Out Forever •
Saving the World and Other Extreme Sports •
The Final Warning • Max • Fang • Angel • Nevermore

Witch & Wizard series
Witch & Wizard (*with Gabrielle Charbonnet*) •
The Gift (*with Ned Rust*) • The Fire (*with Jill Dembowski*) •
The Kiss (*with Jill Dembowski*)

Daniel X series
The Dangerous Days of Daniel X (*with Michael Ledwidge*) •
Watch the Skies (*with Ned Rust*) • Demons and Druids (*with Adam Sadler*) • Game Over (*with Ned Rust*) •
Armageddon (*with Chris Grabenstein*)

Middle School novels
Middle School: The Worst Years of My Life (*with Chris Tebbetts*) •
Middle School: Get Me Out of Here! (*with Chris Tebbetts*) •
Middle School: My Brother Is a Big, Fat Liar (*with Lisa Papademetriou*) • Middle School: How I Survived Bullies, Broccoli, and Snake Hill (*with Chris Tebbetts*)

I Funny
I Funny (*with Chris Grabenstein*) • I Even Funnier (*with Chris Grabenstein, to be published December 2013*)

Treasure Hunters
Treasure Hunters (*with Chris Grabenstein, to be published September 2013*)

Confessions series
Confessions of a Murder Suspect (*with Maxine Paetro*) •
Confessions: The Private School Murders (*with Maxine Paetro, to be published October 2013*)

Graphic novels
Daniel X: Alien Hunter (*with Leopoldo Gout*) • Maximum Ride: Manga Vol. 1–6 (*with NaRae Lee*)

For more information about James Patterson's novels, visit
www.jamespatterson.co.uk

Or become a fan on Facebook

Middle School
The Worst Years of My Life

James Patterson
& Chris Tebbetts

Illustrated by Laura Park

Rafe Khatchadorian has enough problems at home without throwing his first year of middle school into the mix. Luckily, he's got an ace plan for the best year ever, if only he can pull it off. With his best friend Leonardo the Silent awarding him points, Rafe tries to break every rule in his school's Code of Conduct. Chewing gum in class – 5,000 points! Running in the hallway – 10,000 points! Pulling the fire alarm – 50,000 points! But when Rafe's game starts to catch up with him, he'll have to decide if winning is all that matters, or if he's finally ready to face the rules, bullies, and truths he's been avoiding.

Containing over 100 brilliant illustrations, *Middle School* is the hilarious story of Rafe's attempt to somehow survive the very worst year of his life!

CHAPTER 1

I'M RAFE KHATCHADORIAN, TRAGIC HERO

It feels as honest as the day is *crummy* that I begin this tale of total desperation and woe with me, my pukey sister, Georgia, and Leonardo the Silent sitting like rotting sardines in the back of a Hills Village Police Department cruiser.

1

Now, there's a pathetic family portrait you
don't want to be a part of, believe me. More on the
unfortunate Village Police incident later. I need to
work myself up to tell you that disaster story.

So anyway, *ta-da,* here it is, book fans, and all
of you in need of AR points at school, the true
autobio of my life so far. The dreaded middle school
years. If you've ever been a middle schooler, you
understand already. If you're not in middle school
yet, you'll understand soon enough.

But let's face it: Understanding *me* —I mean,
really understanding me and my nutty life—isn't
so easy. That's why it's so hard for me to find
people I can trust. The truth is, I don't know who I
can trust. So mostly I don't trust anybody. Except
my mom, Jules. (Most of the time, anyway.)

So . . . let's see if I can trust you. First, some
background.

That's me, by the way, arriving at "prison"—also
known as Hills Village Middle School—in Jules's
SUV. The picture credit goes to Leonardo the
Silent.

Getting back to the story, though, I *do* trust one
other person. That would actually be Leonardo.

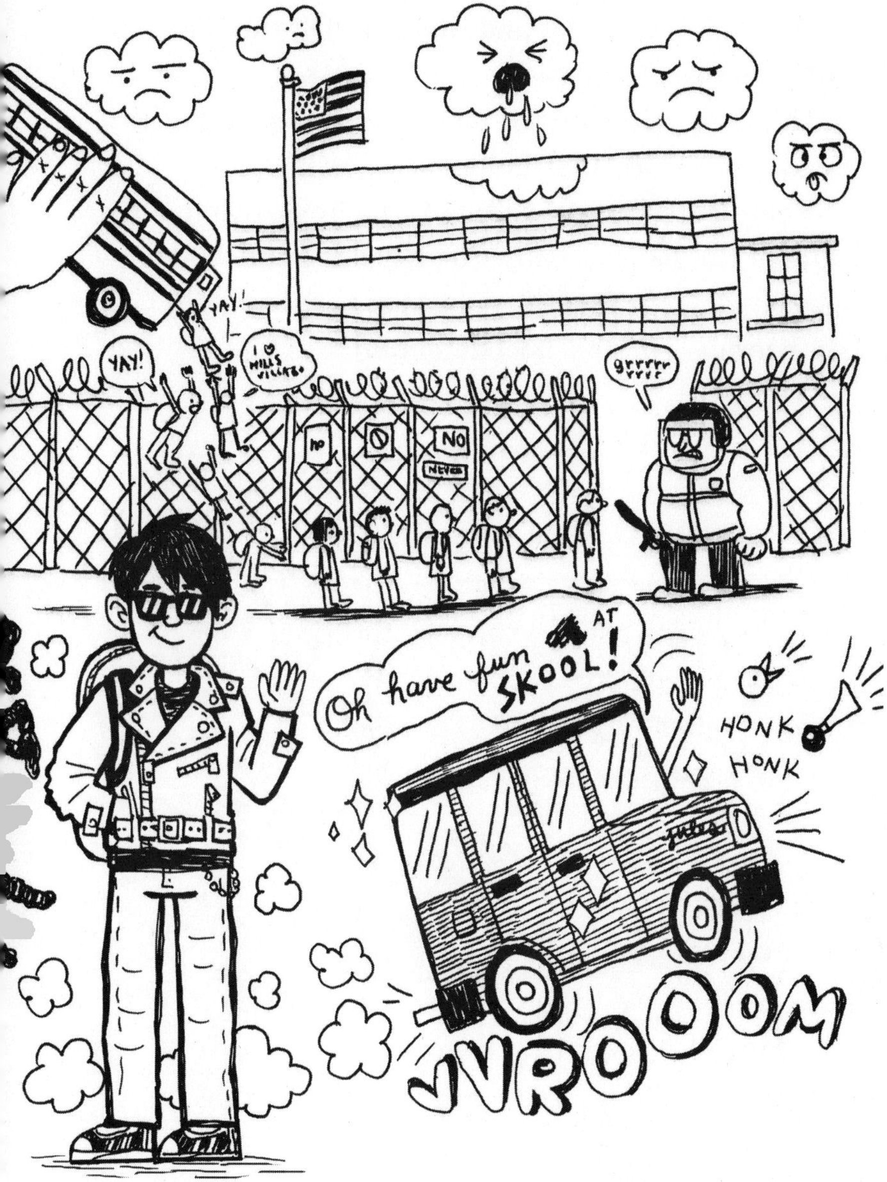
YAY!
YAY!
I ♥ HILLS VILLAGE
grrrrr rrrr
NO
NEVER
Oh have fun AT SKOOL!
HONK
HONK
VVROOOM

Leo is capital *C* Crazy, and capital *O* Off-the-Wall, but he keeps things real.

Here are some other people I don't trust as far as I can throw a truckload of pianos.

There's Ms. Ruthless Donatello, but you can just call her the Dragon Lady. She teaches English and also handles my favorite subject in sixth grade—after-school detention.

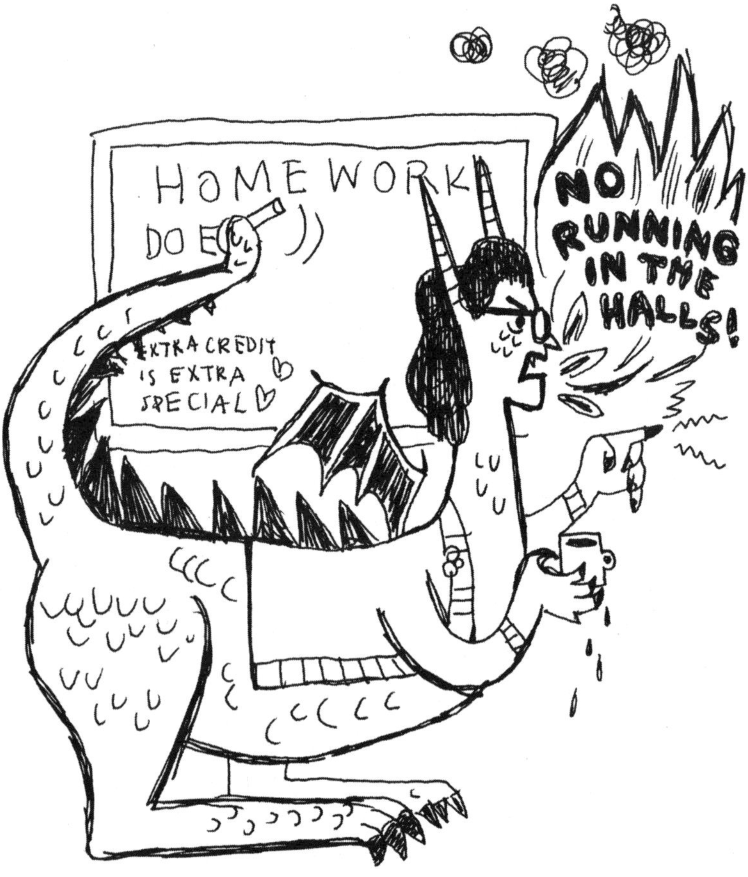
HOMEWORK
DO E
EXTRA CREDIT IS EXTRA SPECIAL
NO RUNNING IN THE HALLS!

SEES ALL!
HEARS ALL!
BEWARE!

Also, Mrs. Ida Stricker, the vice principal. Ida's pretty much in charge of every breath anybody takes at HVMS.

I'M TELLING

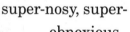

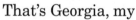

That's Georgia, my super-nosy, super-obnoxious, super-brat sister, whose only good quality is that she looks like Jules might have looked when she was in fourth grade.

There are more on my list, and we'll get to them eventually. Or maybe not. I'm not exactly sure how this is going to work out. As you can probably tell, this is my first full-length book.

But let's stay on the subject of *us* for a little bit. I kind of want to, but how do I know I can trust

you with all my embarrassing personal stuff—like the police car disaster story? What are you like? *Inside,* what are you like?

Are you basically a pretty good, pretty decent person? Says who? Says you? Says your 'rents? Says your sibs?

Okay, in the spirit of a possible friendship between us—and this is a huge big deal for me—here's another true confession.

This is what I *actually* looked like when I got to school that first morning of sixth grade.

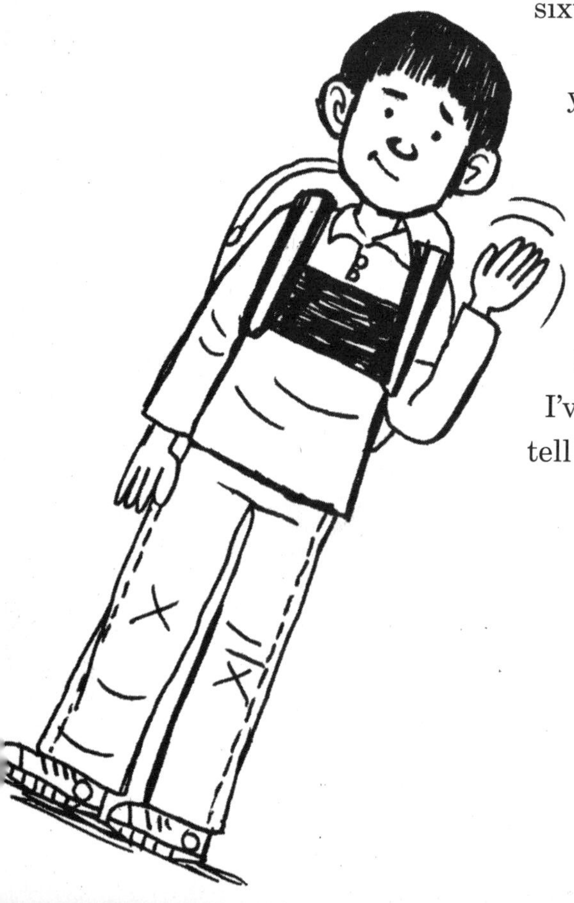

We still friends, or are you out of here?

Hey—don't go—all right?

I kind of like you. Seriously. You know how to listen, at least. And believe me, I've got quite the story to tell you.